SVEC

2002:05

Using the *Encyclopédie*

Ways of knowing, ways of reading

edited by

DANIEL BREWER

and

JULIE CANDLER HAYES

VOLTAIRE FOUNDATION

OXFORD

2002

ISBN 0 7294 0795 0
ISSN 0435-2866

Voltaire Foundation
99 Banbury Road
Oxford OX2 6JX, UK

A catalogue record for this book
is available from the British Library

The correct reference for this volume is
SVEC 2002:05

This series is available on annual subscription

For further information about *SVEC*
and other Voltaire Foundation publications see
www.voltaire.ox.ac.uk

This book is printed on acid-free paper

Typeset in Baskerville by Alden Bookset
Printed and bound by Polestar Scientifica Ltd

Table of contents

Editors' preface, or Dialogue between A and B

A: It seems as though a long time has passed since that conference in Nashville where Tony Strugnell suggested that we consider putting together this volume...

B: We should probably thank him at some point.

A: We certainly should. An editor's task indeed deserves some thanks. But now, as we see the volume nearly complete, what do you think of this project?

B: Other than an undeniable feeling of relief at seeing it all but done, and real gratitude for the hard work of the contributors, I wonder to what extent the actual collection lines up to the description you wrote for our 'Prospectus' a couple of years ago: 'The objective of the present volume of essays is to provide a series of reflections upon the relation between knowledge and history. By returning to the encyclopedists' claim of providing useful knowledge, this volume proposes to consider the use(s) to which the *Encyclopédie* may be put at present in the attempt to analyse the relation to knowledge. Consideration will be given to how the *Encyclopédie* may be read as a text that not only compiles knowledge but also focuses, reshapes, and redirects it. Articles will treat such topics as identity and sensibility, normalcy and monstrosity, the technology of knowledge, medicine and the body, print culture, material culture, nationalism and the question of representing the nation, engendering the self. Despite the wide range of topics treated, corresponding quite naturally to the breadth of the *Encyclopédie* itself, in each instance essays will contain some reflection on "the state of the discipline", on the issues, debates, and paradigms in terms of which critical knowledge is produced in the eighteenth century as well as in the twentieth.'

A: An ambitious agenda. Obviously no collection of essays could ever 'correspond to the breadth of the *Encyclopédie* itself'. The encyclopedists themselves quickly realised that the words and images in their own work could never succeed in reproducing the material world. But they certainly believed it could make that world knowable. In similar fashion I suppose we can hope that the diversity of topics and approaches in our volume at least gestures toward the complexity of the whole.

B: A number of the essays examine a particular topic, theme or sequence of articles, in order to discern the discursive networks, language games, or ideological connections that simultaneously signal their historical distinctiveness and enable a dialogue between past and present.

A: You are referring, no doubt, to Janie Vanpée's reading of the FEMME sequence, Patrick Coleman's reading of the articles under FIGURE, as well as the studies by Robert Morrissey, Pierre Saint-Amand, Downing Thomas, and Cynthia Koepp of larger constellations of articles that concern the issues of nation, civility, taste, and work.

B: Or Anne Vila's and Thomas DiPiero's very different accounts of human corporality, one from a medical standpoint, the other 'anthropological'.

A: On the other hand, other essays interrogate issues relating to the encyclopedic order and the epistemology of reading: Stephen Werner on the internal structure of articles, plates, and cross-references; Philip Stewart on changes in the material conditions of reading and the opportunities afforded by digitisation; David Bates and Fabienne Chauderlot on 'cartography' as a way of coming to terms with concepts of relationality in the work of the *philosophes* as well as in the World Wide Web.

B: But you recall that we realised the essays couldn't be divided simply into two distinct groups. Reading is the experience of the particular, and so questions concerning epistemology and order are linked necessarily to the various specific contexts where knowledge is produced. At the same time reading is always this experience, and so the essays on specific topics provide rich insights into the way these topics, and all topics in the *Encyclopédie*, are constructed, thought, and produced. For example, Ann-Marie Thornton's dissection of the relationship between the *Encyclopédie* and *The Gardner's dictionary* offers a glimpse at the work of translation, textual appropriation, and compilation in the work of the editors.

A: Doesn't the essay on translation, which one of us wrote, aim to show how the particular idea and practice of translation can stand for the work of the *Encyclopédie* in a general sense?

B: Just as the essay on the article PHILOSOPHE takes this self-reflexive entry in the encyclopedic text to stand for a more general social and intellectual self-reflexivity, which extends from eighteenth-century readers to contemporary ones.

A: The essays in this volume teach us much about the complex, dynamic world of the eighteenth century. But they do more than present that knowledge once again. For they also help us understand the chief characteristic of how the encyclopedists thought about their venture, which for them involved above all a self-reflexive concern with how things are known and not just what is known of them. The encyclopedic project of formulating and expressing knowledge had to be coupled with a self-reflexive investigation of the ways that knowledge was generated, represented, and transmitted.

B: So the encyclopedists' question is our own: how do we know the *Encyclo-pédie*? How do we read it? This is the question I wondered about when as a graduate student I first laid hands on this text. Don't the interpretive questions we ask ourselves change at all?

A: Even if certain questions don't seem to change, the answers that scholars provide have. The encyclopedists were well aware of the impact that disciplinary shifts were having on their enterprise. Indeed part of their wager was to find a way to chart those shifts. Contemporary knowledge production involves shifting fields as well. Print culture historians, for instance, have told us much about the importance of the *Encyclopédie*, which was as much a cultural event as a textual one. And issues that shape research in a number of contemporary disciplines – such as gender, nation, power – provide pertinent lenses for fresh readings of the *Encyclopédie*.

B: And if how we read the *Encyclopédie* is our question, then one should not forget the medium in which we 'access' this text's message. The Pergamon reprint of 1969 brought the encyclopedic text out of rare book rooms and onto researchers' desks. Even as we've been at work on this volume, the technologies of reading the *Encyclopédie* have undergone profound changes: the ARTFL electronic version came online in the fall of 1998, and more recently a CD-ROM edition has appeared. On the one hand, the sorts of 'transversal readings' – to borrow Robert Morrissey's phrase – allowed by these innovations would seem to realise in a spectacular way the creative connections and juxtapositions envisioned by Diderot in his article ENCYCLOPÉDIE. Yet on the other hand, as several of the contributors point out, not everything is connected to everything else, and so the semiotic labyrinth is not quite infinite. It was easier to imagine it as such, perhaps, when the material process of reading and consulting the volumes was more arduous. We also know a great deal more about the individuals who produced the *Encyclopédie*, as well as the networks of distribution and reception along which this text travelled.

A: In short, we have exchanged an imaginary endless connectivity for a more textured understanding of the patterns and structures within the network, both historically and transhistorically.

B: Perhaps the same could be said of literary studies of the past thirty years, and the 'cultural turn' they are now negotiating.

A: Well, I hope our preface has successfully avoided what you once referred to as the 'narrativised table of contents'. Perhaps our friends, readers, and contributors will wonder who is A and who is B.

B: They might.

Abbreviations

ARTFL   Project for American and French Research on the Treasury of the French Language

DPV   Denis Diderot, *Œuvres complètes*, ed. Herbert Dieckmann *et al.* (Paris 1975-1995)

SVEC   *Studies on Voltaire and the eighteenth century*

Encyclopédie   *Encyclopédie, ou dictionnaire des arts, des sciences et des métiers*.
All references are to the 17-volume, Paris 1751-1765
edition. The 5-volume Readex / Pergamon reprint of
the *Encyclopédie* published in 1969 is based on this
edition. The first printing of the 1751 edition was used
as the prototype for the on-line version of the *Encyclopédie* developed by the ARTFL project.

Supp.   The 4-volume *Supplément* to the *Encyclopédie*. All references are to the Amsterdam 1776-1777 edition. The
volumes of the *Supplément* are contained in volume 5 of
the Pergamon reprint.

DAVID BATES

Cartographic aberrations: epistemology and order in the encyclopedic map

Cette carte sans bornes est l'Encyclopédie éternelle.

Jacob Moreau, *Essai sur les bornes des connaissances humaines*, 1784

i. The rhetoric of the map and Enlightenment order

How would the *Encyclopédie* function as a guide? The editors did not aim merely to compile knowledge in one particular text. They explicitly rejected an 'alphabetical' model of order, one that would simply juxtapose different modes of inquiry. Although the text was, of course, ultimately arranged alphabetically, the true order of the *Encyclopédie* was to be found elsewhere. One of the key metaphors employed by the editors to explain this elusive order was that of the 'map'. In an age of discovery, the map was a popular eighteenth-century image, used to describe the progress of scientific inquiry. It has been said that 'maps and mapmaking epitomised the Enlightenment practice of science'.[1] In this tradition, the editors of the *Encyclopédie* claimed that it should be understood as a kind of *mappemonde* that would clearly demonstrate the interconnections of the arts and sciences, by tracing out a rigourous 'topography' of knowledge. Each article was a fragment of a vast three-dimensional 'atlas' of human endeavour, and the borders of each individual state, each specific locale, pointed to new regions and new frontiers of discovery.

This intricate map could hardly be represented in one schematic diagram. The great *tableau* that unfolds from the first volume was not, in fact, the one 'true' map of knowledge; it was at best only one, perhaps imperfect, attempt to show its basic outlines.

The encyclopedic text itself, in all its complexity, would reveal the intricate topography of human understanding. Diderot explained it this way:

1. Matthew H. Edney, 'Cartography without "progress": reinterpreting the nature and historical development of mapmaking', *Cartographica* 30 (1993), p.62. Compare Edney, *Mapping an empire: the geographical construction of British India, 1765-1843* (Chicago, Ill. 1997), p.18, on how mapmaking was, for eighteenth-century philosophy, the epitome of an ordered archive of knowledge.

I

l'ordre encyclopédique général sera comme une mappemonde où l'on ne rencontrera que les grandes régions; les ordres particuliers, comme des cartes particulières de royaumes, de provinces, de contrées; le dictionnaire, comme l'histoire géographique & détaillée de tous les lieux, la topographie générale & raisonnée de ce que nous connaissons dans le monde intelligible & dans le monde visible; & les renvois serviront d'itinéraires dans ces deux mondes, dont le visible peut être regardé comme l'Ancien, & l'intelligible comme le Nouveau.[2]

Nothing, it seems, could be clearer than this analogy. Yet, perhaps because maps are in our culture so ubiquitous, and cartographic metaphors so familiar, this important dimension of the *Encyclopédie* has not really been well explored. Here I want to unravel some of the important historical and conceptual complexities of the figure of the map, as a way of illuminating the less than obvious epistemological functions of cartographic order, especially since this order has increasingly come under attack in discussions of Enlightenment. I will suggest, in the end, that both Diderot and D'Alembert were well aware of these complexities. Their use of map imagery was at once explicitly rhetorical and epistemological, and for this reason a reading of the *Encyclopédie* can help point the way to a new understanding of 'truth' in the Enlightenment that evades current polarised views of the period.

For an earlier generation of historians and critics, those post-war liberals who self-consciously aligned themselves with Enlightenment values, the eighteenth-century effort to map the human and natural world according to reason was a great step forward for humanity. Like the bold explorers of that era, the *philosophes* in their own way broke through the artificial borders of tradition and religion, ending a provincial intellectual isolation, consolidating a global territory for themselves while opening up new lands in an ongoing process of discovery. Whatever mistakes the philosophes might have made, this kind of Enlightenment was a necessary element of modernity. As Peter Gay put it, the Enlightenment was about recovering 'nerve'. Projects like the *Encyclopédie* were key weapons in the fight against all the maladies of the past. The new mapping of knowledge was a democratic, rational effort to dethrone illegitimate traditions and crown the forward-looking cosmopolitan citizen.[3] As Ernst Cassirer wrote, in an earlier work on Enlightenment itself aimed at the darker philosophical forces of interwar Germany, the *Encyclopédie* was meant 'not to supply a certain body of knowledge but also to bring about a change in the mode of thinking'.[4]

It is hardly surprising though that the idea of the map has not been celebrated in recent critical debates on the *Encyclopédie*. If Peter Gay could

2. ENCYCLOPÉDIE, DPV vii.216.

3. Peter Gay, *The Enlightenment: an interpretation*, 2 vols (New York 1966-1969), ii.26, 567; i.6, 183, 364, 373.

4. Ernst Cassirer, *The Philosophy of the Enlightenment*, translated by Fritz C. A. Koelln and James P. Pettegrove (Princeton, N.J. 1951), p.14.

write, in the aftermath of mass death, that the world needs more light, many have since questioned the very nature of this 'light' of reason. What has come under intense scrutiny is exactly the comprehensive and totalising order of reason, the kind of order exemplified by the *Encyclopédie* and other Enlightenment projects. The encyclopedic order has been read *rhetorically*, as an exercise of power and not a reflection of reality: 'the encyclopedists' work reveals all orders of knowledge – including their own – to be arbitrary and motivated, mediated through and through by the power deployed and channeled by discourses of order'.[5] The discourse of order mapped by the *Encyclopédie* has, in this context, no important epistemological function. 'The order of things in the *Encyclopédie* is determined above all by the status accorded them as belongings, by their usefulness to an ordering subject. Things in the encyclopedic text do not simply exist, they are meant to be used.'[6] The 'map' of knowledge is an instrument for mercantile expeditions to acquire value. Division and classification is a mode of appropriation.[7]

The *Encyclopédie* may stand as an icon of order, but categories can be shifted, borders altered; no order stands uncontested. In fact Robert Darnton detects in the *Encyclopédie* itself a certain 'anxiety' over the order of knowledge. D'Alembert, he says, sets out to make a comprehensive *mappemonde* in his 'Discours préliminaire', but he only runs into contradictions and obstacles, failing to find his way as he wanders off course. The vast encylopedic text is confused, riddled with inconsistencies, Darnton says, and in the end the celebrated 'order' displayed in the great schematic map that is the Tree of Knowledge is exposed as a mere power play, a motivated effort by the editors to trim previous Trees, excising religion from any position of prominence and replacing it with the new empirical philosophy of the eighteenth century.[8]

Darnton here explicitly follows the lead of Foucault, whose own influential critique of the 'order of things' was occasioned by a reading of a Borges essay, which describes a Chinese encyclopedia that organises the world in a strange and seemingly arbitrary way. But if Darnton (and other critics) are content to believe that the strangeness of alternative orders is enough to show that all order is arbitrary, rhetorical and not ontological, Foucault's discussion of order in *Les Mots et les choses* is a great deal more complex.

5. Daniel Brewer, '1751: ordering knowledge', in *A New history of French literature*, ed. Denis Hollier (Cambridge, Mass. 1989), p.454.

6. Daniel Brewer, *The Discourse of Enlightenment in eighteenth-century France: Diderot and the art of philosophizing* (Cambridge 1993), p.19.

7. Roland Barthes, 'Image, raison, déraison', in *L'Univers de l'"Encyclopédie"* (Paris 1964), p.12. Cf. Grant Holly, 'The allegory in realism', in *Enlightening allegory: theory, practice, and contexts of allegory in the late seventeenth and eighteenth centuries*, ed. Kevin L. Cope (New York 1992), p.150-51.

8. Robert Darnton, 'Philosophers trim the tree of knowledge: the epistemological strategy of the *Encyclopédie*', in *The Great cat massacre and other episodes in French cultural history* (New York 1984), p.192-95, 201-205.

What Foucault found unsettling in Borges's Chinese encyclopedia is not the perverse categories that order the world of animals ('those that tremble as if they were mad', 'those that have just broken a flower vase'), so much as one particular category: 'those that are included in this classification'.[9] Order is fractured by this one self-reflexive category. The monstrous quality of the encyclopedic order is not the oddity of juxtaposition but the destruction of a common ground for any order. What Foucault says here is that these classifications can meet *only in language*, for the space of the order itself is 'unthinkable'. The disorder revealed here is more than mere incongruity. The common locus disappears: there is no world of things 'to be arranged' but only a linguistic practice that creates a world of order. Differences and similitudes, he says, are only the result of an 'operation'. What Foucault wants us to think about, then, is not 'alternative' orders but the possibility of simultaneous orders, a 'heteroclite' world that denies the homogeneity of any one coherent 'order'. Significantly, this linguistic sovereignty of homogeneous order originates, according to Foucault, in eighteenth-century Enlightenment thought, which reduces identity to 'relations' on one systematic 'table' of reality.[10]

Here Foucault looks back to a long tradition of anti-Enlightenment criticism. Beginning with Hegel, who thought that the universalising abstraction of 'reason' was dangerous because it destroyed the concrete particularity of the empirical world, a world marked by essential differentiation, Enlightenment has been seen as the enemy of diversity. 'Order' is not an ontological category, but only a rhetorical performance, a linguistic act that defines and classifies in order to control. The discursive order of the *Encyclopédie*, outlined in the 'Discours préliminaire', is only a 'phantom', a logocentric desire for unity and control. The reality it supposedly represents is a 'mythic entity'.[11] The *Encyclopédie* is linked with the basic Enlightenment desire to systematise through precise analysis, a process that dismembers its own objects. So even as Enlightenment philosophes railed against the 'false unities' of scholastic thought, their own rational method integrated the most disparate fields of inquiry into one collective encyclopedic enterprise.[12]

The very idea of an encyclopedic 'worldmap' of knowledge has been further undermined by much recent work in the history and theory of cartography. Long understood as a representational practice that strives for ever-increasing accuracy, cartography has been subjected to a rhetorical

---

9. Jorge Luis Borges, 'The analytical language of John Wilkins', in *Other inquisitions, 1937-1952*, translated by Ruth L. C. Simms (Austin, Texas 1964), p.103.

10. Michel Foucault, *The Order of things: an archaeology of the human sciences* (New York 1971), p.xvi-xx.

11. See Walter Moser, 'Les discours dans le *Discours préliminaire*', *Romanic review* 67 (1976), p.115-16.

12. Barbara Maria Stafford, *Body criticism: imaging the unseen in Enlightenment art and medicine* (Cambridge, Mass. 1991), p.35.

reading that reveals the many distortions that lie behind supposedly 'objective' maps. In J. B. Harley's influential (if somewhat belated) postmodern turn, his 1989 article 'Deconstructing the map', we are told that every map is necessarily an abstraction from the landscape, and abstraction is always violent. The map is a product of a whole series of rhetorical transformations, but the 'apparent honesty' of the visual image hides the motivations that lie behind its construction. Harley wants to 'break the assumed link between reality and representation which has dominated cartographic thinking, has led it in the pathway of "normal science" since the Enlightenment'. The task is 'to locate the presence of power' in a map that does not represent (whether accurately or not) a reality so much as *create* its own reality.[13] Even cartographic textbooks demonstrate how, in order to create a usable map, any given topography must be creatively distorted, using techniques that echo Freud's dreamwork, such as selective omission, simplification, combination, exaggeration, and displacement. The representational map must freeze what is fluid, fix what is temporally variable, simplify the complex, articulate what is hidden.[14] A map is essentially a lie, a creative distortion that allows the user to 'escape the complexity of the environment'.[15] Any 'map', then, is a fictional construction that can be deconstructed to show the social and political forces shaping its form. As Harley wrote, maps are 'at least as much an image of the social order as they are a measurement of the phenomenal world of objects'.[16]

Yet even this rather ephemeral link with the 'world' has been relentlessly undermined by a 'post-modern' cultural cartography. 'Both truth of signs and truth of maps are intimately linked to processes of conceptual categorisation. We can only know the "true" world in the context of conceptual categories that we apply to organise that world. Different ways of categorising are likely to yield different truths.'[17] The map, in other words, is not simply a *distortion* of reality, or even a particular way of looking at the world as a new, independent reality. Once it could be said that a 'map *is not* the territory'.[18] Now, however, Jean Baudrillard can claim that the map *precedes* the territory, and they are, in a sense, indistinguishable.[19] Which is to say that we approach the world with what are called 'cognitive

13. J. B. Harley, 'Deconstructing the map', *Cartographica* 26, no.2 (1982), p.2, 13-14.

14. J. S. Keates, *Understanding maps* (New York 1982), p.100-101, 139.

15. Mark Monmonier, *How to lie with maps*, 2nd edn (Chicago, Ill. 1996); Phillip C. Muehrcke and Juliana O. Muehrcke, *Map use: reading, analysis, and interpretation*, 4th edn (Madison, Wisc. 1998), p.17-18, 417.

16. Harley, 'Deconstructing the map', p.7.

17. Alan MacEachren, *How maps work: representation, visualization, and design* (New York 1995), p.436.

18. Alfred Korzybski, *Science and sanity: an introduction to non-aristotelian systems and general semantics*, 2nd edn (Lancaster, Penn. 1941), p.72.

19. Jean Baudrillard, *Simulacra and simulation*, translated by Sheila Faria Glaser (Ann Arbor, Mich. 1994), and Baudrillard, *Simulations*, translated by Paul Foss, Paul Patton and Philip Beitchman (New York [c.1983]).

maps', complex ways of ordering our experience. There is no real difference between map and territory because the territory is already a product of 'cultural mapping'.[20] So concrete 'maps' are problematic because they reify particular orders and present them as an objective reality. The individual map defines one version of the world at the expense of other perspectives, excluding them with its appearance of scientific 'accuracy'.

The objective map has, in a sense, become a fetish. We mistake the map, which is only a reification of the material and human world, of life itself, for reality. Fetishes, as Donna Haraway writes, 'obscure the constitutive tropic nature of themselves and of worlds'. The fetishised map makes everything seem clear: itself and the 'world' it supposely represents. The non-tropic map is, however, an error for Haraway, an error located precisely in the fanatical obsession with 'accurate' representation. The map imagines a fixed reality that can then be objectively traced. She writes that 'contingency, finitude, and difference – but not "error" – inhere in the irremediably tropic, secular liveliness. Error and denial inhere in reverent literalness'.[21] Many pleas are made for 'non-tropic' maps, provisional maps, 'deterritorialisation' processes, and so on, all aimed at provoking what might be called, following Foucault, a 'heteroclite' human topography that emphasises the specificity and radical otherness of 'place'.[22]

Although we seem to have strayed far from the *Encyclopédie* and the eighteenth century at this point, in fact this critique of the map leads us straight back to the Enlightenment. For the origins of this fetishistic mode of cartographic representation lie, as Harley and others have suggested, in the peculiar development of Enlightenment rationality.[23] As recent histories of cartography have shown, maps only became 'modern' (in this pathological sense) in the aftermath of the scientific Revolution and the emergence of Enlightenment. Early maps, which often seem distorted and inaccurate to modern eyes, did not attempt to mimic reality in any objective sense. The earliest maps were 'itineraries', highly specific guides to particular paths and routes, with no 'spatial' characteristics at all. Medieval *mappemondes* may often have erred topographically, but the 'truths' they revealed reflected the reality of Christian history and theology.[24] In the feudal period, maps derived from concrete experience and traditional usages, 'place' was more important than the larger spaces of geography. The local region was not linked to a larger world: the outside was mysterious, a threat to be avoided, and not an object of knowledge. In medieval maps and art

---

20. Geoff King, *Mapping reality: an exploration of cultural cartographies* (New York 1996), p.16.

21. Donna J. Haraway, *Modest-witness@second-millennium.femaleman-meets-oncomouse: feminism and technoscience* (New York 1997), p.135-37, from the section 'Fetishism of the map'.

22. See Gilles Deleuze and Félix Guattari, *Mille Plateaux* (Paris 1980), p.20, as well as, more generally, their theory of 'nomadology'. Cf. Haraway's discussion of the fetishism of the map in *Modest-witness*, p.136, and the conclusions in King, *Mapping reality*, p.185.

23. See, for example, Derek Gregory, *Geographical imaginations* (Cambridge 1994), p.7.

24. David Woodward, 'Medieval mappaemundi', in *The History of cartography*, vol.i, ed. David Woodward and J. B. Harley (Chicago, Ill. 1987), p.342.

we find not 'objective' representations of space but instead multiple points of view that reflect varied, particular experiences, and social organisations of space.[25] Only in the Renaissance, with the rediscovery of perspective, did space become somewhat 'homogeneous', and relational accuracy desirable. But even in the Renaissance there was a respect for the individual and the particular. The world was understood to be linked in complex, and not systematic, ways. In early modern texts one can still find, then, two different maps of one territory occupying the same page, each considered a possible path to knowledge.

It was the 'new intellectual regime' of Enlightenment that 'transformed this epistemological multiplicity into self-contradiction; the new epistemological singularity required that at any *one* time, there should be only *one* map of *one* territory'. The foundational technique of this new regime, the story goes, was something now called 'mathematical cosmography'. In the wake of the revolution in physical science, the Enlightenment posited an absolute, abstract space, a homogeneous reality into which everything could be placed with mathematical precision. Knowledge was spatialised in the eighteenth century (metaphorically) because 'space' was understood at the time to be a unitary and stable reality that made possible the precise 'mapping' of any given object of knowledge. So it was not simply any 'map' that epitomised Enlightenment science. A particular kind of map, grounded on a historically specific concept of space, symbolised rational inquiry. Difference now became *error*.[26]

This is why so many critics of Enlightenment have argued that the image of the map was so important, and not just for the editors of the *Encyclopédie*. A homogeneous, abstract idea of empty space justifies *systematic* and comprehensive surveys. There is, then, more than just a poetic connection made between the *Encyclopédie* and Enlightenment cartography. Just as the encyclopedic text rationalises and thus *reconciles* diverse views into one unitary and coherent body of knowledge,[27] the systematic surveying and mapping undertaken by so many powerful states in this era aimed to *produce* not just ideal maps of the given territory but a very real political and social unity that would transcend local and regional differences.[28] Enlightenment cartography, in both its epistemology and its practice, sweeps away local knowledge, particular itineraries, traditional points of reference, redrawing the world according to a comprehensive and rational system of

25. See David Harvey, *The Condition of postmodernity: an enquiry into the origins of cultural change* (Oxford 1989), p.240-41.
26. Edney, 'Cartography without "progress"', p.62, 26.
27. See Alasdair MacIntyre, *Three rival versions of moral enquiry: encyclopedia, genealogy, and tradition* (Notre Dame, Ind. 1990).
28. On the politics of cartography in this period, see for example Marcelo Escolar, 'Exploration, cartography, and the modernization of state power', *International social science journal* 49 (1997), p.68; and *Monarchs, ministers, and maps: the emergence of cartography as a tool of government in early modern Europe*, ed. David Buisseret (Chicago, Ill. 1992).

mathematically controlled points.[29] The concreteness of 'place' is transformed into a mere relative site in infinite space.[30] As an independent discipline, chorography (from the Greek *chora*, place) disappears by 1750, subsumed by the relentless progress of mathematical topographies and geodesic surveys.[31] In the Enlightenment map, as in the encyclopedic map of knowledge, the particular was understood to be a division of a global whole; the 'other' of difference was not so much eliminated as integrated into a larger totality. According to this view of Enlightenment, the process of 'discovery' (epistemological or geographical) was not a confrontation with genuine novelty or difference, only an opportunity for *expansion* of the given: 'Not by chance do the encyclopedists use the metaphor of the voyage to describe reading their text, and that of the map to figure how it structures knowledge. Like the maps used to chart the great voyages of discovery, the encyclopedic *mappemonde* too holds out the promise of territorial expansion, power to be achieved, and wealth to be had.'[32]

What has been questioned in some recent work on the *Encyclopédie* is the status of totalising, graphic metaphors such as the 'map', the 'tree' and the *tableau*. To rehabilitate the project, critics have tried to show how the encyclopedic text in fact subverts rigid order in different ways. The *Encyclopédie* is thereby disengaged from the repressive cartographic mode and shown to be the vehicle of polyphonic communication. A good example of this is Jean Starobinski's concise commentary on Diderot's article ENCYCLOPÉDIE, where various metaphors of encyclopedic practice are analysed. Diderot first described individual sciences organically, likening them to trees with clearly defined roots, trunks, branches, leaves. Science was ordered; all aspects of inquiry could be placed relative to solid foundational principles. Diderot then changes perspective, Starobinski says, when it is pointed out that all these individual trees can be located in a larger space: 'le modèle topologique se substitue au modèle biologique, et, dès lors, chaque science particulière vient occuper un *espace* plan, découper une région singulière, dont les frontières marquent le commencement d'une autre science: le Tout encyclopédique est constitué par la juxtaposition de ces territoires limitrophes.' All the sciences can be displayed on maps of various scales. But, Starobinski points out, a final dimension of the text, the 'jeu des *renvois*', disrupts this topological order. This 'polysemic' network of words reorients the encyclopedic text, according to Starobinski. Within this heterogeneous space, 'le Système, confié aux *Discours* et aux *Prospectus*, au grand *Tableau*

29. Edney, 'Cartography without "progress" ', p.62-63. See as well Fredric Jameson, *Postmodernism, or the cultural logic of late capitalism* (Durham, N. Carolina 1991), p.52, on the historical move from the local chart to the comprehensive survey, and beyond to the abstraction of the world projection.

30. Edward S. Casey, 'Smooth spaces and rough-edged places: the hidden history of place', *Review of metaphysics* 51 (1997), p.286-87.

31. Edney, *Mapping an empire*, p.43.

32. Brewer, *Discourse of Enlightenment*, p.22.

figuré, prend l'aspect d'une structure adventice ou d'une résultante virtuelle'. The true nature of the encyclopedic text is not found in these rigid orders: 'Pour qui parcourt l'*Encyclopédie*, l'évidence est celle de la particularité, de la multiplicité des objets différenciés.' And so Starobinski links the encyclopedic project not with the systematic mapping surveys of the absolutist state, but rather with the eighteenth-century opening up of the *voies de communication*.[33]

This interpretive move – the move to resist cartographic order in the *Encyclopédie* by focusing on its complexity – has been repeated in a number of contexts. Jean Ehrard, for example, cites Foucault and Darnton on the 'epistemological anxieties' associated with the encyclopedic order, expressed in the great 'système figuré' of knowledge, but tries to show, with Starobinski, that the text does not really operate according to this schematic figure. The richness of the text, he says, is really in the unstable multiplicity of the *renvois*. This textual 'labyrinth' defies any strict representational mapping; it is, like nature itself, 'un réseau infiniment complexe d'interférences, de ramifications, de chevauchements'. We have, Ehrard claims, overestimated the importance of the graphic metaphors: 'Laissons donc se dessécher l'arbre, et engageons-nous dans le labyrinthe.'[34] Others have pointed to similar conclusions. The actual effect of the labyrinthine encyclopedic text, with its disorienting cross-references, has been characterised as a 'desystematisation' of the global order.[35] The *Encyclopédie* seems to rely on a fixed, unvarying object to maintain its representational status, but it fails, because it needs the endless supplementary network of *renvois*, which destabilises knowledge and make the order of the text a 'proleptic' one.[36] More recently, the *Encyclopédie* has been called an 'unintegrated juxtaposition', with only a superficial order arising from the arbitrary alphabetical series. The intention of the text, we hear, is 'to initiate a series of innovative intersections and confluences' in a world without fixed divisions. The *Encyclopédie* is part of a rediscovered 'heteroclite' Enlightenment culture fascinated with the 'multiple, chaotic, and subversive fruits of the moment', a culture that heroically resists the imposition of encyclopedic and narrative structures of control.[37]

So we have come a long way from the dark world of *Dialectic of Enlightenment*, with its Hegelian vision of Reason gone mad, liquidating the individual entities of concrete existence. We now have two Enlightenments.

33. Jean Starobinski, 'Remarques sur l'*Encyclopédie*', *Revue de métaphysique et de morale* 75 (1970), p.285-86.

34. Jean Ehrard, 'L'arbre et le labyrinthe', in *L'Encyclopédie, Diderot, l'esthétique: mélanges en hommage à Jacques Chouillet*, ed. Sylvain Auroux *et al.* (Paris 1991), p.233, 235, 239.

35. Georges Benrekassa, 'La pratique philosophique de Diderot dans l'article "Encyclopédie" de l'*Encyclopédie*', *Stanford French review* 8 (1984), p.203-204, 190-91.

36. James Creech, ' "Chasing after advances": Diderot's article "Encyclopédie" ', *Yale French studies* 63 (1982), p.185-88.

37. Thomas Kavanagh, *Esthetics of the moment: literature and art in the French Enlightenment* (Philadelphia, Penn. 1996), p.14, 275.

9

Besides the abstract universalism reflected in the great universal grids of cartographic and encyclopedic practice, we have an almost post-modern eighteenth century, a cultural labyrinth of fluidity, errancy, and dialogical intersection. What is interesting is that both Enlightenments still figure prominently in the *Encyclopédie*. At times these opposing tendencies are personified by the editors themselves: 'Au point de vue pyramidal de d'Alembert, position idéale du philosophe faisant tournoyer autour de lui la carte des sciences, Diderot oppose un univers multicentré', explored via the *renvois*.[38] As we see here, the metaphor of the map can, at least in today's largely post-modern critical environment, only be associated with the darker Enlightenment effort to abstract from the fluid and diverse world of human reality a rational and coherent 'graticule': 'les images du tableau, de la carte, de la mappemonde [...] banalisent la complexité encyclopédique'.[39] The map, as rhetorical text, represses difference and blinds us to the dynamic nature of life itself.

Strangely enough, the editors of the *Encyclopédie* seemed to have understood the problematic status of their map quite well, constantly remarking, from the *Prospectus* forward, on the arbitrary nature of their epistemological cartography. This raises an important question. Why would they simultaneously admit the 'arbitrary', rhetorical nature of their ordering map *and* insist on its critical epistemological importance? It is difficult to think of the map in both contexts. One must, it seems, choose sides in the battle over Enlightenment: the *Encyclopédie* was really for or against order, and the map represents, clearly, order, for what else could it represent? Given the confusion, it makes sense, it seems to me, to focus our attention again on the encyclopedic map as it emerges in the actual texts. Perhaps it had another kind of function.

ii. Truth and the map in the *Encyclopédie*

> Engagez-vous dans les sinuosités & dans les replis tortueux des rues d'une Ville immense: elle vous paroît un labyrinthe inextricable. Vous ne rencontrez qu'embarras, obscurités: tout vous arrête. [...] Montez sur une tour élévée, & regardez la Ville à vue d'oiseau. Les issues se multiplient, les incertitudes cessent.
>
> F. L. d'Escherny, *Les Lacunes de la philosophie*, 1783

At a certain point in the 'Discours préliminaire' D'Alembert gives the reader a rest: 'Arrêtons-nous un moment ici, & jettons les yeux sur l'espace que nous venons de parcourir.' What we see, however, is rather unsettling. For we have been travelling without a really clear idea of where we

---

38. Pierre Saint-Amand, *Diderot: le labyrinthe de la relation* (Paris 1984), p.73. See also Wilda Anderson, *Diderot's dream* (Baltimore, Md. 1990), for a similar comparison of the two editors.
39. Saint-Amand, *Diderot*, p.73.

are going. Yes, we are sure of our existence. Yes, we can rely on a few mathematical propositions. But in fact the human mind, in this epistemological topography, is lost:

Entre ces deux termes est un intervalle immense, où l'Intelligence suprème semble avoir voulu se jouer de la curiosité humaine, tant par les nuages qu'elle y a répandus sans nombre, que par quelques traits de lumiere qui semblent s'échapper de distance en distance pour nous attirer. On pourroit comparer l'Univers à certains ouvrages d'une sublime obscurité, dont les Auteurs en s'abaissent quelquefois à la portée de celui qui les lit cherchent à lui persuader qu'il entend tout à-peu-près. Heureux donc, si nous nous engageons dans ce labyrinthe, de ne point quitter la véritable route; autrement les éclairs destinés à nous y conduire, ne serviroient souvent qu'à nous en écarter davantage.[40]

Clearly, without a guide in this dangerous wilderness, the mind cannot tell the flash of truth from the misleading lights of the dark forest. However, it is not so clear how the lost traveller can create his own map given his predicament. Given that the *Encyclopédie* obviously was meant to function in this capacity, it is important to remember this striking analogy, for whatever goals the encyclopedists may have had, an essential limitation explains both the need for clear paths, and the ever present risk of marking a path to an *obscured* truth.

The perfect mimetic map would, of course, be absolutely useless, as Borges once suggested in the following fragment of a fictional seventeenth-century text:

In that empire, the craft of Cartography attained such Perfection that the Map of a Single province covered the space of an entire City, and the Map of the Empire itself an entire Province. In the course of Time, these Extensive maps were found somehow wanting, and so the College of Cartographers evolved a Map of the Empire that was of the same Scale as the Empire and coincided with it point for point. Less attentive to the Study of Cartography, succeeding Generations came to judge a map of such Magnitude cumbersome, and, not without Irreverence, they abandoned it to the Rigors of Sun and Rain. In the western Deserts, tattered fragments of the Map are still to be found, Sheltering an occasional Beast or beggar; in the whole Nation, no other relic is left of the Discipline of Geography.[41]

It is in fact the manipulation of scale and perspective that makes a map useful, but the use of scale and perspective always introduces error.[42] The new cartography stems from this insight into the essential errancy of maps. But in the move toward rhetorical deconstruction of the map, the epistemological potential of these errors has been neglected. Only the aberrant relationship between map and 'object' has been examined in any detail. But we can ask, what unknown relations might be revealed by the inevitably

---

40. 'Discours', i.vii.
41. Jorge Luis Borges, 'Of exactitude in science', in *A Universal history of infamy*, translated by Norman Thomas di Giovanni (New York 1972), p.141. Borges may well have lifted this image from Lewis Carroll, who made the same point in his *Sylvie and Bruno*.
42. Keates, *Understanding maps*, p.135.

aberrant perspectives that make up the multiple maps/texts of the *Encyclopédie*?

In the 'Discours préliminaire', perhaps the most important examination of the encyclopedic project, we can see that D'Alembert is certainly aware of the fact that this vast map of knowledge is, fundamentally, an error of sorts. We also see clearly the idea that the very aberration of 'order' in the *Encyclopédie* is what makes possible a certain kind of insight. D'Alembert, in a series of explanations, tells us that the systematic representation of knowledge that is graphically displayed in the great 'tree', cannot be constrained by the *real* history or the *real* practices of actual human subjects: 'il ne faut pas croire que l'arbre encyclopédique doive ni puisse même être servile-ment assujetti à cette histoire' (i.xiv). Although the facts of historical development are of necessity the starting point for the project to map scientific practice, this development is not quite the ultimate *object* of this expedition.

For one, D'Alembert points out in another spatial metaphor, the course of scientific activity has been too chaotic, a random tale full of missed paths, obstacles, missteps, and inconsistent progress. In a famous passage D'Alembert writes that the 'système général des Sciences & des Arts est une espece de labyrinthe, de chemin tortueux où l'esprit s'engage sans trop connoître la route qu'il doit tenir'. The discontinuities and disorders of inquiry, D'Alembert says with great candour, 'défigureroit, ou plûtôt anéantiroit entiere-ment un Arbre encyclopédique dans lequel on voudroit le représenter' (i.xiv). And that is not all: the actual history of scientific progress is all backwards, according to D'Alembert. The foundational sciences such as logic and mathematics appear late, invented after the sciences that must be derived from them. The paradox emerges from the unfortunate fact that certain general properties of things can only emerge from long and careful study, even though *logically* these general properties must be the foundation of any true scientific enterprise. And so his map of knowledge will *reverse* the aberration that is empirical historical reality.[43] Finally D'Alembert points out another problem. In reality, many different paths are followed in the sciences at the same time, but it is impossible to represent simultaneity. So the encyclopedic order must create a successive chain of development, if it is going to show the formal links between different studies.

In what seems to be an overt act of ruthless Enlightenment abstraction, then, D'Alembert confidently insists that his encyclopedic order will have none of the inconveniences of this heterogeneous, complex historical reality. But D'Alembert is saying something quite important here. He is suggesting, in fact, that the immediacy of actual experience, the long history of human endeavour, conceals something very real in its disorder, another kind of conceptual order made accessible by the genealogical and

43. Daniel Rosenberg has recently made this same point, in 'An eighteenth-century time machine: the *Encyclopédie* of Denis Diderot', *Historical reflections / réflexions historiques* 25 (1999), p.248.

conceptual rewriting of that history. In his words, the encyclopedic mode allows us to *escape* the discordant experiences that conceal a larger truth. The encyclopedic order, he writes,

consiste à les rassembler dans le plus petit espace possible, & à placer, pour ainsi dire, le Philosophe au-dessus de ce vaste labyrinthe dans un point de vûe fort élévé d'où il puisse appercevoir à la fois les Sciences & les Arts principaux; voir d'un coup d'œil les objets de ses spéculations, & les opérations qu'il peut faire sur ces objets; distinguer les branches générales des connoissances humaines, les points qui les séparent ou qui les unissent; & entrevoir même quelquefois les *routes secretes* qui les rapprochent.[44]

This last phrase is especially important. The admittedly artificial and 'abstract' order of the encyclopedia prepares one to glimpse (*entrevoir*, to see *between* what is immediately visible) the secret connections that are simply unobservable if one is caught in the middle of the labyrinthine reality of experience.

And so, for D'Alembert, the encyclopedic text is literally a map, a guide that becomes necessary precisely because one is *lost* somewhere. This map would hardly be useful if it offered a mimetic representation of a labyrinthine territory. The map must instead elevate us above that territory and show us connections and paths that can be seen only in this 'virtual' or 'adventitious' order (to use Starobinski's terms). Note the importance of the 'path' in this description of the encyclopedic order (i.xv):

C'est une espece de Mappemonde qui doit montrer les principaux pays, leur po- sition & leur dépendance mutuelle, le chemin en ligne droite qu'il y a de l'un à l'autre; chemin souvent coupé par mille obstacles, qui ne peuvent être connus dans chaque pays que des habitans ou des voyageurs, & qui ne sauraient être montrés que des cartes particulieres fort détaillées. Ces cartes particulieres seront les différens articles de notre Encyclopédie, & l'arbre ou système figuré en sera la mappemonde.

The straight path can be found only *after* difficult, tortuous explorations.

The difficulty, for any situated individual, lies in actually constructing this map. One cannot, of course, literally rise above the labyrinth at will in order to see clearly every twist and turn. Some technique must be found that will allow one to move *from* the labyrinth toward greater insight. As D'Alembert suggests, a virtual perspective must be created by *reconfiguring* the complex and often chaotic world of factual experience. Like eighteenth-century conjectural histories, this perspective is artificial and arbitrary, yet also epistemologically critical (i.xv):

Mais comme dans les cartes générales du globe que nous habitons, les objets sont plus ou moins rapprochés, & présentent un coup d'œil différent selon le point de vûe où l'œil est placé par le Géographe qui construit la carte, de même la forme de l'arbre encyclopédique dépendra du point de vûe où l'on se mettra pour envisager l'univers littéraire.

44. i.xv, emphasis added.

To rise above the labyrinth, a perspective must be chosen to organise the virtual representation. The one perspective chosen is for this reason 'arbitrary', but we should note that the root of this word is related to *judgement*. One decides on a point of view that will reveal certain kinds of connections: 'On peut donc imaginer autant de systèmes différens de la connoissance humaine, que de Mappemondes de différentes projections; & chacun de ces systèmes pourra même avoir, à l'exclusion des autres, quelque avantage particulier.' The map, according to D'Alembert, does not function mimetically. Rather, the map must *reveal* something not given in the immediate cartographic object: that is why the projection can take any number of forms. The map is a transformation of its object, but like all rhetorical transformations, it is at once both a resemblance and an aberration. In this case, however, it is the *aberration* of the encyclopedic *mappemonde*, the violation of actual scientific practice and experience, that makes this transformation valuable. In the end D'Alembert says that the best map is not so much the most 'accurate' (for that would simply replicate the confusions of the labyrinth) as that which reveals the most relationships: 'celui de tous les arbres encyclopédiques qui offriroit le plus grand nombre de liaisons, & de rapports entre les Sciences, mériteroit sans doute d'être préféré' (i.xv).

The problem is the very fact that these relations and connections remain invisible without the process of mapping, which means that any one map is potentially incomplete, or even mistaken, if it fails to reveal important links between the zones of human knowledge. D'Alembert pointedly wonders whether or not the *Encyclopédie* has 'seized' that perfect order. The problem is twofold: since Nature itself does not reveal its inner secrets, the myriad relations that interconnect the universe of phenomena, our own scientific classifications and modes of inquiry are potentially in error. This means that any subsequent mapping of the sciences and arts is subject to error on two levels: not only might the map be imperfect, concealing relations between zones of knowledge, but these zones themselves, the starting point of the encyclopedic map, might be in error. Yet this is not a statement of despair. The mapping of nature that is science is not some arbitrary imposition of order on a chaotic set of individual and discrete objects. As D'Alembert says, the object of this scientific mapping is the same as the encyclopedic task: to reveal hidden relations. Our classifications aim to do this, even if the very act of organisation introduces the possibility of error (i.xv):

La Nature, nous ne saurions trop le répéter, n'est composée que d'individus qui sont l'objet primitif de nos sensations & de nos perceptions directes. Nous remarquons à la vérité dans ces individus, des propriétés communes par lesquelles nous les comparons, & des propriétés dissemblables par lesquelles nous les discernons; & ces propriétés désignées par des noms abstraits, nous ont conduit à former différentes classes où ces objets ont été placés. Mais souvent tel objet qui par une ou plusieurs de ses propriétés a été placé dans une classe, tient à une autre classe par d'autres propriétés, & auroit pû tout aussi-bien y avoir sa place. Il reste donc nécessairement de l'arbitraire dans la division générale.

Still, without this attempt to move *beyond* the immediacy of sensation, the immediacy of the individual objects that present themselves to our sensations, we would have absolutely no indication of the vast structure that is nature. For D'Alembert the order of human classification is an error but not an outright mistake. It is an aberration of the truth of nature's complexity, but for that reason a partial insight into truth. The perfect system, the perfect order, he says, is one that reveals what is on the surface imperceptible: 'L'arrangement le plus naturel seroit celui où les objets succéderoient par les nuances insensibles qui servent tout à la fois à les séparer & à les unir.' Human limitation makes our orders imperfect: 'Mais le petit nombre d'êtres qui nous sont connus, ne nous permet pas de marquer ces nuances. L'Univers n'est qu'un vaste Océan, sur la surface duquel nous appercevons quelques îles plus ou moins grandes, dont la liaison avec le continent nous est cachée' (i.xv).

Diderot, in the 'Prospectus', made the same point concerning the relationship between nature, science, and the *Encyclopédie*. 'La nature', he writes, 'ne nous offre que des choses particulières, infinies en nombre & sans aucune division fixe & déterminée.' He goes on to admit that 'sur cette mer d'objets qui nous environne, s'il en paraît quelques-uns, comme des pointes de rochers, qui semblent percer la surface & dominer les autres, ils ne doivent cet avantage qu'à des systèmes particuliers, qu'à des conventions vagues, & qu'à certains événements étrangers à l'arrangement physique des êtres, & aux vraies institutions de la philosophie.' Our efforts do seem 'arbitrary' here. But significantly, Diderot says something else about 'nature' between these sentences: 'Tout s'y succède par des nuances *insensibles*.'[45] The order of relations we create is not, then, wholly arbitrary; it is, rather, a crude error, an aberrant version of nature's infinite complexity of relations. The map of knowledge that is the *Encyclopédie* functions in the same way. The individual arts and sciences do not exist in isolation, Diderot noted, they are linked by a myriad of intricate relations. The *tableau général* that maps out these relations aims, he says, to 'faire sentir les secours mutuels qu'ils se prêtent' (DPV v.87). This effort is inevitably incomplete, yet the encyclopedic order, as Diderot explains, allows us to move between different zones of knowledge, and we become increasingly aware of their interconnection in the process. This order allows us to 'faire sans égarer le tour du monde littéraire' (DPV v.89). The map shows us where we are and where we might go, even if it cannot show all the possible paths of interconnection. In fact, the map that is the *Encyclopédie* must be 'arbitrary' or risk becoming unreadable.

In the article ENCYCLOPÉDIE Diderot repeats this idea that any division and classification must be somewhat arbitrary, because the complexity of things does not lend itself to simple orders. All the distinctions between various kinds of human knowledge must be decided,

45. Diderot, 'Prospectus', DPV v.91 (emphasis added).

created, distributed: 'Il est donc impossible de bannir l'arbitraire de cette grande distribution première' (DPV vii.217). Or rather, Diderot goes on to say, the only system from which arbitrariness would be excluded is the eternal one of the will of God. Whatever the theological implications of this statement, this ideal perspective serves a specific rhetorical and epistemological function. Diderot is saying here that the arbitrary (because incomplete) human systems of thought are failures not because of their 'arbitrary' character, but because they fail to attain the perfect insight that reveals all those 'imperceptible nuances' that interconnect reality. Without this perfect vision, we must start somewhere, map certain relations, and this beginning point is, of course, wholly arbitrary. Diderot explains the problem of understanding any complex object (DPV vii.211):

En général la description d'une machine peut être entamée par quelque partie que ce soit. Plus la machine sera grande & compliquée, plus il y aura de liaisons entre ses parties, moins on connaîtra ces liaisons; plus on aura de différents plans de description. Que sera-ce donc si la machine est infinie en tout sens; s'il est question de l'univers réel & de l'univers intelligible, ou d'un ouvrage qui soit comme l'empreinte de tous les deux? L'univers soit réel soit intelligible a une infinité de points de vue sous lesquels il peut être représenté, & le nombre des systèmes possibles de la connaissance humaine est aussi grand que celui de ces points de vue.

Still, these points of view allow one to see the 'machine' in its complexity, not just as a collection of parts that could be catalogued. The encyclopedic order, then, is only one point of view but it is an act of understanding, even if it is not a perfect insight.

But Diderot goes further: he says, rather remarkably, that the perfect view that excludes everything arbitrary would not be very effective even if we had access to it. He gives us his own rather Borgesian analogy that shows again how important the very *error* of organised representation is as an essential tool of the intellect (DPV vii.211):

Quant à ce système général d'où l'arbitraire serait exclu, & que nous n'aurons jamais, peut-être ne nous serait-il pas fort avantageux de l'avoir; car quelle différence y aurait-il entre la lecture d'un ouvrage où tous les ressorts de l'univers seraient développés, & l'étude même de l'univers? presque aucune: nous ne serions toujours capables d'entendre qu'une certaine portion de ce grand livre; & pour que l'impatience & la curiosité qui nous dominent & interrompent si communément le cours de nos observations, jetassent de désordre dans nos lectures, nos connaissances deviendraient aussi isolées qu'elles le sont.

The perfect text would be as complex as the universe itself, and would end up being as labyrinthine as its object. This vast text would have to be read in fragments, which means starting somewhere, following traces, and potentially getting lost. The human intellect has to limit its view precisely to maintain some insight into the 'whole', a whole that escapes our direct apprehension. Otherwise, 'perdant la chaîne des inductions, & cessant d'apercevoir les liaisons antérieures & subséquentes, nous aurions bientôt les mêmes vides & les mêmes incertitudes'. It is bad enough that we are continually seeking new relations and new discoveries in nature; 'nous nous occuperions à les remplir, en méditant un volume immense qui n'étant pas plus parfait à nos yeux que l'univers, ne serait pas moins exposé à la témérité de nos doutes & de nos objections' (DPV vii.212).

So Diderot reorients his discussion. We need to rise above the complexity to attain some understanding of our world, yet 'la perfection absolue' of a divine perspective would not in any way supplement or improve our rather limited human understanding. And so, he writes, we must find our own path to this insight, which means we must construct our own view, as D'Alembert also advocated: 'attachons-nous à ce qui convient à notre condition d'homme, & contentons-nous de remonter à quelque notion très générale'. These higher views are not mimetically perfect; actually, just the opposite is the case. The general human perspectives are aberrations of singular experiences, but through that aberration they move us out of the labyrinth and into the light of knowledge (DPV vii.212):

Plus le point de vue d'où nous considérons les objets sera élévé, plus il nous découvra d'étendue, & plus l'ordre que nous suivrons sera instructif & grand. Il faut par conséquent qu'il soit simple, parce qu'il y a rarement de la grandeur sans simplicité; qu'il soit clair & facile; que ce ne soit point un labyrinthe tortueux où l'on s'égare & où l'on n'aperçoive rien au delà du point où l'on est.

Like D'Alembert, Diderot faces the question of how to rise to this level of insight, given that, like cartographers of the eighteenth century, the philosopher is 'earth bound', rooted in the concrete, in a specific place and time. As Diderot asserts, the perspective he seeks must be *constructed*; it is an artificial point by definition. Like D'Alembert, Diderot believes that intellectual order must not follow the twisting paths of a complex reality, 'mais une grande & vaste avenue qui s'étend au loin, & sur la longueur de laquelle on en rencontre d'autres également bien distribuées, qui conduisent aux objets solitaires & écartés par le chemin le plus facile & le plus court'. These roads are an explicitly human intervention into the landscape, according to Diderot, but this is what makes them so useful. It is one thing to map the difficult terrain in detail, but if one wants to move with ease between zones, it is best to construct a straight road. This is, in essence, the function of the *Encyclopédie*, conceived of as a *mappemonde*. It at once constructs and maps a network of easily navigable roads, radiating from the centre that is man himself, just as the construction of actual highways in France transformed the landscape: 'Irregularity gave way to regularity; discontinous itineraries were replaced by continuous ones', and regions were no longer *isolated*. The mastery of space increased the flow of goods, people, and information.[46] Similarly, Diderot acknowledges that the

---

46. Daniel Roche, *France in the Enlightenment*, translated by Arthur Goldhammer (Cambridge, Mass. 1998), p.46. See also Henri Cavaillès, *La Route française: son histoire, sa fonction* (Paris 1946), especially p.66.

artifice of the 'straight' road may be an error with respect to the complex curves of the topography (the road has no 'real' counterpart in nature), but these roads serve that topography. These constructions allow us to move with ease between multiple zones of inquiry, zones that would never directly reveal their own secret itineraries.

Denied access to perfect insight, acts of human understanding move the mind, in an errant fashion, in the direction of possible insight. That is why the inevitability of cartographic error must not deter us from constructing maps. What must be recognised, as D'Alembert points out, is that the map is a tool for provoking knowledge, not fixing it in one place. It is not a static representation of reality: 'Nous ne voulons point ressembler à cette foule de Naturalistes qu'un moderne a eu tant de raison de censurer, & qui occupés sans cesse à diviser les productions de la Nature en genres & en especes, ont consumé dans ce travail un tems qu'ils auroient beaucoup mieux employé à l'étude de ces productions mêmes' (i.xvi). Like the architect whose goal is to build something, not pass his life drawing plans, the encyclopedists aim to create a map that will allow the individual explorer to *do* something, namely, return to the concrete contexts of scientific inquiry. The map is not meant to be a representational (or fetishised) substitute for the activity of science itself (i.xix):

pour ne point sortir de la comparaison que nous avons tirée plus haut des Cartes géographiques, celui qui tiendroit à l'Arbre encyclopédique pour toute connois-sance, n'en auroit guere plus que celui qui pour avoir acquis par les Mappemondes une idée générale du globe & de ses parties principales, se flateroit de connoître les différens Peuples qui l'habitent, & les Etats particuliers qui le composent.

The actual study of concrete reality prepares the way for future discovery that may well in fact supplant the encyclopedic order as it now stands.

So for D'Alembert the human mind is caught in a kind of twilight, cut off from clear insight into the workings of nature even as it escapes the darkness and confusion of immediate experience in its efforts to grasp relationships and laws. D'Alembert's conjectural history of human thought explains this strange situation. What began as a mere tool for survival – the faculty of reason – became for humans a complex gift at a certain point in history. As D'Alembert relates at the start of the 'Discours préliminaire', as soon as the human mind discovers, through repeated observation of the environ-ment, just one of the secrets of nature, an unquenchable desire – curiosity – is awakened. The continuing effort to map all these hidden relations is a sign of both a remarkable ability to break out of our limited existence and of an inherent imperfection. In his critique of Descartes's overly confident geometric method, D'Alembert explains the human predicament in this way:

En formant un ouvrier, Dieu a mis en lui les principes propres à diriger ses opéra-tions; mais destinant l'homme à faire usage du monde, & non à le construire, il s'est contenté de lui en faire connoître sensiblement & expérimentalement les qualités usuelles; il n'a pas jugé à propos de lui accorder la vûe claire de cette machine immense.[47]

Any human system of knowledge, any order, any map, must break free of the merely sensible to glimpse that other reality, which is always outside our reach. The error of the map is an error on the way to a hidden truth, one concealed by the very nature of human understanding.

While a map is a mode of discourse, the rhetorical transformations that make up the cartographic 'text' do not necessarily undermine its ability to represent, if we take care to figure out what it is the map is really trying to represent. The creative distortions of the landscape or territory that are revealed by any rhetorical reading of the map may in fact serve to prepare insight into another kind of reality even as these acts violate the initial object of representation. The map then is not merely a transmitter (more or less accurate) of previously existing facts; it is a process of constructing a new knowledge that did not actually exist prior to the representational act.[48] In other words the map *qua* rhetorical construct provides a vehicle for the representation of a hidden dimension of experience unavailable without the 'fiction' of the map itself. 'Maps enable us', wrote Hans Speier some years ago, 'to perceive visually relationships within a context, as on a symbolic plane we can see what would not be clear to us if we had to rely on immediate sense and experience. Thus maps help us not only to visualise the meaning of remote facts, but they also organise details in a whole which, without the help of the map, would be lost because of our limitations.' The symbolic values help us identify 'unknown relationships'.[49] The point is that the map reveals something only *when* it creatively transforms the immediacy of experience. The error of the map makes possible a representation of something hidden. In his book on the history of cartography in France, Josef Konvitz cites an eighteenth-century version of this idea. 'The use of maps', he writes, 'was advocated in the belief that to look at a map was to see patterns that exist in space but are not apparent to a observer who stands in the landscape.'[50]

And so the encyclopedic map was not an exercise in domination, a pathological 'fetish' or delusion of mimetic perfection imposed on an unruly world. In fact the encyclopedic order was understood as a guide for future discovery, discovery that was not at all predetermined by existing knowledge. In a later text D'Alembert cautioned the philosopher against the temptation to totalise the map, to pretend it had a global extent. Given the inevitable imperfections of our understanding, he advises caution: 'à imiter enfin ces géographes qui, en détaillant avec soin sur leur cartes les régions connues, ne craignent point de laisser des espaces vides à la place des terres

47. CARTÉSIANISME, ii.719.

48. MacEachren, *How maps work*, p.459.

49. Hans Speier, 'Magic geography', *Social research* 8 (1941), p.311, 310.

50. Josef Konvitz, *Cartography in France, 1660-1848: science, engineering and statecraft* (Chicago, Ill. 1987), p.104.

ignorées'.[51] Furthermore, D'Alembert suggestively noted, there was no guarantee that exploration of these lands would result in a continuous, homogeneous map of knowledge.[52] Many connections escape us, and it sometimes happen●that truths do not operate on the same plane. D'Alembert calls these disorienting zones 'isolated and floating' truths. Not exactly incompatible with other systems of knowledge, these strange facts and observations fail to cohere easily with the known terrain. If their exceptional status is only apparent, he says, given the ultimate unity of nature, we nonetheless cannot penetrate the obscurity; our 'carte générale des vérités' remains fractured, at least from our limited perspective.[53] 'Il y a peut-être un phénomène central qui jetterait des rayons non seulement à ceux qu'on a, mais encore à tous ceux que le temps ferait découvrir, qui les unirait, et qui en formerait un système. Mais au défaut de ce centre de correspondance commune, ils demeureront isolés.'[54] Without insight into the whole, we can never be assured of our patterns of order.[55]

The *Encyclopédie* was a map of knowledge, one that represented a hidden reality concealed in the complex and labyrinthine terrains of mind and nature. Given that this cartographic object was never fully visible, the encyclopedic map was always provisional, always in error. The map created an artificial space that allowed the mind to escape the mute specificity of empirical reality, even as it failed to attain the ultimate perspective of divine insight.

51. D'Alembert, *Essai sur les éléments de philosophie*, in *Œuvres complètes* (Paris 1821), i.152.

52. It has been argued that D'Alembert left the *Encyclopédie* in part because he thought the idea of a unified knowledge naive. See Wilhelm Treue, 'D'Alemberts Einleitungen zur Enzyclopädie – heute gelesen', *Blätter für Techniksgeschichte* 51-52 (1989-1990), p.173-86.

53. D'Alembert, *Essai sur les éléments*, p.137-38.

54. Diderot, *Pensées sur l'interprétation de la nature*, DPV ix.73.

55. In an article where one would expect statements of Enlightenment totality D'Alembert notes that many zones of human knowledge remain isolated, unintegrated with other bodies of truth; see COSMOLOGIE (*Ordre Encycl. Entendement. Raison. Philosophie ou Science, Science de la Nature, Cosmologie*), iv.294. Similarly, in the article ORDRE (*Métaphysique*), xi.596, it is said that only a Supreme Being could ever know the principles underlying the ultimate order of the 'vast machine' that is the universe. Human beings are limited to insight into partial modes of order.

DANIEL BREWER

•

Constructing philosophers

THERE is something daunting about wishing to say anything more about the *Encyclopédie*. The time of path-breaking discoveries or of grand, conclusive overviews appears over, and little seems needed to be added to the work of scholars such as Jacques Proust, John Lough, and Robert Darnton.[1] Perhaps we must resign ourselves to performing modest, regional incursions into this massive work, attempting to avoid already trodden pathways in our search for unexplored ones, remaining aware of the risk of encountering dead ends or what may be worse, threads and crevices of increasingly narrow significance. If this is the situation today's scholars of the *Encyclopédie* may feel they face, it results from objective, tangible circumstances: the increased accessibility of this particular text, which has moved from rare book rooms to reprint editions such as the 1985 Pergamon reprint, to the internet via the ARTFL project, and to a CD-ROM format in 2000; the broad, scholarly attention the *Encyclopédie* has received from individual scholars and international research teams; and the development of new research areas, to which the *Encyclopédie* has provided access and which have resulted in fact from the work's very accessibility both as print text and as searchable data base.

But somewhat more abstract, theoretical reasons also explain the difficulty we face in speaking of this text. Quite simply, we are not as certain nor as confident as the encyclopedists themselves were about how to navigate the encyclopedic tree of knowledge, this metaphor figuring what could also be called, at the risk of infusing life into a metaphor best left unturned, the information superhighway of the eighteenth century. The criteria the encyclopedists invoked for determining their relationship to knowledge, together with the language they devised to figure that relationship, seem both transparent and suspect. The values of encyclopedism have become naturalised, especially those values that belong to the Enlightenment project of developing new knowledge and new ways of knowing in order to empower individuals as thinkers and as social subjects. Yet these values also give pause as we consider the various consequences that empowerment may generate. A comment of Diderot's concerning the structure of the *Encyclopédie* illustrates this double bind. Reflecting on the arbitrary epistemological

---

1. Jacques Proust, *Diderot et l'Encyclopédie* (Paris 1962); John Lough, *Essays in the 'Encyclopédie' of Diderot and d'Alembert* (London 1968); Robert Darnton, *The Business of Enlightenment: a publishing history of the 'Encyclopédie', 1775-1800* (Cambridge 1979).

order that the alphabetical structuring of knowledge produces, he notes that a second, properly encyclopedic order can be derived by structuring knowledge in relation to 'man'. 'Pourquoi n'introduirons-nous pas l'homme dans notre ouvrage,' Diderot asks, 'comme il est placé dans l'univers? Pourquoi n'en ferons-nous pas un centre commun? [...] L'homme est le terme unique d'où il faut partir, & auquel il faut tout ramener' (v.641). This other encyclopedic order is represented in the *arbre généalogique des connaissances*, which displays the interconnection of all branches of knowledge based on the encyclopedists' understanding of the working of human thought. What the *arbre* encourages its viewers to believe is that 'man's position' within the world is that of universal thinking subject. That position is far from stable, however, for its universality can be won only by transcending particularities that will not disappear so simply. The place of 'man' in the encyclopedic ordering of knowledge often enough turns out to be occupied by a subject defined by gender, class, and race, to say nothing of place and affect.

Thus, reading the *Encyclopédie* today, we are less certain than its editors were of the legitimacy of key metaphors such as 'man', as well as the master narratives to which they belong. The founding terms and foundational values of encyclopedism, and with them the Enlightenment in general with which they overlap, have been subjected to increasing critical scrutiny. We are certainly more sceptical towards the ideal of universal knowledge, which may well have already become an outmoded epistemological perspective. Universal knowledge, despite the universalising, imperial claims made in its name, is not sufficiently productive knowledge, and thus it is at a kind of technological disadvantage, a situation upon which producers of other kinds of knowledge cannot fail to capitalise.[2] Local knowledges, or know-how, outperform universal knowledge, which is edged out by bodies of information that are designed, distributed, and assessed in function of their use value. Moreover, we are skilled in detecting the place of particular interests within any statement of knowledge, especially that knowledge that claims objective disinterestedness. The danger to which this skill leads, of course, is an agnostic rejection of knowledge, which is quite different from a critical awareness of the way in which all knowledge is situated knowledge, determined by its relation to subjects.

The operative assumption of the following pages is that in returning to the *Encyclopédie* we must determine not only the encyclopedists' admittedly interested relation to the knowledge they sought to produce, shape, and judge, but also our own critical and contemporary relation to that knowledge. To set forth that double relation, I propose to investigate one of the founding images of encyclopedism, the construction of a privileged subject

---

2. In *The Postmodern condition* (Minneapolis 1984), Jean-François Lyotard analyses this shift in the state of knowledge, suggesting an avenue of further inquiry into the transformations of the function and configurations of the university, where knowledge is produced.

of knowledge figured in the pages of the *Encyclopédie* and also in the culture of the *ancien régime*, that of the *philosophe*. The objective here will be to analyse how the encyclopedic text provides a means for its writers and readers to construct a 'modern' subject, and thereby to phrase their relation to their own emergent modernity.

Writers and philosophers, *ancien régime*

The French *philosophe* is a familiar figure. Writer, thinker, and sometimes activist, the *philosophe* is exemplified by canonised individuals such as Voltaire, Diderot, D'Alembert, and Condillac, but also by numerous other members of the literate class, writers and *gens de lettres* that history remembers less well. Not a philosopher in a contemporary, disciplinary, institutional sense, the *philosophe* is a distant precursor of today's public intellectual. These two are not synonymous of course, for they designate cultural realities as different as the *ancien régime* and twentieth-century republican France. Each is a particular phase in a common cultural genealogy. Thus the *philosophe* can be thought of as an historically determined symbolic construction, produced in the eighteenth century and available to us today as a kind of cultural 'memory site', to borrow a notion from Pierre Nora, through which we can phrase the relation between past and present.[3] Precursor of the public intellectual, the figure of the *philosophe* has its own precursors as well. Chief among them is that of the writer, whose 'birth' in seventeenth-century France made possible the emergence of the *philosophe* in the shape this figure would assume in the next century.[4]

If the writer was born in the seventeenth century, it was due in no small measure to the cultural policy of the absolutist state, which set institutions in place that supported the production of elite culture. This support helped produce increasingly autonomous high cultural spaces. Academies quickly became centres that socialised artists and writers, providing them with contacts, mutual support, and social recognition. Because of the privileges these state-sponsored academies afforded, they risked becoming institutions that served to maintain the status quo, mediocrity, and gerontocracy. Representing a counter-force to this development, numerous salons were founded that also served to socialise artists and writers. These salons were places where literary issues were discussed, but also where a discourse of cultural politics was developed that provided salon-goers with a mode of

---

3. See Nora's essay on cultural identity formation, 'Entre mémoire et histoire: la problématique des lieux', in *Les Lieux de mémoire* (Paris 1984-1992), i.xvii-xlii.
4. Numerous cultural, literary, and book historians have provided a detailed analysis of this event. See for example Roger Chartier, *Lectures et lecteurs dans la France d'Ancien Régime* (Paris 1987), and *Culture écrite et société* (Paris 1996); Eric Walter, 'Les auteurs et le champ littéraire', in *Histoire de l'édition française*, ed. Henri-Jean Martin, vol.ii: *Le Livre triomphant (1660-1830)* (Paris 1984), p.383-409; Alain Viala, *La Naissance de l'écrivain: sociologie de la littérature à l'âge classique* (Paris 1985).

strategic resistance, albeit limited, to the hegemony of court culture.[5] Both academic and salon culture helped bring about the emergence of the writer, who was relieved although not entirely freed from the constraints of aristocratic patronage, and newly subjected to the pressure of state patronage. The writer of the seventeenth century is no longer the scribe of the previous century, the term *écrivain* coming to designate the creator of works possessing an esthetic element. The three major dictionaries of the period, produced by the Académie française, Furetière, and Richelet, illustrate this semantic shift. The term *écrivain* first becomes synonymous with *auteur*, then in successive editions outstrips it, designating an activity to which greater and greater prestige or cultural capital is attached. A further consequence of this reconfiguration of the cultural field during the seventeenth century is the development of new reading publics, and especially of writers' sense of their power to shape these publics' sensibility. What occurs, finally, in the flourishing of court culture during the reign of Louis XIV is the production of 'literature', with the literary field designating a specific and increasing autonomous social space.

The emergence of the literary field in the seventeenth century is part of the larger process, the development of what Pierre Bourdieu has called the intellectual field in Western culture. For Bourdieu culture is a structured system of relations comparable to the forces of a magnetic field, where the power and authority of individual elements or agents are determined by their dynamic relation to other components of the field. Bourdieu's field theory aims at accounting for culture not only structurally but temporally, claiming that elements of culture must be understood in their ultimately historical dimension. In the case of the intellectual field, this means viewing it as resulting from an historical process of increasing differentiation and autonomy. Thus the development of seventeenth-century court culture is but one moment in the gradual organisation of cultural life into an intellectual field taking place during the Middle Ages and Renaissance, as creators of high culture free themselves both economically and socially from court and church. That story continues in France beyond the Ancien Régime, with the more extensive development of institutions that strengthen and expand the intellectual field, such as the school and university systems of post-revolutionary republican France, and the publishing and communications industry of more recent times. The elements of this more recent development of the intellectual field have been analysed extensively by Bourdieu and others.[6]

---

5. See Carolyn Lougee, *Le Paradis des femmes: women, salons, and social stratification in seventeenth-century France* (Princeton 1976), and Joan DeJean, *Tender geographies: women and the origins of the novel in France* (New York, 1991).

6. See Pierre Bourdieu, *Distinction: a social critique of the judgement of taste*, translated by Richard Nice (Cambridge, Mass., 1984). An extensive literature exists on the post-revolutionary development of the intellectual field. See Christophe Charle, *Naissance des 'intellectuels' 1880-1900* (Paris 1990). Régis Debray analyses the transformation of modern French

To avoid the risk of conflating description and analysis, a risk to which field theory often leads, we would do well to recall that in seeking to understand the cultural field Bourdieu starts from the assumption that its workings are not obvious. The cultural field can govern intellectual operations, but without being apprehended from within the field itself. The enabling conditions of intellectual production remain the unspoken of the cultural field, mediating and governing all operations there, all the while remaining unstated. But this silence is not that of what is simply unsaid. It is as if there were something about the cultural field that resists analysis and understanding, a kind of cultural unconsciousness that cannot be understood in terms of individuals' awareness but that nonetheless receives material form in the cultural practice of symbolic production, notably in textual practices. That symbolic production in turn must be analysed through the inevitable tension between what the text of culture 'says' and what remains unsaid. Because of this tension, one might conclude that the texts of culture can never simply be paraphrased, at least not without running the risk of simply pursuing and perpetuating the ideological work of the text.[7]

Given these extensive theoretical concerns, which have inescapable consequences for the practice of interpretation, how do we go about understanding the figure of the *philosophe* that is constructed in the eighteenth century? There are numerous textual entry points for beginning such an analysis, from prose fiction to letters, memoirs, and reception speeches.[8] Let us begin by identifying one of most influential texts to construct this image, the article PHILOSOPHE of the *Encyclopédie*. Commonly attributed to César Chesneau Dumarsais, the *grammairien-philosophe* associated with the Ecole royale militaire and who wrote a number of articles on grammar for the *Encyclopédie*, this article is an abridged version of a short treatise that appeared earlier in 1743 under the title 'Le Philosophe'. From the moment of its publication, this text was widely circulated and was to be found, says Voltaire, 'dans le portefeuille de tous les curieux'.[9] Voltaire published the article in 1773 and it appeared in an edition of Helvétius's works. The article is important, from a literary historical perspective, because of its place in the clandestine literature of the period, the French literary underground. It was highly instrumental in consolidating a semantic,

intellectuals into teachers, writers, and celebrities, which is roughly the English translation of his *Le Pouvoir intellectuel en France* (Paris 1979).

7. This notion of the unsaid is of course the cornerstone of the most productive theoretical understandings of ideology. See Fredric Jameson, *The Political unconscious* (Ithaca, N.Y. 1981).

8. I undertake this more extensive analysis in *Instituting Enlightenment*, ch.1 (forthcoming).

9. For an evaluation of this text's significance within the Enlightenment, see Herbert Dieckmann, *Le Philosophe: texts and interpretation* (St Louis 1948), here p.9; and Ira O. Wade, *The Clandestine organization and diffusion of philosophic ideas in France from 1700 to 1750* (Princeton 1938).

intellectual, and sociological shift under way in France at the time.[10] Less and less was the kind of writing designated by the term 'philosophy' represented as marginal with respect to the social order, whether this marginality was viewed as harmless or on the contrary as subversive. Instead, philosophy was portrayed with increasing frequency as serving an essentially critical role within society.

An indication of this shift is seen by comparing earlier representations of the figure of the *philosophe*, such as the entry *'philosophe'* in the *Dictionnaire de l'Académie française*. In the editions of 1694, 1718, and even until 1740, the *Dictionnaire* defined the *philosophe* first in relation to logical inquiry, second in terms of a mode of behaviour, a secluded and modest life, and third as incarnating a potentially disruptive way of thinking. The third definition reads as follows: '[philosophe] se dit aussi quelque fois absolument, d'un homme, qui, par libertinage d'esprit, se met au dessus des devoirs et des obligations ordinaires de la vie civile et chrétienne. C'est un homme qui ne refuse rien, qui ne se contraint sur rien, et qui mène une vie de Philosophe.' Linked to a critical libertinage tradition, the *philosophe* is represented here as incarnating a potential threat both to good manners and to religion.[11] By 1743, however, the *philosophe* of the Academy's *Dictionnaire* was a *philosophe* in name only, that is, an outmoded figure that Dumarsais's text will attempt to displace and do away with from its opening lines: 'Il n'y a rien qui coûte moins à acquérir aujourd'hui que le nom de philosophe; une vie obscure et retirée, quelques dehors de sagesse avec un peu de lectures suffisent pour attirer ce nom à des personnes qui s'en honorent sans le mériter.'[12] In this passage a strategy is employed of which the encyclopedists frequently avail themselves, that of affirming the relation between name and thing as a matter of convention. Socially determined and not fixed by nature, this relation is arbitrary and thus is subject to revision. Nothing is easier to acquire than the *name* of philosopher – the proper manner and some well-placed references will suffice. But this means the conventional definition of *philosophe* can be rewritten according to other, more 'useful' criteria – useful knowledge being highly valorised by the encyclopedists – in other words more critical and productive ones. The article PHILO-SOPHE rewrites prior definitions in just this fashion, rejecting the image of the *philosophe* as a simple libertine, whether deist or atheist, who had 'la force de se défaire des préjugés de religion en matière de religion'. The

10. For an overview of this shift that focuses on the figure of the writer, see Roger Chartier, 'The man of letters', in *Enlightenment portraits*, ed. Michel Vovelle, translated by Lydia Cochrane (Chicago 1997), p.142-89.

11. These earlier representations of the figure of the *philosophe* merit careful attention. While the *Dictionnaire de l'Académie* displays already in 1694 a certain uneasiness regarding the threatening libertinage the philosophe may foster, the Jesuits' *Dictionnaire de Trévoux* gives no indication of such a threat until after 1743. As Dieckmann notes, this change of attitude provides an interesting indication of the development of the anti-philosophe movement in eighteenth-century France, as well as the Jesuit order's relation to Enlightenment.

12. Quotations from PHILOSOPHE are from the Dieckmann edition; here, p.30.

philosophe fashioned here differs from that of the Academy's *Dictionnaire* in that this article works to represent a more 'modern', enlightened subject. The article goes on to describe this subject in terms of two constitutive traits, namely, a particular type of philosophical inquiry and social behaviour.

The first of the *philosophe*'s traits defined here is the particular type of knowledge this figure represents. Imbued with an 'esprit philosophique', 'un esprit d'observation et de justesse qui rapporte tout à ses véritables principes', this version of the *philosophe* belongs to early mainstream Enlightenment thinking. Exemplifying the move away from Cartesian idealism, this text rejects 'méditation' as a source of knowledge, maintaining that truth must be grounded on empirical observation, not on pure speculation. Affirming the sensationalist credo that all knowledge comes from the senses, the *philosophe* acquires a new empowered self-sufficiency insofar as he quite literally embodies knowing. (Diderot will explore the limit case of this way of knowing through the epistemological set-up of *Le Rêve* – knowing through the body.) In search of first causes, the *philosophe* need go no further than the very body, for thought itself is a kind of sense. The fantasmatic image proposed here to illustrate this epistemology is that of the clock that winds itself. (No mention is made of any clockmaker, the issue of divine existence or action being one this text resolutely skirts.) If Enlightenment discourse is marked by an intellectual, social, and ideological struggle, the scene of eighteenth-century culture wars, then the article PHILOSOPHE too can be seen not only as affirming new 'true' principles, but also as seeking to found them rhetorically by contesting and displacing others. Quite expectedly, the rationalism affirmed here is radical and intransigent, designed to replace not only speculative metaphysics and idealism, but also religion: 'La raison est à l'égard du philosophe ce que la grâce est à l'égard du chrétien [...]. La grâce détermine le chrétien à agir volontairement; la raison détermine le philosophe, sans lui ôter le goût du volontaire' (p.32).

It is claimed not only that rationalism replaces religion but that a new sociability does as well, which constitutes a second aspect of the image of the *philosophe* the article develops: 'Le philosophe est jaloux de tout ce qui s'appelle honneur et probité: c'est là son unique religion. La société civile est, pour ainsi dire, la seule divinité qu'il reconnaisse sur la terre; il l'encense, il l'honore par la probité, par une attention exacte à ses devoirs et par le désir sincère de n'en être pas un membre inutile ou embarrassant' (p.46). The *philosophe*'s intellectual pursuits, even those that aim at dislodging the wisdom of tradition, do not preclude him from being an essentially social creature. Here we see an important difference between the mid-eighteenth-century image of the *philosophe* and that of a half-century earlier. One of the chief traits of the *philosophe* of earlier generations was retreat, a willed withdrawal from social pressures and obligation in favour of a simpler, more honest life of philosophical reflection. In the philosophical tradition, this notion of speculative retreat is a common-place. What does it signify, however, when read in relation to the social and cultural context in which it is activated?

In the highly integrated Parisian court culture of Louis XIV, the concept of retreat was a complicated one. For the court nobility, such retreat was in fact a kind of exile, tantamount to the loss of wealth, privileges, and power. For the nobility that derived its sense of identity from its place within court culture, choosing such retreat was unthinkable. For other groups, however, anxious to imagine ways of constructing forms of social identity removed from court culture if not entirely independent of it, the notion of retreat was a more appealing one. As freely chosen state, retreat was not necessarily exile, and thus it signified potentially a certain degree of autonomy and difference. One of the best-known novels of the seventeenth century, La-fayette's *La Princesse de Clèves*, ends with a scene of retreat, as the novel's heroine leaves Paris to spend the remaining few years of her life in seclu-sion. Generations of readers of this novel have grappled with the meaning of this final act. Is it a tragic and fatal ending, which befalls a heroine no longer able to resolve competing exigencies of love and duty? For long it seemed that seventeenth-century readers must have interpreted the novel through the same lens as the one they used to view the classical tragedies of Corneille and Racine, where the logic of the tragic genre meted out a similar mortal fate. In these plays the tragic hero is a victim whose individ-ual death affirms the survival of a collective order, be it moral, social or political. Recently, however, the retreat of the Princess has been seen as a form of affirmative resistance, an act whereby the heroine removes herself from the competing demands of husband and lover, as well as from a social order that defines her place in terms of such demands. Despite the interest of this new reading of the Princess's act, it remains a 'literary' retreat. In actual social practice, retreat took place in a limited number of instances, the most notable of which are perhaps the literary salons established by women such as Mlle de Scudéry. Retreat occurred as well in religious institutions such as Port-Royal (even if convents functioned more often as spaces of imprisoning exile for girls and women). In terms of its symbolic function, however, as an image that may not have reflected reality but that produced effects that were nonetheless real, the image of retreat doubt-less served to affirm and in fact perform the idea of withdrawal, to maintain it as an act that could be realised, if only in an imaginary, symbolic way. It would have been all the more important to make such withdrawal appear possible, given the regulative pressures of a courtly society.[13]

By the eighteenth century the need for such a symbolic escape valve was less pressing. Accordingly, the imaginary spaces constructed in literature and other forms of educated writing were configured differently and served other purposes. The established genre of utopian literature

13. See Norbert Elias, *The Court society*, translated by Edmund Jephcott (New York 1983).

continues, intersecting with a flourishing new genre of travel literature. In both cases, however, the symbolic exteriority provided by the fictional, narrative elaboration of 'exotic' other spaces tended to affirm the cultural order instead of offering a retreat or escape from it. In the case of the *philosophe* the voluntary withdrawal of the previous century tends increasingly to be rewritten as an intellectual exteriority affording critical insights concerning arbitrary and dogmatic norms, insights that contribute to intellectual and social change. Viewing themselves as both agents and instruments of that change, eighteenth-century *philosophe*-writers claim to be necessary members of the social order, yet they argue with equal conviction that they wish to remain free from what they see as its contingent and arbitrary determinations. For Jean Marie Goulemot, the numerous, almost obsessively repetitive gestures of self-representation on the part of eighteenth-century *philosophes* constitute the beginnings of the modern notion of writer and writing: 'Fonder la vérité de ce que l'on dit sur sa vocation malheureuse, sa marginalité, son ego ou la rigueur de sa vie, voilà qui représente l'archéologie d'un discours actuel sur l'écriture [...]. Ce qui aujourd'hui constitue l'image de l'écrivain comme rebelle, un opposant par nature, un marginal par obligation et écriture, vient de loin.'[14] Following Goulemot, we might view Jean-Jacques Rousseau as the most modern of eighteenth-century writers, for the truth that Rousseau makes public in the *Confessions*, the *Rêveries d'un promeneur solitaire*, and other intimate writing is a personal, private one. The truth these texts recount is that of an alienated individual, an 'ex-centric' subject whose individual experience is presented nonetheless as transcending that particularity to serve as the foundation of a new social order based on a kind of general particularity, which can be theorised in literary terms through Rousseau's autobiographical writing and in political terms through his notion of the general will.

The case of Rousseau must be set within the context of the changing socio-economic conditions of literary activity of *ancien régime* France. The sphere of educated writing, *les lettres*, was reshaped as the writer's dependence on an aristocratic patronage system weakened. That system was being replaced by a market economy in which publishers' sales figures, not the will of the aristocratic wealthy, determined who would write, what would be written, and most significantly what would be published. Consequently, authors came to see themselves as producing works to which it was possible to have rights, which moreover had economic value. The publishing industry is not yet the sole source of support for the eighteenth-century writer, and market economy capitalism is not yet seen as sufficient for explaining the work of writing and writer. For the economic sphere of

14. Jean-Marie Goulemot and Daniel Oster, *Gens de lettres, écrivains et bohèmes: l'imaginaire littéraire, 1630-1900* (Paris 1992), p.9, 11. Edward Said extends this idea of the marginalised, alienated writer to include the intellectual whose viewpoint, he argues, is always 'exilic', as she or he moves away from and against centralising authority and towards margins: *Representations of the intellectual* (New York 1994).

the book trade intersected with another economic sphere, that of the state and its extensive system of privileges. Writers may have amassed social capital from being admitted to the salon world, but they acquired real wealth from membership in the numerous academies and other institutions of elite culture. Robert Darnton argues that two distinct literary worlds take shape after mid-century: the 'high' Enlightenment where writers form a part of the social and cultural elite, moving easily between salons and academies; and the 'literary underground', composed of still aspiring – or already failed – *philosophes*, writers, and critics.[15] The literary world may not have been as dichotomous as the binary metaphors of 'high' and 'low' suggest though. Sizeable numbers of mid-level writers existed – journalists, editors, translators, and compilers – who propagated Enlightenment without necessarily producing it originally.[16]

These entwined issues of philosophical reflection, social integration, and economic benefit traverse the article PHILOSOPHE. The *philosophe* may establish a critical remove from traditional thinking, but he is not some marginalised rebel who proclaims the purifying value of alienation. Such solitude is in fact presented here as unthinkable, amounting to a kind of monstrosity: 'L'homme n'est point un monstre qui ne doive vivre que dans les abîmes de la mer ou dans le fond d'une forêt' (p.42). Invoking the idea of an intrinsic, essential sociability in the individual, the text affirms that the *philosophe*'s place is located quite naturally in the social order: 'Notre philosophe ne se croit pas en exil dans ce monde; il ne croit point être en pays ennemi' (p.44). It is only natural that the *philosophe* would be sociable in this world, for there can be no hope of gain or punishment in any future one. The religious paradigm is replaced by the social paradigm, just as it was by the sensationalist paradigm earlier in the text.

Sociability does not remain an abstract principle and universal value for long here, for it is soon linked to a well-defined system of exchange, interest, and benefits. This linkage is suggested by the following lapidary definition of the *philosophe*'s social character: 'c'est un honnête homme qui veut plaire et se rendre utile' (p.44). The term *honnête homme* designated a complex cultural formation in *ancien régime* France. In the texts of seventeenth-century moralists, *honnêteté* refers to a specific kind of moral character that

---

15. Robert Darnton, *The Literary underground of the Old Regime* (Cambridge 1982).

16. Geoffrey Turnovsky proposes an alternative view of the literary field, which he argues is characterised 'by a trend not towards disequilibrium and proletarianisation, but towards the development of a mid-level field of opportunities, between High and Low, in which aspirants who were not destined for glory were able nonetheless to sustain viable, desirable livelihoods', 'Reconsidering the literary underground in France, 1750-1789' (unpublished paper). Gregory Brown also argues for a more nuanced view of the eighteenth-century writer's situation that avoids projecting a twentieth-century antithesis between individual autonomy and state repression, 'Reconsidering the censorship of writers in eighteenth-century France' (unpublished paper). Cf. Rémy Saisselin, *The Literary enterprise in eighteenth-century France* (Detroit 1979); Elizabeth Eisenstein, *Grub Street abroad: aspects of the French cosmopolitan press from the age of Louis XIV to the French Revolution* (New York 1992).

individuals may possess regardless of social class. But moral values and social structures are seldom so easily separated. *Honnêteté* is not a classless ideal. If it appeared as such to some, this is because of the term's rhetorical and ideological function in the discourse of a changing social order. As Michael Moriarty has argued, *honnêteté* was 'the site of a class's renegotiation of its position, a renegotiation that took account of new recruitment to this class and a new relationship of this class to other social groups'.[17]

By 1743 when 'Le Philosophe' was written, the renegotiation of social position and cultural capital that had taken place in the previous century through the discourse of *honnêteté* was essentially a fait accompli. Consequently, through reference to the figure of the *honnête homme* in 1743, particular moral values are introduced into the discussion of what constitutes a *philosophe*; at the same time, reference to this figure also recalls a discursive strategy for forming an emergent social figure. Values and interests dovetail here in the construction of the figure of the *philosophe*, a figure located far more explicitly in the economic sphere than was the *honnête homme* of the seventeenth century. If the *philosophe* is defined as wanting to please and be useful, it appears that this *utilité* or usefulness is inseparable from a certain self-interest, which is phrased here in terms of pleasure and economic advantage: '[Notre philosophe] veut jouir en sage économe des biens que la nature lui offre; il veut trouver du plaisir avec les autres, et pour en trouver il faut en faire. Ainsi, il cherche à convenir à ceux, avec qui le hasard ou son choix le font vivre, et il trouve en même temps ce qui lui convient' (p.44). Seeking to combine *sagesse, économie,* and *jouissance* ('jouir en sage économe'), the *philosophe* works to set up a situation in which it is by giving others pleasure that the *philosophe* finds what suits him, what is appropriate, what he desires.

Pleasure and happiness are subjected to demanding calculation moreover: 'Le vrai philosophe n'est point tourmenté par l'ambition; mais il veut avoir les douces commodités de la vie. Il lui faut, outre le nécessaire précis, un honnête superflu nécessaire à un honnête homme, et par lequel seul on est heureux' (p.60). How are we to understand terms such as 'douces commodités' and 'honnête superflu', which constitute the *philosophe*'s happiness? Are these the creature comforts of a developing consumer society, praised by Voltaire in *Le Mondain*?[18] Or do these lines betray a thrifty wisdom on the part of our 'sage économe', ever first to calculate the benefits to be derived from each word and act, according to an economic principle that legitimates excess (the 'honnête superflu') without asking at whose particular expense this excess is derived. Phrasing this question in admittedly far

---

17. Michael Moriarty, *Taste and ideology in seventeenth-century France* (Cambridge 1988), p.52.

18. 'J'aime le luxe et même la mollesse, / Tous les plaisirs, les arts et toute espèce, / La propreté, le goût, les ornements: / Tout honnête homme a de tels sentiments / [...] Ah! le bon temps que ce siècle de fer!' Although more restrained in his *Défense du Mondain* (1737) and more nuanced in his *Discours en vers sur l'homme* (1738), Voltaire's epicureanism will remain a constant ideal in his writing.

broader terms, we can ask whether it is sufficient to borrow the Enlightenment writer's own terms to describe the writer's situation, thereby reproducing the image that writers produced of themselves? Or should we instead seek ways to resist the lure of that tantalising image, refusing paraphrase and striving to resituate powerful concepts and the values they convey? I would argue that such a resistant reading should be precisely the goal of critical interpretation. Here follows a brief example of one direction such a resistant reading of the image of the *philosophe* might take.

The first step in such a reading involves determining how a text such as 'Le Philosophe' can be understood historically as symbolic construction rather than as unmediated reflection. Herbert Dieckmann's commentary on 'Le Philosophe' illustrates the latter understanding of the text. For Dieckmann, 'Le Philosophe' both belongs to and reflects an historical moment of transition, in which the seventeenth-century notion of aristocratic civility was losing its intellectual force and regulative function. The *honnête homme* of the court was becoming the urban, cosmopolitan *philosophe*. As Dieckmann puts it, 'the philosopher freed himself from the standards of polite society; he felt no longer bound to its code, but to the *bien public* and the *genre humain*; from an observer of the "bienséances" and the "délicatesses sensibles" he became a guide and leader of humanity; it was to the larger world that he was going to devote his thought and actions.'[19] Now it is surely correct to point to a general decline in the power of eighteenth-century court culture to produce or shape significant intellectual or esthetic works. But we should exercise slightly more caution than Dieckmann does in linking that historical context to a reading of its texts. Most notably, his commentary collapses the distinction between actual writers (the *philosophes* or those who aspired to such a state) and the image of this social type constructed by these writers, an image that tacitly performed a strategic symbolic function. As a result of collapsing the distinction between historical context and its representation, the interpretive perspective that I am using Dieckmann to illustrate here in fact continues the rhetorical, performative work that the image of the *philosophe* originally was designed to do. In presenting the *philosophe* as someone able, as if at will, to free himself from society's constraints and become a citizen of the world, this perspective essentially repeats the gesture of numerous eighteenth-century writers who represented themselves as free from historical determination. Such a state is a paradise soon to be lost, as Roland Barthes puts it in an essay on Voltaire, arguing that history soon enough catches up with these writers, and all who imagine themselves beyond it. Interestingly enough, Barthes's early essay condenses into the figure of Voltaire an image of the eighteenth century that Jean-Paul Sartre had developed two decades earlier in *Qu'est-ce que la littérature?* For Sartre the situation of the eighteenth-century writer was perfectly utopian, for

19. Dieckmann, p.91-92.

although he imagined himself as liberated from court culture he had not yet become alienated from bourgeois society.[20] Thus it seemed both possible and legitimate to espouse universally applicable values, ideals, and prescriptions that in fact were derived from the writer's particular situation. An especially pointed critique of this strategy is given by Louis Althusser. 'When during the eighteenth century, the "rising class", the bourgeoisie, developed a humanist ideology of equality, freedom and reason,' he argues, 'it gave its own demands the form of universality, since it hoped thereby to enroll at its side, by their education to this end, the very men it would liberate only for their exploitation.' The relation between this class and its own ideology was not 'an external and lucid relation of pure utility and cunning', for the bourgeois subject lives out in the ideology of freedom 'the relation between it and its conditions of existence: that is, its real relation (the law of a liberal capitalist economy) but invested in an imaginary relation (all men are free, including the free laborers)'.[21] Following · Althusser, one can ask to what extent 'Le Philosophe' too involves a real relation – intellectual work – but set in an imaginary relation – the writer free to become through his writing a citizen of the world, a state presented as available to all enlightened subjects. To the extent that it can be read according to this paradigm, 'Le Philosophe' deploys a strategy designed above all to provide a symbolic resolution to particular social contradictions. The image of the *philosophe* constructed here thus works to paper over the kind of contradictions Althusser describes, or more precisely to stabilise and neutralise them.

The article PHILOSOPHE, I have suggested, presents an image of the *philosophe* that is defined by the ultimately unsuccessful attempt to stabilise the essentially contradictory nature of this figure. Other versions of the eighteenth-century *philosophe* suggest much more wariness towards such a goal. Diderot, for instance, presents in *Le Neveu de Rameau* a figure of the *philosophe* that is in fact double, represented by both of the characters of the text, Moi and Lui. Moi may be referred to by Lui as 'Monsieur le philosophe', but each of them has his own relation to truth, and each provides a particular way to 'démêler son monde'. As is inevitably the case in Diderot's writing, apparent unity is destabilised in this text, and the image of the *philosophe* is rent in two. In this split, any number of oppositions – between the universal and the particular, the general good and individual self-interest, the useful *philosophe* and the deceptive social parasite – are forcefully played out in all their problematic consequences. One of these consequences involves posterity, the *philosophe*'s successors, those who may have 'the last laugh' the Nephew refers to. Diderot's text thus reminds us that the question regarding the image of the *philosophe* is not, and cannot be, limited to the

---

20. Roland Barthes, 'Le dernier des écrivains heureux', in *Essais critiques* (Paris 1964); Jean-Paul Sartre, *Qu'est-ce que la littérature?* (Paris 1945).

21. Louis Althusser, *For Marx*, translated by Ben Brewster (London 1969), p.234.

eighteenth century, for the cultural field of the Enlightenment is one to which we too are linked, however uneasily at times we occupy this field and despite all too justifiable misgivings. The image of the *philosophe* must be read as prefiguring, however remotely, another figure in and through which another modern moment is represented once again, through another symbolic construction or *image tutélaire*, that of the intellectual. How might one imagine a possible linkage between these two moments? Moreover, how does such a linkage exemplify the resistant reading strategy in which we are engaged?

In the eighteenth century 'un monde naît, qui deviendra plus tard celui des intellectuels, dans lequel au philosophe de type nouveau sont reconnus une universelle compétence et un droit illimité d'intervention dans les affaires de la cité. L'écrivain se veut juge, guide, seul capable d'inscrire la totalité du monde réel dans les mots et les pages, privilège dont *Encyclopédie* offre l'illustration la plus achevée.'[22] At present, however, that utopian world of proto-intellectuals seems distant. Or rather, it is constituted by a way of speaking in which it has become difficult to engage. This is the position taken by Jean-François Lyotard, who proposes understanding the term intellectual as designating not a person to be described in professional, institutional or sociological terms, but rather a specific type of discourse:

Les intellectuels sont [...] des esprits qui, se situant à la place de l'homme, de l'humanité, de la nation, du peuple, du prolétariat, de la créature ou de quelque entité de cette sorte, c'est-à-dire s'identifiant à un sujet doté d'une valeur universelle, décrivent, analysent de ce point de vue une situation ou une condition et prescrivent ce qui doit être fait pour que ce sujet se réalise ou du moins pour que sa réalisation progresse.[23]

Intellectual discourse is based on the assumption that its particular subject can identify (or be identified) with a universal subject.

Thus the intellectual is completely distinct from information 'managers' of what Lyotard calls the new 'techno-sciences of language' whose responsibilities are designed to realise maximum efficiency (by maximising profit), not to question the limits and conditions of those responsibilities. The intellectual is also distinct from the writer, the artist, and the philosopher, whose responsibility involves testing the limits of his/her domain, questioning the accepted criteria of judgement in writing, painting or thought. What has made the intellectual's situation critical, argues Lyotard, is that since the mid-twentieth century there has been no way to think universality, to justify claims made in the name of a universal subject.[24] 'Enlightenment' is the term used by Lyotard to designate universalising thinking (although one should note that in the writings of modern French philosophers, the

---

22. Goulemot, p.8.
23. Lyotard, *Tombeau de l'intellectuel* (Paris 1984), p.12.
24. Lyotard explains the historical specificity of this remark and pursues this reflection in his essay, 'Discussions, ou: phraser "après Auschwitz"', *Les Fins de l'homme* (Paris 1981), p.283-308. See also *Le Différend* (Paris 1983).

term tends to refer more to a rather Hegelian dialectic than to an indigenous *pensée des Lumières*). In any event, Enlightenment thought 'est tombée en desuétude', asserts Lyotard, not because it is obsolete and must somehow be modernised, but because it has fallen into disuse, its laws now in abeyance. With the decline of Enlightenment thought comes the inability to mount a defense of ethical values derived from it and that would be based upon the notion of what Lyotard calls a 'universal victim-subject'. Can one no longer justify acting to defend the cause of someone who has suffered an injustice? Lyotard maintains that such intervention is necessary because of 'une responsabilité éthique et civique', yet he cautions against extending beyond the limits of local and defensive interventions the point of view that would justify them. Such a move towards universality, he claims, 'peut égarer la pensée, comme il a égaré celle de Sartre'. The intellectual as portrayed by Lyotard seems to be left with a kind of negative freedom to act in the postmodern condition. With the idea of universality in ruins, thinking is perhaps newly unfettered from its tantalising obsessions. But what actions become possible? What ethical, political actions are to be performed, and what discourse can legitimate or defend them? It is in terms of these questions that the debate over the legacy and aftermath of Enlightenment will and must be couched.

As for the figure of the *philosophe* that we encounter in the *Encyclopédie*, it may be that this image has become too outmoded, too untimely, to be of much use any more in figuring a subject whose call we would wish to hear and heed today. It may be too that even the image of the intellectual has been eclipsed; champion of ethical modernity in the time of the Dreyfus Affair, the intellectual appears more frequently now as a shady figure with a past, and an imperfect one as well, a figure all too often displaced by others better able to perform the role of intellectual, to present a simulated image or simulacrum of that figure.[25] Perhaps finally all we can do is attempt to gauge our distance from those images, reactivating them without nostalgia for what may have been lost and without satisfaction over an identity regained and affirmed, acknowledging instead quite simply these images' incommensurability with our present. For in that recognition of incommensurability lies historical understanding, of a kind moreover that will permit us to resist Enlightenment without rejecting it, to put it to use once again, but hopefully without delusion.

25. See the special issue of *L'Esprit créateur* on the subject of the intellectual, including my essay, 'The French intellectual, history, and the reproduction of culture', 37:2 (1997), p.16-33.

FABIENNE-SOPHIE CHAUDERLOT

Encyclopédismes d'hier et d'aujourd'hui: informations ou pensée? Une lecture de l'*Encyclopédie* à la Deleuze

ALORS qu'il est toujours relativement compliqué, en France, de souscrire un abonnement à un serveur du réseau Internet, ces deux ou trois dernières années ont vu la commercialisation d'un nombre remarquable d'"encyclopédies numériques', aussi appelées encyclopédies multimédia ou cédéroms encyclopédiques.[1] L'événement est sans doute lié à l'apparition des ordinateurs dans le cadre familial. Celle-ci est beaucoup plus lente qu'aux Etats-Unis mais tout aussi inéluctable. Elle résulte souvent, en France, des désirs des adolescents qui utilisent comme argument de conviction leurs besoins scolaires. Les plus grandes maisons d'édition de dictionnaires traditionnels proposent ainsi des ouvrages généraux tels qu'un *Dictionnaire Hachette multimédia encyclopédique*, une *Encyclopédie science interactive* (Hachette multimédia, 1997), un *Petit Larousse illustré* (Liris interactive, 1997). L'entrée des ordinateurs dans la sphère privée répond donc à l'ouverture d'un marché en processus de création, comme le faisait déjà l'*Encyclopédie* de Diderot et D'Alembert.[2] Mais la prolifération de telles sommes électroniques est également symptôme d'une modification plus fondamentale de l'accès au savoir. Elle s'explique certainement par l'attrait du grand public pour ces formes souples d'organisation des connaissances. Etonnant, par contre, est le renouveau du genre lui-même que manifeste et/ou encourage la publication d'innombrables dictionnaires et encyclopédies, eux sur papier.

La revue *Critique* consacrait récemment un numéro spécial au phénomène qu'elle intitule *Dicomania*.[3] Dans sa présentation, l'éditeur parlait d'"avalanche', de raz-de-marée et de déferlement des dictionnaires et encyclopédies. Il y voyait 'le mouvement éditorial le plus frappant de ces dernières années' (p.970). Au fil des articles d'experts, on y rencontre, entre autres, un *Dictionnaire européen des Lumières*, un *Dictionnaire Jean-Jacques Rousseau*, une *Histoire et dictionnaire du temps des Lumières*. En parallèle à la séduction de l'informatisation de l'information, il est donc clair que c'est le concept même de 'concentré' de connaissances – 916 dictionnaires et 251 encyclopédies ont vu le jour entre 1994 et 1996 – qui rencontre un tel intérêt.

---

1. Cette orthographe a été finalement adoptée par l'Académie française.
2. Voir Dena Goodman, *The Republic of letters* (Ithaca 1994), p.26-33.
3. *La Folie des dictionnaires*, *Critique* 608-609 (Paris 1998).

Ce qui est surprenant car, au-delà de l'apparente liberté que procure la manipulation interactive des données sur cédéroms et les nouvelles pratiques d'apprentissage et de lecture qu'elle engendre, ces outils participent d'une conception considérée comme humaniste du savoir. Il s'agit de celle-là même, restrictive, élitiste et eurocentrée, qu'auraient irrémédiablement ébranlée les théories post-modernes. Si l'on postule, par exemple, que le post-modernisme, amplifiant le post-structuralisme, refuse l'existence de centres de vérité qui échapperaient à la portée idéologique du langage, alors les principes structurants des encyclopédies – recensement, totalisation, classification de tous les savoirs jugés officiels par une équipe de spécialistes à une époque donnée – apparaissent non seulement dépassés mais illégitimes. Même si, comme en témoignent les positions variées de penseurs tels que Jürgen Habermas, Terry Eagleton, Christopher Norris, et Peter Dews entre autres, il est bien évident que le concept de raison est, au dix-huitième siècle, beaucoup plus complexe que ne le présentent certains des détracteurs des Lumières, c'est à une forme spécifique de rationalisme et de vérité que renvoie toute approche du savoir de l'époque.[4]

En parallèle à toutes les nuances que les recherches récentes ont introduites dans notre conception des Lumières, il n'en reste pas moins clair que la foi en un progrès infini de la connaissance, en des définitions rigoureuses de l'intelligence et de la légitimité scientifique, en une amélioration de la société par la morale, en un développement du genre humain tout entier axé sur un mieux-être universel, animait les penseurs de la période.[5] Mais c'est précisément cette foi qui a été irrémédiablement ébranlée et par l'histoire et par la pensée de la deuxième moitié de notre siècle. Si l'on considère, ainsi que le postule Daniel Brewer, que 'the *Encyclopédie* is also the text most representative of the French Enlightenment, providing massive testimony to the Enlightenment belief in the value of unfettered inquiry into all sectors of human knowledge',[6] alors il est difficile de comprendre cet engouement pour une nouvelle vague d'encyclopédisme. Dans le cadre d'une vision post-moderne des Lumières, où les intellectuels au sens large, détenteurs des contenus et dessinateurs des contours du savoir, auraient, jusqu'à présent et depuis le dix-huitième siècle, tendu à légitimiser la notion de vérité ultime de leurs connaissances, le genre encyclopédique devrait être en voie de disparaître comme le sont les concepts attenants

---

4. Voir aussi les travaux de David Harvey, *The Condition of postmodernity* (Oxford 1990); Alex Callinicos, *Against postmodernism* (Cambridge 1989); Kate Soper, *Humanism and anti-humanism* (London 1986).

5. Pour une analyse détaillée du profil humaniste, consulter Paul Bénichou, *Le Sacre de l'écrivain: 1750-1830* (Paris 1985), et Didier Masseau, *L'Invention de l'intellectuel dans l'Europe du XVIIIe siècle* (Paris 1994). Pour une vision réaliste de l'intellectuel d'aujourd'hui, voir Jean-François Lyotard, 'Tombeau de l'intellectuel', in *Tombeau de l'intellectuel et autres papiers* (Paris 1984), p.11-22.

6. Daniel Brewer, *The Discourse of Enlightenment in eighteenth-century France* (Cambridge 1993), p.13.

d'Intellectuel, de Culture et de Canon.[7] De plus, comme le démontre clairement Jean-François Lyotard, la notion même d'intellectuel a été profondément bouleversée, si ce n'est irrémédiablement détruite, par les réformes de l'enseignement des puissances industrielles et commerciales. En France, comme aux Etats-Unis, 'on n'attend pas aujourd'hui, de l'enseignement, partout déconsidéré, qu'il forme des citoyens plus éclairés, mais seulement des professionnels plus performants'.[8] Les encyclopédies proposent, au contraire, l'ultime outil de la recherche abstraite d'un savoir considéré comme 'pur', pour un esprit en quête de connaissances toutes aussi universelles que peu analytiques ou fonctionnelles. Elles devraient ainsi être vouées à l'extinction comme d'autres instances de la même espèce en voie de disparition telle que 'l'intellectuel' au sens humaniste du terme, précisément:

Il ne devrait donc plus y avoir d'"intellectuel", et s'il y en a, c'est qu'ils sont aveugles à cette donnée nouvelle dans l'histoire occidentale depuis le XVIIIe siècle: il n'y pas de sujet-victime universel, faisant signe dans la réalité, au nom duquel la pensée puisse dresser un réquisitoire qui soit en même temps une conception du monde.[9]

Comment justifier, dès lors, la popularité de ces sommes qui façonnent tout autant qu'elles décrivent les mondes bien précis que leurs auteurs veulent circonscrire? Surtout si l'on voit dans le World Wide Web / hypertoile la réalisation parachevée d'une volonté universelle de rassemblement des connaissances doublée d'un effort de démocratisation d'accès au savoir.[10] Et que l'on considère, comme je vais essayer de le montrer, qu'on trouve dans l'*Encyclopédie* précisément ses origines et son modèle épistémologiques.[11]

On peut argumenter que ces bilans littéraires, artistiques, scientifiques et culturels compensent une peur endémique de la déconstruction de la certitude du savoir, le délire de la surmultiplication des spécialités, le chaos de la fragmentation des disciplines. Ils semblent même offrir une possibilité de

7. Les majuscules sont explicites. Voir, à ce sujet, l'essai dans la quatrième partie de *La Défaite de la pensée* d'Alain Finkielkraut, intitulée très sérieusement mais non sans humour: 'Une paire de bottes vaut Shakespeare' (Paris 1987). Sur la redéfinition de la fonction des intellectuels, on consultera également *Le Pouvoir intellectuel en France* de Régis Debray paru en anglais sous le titre étrange de *Teachers, writers, celebrities: the intellectuals of modern France* (London 1981).

8. Lyotard, *Tombeau de l'intellectuel*, p.20.

9. Lyotard, *Tombeau de l'intellectuel*, p.20.

10. Une telle démocratisation est évidemment motivée par des facteurs économiques plus qu'humanistes, et elle reste aussi illusoire qu'au dix-huitième siècle, mais il s'agit là d'un autre débat. La mise en circulation sur Internet garantit un potentiel d'accès universel. Les lecteurs intéressés par une approche sémantique du problème de l'universalité pourront s'attacher aux questions de traduction générée par le World Wide Web. Pour le français, ils trouveront une traduction extensive du champ sémantique des néologismes multi- et hyper-médiatiques. Elle est proposée par l'Université de Strasbourg. On la trouve sur le site: www.chimie.u-strasb.Fr/membres/GB/FLexique.html.

11. Voir le deuxième chapitre: 'Histoire de la "manufacture encyclopédique"', dans *Diderot et l'Encyclopédie* de Jacques Proust (Paris 1982).

résistance au pur vertige cognitif que procure la profondeur insondable des textes électroniques. Il est également compréhensible que l'accélération, exigée par les universités, des rythmes de production d'ouvrages académiques – articles, conférences, livres, interventions sur Internet – ait généré un besoin d'immobilisation des sources de réflexion. Dans une période où les auteurs sont morts et les lecteurs décentrés, comment rester indifférent à l'anonymat d'un dictionnaire ou insensible à la solide logique de son alphabet, en dépit des échos d'exhaustivité, de totalitarisme, de simplification et d'exclusions que le genre renvoie?

On expliquerait le phénomène paradoxal, dans son présent, par une dynamique du besoin professionnel ou une politique des désirs personnels. Mais on peut aussi réexaminer, à partir de leur 'descendance' multimédiatique, les principes du savoir encyclopédique élaborés systématiquement dans des textes tels que le 'Prospectus', le 'Discours préliminaire' et l'article ENCYCLOPÉDIE lui-même. Il s'agirait de se demander, non nécessairement pourquoi, mais surtout comment ils restent d'actualité dans une actualité qui se fonde par opposition à eux et alors qu'ils transmettent souvent un savoir, en soi, désuet.

Cet article propose une relecture de l'*Encyclopédie* dans une telle perspective, et à la suite d'une série de récentes approches critiques offrant une vision exhaustive mais nuancée de la démarche des philosophes.[12] Il ne s'agira pas ici de traiter l'immense ouvrage en tant que profession de foi humaniste, ni même comme première tentative d'homogénéisation du sens et de contrôle des publics élargis. Ces aspects ont déjà largement été accentués, notamment par les analyses imprégnées de théorie marxiste. Au lieu de considérer la philosophie en général, et celle du dix-huitième siècle en particulier, comme un discours conceptuel de propositions auto-validantes et organisateur d'un processus de normalisation, je propose de voir dans l'aventure encyclopédique et, par extension dans celle de sa lecture contemporaine, une… aventure précisément.

Par aventure, j'entends l'adoption d'une attitude de distanciation par rapport aux systématisations antérieures et d'expérimentation. Elle s'accompagne à la fois d'une connaissance des positions précédentes et d'une valorisation de l'inconnu. Elle nécessite que l'on embrasse le doute et prise la panique qui sous-tendent encore, à juste titre, notre relation au savoir. Mais il s'agit aussi, avant de s'y lancer, de prendre conscience que l'aventure n'est plus, comme l'écrivent brillamment Pascal Bruckner et Alain Finkielkraut, 'seulement liée au risque et à l'exploit'.[13] Elle ne saurait consister en la recherche d'un exotisme désormais illusoire, ni en

---

12. Mes propos font notamment écho aux analyses de James Creech, *Diderot: thresholds of representation* (Columbus 1986); Wilda Anderson, *Diderot's dream* (Baltimore 1990); Pierre Saint-Amand, *Les Lois de l'hostilité* (Paris 1992); Georges Benrekassa, *Le Langage des Lumières* (Paris 1995); Julie Candler Hayes, *Reading the French Enlightenment: system and subversion* (Cambridge 1999); et l'ouvrage de Daniel Brewer déjà cité.

13. Pascal Bruckner et Alain Finkielkraut, *Au coin de la rue l'aventure* (Paris 1979).

l'impensable glorification d'exploits guerriers ou mêmes académiques. Elle ne désigne plus, non plus, les prouesses physiques que la science semble pouvoir générer sur simple demande de nouveaux records. L'aventure est, en fait, aujourd'hui bien plus difficile à trouver. Elle implique le déploiement de ce que l'on nomme communément des lignes de fuite, lignes que j'envisage à partir du projet de 'déterritorialisation' de Gilles Deleuze et Félix Guattari.[14] Au-delà d'une conception fort complexe de l'aventure à la Bruckner et Finkielkraut ou à la Deleuze et Guattari, il s'agit en fait simplement d'échapper à l'emprise du sentiment de banalité qu'engendrent les techniques de banalisation du savoir. Et, pour ce faire, de redonner à l'acte commun de lecture toute son intensité.

Je lirai donc l'*Encyclopédie* à partir de sa limite, le réseau du World Wide Web, afin d'en dégager les éléments qui préfigurent à l'événement encyclopédique d'aujourd'hui. Notamment ceux qui, au-delà du recensement des connaissances, interpellent précisément la difficulté de la totalisation des connaissances, les défis de sa sélection, la problématique de son accès, l'impossibilité de sa certitude. Bien loin de vouloir combler ces fissures du rationalisme cartésien grâce au contrôle omnipotent du savoir par le sujet pensant, Diderot, il me semble, les a révélées, dès l'*Encyclopédie*, pour mieux les confronter. D'où toute la sémantique de la confusion, de la digression, celle du décousu, du discontinu qui le caractérisent, en apparence négativement, depuis Barbey d'Aurevilly jusqu'au tribut collectif payé à sa dispersion dans le volume *Diderot* édité par Jack Undank et Herbert Josephs.[15]

---

14. Voir leurs deux volumes *Capitalisme et schizophrénie* (Paris 1972-1980), mais aussi l'œuvre toute entière de Gilles Deleuze. S'il n'utilise le terme d'aventure que rarement, sa conception de la philosophie comme activité créative de concepts en est une remarquable illustration. De même sa définition du style chez un grand écrivain: 'c'est toujours aussi un style de vie, non pas du tout quelque chose de personnel, mais l'invention d'une possibilité de vie, d'un mode d'existence', inscrit l'activité intellectuelle dans une recherche du nouveau, une pratique de l'inconnu et un désir d'engagement actif à l'expérimentation. Voir 'La vie comme œuvre d'art', dans *Pourparlers* (Paris 1990), p.138. Il me semble que toutes les incursions de Deleuze dans la psychanalyse, la linguistique, l'ethnologie, le cinéma, la peinture et, bien entendu, la littérature constituent une véritable aventure d'une pensée qui ouvre sur 'une lecture en intensité' où 'quelque chose passe ou ne passe pas'. Dans laquelle 'il n'y a rien à expliquer, rien à comprendre, rien à interpréter'. Mais où les flux de lecture 'entrent dans des rapports de courant, de contre-courant, de remous avec d'autres flux, flux de merde, de parole, d'action, d'érotisme, de monnaie, de politique, etc.' ('Lettre à un critique sévère', dans *Pourparlers*, Paris 1990, p.17-18). Comme l'ont dit et répété Deleuze et Foucault, s'il reste une aventure aujourd'hui, et l'importance des sciences cognitives le montre, c'est bien celle de penser autrement: 'Il y a des moments dans la vie où la question de savoir si on peut penser autrement qu'on ne pense et percevoir autrement qu'on ne voit est indispensable pour continuer à regarder ou à réfléchir [...] [Q]u'est-ce donc que la philosophie aujourd'hui – je veux dire l'activité philosophique – si elle n'est pas le travail critique de la pensée sur elle-même? Et si elle ne consiste pas, au lieu de légitimer ce qu'on sait déjà, à entreprendre de savoir comment et jusqu'où il serait possible de penser autrement?' (Michel Foucault, *L'Usage des plaisirs*, Paris 1984, p.14-15).

15. Voir l'enthousiasme effréné des accusations de Jules Barbey d'Aurevilly dans son *Contre Diderot* (Paris 1986) et celui si bien tempéré des analyses dans *Diderot, digression and dispersion: a bicentenial tribute*, ed. Jack Undank et Herbert Josephs (Lexington 1984).

Ainsi, postulant que le post-moderne n'est pas ce qui vient après le moderne mais plutôt ce qui en révèle les failles, les troubles et les contradictions, je montrerai que l'*Encyclopédie* – bien avant le réseau appelé, en français, hypertoile – déploie déjà un espace où l'hétérogène est privilégié. Pour suggérer, en conclusion, que la conception de la relation au savoir que cédéroms et Internet revendiquent, relation fondée sur la fluctuation subjective non seulement entre les différents sujets d'interrogation mais aussi entre le concept de pensée et celui d'information, sous-tendait déjà le projet encyclopédique. Le but étant, finalement, de contribuer au dépassement de la dichotomie Lumières/post-modernisme et d'établir que le savoir, de nos jours, réside tout autant dans leur entente réciproque que dans notre entendement de leur complémentarité.

Le mot *encyclopédie* signifie enchaînement des sciences. Il est composé de *en*, de *cercle*, et de *institution* ou *science*. Ceux qui ont prétendu que cet ouvrage était impossible, ne connaissaient pas, selon toute apparence, le passage qui suit; il est du chancelier Bacon. '*De impossibilitate ita statuo: ea omnia possibilia, & praestabilia esse censenda, quae ab aliquibus perfici possunt, licet non a quibusvis; & quae a multis conjunctim, licet non ab uno; & quae in successione saeculorum, licet non eodem aevo; & denique quae multorum cura & sumptu, licet non opibus & industria singulorum. Bac., lib. 2, de Aug. Scient., cap. I, p. 103.*[16]

Dans le 'Prospectus' mis en circulation en 1750, Diderot préface la description et, en quelque sorte, rédige l'annonce publicitaire de l'*Encyclopédie* par cette citation dont les échos intellectuels, sociaux et politiques ne résonnent peut-être qu'aujourd'hui dans toute leur ampleur. La première raison d'une telle actualité est évidente. La 'collectivité', ou plutôt multiplicité, qu'invoquait Bacon, libérée des contraintes temporelles – 'dans la succession des siècles' – et pourvue du moyen d'abolir les distances – 'ressources, gens isolés' – est non seulement possible mais réalisée, grâce au World Wide Web. Repenser, dès lors, l'entreprise didactique tout autant que cognitive des encyclopédistes à partir de l'outil informatique qui structure quotidiennement notre propre accès au savoir s'impose.

Les points communs se révèlent vite multiples, en effet, que l'on compare les deux moyens de connaissance du point de vue de leurs projets, structure, formulation ou même conception. La plupart des travaux récents sur l'entreprise intellectuelle des philosophes des Lumières met en valeur l'environnement de leur activité. Ce n'est plus seulement le contenu mais les conditions pratiques de leur production textuelle qui caractérisent la période. Dans son livre sur *L'Invention de l'intellectuel dans l'Europe du XVIIIe siècle* Didier Masseau recense les facteurs historiques, économiques et

16. 'Prospectus', DPV v.85. Selon la traduction DPV: 'Quant à l'impossibilité, voici ce que je pense sur ce sujet. Je regarde comme possible et excellent tout ce qui peut être exécuté par certains hommes sans pouvoir l'être par toutes sortes de gens; par plusieurs individus réunis, sans pouvoir l'être par un homme isolé; par la succession des siècles, sans être possible à un seul siècle; enfin par les soins et les dépenses DE BEAUCOUP, sans être à la portée des moyens et de l'industrie des particuliers' (DPV vi.85n).

épistémologiques qui concourent au renouveau de la pensée et à sa spécificité. Il cite 'l'effet des changements qui affectent l'imprimerie, les lecteurs et la population écrivante'; 'la diversification des modèles éditoriaux'; l'adaptation à 'un public plus hétérogène et plus étendu'; la naissance du 'grand capitalisme éditorial'; 'la croissance de la production livresque' et 'l'essor des réseaux de distribution'. Masseau souligne aussi la multiplication des formes d'intervention des intellectuels qui peuvent 'exercer leur fonction dans plusieurs lieux à la fois et avoir le sentiment exaltant d'être en mesure d'élargir toujours leur audience'.[17] Si l'on transpose tous ces éléments dans le contexte technologique de notre époque, on comprend à quel point les composantes des deux phénomènes correspondent à la 'révolution' aujourd'hui hâtée par 'les maîtres du monde' qu'annonçait l'avertissement du tome viii de l'*Encyclopédie*.[18] Les différences concernent les formes mais non la nature de l'événement. Ce ne sont plus des livres qui sont publiés mais des pages de sites, pour un public des lecteurs qui n'a, théoriquement, pas de limites. Historiquement, le World Wide Web apparaît au moment où l'essor d'un capitalisme global semble inéluctable. De plus, comme l'explique André Leroi-Gourhan et l'approfondit, à sa suite, l'historien Jacques Le Goff, l'imprimerie – et aujourd'hui le Web – se développent à la fois parce que fixer les nouvelles connaissances devient impossible et pour créer un outil de mémorisation qui palie aux limites de la mémoire humaine. Pour Leroi-Gourhan, que Le Goff cite, l'avènement de l'imprimerie a eu un effet double. D'une part le lecteur s'est vu confronté à une somme de savoirs qu'il ne pouvait plus assimiler en totalité et qui formait donc une énorme mémoire désormais collective. D'autre part, ce lecteur s'est trouvé plus fréquemment capable de se servir de nouvelles œuvres. La nature du phénomène aurait engendré une extériorisation de la mémoire individuelle, tout texte imprimé étant orienté depuis l'extérieur.[19] On constate ainsi, aux moments de l'apparition des manuscrits, de la publication de l'*Encyclopédie* et de la vulgarisation de l'hypertoile, une surmultiplication accélérée des informations similaire et un comparable défi posé par leurs inscription et regroupement. L'argument de Le Goff qui considère tout document depuis les lettres sur cire de Mésopotamie jusqu'au papier en passant par les feuilles de palmier en Inde, les coquillages en Chine, le papyrus et le parchemin, est tout aussi valide à propos du Web qui remplit le plus efficacement que possible la fonction de ces types de supports:

---

17. Masseau, *L'Invention de l'intellectuel*, p.45-47.

18. 'On ne pourra du moins nous contester, je pense, que notre travail ne soit au niveau de notre siècle, & c'est quelque chose. L'homme le plus éclairé y trouvera des idées qui lui sont inconnues & des faits qu'il ignore. Puisse l'instruction générale s'avancer d'un pas si rapide que dans vingt ans d'ici il y ait à peine en mille de nos pages une ligne qui ne soit populaire! C'est aux Maîtres du monde à hâter cette heureuse révolution' (Diderot, 'Avertissement', viii.ii).

19. André Leroi-Gourhan, *Le Geste et la parole* (Paris 1964). Voir plus particulièrement le deuxième volume: *La Mémoire et les rythmes*.

'information storage, which allows communication across time and space and provides men with a means of marking, memorizing and registering'.[20]

Les ressemblances de contexte et d'enjeux entre ces deux périodes sont saisissantes. Même les 'mirages' que Masseau mentionne préludent de façon étrange à ce que nous vivons aujourd'hui. 'Le pouvoir de fascination [de l'imprimerie] sur les intellectuels et en particulier sur les philosophes des Lumières' est tout à fait comparable à celui qu'exerce le Web sur une grande partie de la population éduquée aux Etats-Unis et ailleurs. 'Le rêve d'exercer un pouvoir à distance' est clairement réalisé par les enseignants d'université qui se voient contacté(e)s à propos d'un article depuis partout dans le monde. Quant à l'imprimé qui 'semble fixer une voix, incorporer une présence, donner forme à une pensée qui demeurait incertaine tant qu'elle n'était pas suffisamment diffusée pour susciter échos et réactions', on peut aisément y substituer tous les phénomènes de créations de subjectivité, d'identification et d'auto-glorification que la présence virtuelle entraîne, sans parler de la valeur de vérité aveuglément attribuée à l'information distribuée par Internet.

Sans aller, bien entendu si loin, les ambitions de Diderot, d'après le 'Prospectus', dans cette phase particulièrement unifiée d'une œuvre globale fort hétérogène, sont à la fois conformes et à l'esprit des Lumières et à celui de notre époque. L'*Encyclopédie* est présentée comme le moyen par excellence d'organiser la libre circulation des idées du passé comme celle des théories nouvelles. Elle reste exemplaire de la volonté de diffusion de la connaissance exprimée tout au long du siècle, diffusion que l'on appellerait aujourd'hui, au sens large, dissémination dans la mesure où sa lecture génère une prolifération infinie d'exégèses possibles. Son but officiel est de faciliter et d'accélérer la divulgation des techniques traditionnelles comme celle des moyens de fabrication récents ou en cours de développement, de permettre l'appréciation des Beaux-Arts comme l'apprentissage des arts mécaniques.[21] L'*Encyclopédie*, que Diderot entend bel et bien commercialiser grâce à son *Prospectus*, se veut, selon ses propres mots, 'un sanctuaire où les connaissances des hommes soient à l'abri des temps & des révolutions' (DPV v.99). Il s'agit de composer 'un livre qu'on pût consulter sur toutes les matières' (DPV v.86-87). Conformément à la volonté pédagogique des penseurs éclairés, la somme alphabétique est destinée aux enseignants: 'ceux qui se sentiraient le courage de travailler à l'instruction des autres' comme aux curieux autodidactes 'ceux qui ne s'instruisent que pour eux-mêmes' (DPV v.87). Les mêmes aspects de conservation de patrimoines artistique et littéraire, de propagation d'informations récentes ou de valeur comme outil pédagogique sont à nouveau les composantes-clés du marketing des ordinateurs, des abonnements aux serveurs du réseau, des

---

20. Le Goff, *History and memory*, p.59.
21. Tous aspects accessibles également sur le Web, que l'on veuille se promener au Louvre ou construire une bombe.

programmes d'enseignement sur cédéroms et, naturellement, des encyclopédies informatisées.[22]

Mais, au-delà de ces manières communes de savoir, c'est aussi une approche similaire de la lecture que l'*Encyclopédie* et le Web préconisent, facilitent et surtout valorisent. Toujours dès le 'Prospectus' se trouve également accentué le concept, original alors, de renvoi. Naturelle pour l'usager contemporain des 'navigateurs, butineurs, visualiseurs et autres feuilleteurs', l'idée de renvois d'un article à un autre est cependant paradoxale.[23] Posé par Diderot comme moyen de palier à l'organisation somme toute aveugle du simple dictionnaire, le terme opère une fonction double et contradictoire.[24] Le suivi de renvois est proposé comme méthode de structuration, c'est-à-dire de ramifications centralisées autour d'un article. Or c'est en un décentrement qu'il résulte, dans la mesure où les voies de connaissance ouvertes par les suggestions de renvois restent soumises à l'arbitraire des auteurs. Cependant, comme le démontre Daniel Brewer, les renvois sont aussi l'arme d'une 'machine de guerre' encyclopédique visant les points forts du savoir classique: dogmes, perspective unique et autoritaire, auteur omniscient, lecteur impuissant.[25] Livrées à la subjectivité des lecteurs que rien ne contraint à les emprunter, ces destinations potentielles leur donnent le pouvoir de transformer 'l'acte de lecture' en 'pratique critique' régénérée et revalidée à chaque nouvelle combinatoire.

Comme garantie théorique de cohérence dans le 'Prospectus', la possibilité de libre passage d'un article à un autre manifestait et incorporait le principe essentiel éclairant la conception du savoir chez les citoyens de la République des Lettres. Ce principe avait été énoncé et développé par Condillac dans son *Essai sur l'origine des connaissances humaines* de 1746: 'C'est qu'il n'est point d'objets auxquels nous n'ayons le pouvoir de lier nos idées et qui, par conséquent, ne soient propres à faciliter l'exercice de la mémoire et de l'imagination. Tout consiste à savoir former ces liaisons conformément au but qu'on se propose et aux circonstances où on se trouve.'[26]

Reprise notamment dans le *Discours préliminaire* sous le terme de 'rapports' – il y apparaît quatorze fois – l'idée de liaison préside à celles de savoir, de connaissance et même de philosophie depuis Condillac jusqu'à

22. Consulter, pour s'en convaincre, l'encyclopédie multimédia Grolier.

23. Tous ces termes poétiques traduisent l'anglais *browser*.

24. Prévenant et étouffant dans l'œuf les critiques à venir, Diderot concluait la dernière partie de son prospectus précisément intitulée *Système des connaissances humaines* par cette affirmation sans équivoque: 'Si l'on nous objecte que l'ordre alphabétique détruira la liaison de notre système de la connaissance humaine, nous répondrons que, cette liaison consistant moins dans l'arrangement des matières que dans les rapports qu'elles ont entre elles, rien ne peut l'anéantir, et que nous aurons soin de la rendre sensible par la disposition des matières dans chaque article, et par l'exactitude et la fréquence des renvois' ('Prospectus', DPV v.118).

25. Brewer, *The Discourse of Enlightenment*, p.48-49.

26. Condillac, *Essai sur l'origine des connaissances humaines* (Paris 1998), p.294.

Kant.[27] Mais elle prend une dimension résolument contemporaine quand on la suit dans certains de ses développements. A propos de l'étude de la physique par exemple, les auteurs constatent qu''il nous suffit d'avoir trouvé quelquefois un avantage réel dans certaines connaissances, où d'abord nous ne l'avions pas soupçonné, pour nous autoriser à regarder toutes les recherches de pure curiosité, comme pouvant un jour nous être utiles' (i.iv). Par delà l'application spécifique au domaine des sciences de la nature, l'alliance renvois-curiosité préconise tout un type d'apprentissage nouveau, une entrée dans le savoir liée au libre arbitre de chacun, une connaissance non seulement conçue comme accumulation purement subjective mais encore détachée de l'exigence d'une efficacité immédiate et certaine. La différence de visées engendre une différance de vérité. Dans la mesure où l'utilité du savoir est déplacée sur un des mondes futurs possibles, son authenticité n'est plus primordiale non plus. La connaissance est ainsi envisagée pour ce que Georges Benrekassa appelle 'une universalité transitoire, conçue dans le temps'.[28] Les quatre types de renvois détaillés dans l'article ENCYCLOPÉDIE en cachent donc une cinquième sorte, celle qui envoie à l'au-delà du soi théorique et exclusif de l'*Encyclopédie*, c'est-à-dire à une pratique généralisée de lecture par options.

L'on a communément compris, jusqu'à présent, ces renvois selon les directives explicites de Diderot et comme un 'système destiné à assurer l'unité [de l'ouvrage] à l'arrivée'.[29] Peut-être faut-il désormais, si l'on accepte de voir en le réseau informatique une extension pragmatique de l'*Encyclopédie*, aussi leur accorder une fonction de subversion de cette volonté unificatrice. Diderot est clair. Dans l'article ENCYCLOPÉDIE les renvois doivent opérer à la fois une fonction de liaison – ils 'rappellent les notions communes et les principes analogues; fortifient les conséquences [...] et donnent au tout cette unité si favorable à l'établissement de la vérité' – et son contraire: 'ils opposeront les notions [...] si l'auteur est impartial, ils auront toujours la double fonction de confirmer et de réfuter; de troubler et de concilier' (v.642a). Les renvois servent donc deux objectifs opposés. D'une part, certains tissent un réseau de rappels, d'approfondissements et de confirmations sous-tendant le postulat de vérité. Au contraire, mais simultanément, d'autres tendent à déjouer l'illusion d'un savoir définitif dans laquelle auteurs ou lecteurs peu critiques voudraient s'installer. Ce double mouvement d'établissement apparent et de sapement interne d'un sens officiel et définitif n'est pas sans anticiper les intentions poststructuralistes de déconstruction. Par les renvois, il s'agit d'affirmer un savoir possible tout en démentissant ('réfuter') les revendications de

27. Dans sa *Critique de la raison pure* Kant voit en la philosophie une recherche du rapport entre les connaissances et les fins de la raison humaines.

28. Georges Benrekassa, *Langage des Lumières*, p.245.

29. Voir Laurent Versini, introduction à l'*Encyclopédie*, in Diderot, *Œuvres*, 5 vols (Paris 1994-1997), i.203. Quant à Diderot, voir l'article ENCYCLOPÉDIE.

certitude et de vérité par la révélation ('troubler') de l'instabilité fondamentale du langage dont elles dépendent.

De même, l'accès au 'savoir' contenu dans l'*Encyclopédie* est bien moins linéaire et systématique que le diagramme détaillé fourni à la suite du 'Prospectus' ne s'efforce de l'indiquer. En fait, se dégageant radicalement des moules téléologiques traditionnels, il est même tout à fait à l'opposé du schéma donné comme organisateur de l'*Encyclopédie*, à savoir la figure de l'arbre des connaissances qui revient en *leit-motiv* justificateur dans le 'Prospectus' et le 'Discours préliminaire'. Bien que reprenant le paradigme vertical et généalogique classique à plusieurs reprises, Diderot et D'Alembert remettent en question la validité du modèle tout aussi régulièrement: 'Cet arbre de la connaissance humaine pouvait être formé de plusieurs manières, soit en rapportant aux diverses facultés de notre âme nos différentes connaissances, soit en les rapportant aux êtres qu'elles ont pour objet. Mais l'embarras était d'autant plus grand, qu'il y avait plus d'arbitraire. Et combien ne devait-il pas y en avoir?' ('Prospectus', DPV v.90-91). Loin de proposer, avec assurance, un principe singulier ordonnateur des recueils, et de poser son choix comme objectif, D'Alembert dévoile la nature subjective du recensement de la connaissance après avoir seulement suggéré cette dernière en faisant des renvois la structure d'accès et de lecture. Reprenant le plurimorphisme de ce fameux arbre, Diderot le problématise et précise que 'former cet arbre généalogique de toutes les sciences et les arts' n'est ni 'une chose facile' ni une démarche évidente. Ainsi, dans le 'Prospectus', il propose, au contraire, l'image d'une horizontalité de la réalité (DPV v.91):

La nature ne nous offre que des choses particulières, infinies en nombre et sans aucune division fixe & déterminée. Tout s'y succède par des nuances insensibles. Et sur cette mer d'objets qui nous environne, s'il en paraît quelques-uns, comme des pointes de rochers, qui semblent percer la surface & dominer les autres, ils ne doivent cet avantage qu'à des systèmes particuliers, qu'à des conventions vagues, & qu'à certains événements étrangers à l'arrangement physique des êtres, & aux vraies institutions de la philosophie.

Un paragraphe du 'Discours préliminaire' semble prolonger exactement ces remarques et continuer d'aplanir le modèle (i.xiv):

Le système général des Sciences et des Arts est une espèce de labyrinthe, de chemin tortueux, où l'esprit s'engage sans trop connaître la route qu'il doit tenir. Pressé par ses besoins, et par ceux du corps auquel il est uni, il étudie d'abord les premiers objets qui se présentent à lui, pénètre le plus avant qu'il peut dans la connaissance de ces objets; rencontrent bientôt des difficultés qui l'arrêtent, et soit par l'espérance ou même par le désespoir de les vaincre, se jette dans une nouvelle route; revient ensuite sur ses pas, franchit quelquefois les premières barrières pour en rencontrer des nouvelles; & passant rapidement d'un objet à un autre, fait sur chacun de ces objets à différents intervalles & comme par secousses, une suite d'opérations dont la génération même de ses idées rend la discontinuité nécessaire. Mais ce désordre tout philosophique qu'il est de la part de l'âme, défigurerait, ou plutôt anéantirait entièrement un arbre encyclopédique dans lequel on voudrait le représenter.

La mention, en une phrase, de l'arbre encyclopédique est superflue après une longue description d'un apprentissage par déplacements, hésitations et digressions latérales. Les auteurs semblent s'être heurtés au modèle traditionnel d'un monde cognitif ordonné officiellement, comme celui de la politique ou de la métaphysique, de haut en bas. Mais leur insistance sur les renvois et leur description du dédale du savoir découvre l'artifice et promeut, en fait, une acquisition horizontale et erratique des connaissances, la plus conforme au 'système général des Sciences et des Arts'.

Le véritable projet de Diderot apparaît donc bien plus comme éclaté et décentré par la curiosité et les aléas de la subjectivité que comme enraciné dans une transcendance et lié à la seule poursuite de la vérité. S'il est vrai que D'Alembert reste prisonnier, dans le 'Discours préliminaire', de sa volonté d'ériger, à tout prix, un 'arbre naturel, non arbitraire', Diderot, lui, insiste trop sur l'étalement visible et l'errance nécessaire du parcours intellectuel pour qu'on le croie semblablement attaché à l'unicité du modèle.[30] A l'ordre symbolique qu'érige la figure de l'arbre, on substitue une série de 'cartes particulières' établie par chacun 'selon le point de vue où l'on se mette pour envisager l'univers littéraire' (i.xv). Impossible à saisir, l'organisation des connaissances est livrée à la subjectivité de chaque savant qui le tisse à partir et autour de lui. A la place d'un dessin unique, il y aurait donc une multiplicité de ce que Deleuze appelle 'diagrammes', à savoir les cartes des rapports entre les 'formes du savoir: le Visible, l'Enonçable, bref l'archive' et les 'forces du pouvoir', invisibles, indicibles mais qui président à l'élaboration et la saisie de la connaissance.[31] Dans le 'Discours préliminaire', le long développement sur la mappemonde, et, surtout, sur la validité de toutes ses variantes suggère la nécessité d'un modèle beaucoup plus souple et subjectif que celui de l'arbre. Il préface aux connections en rhizome que Deleuze et Guattari proposent et dessine les plis qu'ils explorent en alternative à la rigidité arborescente et imposante que le classicisme avait consacrée. C'est précisément ce type de fluidité au sein d'une structure ouverte que le réseau Internet concrétise. Le World Wide Web met en place et en priorité ces tiges de rhizome qui 'n'arrêtent pas de sortir des arbres', d'où 'les masses et les flux ne cessent pas de s'échapper', pour 'inventer des connexions qui sautent d'arbre en arbre, et qui déracinent'.[32] Mais il me semble que la possibilité d'une telle appréhension des connaissances était déjà entrevue et encouragée par l'érosion de l'évidence d'un ordre unique, absolu et stable du savoir caracteristique de l'œuvre de Diderot tout entière.

30. Julie Hayes explique les deux modèles en les réconciliant, fort justement, dans la dialectique 'esprit systématique/esprit de système'. L'Arbre de D'Alembert 'rooted both in the urge to liberation and progress' participerait et de l'esprit systématique et de celui de système qui lui donne un pouvoir totalisateur (*Reading the French Enlightenment*, p.44).

31. Deleuze, 'Fendre les choses, fendre les mots' in *Pourparlers*, p.126.

32. Gilles Deleuze et Felix Guattari, *Mille Plateaux* (Paris 1980), p.632.

L'*Encyclopédie* ne représenterait donc pas le texte exemplaire d'un esprit philosophique purement rationaliste, systématique, et persuadé et de sa fondation dans le Bien et de son bien-fondé universel. Pas plus que Diderot – comme le prouve James Creech – ne 'distille les courants [de pensée] de son temps', l'*Encyclopédie*, en dépit de ses ambitions démesurées et ses massives dimensions, ne constituerait l'œuvre monolithique témoin d'une ère de pensée unifiée.[33] Elle articulerait, par contre, les débats internes et les contradictions qui scindaient un domaine cognitif à la recherche de sa structuration. J'y vois le lieu non unique mais privilégié des tensions qui traversent l'entreprise intellectuelle de son époque. En compagnie des 'autres' dix-huitièmes siècle, celui des *Confessions* ou de la politique à la Rousseau, du théâtre de Beaumarchais, ou celui des fantasmes de Sade, par exemple, l'*Encyclopédie* ne propose qu'une des méthodes de recherche du sens. Mais c'est une stratégie correspondant, et désormais adaptée par la technologie, aux paramètres de notre propre quête de la connaissance.

La somme encyclopédique ne saurait donc plus constituer le premier des deux types de livres que distinguent Deleuze et Guattari:

le livre-racine. L'arbre est déjà l'image du monde, ou bien la racine est l'image de l'arbre-monde. C'est le livre classique, comme belle intériorité organique, signifiante et subjective (les strates du livre). Le livre imite le monde, comme l'art, la nature: par des procédés qui lui sont propres, et qui mènent à bien ce que la nature ne peut pas ou ne peut plus faire. La loi du livre, c'est celle de la réflexion, le Un qui devient deux [...]. Autant dire que cette pensée n'a jamais compris la multiplicité.[34]

Au contraire, l'*Encyclopédie* matérialiserait plutôt le second genre de livres qu'ils définissent comme

système-radicelle ou racine fasciculée dont notre modernité se réclame volontiers. Cette fois, la racine principale a avorté ou se détruit vers son extrémité; vient se greffer sur elle une multiplicité immédiate et quelconque de racines secondaires qui prennent un grand développement. Cette fois, la réalité naturelle apparaît dans l'avortement de la racine principale, mais son unité n'en subsiste pas moins comme passée ou à venir, comme possible.[35]

Que ce soit la fameuse et incomparable multiplicité des collaborateurs à l'*Encyclopédie*, la célébration originale de la curiosité en parallèle aux louanges systématiques de la réflexion et, naturellement, l'insistance sur les renvois, tout dans la façon d'écrire, et par conséquent de lire, que propose Diderot, à l'instar de ses personnages, exige un processus cognitif aux multiples entrées, aux vitesses variables et aux flux saccadés. Pierre Saint-Amand l'a bien vu, qui établit un parallèle entre l'*Encyclopédie* et *Le Neveu de Rameau*, son 'précipité fictionnel' où se 'condense la polémique' entre

---

33. Voir son analyse de *La Lettre sur les aveugles*, dans *Diderot: thresholds of representation*, p.104.
34. Deleuze et Guattari, *Mille Plateaux*, p.11.
35. Deleuze et Guattari, *Mille Plateaux*, p.12.

philosophes et anti-philosophes.[36] Il est vrai que le corpus encyclopédique ne donne que l'illusion de l'unité que l'on s'attendrait à trouver dans le 'monument à la gloire des Philosophes', manifeste, selon Saint-Amand, de 'la réussite d'une communauté pacifiée [...] une société qui a su éviter des dissensions fatales'. De même, il est exact que Diderot prend, dans *Le Neveu*, 'sa revanche en quelque sorte d'avoir été le médiateur des contradictions'.[37] Cependant, les contradictions sont déjà présentes au sein de l'*Encyclopédie* non seulement celles de ses acolytes ou de ses détracteurs, mais les siennes propres.

Peut-être, est-ce pour cela qu'au lieu de passer de A à B et de B à C, le lecteur de l'*Encyclopédie* est invité à suivre, avant la lettre et celles du WWW, des bio-rythmes personnels et à progresser dans la découverte des savoirs comme lors de celle d'un territoire inconnu. Ici, la connaissance ne s'établit pas sous la forme de fixité et d'enfermement que produirait l'essai, autre genre majeur, à l'époque, dans la compréhension et l'exercice de l'entendement. Dans l'*Encyclopédie*, ces derniers demandent l'opposé: souplesse, versatilité et ils dépendent des rencontres et de leur hasard. Comprendre, apprendre et savoir entraînent, dès lors, un parcours accidenté, des digressions, des excursions, des retours en arrière, des détours, des sauts latéraux ou bonds en avant. En corollaire, il faut que la lecture se fasse tout sauf linéaire, puisqu'il s'agit de lire un texte 'that all but prohibits linear reading'. Comme le montre Julie Hayes à travers sa comparaison entre hiéroglyphe et hypertexte, les encyclopédies 'fascinent' justement parce qu'elles sont illisibles, vu leurs proportions, et le défi qu'elle pose à un esprit cherchant la synthèse et la cohérence constitutives de toute figure circulaire.[38]

D'où la nouvelle image, une mappemonde, qui s'insinue vers la fin du 'Discours préliminaire' pour se superposer à celle de l'arbre et la recouvrir. Si cette métaphore est loin d'être originale durant un siècle fortement engagé dans la cartographie systématique d'un territoire connu en pleine expansion, elle se pose cependant en fort contraste par rapport à celle de l'arbre, en dépit des efforts de la part des auteurs du 'Discours' pour en contourner l'importance (i.xv):

[L'ordre encyclopédique] est une espèce de Mappemonde qui doit montrer les principaux pays, leur position & leur dépendance mutuelle, le chemin en ligne droite qu'il y a de l'un à l'autre; chemin souvent coupé par mille obstacles qui ne peuvent être connus dans chaque pays que des habitans ou des voyageurs, & qui ne saurroient être montrés que dans des cartes particulieres fort détaillées [...]. Mais

36. Saint-Amand, *Les Lois de l'hostilité*, p.157.
37. Saint-Amand, *Les Lois de l'hostilité*, p.158.
38. 'The *Encyclopédie*, of course, comes immediately to mind as a text that all but prohibits a linear reading. Encyclopedias fascinate from their very "unreadability", both because of their physical proportions and typography, and because of the mental challenge of imagining the "circle of knowledge" enclosed within a single work' (Hayes, *Reading the French Enlightenment*, p.145).

comme dans les cartes du globe que nous habitons, les objets sont plus ou moins rapprochés, & présentent un coup d'œil différent selon le point de vûe où l'œil est placé par le Géographe qui construit la carte, de même la forme de l'arbre encyclopédique dépendra du point de vûe où l'on se mettra pour envisager l'univers littéraire. On peut donc imaginer autant de systèmes différens de la connoissance humaine, que de Mappemondes de différentes projections; & chacun de ces systèmes pourra même avoir, à l'exclusion des autres, quelque avantage particulier [...]. Quoiqu'il en soit, celui de tous les arbres encyclopédiques qui offrirait le plus grand nombre de liaisons & de rapports entre les Sciences mériteroit sans doute d'être préféré. Mais peut-on se flatter de le saisir?

La mention rapide, encore une fois, des arbres encyclopédiques, mais surtout la suggestion de leur multiplicité, leur mérite conditionnel et leur existence évasive destabilisent l'impression de solidité et de certitude qu'ils symbolisent. L'approche de la saisie des connaissances que détaille ce passage du 'Discours préliminaire' correspond, en fait, précisément à celle dont nous avons aujourd'hui l'expérience quotidienne. L'ordre encyclopédique, est-il précisé, 'consiste à rassembler [nos connaissances] dans le plus petit espace possible' pour voir 'd'un coup d'œil les objets des spéculations du philosophe et les opérations qu'il peut faire sur ces objets' (i.xv). Du modèle naturel de l'arbre, on est passé insensiblement à celui culturel du géographe. Il s'agit là des géographes de l'époque, voyageurs ne disposant d'autres instruments que leurs propres yeux et dessinant donc le monde comme autant de visions fragmentaires et centrées sur eux.[39]

Ainsi, procédant, apparemment, d'un parti-pris généalogique où l'on ajouterait un contenu fixe et limité à un autre contenu de même type, celui de chaque article, D'Alembert est forcé d'envisager la poursuite de connexions, et de valoriser l'étude des intervalles qui relient les informations. Dans l'affrontement des modèles et des démarches, le grand vainqueur est l'ordre – ou son désordre – du subjectif. Révélant les remarquables consonances des mots *arbre, arbitraire* et *labyrinthe*, Hayes dégage toutes les contradictions qui fissurent la croyance des encyclopédistes en l'Arbre comme ultime métaphore du savoir. Son analyse prouve que la bataille qui consistait à maintenir l'arbitraire en retrait était perdue d'avance pour D'Alembert.[40] Il est légitime d'induire, à la lecture du reste de son œuvre, qu'elle l'était aussi pour Diderot. C'est pourquoi le principe de cartographie de l'espace intelligible remplace, à cette intersection de tension dans la

---

39. La notion de cartographie est essentiellement différente aujourd'hui. Considérant la multiplicité des espaces aussi bien visibles qu'invisibles que la technologie et la théorie permettent de saisir et de représenter (voir les images par résonnance magnétique, les photos prises de l'espace, les simulations par ordinateurs, etc., mais aussi les nouveaux espaces mathématiques ou même sociologiques) il est clair que le désir d'une visualisation globale de la mappemonde qui animait les encyclopédistes et les explorateurs est totalement dépassé. Il est aussi évident que le concept d'espace si crucial à la pensée post-moderne a irrémédiablement changé. Mais l'idée de regroupement, de rassemblement en un seul lieu de la totalité de la connaissance, elle, reste une constante et me semble être tout aussi illusoire pour les utilisateurs du Web que pour les encyclopédistes. Ce qui ne la rend pas moins fascinante.

40. Hayes, *Reading the French Enlightenment*, p.45.

modernité et d'extension vers la post-modernité, celui de l'étalement linéaire du savoir.

Ce que l'*Encyclopédie* offre d'original est, par conséquent, bien plus une manière de penser qu'une somme d'informations. Les informations existent, elles sont nécessaires pour dresser un bilan de l'état des connaissances, mais les encyclopédistes sont conscients de leur quasi-immédiate obsolescence. L'article ENCYCLOPÉDIE lui-même en témoigne, en se préoccupant longuement de l'effet du temps de rédaction sur la validité des informations et en rappelant la diversité qui 's'introduit tous les jours dans la langue des arts, dans les machines et dans les manœuvres' (v.636a). Bien plus que la matière inscrite dans les volumes ou dessinée sur les planches, ce qui importe est la manière dont le lecteur va l'appréhender, en clair: comment les encyclopédistes vont lui réapprendre à lire.

A nouveau, une comparaison avec la conception deleuzienne du livre s'impose et illumine celle des philosophes éclairés. Pour Deleuze, la conception du second livre, celui qu'il considère moderne, apparaît non pas quand la pensée a finalement pu 'rompre vraiment avec le dualisme, avec la complémentarité d'un objet et d'un sujet' – dans le cas de l'*Encyclopédie* le savoir et l'auteur –, mais quand 'le monde a perdu son pivot; le sujet ne peut même plus faire de dichotomie, mais accède à une plus haute unité, d'ambivalence ou de surdétermination, dans une dimension toujours supplémentaire à celle de son objet. Le monde est devenu chaos, mais le livre reste image du monde, chaosmos-radicelle, au lieu de cosmos-racine'.[41]

D'une certaine façon, le pivot (in?)volontairement perdu dans ou par l'encyclopédisme est celui que l'arbre érigeait. Même si l'information s'organise autour de cet axe, ce n'est qu'artificiellement. La structure se doit d'être secondaire comme le démontre, dans le *Discours préliminaire*, l'exemple par l'absurde de l'architecte qui 'ayant à élever un édifice immense, passerait toute sa vie à en tracer le plan' (i.xv). L'information existe, elle compose le Dictionnaire et en écrit les volumes, mais c'est la pensée du lecteur qui le 'raisonne', c'est-à-dire l'anime et le transforme, par sa lecture, en Encyclopédie. La dimension supplémentaire à l'objet qu'évoquent Deleuze et Guattari, est celle déjà exigée dans l'article ENCY-CLOPÉDIE et qui reste toujours à ajouter: 'C'est à l'exécution de ce projet étendu, non seulement aux différents objets de nos académies, mais à toutes les branches de la connaissance humaine qu'une Encyclopédie doit suppléer' (v.636).

Ce supplément, chez Diderot et Deleuze, ne provient plus du seul écrivain qui penserait l'information en la rédigeant mais d'une multiplicité de subjectivités qui ne consiste pas en une factice 'habileté typographique, lexicale ou même syntaxique'. Rien ne sert de dire 'nous', 'le multiple', comme l'écrit Deleuze, 'il faut le faire'.[42] Le canevas d'une telle multiplicité, pour les

---

41. Deleuze et Guattari, *Mille Plateaux*, p.12-13.
42. Deleuze et Guattari, *Mille Plateaux*, p.13.

encyclopédistes, est sous-tendu par la volonté d'utiliser les talents d'une 'société de gens de lettres et d'artistes [...] épars'. Epars 'parce qu'il n'y a aucune société subsistante d'où l'on puisse tirer toutes les connaissances dont on a besoin' (vi.636). Mais ce qui le tisse, et en fait une (hyper?) toile, ce sont les lecteurs, ces anonymes, qui comblent, d'un renvoi suivi à un autre négligé, les interstices et les fractures inévitables de tout écrit comme de tout savoir.

La démarche encyclopédique ne procède donc pas d'une 'information sur' donnée par les auteurs mais d'une 'pensée entre' générée au fur et à mesure que les lectures se déroulent et dans les espaces et dans leur temps. Elle s'accomplit dans le sujet collectif qui écrit le texte, mais aussi *via* celui à qui il est destiné et dont l'identité, selon l'analyse de Georges Benrekassa, 'reste perpétuellement à définir, car il est radicalement différent de toutes les sociétés savantes existantes, et même de tous les modèles de sociétés savantes existantes ou d'académies possibles'. Comme Benrekassa le précise, de telles sociétés ne peuvent exister, considérant que 'c'est la définition de l'objet réel du savoir encyclopédique' qui 'subvertit leur existence'.[43] La connaissance ne résiderait donc ni dans 'les savantes compagnies' de philosophes, ni dans leur tentative de totalisation encyclopédique. Elle serait, comme le dit Kundera de la vie elle-même, ailleurs, hors du livre, hors de la structure.[44] Qui sait? Dans un simple savoir-mouvement, savoir-temps.

Dès lors, ce n'est plus seulement à Deleuze et Guattari qu'on peut se référer pour demander une lecture de l'*Encyclopédie* et humaniste et postmoderne mais encore à Foucault qui articulait, quelques années avant eux, le concept de 'pensée du dehors'. Caractéristiques, ou tout au moins indicatrices de cette forme de pensée, sont, en résumé, ses considérations suivantes. Tout d'abord le sujet, au sens classique du terme, est exclu du langage qui re-trace 'l'expérience du dehors'.[45] Ensuite, cette expérience grâce à laquelle 'il s'agit bien de passer hors de soi', s'annonce dans le seul geste d'écrire comme dans les tentatives pour formaliser le langage [...] dans la recherche aussi de ce Logos qui forme comme le lieu de naissance de toute la raison occidentale'. L'écriture de la pensée du dehors aurait pour but de 'retrouver l'espace où elle se déploie', espace ouvert par la réalisation d'une 'béance qui longtemps nous est demeurée invisible' où 'l'être du langage n'apparaît que pour lui-même dans la disparition du sujet'.

C'est au 'monologue ressassant de Sade' que Foucault recourt pour illustrer sa théorie et il en fait une exception à l'époque de Kant 'où jamais sans

---

43. Benrekassa, *Langage des Lumières*, p.248.
44. D'une certaine manière parce qu'elle s'applique à Diderot et non seulement à l'éditeur de l'*Encyclopédie*, mais de façon certaine, le texte de Milan Kundera, *Jacques et son maître, hommage à Denis Diderot en trois actes* (Paris 1981), illustre tout à fait ce que j'entendais plus haut par 'cinquième sorte [de renvoi]', celle qui envoie à l'au-delà du soi théorique encyclopédique, c'est-à-dire à sa pratique.
45. Michel Foucault, *La Pensée du dehors* (Paris 1986), p.15-18. Cette citation et les suivantes sont tirées de cette édition. Le texte parut, d'abord, dans *Critique* 229 (1966).

doute l'intériorisation de la loi de l'histoire et du monde ne fut plus impérieusement requise'. Je proposerais, au contraire, de voir en l'*Encyclopédie* cette 'première déchirure par où la pensée du dehors s'est fait jour pour nous', et qui a ouvert, dans une époque d'unification, la recherche d'une esthétique du discontinu. C'est celle, précisément, que l'œuvre propre de Diderot incorpore si résolument ou qui caractérise son personnage du Neveu. Une telle rupture résultera en la sublime errance sadienne.

Je ne crois pas, cependant, que ce soit cette encyclopédie-là qui ait été disponible aux contemporains de ses auteurs, ou nous le soit aujourd'hui dans quelques sections 'livres rares' des bibliothèques mondiales. Ce qui permet à l'*Encyclopédie* de devenir 'cette pensée qui se tient hors de toute subjectivité pour en faire surgir comme de l'extérieur les limites, en énoncer la fin, en faire scintiller la dispersion et n'en recueillir que l'invincible absence' réside, paradoxalement, dans son accessibilité à tous les types de sujets. A partir de son oblation aux Dieux actuels de la connaissance, à savoir les utilisateurs hétéroclites de 'l'hypertoile' – 'l'humanité en pointillé' pour adapter l'expression saisissante de Benrekassa – l'encyclopédisme pourrait aujourd'hui produire les 'ouvrages meilleurs' que Diderot pressentait pour son avenir.[46] Et ils ne seraient autres qu'une infinité de versions alternatives d'une *Encyclopédie* prise dans le processus actif d'un éternel retour à et sur elle-même.

Pour Foucault c'est Sade et Hölderlin qui auraient 'déposé dans notre pensée, pour le siècle à venir, mais en quelque sorte chiffrée, l'expérience du dehors'. Certes, mais avant ces deux écrivains, je trouve en Diderot les 'principes de connexion et d'hétérogénéité' et vois dans la lecture informatisée de l'*Encyclopédie* la possibilité de formation 'des agencements collectifs d'énonciation' qu'analysent Deleuze et Guattari.[47] Ceux-là même qui permettent, selon Foucault cette fois, et à mon humble avis, de 'convertir le langage réflexif [...] de le tourner non pas vers une confirmation intérieure – vers une sorte de certitude centrée d'où il ne pourrait plus être délogé – mais plutôt vers une extrémité où il lui faut toujours se contester: parvenu au bord de lui-même, il ne voit pas surgir la positivité qui le contredit, mais le vide dans lequel il va s'effacer'.[48]

Mais au-delà de l'intersection de théories et de textes, qu'est-ce à dire? Que les banques de données du World Wide Web n'ont pas inventé grand-chose? Que, de la volonté de vérité et de totalité du savoir, si décriée aujourd'hui, motivant les philosophes du dix-huitième siècle à l'illusion d'absolu créée et entretenue par les multinationales détentrices d'innombrables sites, on compte plus de deux cent cinquante années, mais il n'y a qu'un pas? Que, si l'on analysait l'hypertoile en terme d'encyclopédie, on déstabiliserait l'argument des fervents d'un post-modernisme myope

---

46. Benrekassa, *Langage des Lumières*, p.248.
47. Deleuze et Guattari, *Mille Plateaux*, p.13. Il s'agit, bien sûr, d'une schizo-analyse.
48. Foucault, *La Pensée du dehors*, p.22.

posant leur saisie du monde à l'opposé de celle des Lumières pour reconsidérer celui des dix-huitiémistes qui, dans la lignée de Anderson, Brewer et Hayes notamment, intiment la nécessité de les réconcilier?[49] Sans doute. De telles conclusions sont aussi logiques que chronologiques. Elles permettent d'adopter une vision humaniste de l'accès informatisé à la connaissance, de le considérer comme évolution, progrès autant que comme révolution, rupture. Et d'en dépasser la dialectique.

En fait, ce n'est pas son contenu qui est en jeu dans la course effrénée au savoir. Pas plus qu'il ne l'était dans le marathon, épuisant, des encyclopédistes, eux aussi à la poursuite d'un horizon cognitif inapprochable. L'important, alors et maintenant, étant l'entraînement. On pourrait ainsi lire, dans les prémisses de l'*Encyclopédie*, l'intuition concrète du type d'appréhension des savoirs à venir et retracer, dans son aventure, les principes d'un apprentissage post-moderne. L'aventure n'aurait pas été de parvenir à faire publier, en dépit de tout et de presque tous, la série complète des volumes. Elle n'aurait pas consisté non plus en la prouesse de réunir tant de données sur tellement de sujets, ni d'ailleurs en la réalisation d'un projet aussi démentiel. Elle ne résiderait pas dans la gloire des auteurs mentionnés, ni dans le prestige des rédacteurs. Mais elle consisterait dans le défi de montrer comment, depuis le cœur d'une longue tradition d'exégèse rigoureuse, et sous son couvert, on peut tracer de nouvelles lignes de fuite mentales en réapprenant à lire. Quoi de plus banal, quoi de plus risqué?

Il est temps, parce que le virtuel le rend réalisable, de traiter l'*Encyclopédie* comme le livre-rhizome de Deleuze et Guattari. On peut en déchiffrer sa pensée et celle qu'elle déploie à partir de ses ex-tensions et tendre vers 'ce dont la lumière, absolument fine, n'a jamais reçu langage'.[50] Il s'agit de concevoir la liaison que, dans le 'Discours préliminaire', 'les découvertes ont entr'elles' comme les 'chaînons sémiotiques de toute nature' qui traversent les rhizomes. Bref, pour suivre la recommandation des encyclopédistes de ne pas 'renfermer [ces connaissances] en un système qui soit un', l'*Encyclopédie*, sous influence informatique, ne saurait plus être un ordinateur, imposant son organisation à la totalité de la connaissance humaine et érigeant un 'monument', comme dirait Foucault, à l'omnipotence de la Raison. Je la vois 'computeur', rassemblement anorganique, agencement, reterritorialisation absolue.[51] Ce que l'*Encyclopédie* inscrirait ainsi serait précisément le constat, serein, de la perte d'un ordre des choses et celui, joyeux, d'un regain des mots. Elle ne traduirait pas le besoin classique de construire et contenir linéairement les savoirs, c'est-à-dire le tronc de la société. Elle exprimerait, en l'imprimant, la nécessité éminemment post-moderne

---

49. Voir l'introduction de Wilda Anderson à *Diderot's dream* et le développement sur les savants et les philosophes de son troisième chapitre, p.90-98.

50. Foucault, *La Pensée du dehors*, p.25.

51. Il est impossible, dans l'espace restreint d'un article, de s'étendre sur ces concepts difficiles. Mais le lecteur curieux trouvera un résumé dans le lexique qui conclut *Mille Plateaux* sous 'D: Déterritorialisation'.

d'apprendre une écriture et lecture du monde plus adéquates, par fragments juxtaposés, et de tracer des voies courbes, parallèles et/ou perpendiculaires à celle de la rationalité.

Pour preuve le fait que, à la transcendance apparente que l'on s'accorde à voir en la Raison comme principe et outil de la pensée des Lumières, les auteurs du 'Discours' substituaient l'immanence des sensations qui nous assiègent de toutes parts et qui nous arrachent à la solitude où nous resterions sans elles. Avant d'aborder l'apprentissage des sciences, des arts et des métiers, ils rappelaient que 'la première chose que nos sensations nous apprennent, et qui même n'en est pas distinguée, c'est notre existence' et que 'la seconde connaissance que nous devons à nos sensations est l'existence des objets extérieurs, parmi lequel notre propre corps doit être compris' (i.ii).

En exergue à l'*Encyclopédie*, ces remarques qu'il développe ensuite sur plusieurs pages font des postulats du sensualisme une véritable ontologie: je sens donc je suis. De même, elles déplacent l'être et le mettent en et dans le mouvement d'un parcours, d'un 'feuilletage', quasi aléatoire: 'enfin le système de nos connaissances est composé de différentes branches, dont plusieurs ont un même point de réunion; et comme en partant de ce point il n'est pas possible de s'engager à la fois dans toutes les routes, c'est la nature de différents esprits qui détermine le choix' (i.xv).

Ce que l'*Encyclopédie* lègue donc à la postérité, à laquelle elle est destinée tant Diderot est 'persuadé que la perfection dernière d'une encyclopédie est l'ouvrage des siècles', n'est vraiment pas un condensé lisse des connaissances d'une période.[52] Nous sommes aujourd'hui, au contraire, confronté à un corpus qui exige l'appréhension erratique d'une réalité que les enjeux du savoir ont, paradoxalement, commencé à strier dès le dix-huitième siècle et qu'ils continuent tous les jours d'écarteler en millions de pages de base.[53] Voilà peut-être la raison pour laquelle les arguments de promotion de l'*Encyclopédie* française résonnent comme un slogan publicitaire d'America On Line:

D'où nous inférons que cet ouvrage pourrait tenir lieu de bibliothèque dans tous les genres, à un homme du monde; et dans tous les genres, excepté le sien, à un savant de profession; qu'il suppléera aux livres élémentaires; qu'il développera les vrais principes des choses; qu'il en marquera les rapports; qu'il contribuera à la certitude & au progrès des connaissances humaines, & qu'en multipliant le nombre des vrais savants, des artistes distingués, & des amateurs éclairés, il répandra dans la société de nouveaux avantages.[54]

Et ce à juste titre, car il semble en effet que l'*Encyclopédie* ait été conçue pour une mise sur réseau. En témoigne et le démontre le Projet ARTFL

---

52. 'Il a fallu des siècles pour commencer; il en faudra pour finir' (Diderot, 'Prospectus', DPV v.224).
53. Une des traductions courantes du terme *homepage* aussi appelé page d'accueil, enseigne ou portail.
54. 'Prospectus', DPV v.104.

développé par un groupe de chercheurs de l'Université de Chicago.[55] Une heure de feuilletage virtuel des pages encyclopédiques suffit à convaincre de la modernité réelle d'une telle structure cognitive. La saisie du texte par engin de recherche donne à l'hétérogénéité du stock d'informations à la fois toutes ses surfaces et une impression de profondeur d'autant plus vertigineuse qu'elle est refaçonnable à chaque série d'investigations.

Dans le cadre de mon propre questionnement sur les modalités d'apprentissage et les façons de lire, je me suis concentrée sur les termes de 'savoir', 'lecture' et 'connaissance/s'.[56] 'Savoir' a généré 116 occurrences dans les articles les plus divers, 'lecture' 613 et 'connaissance' au singulier et/ou au pluriel en a produit 4627.[57] L'analyse sémantique d'un grand nombre de ces occurrences démontre que par 'savoir', les encyclopédistes entendaient une forme de connaissance abstraite, souvent mise en parallèle à une série d'autres termes valorisés tels que 'mœurs, réputation, mérite, jugement, vertu, solidité des principes, intelligence, philosophie, talents, goût, liberté, fortune, amour de la vérité, génie' qui reviennent constamment. Au contraire, la connaissance est toujours posée par rapport à un objet précis et relativement ciblé du savoir. La connaissance est celle de Dieu, de soi-même, des règles d'un art, du cœur humain, des événements, des faits, d'une technique, de théories.[58] Mais elle est aussi hiérarchisée, alors que le savoir reste toujours de la plus haute valeur. La connaissance peut venir des sens ou bien en être trompée (voir AVEUGLE et CERTITUDE). Chez l'homme, elle est différente de celle des animaux, connaissance que nous aurions, du reste, perdue (voir PHENOMÈNES). Elle est 'plus ou moins étendue' (voir l''Avertissement des éditeurs'), et appartient à différents ordres (voir CHIMIE).

Une telle approche des textes encyclopédiques est remarquablement facilitée par sa mise sur réseau, mais elle n'en est pas particulièrement régénérée et revient, en fin de compte, à traiter l'*Encyclopédie* comme 'le livre classique, comme belle intériorité organique, signifiante et subjective' que

55. Je tiens à remercier tout particulièrement Mark Olsen pour son aide si précieuse dans ma propre découverte de cet outil magique.

56. Voir, en appendice, l'impression de la liste des résultats préliminaires affichés sur l'écran.

57. A titre purement indicatif, voir dans l'appendice la liste des articles dans lesquels 'savoir' apparaît comme nom ou verbe.

58. L'énumération exhaustive des citations est clairement impossible. Mais en voilà des échantillons numérotés par leur ordre d'apparition dans les articles du texte entier. Occurrences #364 CHAMBRE DE LA MARÉE: connaissance d'un Dieu; les occurrences #827 à 984 se trouvent toutes dans l'article CONNOISSANCE; #1008 CONSONNE: connaissance des causes; #1127 CURIOSITÉ: 'La curiosité de l'homme et la plus digne de toutes, je veux dire le désir qui l'anime d'étendre ses connaissances'; #1280 DISSECTION: connaissances que leur procure la dissection; #2336 HÉRÉSIE: la connaissance en appartient au juge d'Eglise; #3361 PARLEMENT DE PARIS: connaissance des crimes; #3871 PYTHIE: connaissance de l'avenir; #3834 RAISON: 'une telle soumission de notre Raison à la Foi ne renverse pas pour cela les limites de la connaissance humaine'; #4105 SHROPSHIRE: la profonde connaissance de la nature; #4439 VITRIOLIQUE: pénétrer par la théorie dans la connaissance des choses; #4515 USAGE: la connaissance de la véritable analogie.

Deleuze et Guattari définissaient en premier lieu. A ce genre d'*Encyclopédie*, celui dans lequel on l'a classifiée traditionnellement, correspond la première 'manière de lire' que Deleuze décrit en réponse à une critique de *L'Anti-Œdipe* et de son concept inaugural de rhizome: 'C'est qu'il y a deux manières de lire un livre: ou bien on le considère comme une boîte qui renvoie à un dedans, et alors on va chercher des signifiés, et puis, si l'on est encore plus pervers ou corrompu, on part en quête du signifiant.'[59]

Rien de plus légitime, en effet, que d'utiliser un système mécanique particulièrement efficace comme le site ARTFL pour produire une analyse éminemment systématique d'un ou plusieurs concepts. Rien de moins nouveau cependant. Là où la consultation en ligne des volumes devient véritablement révolutionnaire, c'est quand elle est faite de façon non linéaire justement, selon le second type de lecture que Deleuze ébauche:

> Ou bien l'autre manière: on considère un livre comme une petite machine a-signifiante; le seul problème est 'est-ce que ça fonctionne, et comment ça fonctionne?' Comment ça fonctionne pour vous? Si ça ne fonctionne pas, si rien ne passe, prenez donc un autre livre. Cette autre lecture, c'est une lecture en intensité: quelque chose passe ou ne passe pas. Il n'y a rien à expliquer, rien à comprendre, rien à interpréter. C'est du type branchement électrique.[60]

A ce moment-là Deleuze rejoint Foucault:

> Cette autre manière de lire s'oppose à la précédente, parce qu'elle rapporte immédiatement un livre au Dehors. Un livre, c'est un petit rouage dans une machinerie beaucoup plus complexe extérieure. Ecrire, c'est un flux parmi d'autres, et qui n'a aucun privilège par rapport aux autres, et qui entre dans des rapports de courant, de contre-courant, de remous avec d'autres flux.[61]

Pour clarifier, prenons l'exemple – prégnant – de l'article SENS, dont l'acception grammaticale est rédigée par Beauzée. Le terme de 'connoissance/s' y revient 15 fois, 'lecture' une et celui de 'savoir' n'y figure jamais. Toutes sortes de conclusions sont envisageables, à partir de ces données, mais une seule lecture est possible. Si l'on se détache, par contre, de la volonté de faire signifier quelque chose à l'article SENS, et qu'on lui demande de 'fonctionner', une autre manière de lire – que Deleuze considérerait sans doute 'en intensité' – prend forme grâce au format électronique. Un second réseau, ou rhizome, de renvois se dégage, en effet, qui s'intercale à celui, officiel, de l'auteur. Beauzée suggère impérativement ('Voyez') de consulter les articles ESPRIT, RÉGIME, TROPE, ANALOGIE, VERSION, PASSIF, RELATIF, IDIOTISME ET SUPERLATIF, ALLEGORIE, CONTRE-SENS, LITTÉRAL, FIGURE, MYSTIQUE. Mais la mise en page interactive signale également tous les termes traités isolément dans le cadre d'un article qu'ils intitulent. L'exploration des ramifications du mot 'sens' entraîne aussi à lire toutes, quelques ou aucune

---

59. Deleuze, *Pourparlers*, p.17.
60. Deleuze, *Pourparlers*, p.17.
61. Deleuze, *Pourparlers*, p.17.

connexions latérales. Figurant ainsi en liens hypertextuels, bien que d'une autre couleur que le bleu symbolique des renvois originels, se trouvent les mots 'acception', 'savant', 'feu', 'lumière', 'clarté', 'aide', 'secours', 'se gâter', 'mémorisation', 'homme', 'vieillard', 'verbum'.

Je doute que l'on puisse, raisonnablement, enfermer dans une explication ou interprétation quelconque une telle prolifération sémantique. Elle existe pourtant, et il est évident que le mode de lecture, et en conséquence, celui d'apprentissage en sont radicalement bouleversés. A l'intérieur de ces surfaces dites intelligentes, se construit tout un appareil de sens dont la signification n'est ni prédéterminée par les auteurs ni commune aux lecteurs. Fait grâce à la vitesse, le pragmatisme et, en quelque sorte, l'aveuglement des rapports informatiques qui traitent toute information sur un plan à la fois unique – original – et multiple – celui des strates de l'accès au texte – l'information prend les dimensions d'une base non de données précises, strictes et toujours déjà limitées, mais d'un vecteur de pensée erratique, hérétique et multiple. Grâce à l'informatisation de l'*Encyclopédie*, toutes les possibilités de 'textualité multiple' sont réalisées: celle du nombre remarquable, pour l'époque, de ses auteurs n'a d'égale que celle quasi-infinie non seulement de ses lecteurs mais de ses lectures par chacun des lecteurs réécrivant leurs propres liaisons.

Qui pourrait, en effet, prédire quel sens aura le mot 'sens' à la fin de chaque consultation du site ARTFL? Et, par là, qui voudrait encore s'y attacher? Une telle recherche, que les auteurs d'encyclopédies numériques qualifient de 'multicritères', engage un dialogue avec la matérialité du savoir qui ne recourt plus aux trois fonctions articulant le 'système des connaissances humaines' des encyclopédistes. Le lecteur n'a plus besoin de *mémoire*, la somme textuelle est accessible dans son intégralité, à tout moment et quasi immédiatement. Il est invité à se laisser guider par son désir et sa curiosité plutôt que par la *raison*, dans sa décision du parcours de lecture à suivre. Et, dans la mesure où tout est imagé – mis sur l'écran en image – son *imagination* ne participe que fort peu de ce type de processus cognitif.

Ce qui entre dans cette nouvelle forme de lecture, c'est-à-dire d'intériorisation, de l'*Encyclopédie*, c'est donc bien l'extérieur au savoir, le Dehors. Devenu pur langage, mais non pas langage pur, le texte sur réseau échappe aux bornes dans lesquelles le temps, l'avance technologique, les études culturelles l'enfermaient.[62] Qu'importe, par exemple, que des préoccupations d'alors n'aient plus cours aujourd'hui ou que les auteurs, références ou théories qui parlaient si clairement aux lecteurs du passé aient perdu toute substance pour nous? Entre les lignes de la toile encyclopédique et les réseaux de l'hypertoile informatique, l'appareil de pensée qui fonctionne est enfin celui dont les encyclopédistes eux-mêmes avaient besoin pour

---

62. Par 'langage pur' je fais référence, par exemple, au concept de *Ursprache* développé par W. Benjamin dans ses écrits sur 'la tâche du traducteur' publié dans le recueil *Illuminations*.

passer de la connaissance, figée, des objets à celle, différentielle et illogique, de leurs rapports.

L'extériorité prend plusieurs formes concrètes: celle du cerveau machinique qui mémorise les textes; celle du formulaire de recherche qui déterritorialise les auteurs, concepts, mots-clés pour les localiser sur le cadre d'un écran; celle, perçue, du renvoi que l'on consulte ou qui reste inconnue pour celui que l'on néglige; celles infinies des autres entrées qui auraient pu être demandées, des associations illimitées que les opérateurs logiques 'et', 'ou' ainsi que 'et/ou' auraient générées.

Mais le dehors est aussi psychique. Si les parcours ne sont pas nécessairement suivis au hasard, ils le sont certainement de façon inconsciente. Ce qui pousse à consulter un renvoi recommandé ou à passer à un article connecté est ressenti par le lecteur comme aléatoire, même s'il peut y trouver, *a posteriori*, l'évidence, rassurante mais illusoire, d'une motivation ou la preuve intangible d'une logique. Et, finalement, il est social dans la mesure où ce dehors, bien qu'"internalisé' par les receuils de connaissances livresques ou multimédiatiques, constitue ce que Le Goff appelle une 'nouvelle mémoire collective'.[63]

Soumise à des nouvelles lois cognitives telles qu'un incessant renouvellement des approches, un débordement constant des concepts, une accélération effrénée de la confrontation au corpus, une fragmentation locale des sens réels aussi rapide que la reconstruction perpétuelle et différée des significations potentielles, la lecture contemporaine, depuis ses extériorités, de l'*Encyclopédie* est intense mais aussi toute entière parcourue d'intensités. Elle suit tous les flux de subjectivités sans jamais appartenir à aucun sujet. Avalanche d'informations, l'*Encyclopédie* sur le Web peut aussi se faire courants déchaînés de pensée et permettre de repenser et le livre et les manières de lire.

En outre, la mise sur réseau informatique – moyen cognitif et culturel post-moderne par excellence – contribue à dépasser les caractéristiques décriées du savoir humaniste. En antidote à l'essentialisme des points de vue, la lecture par engin de recherche permet une approche fondée sur le choix, faite en toute liberté et donc délibérément existentielle des informations. A l'encontre des critiques d'arbitraire accompagnant toute pensée universaliste, le feuilletage électronique facilite et encourage une appréhension des connaissances individualisée et individualiste. En réponse aux arguments reprochant au dix-huitième siècle son logocentrisme et l'irrationalité de sa Raison omnipotente, l'*Encyclopédie* via ARTFL et ses significations sont toute entières liées aux jeux de la passion et du hasard.

---

63. 'To be sure, this new collective memory constitutes its knowledge in the traditional vehicles, but it conceives them differently. Compare for example the *Enciclopedia Einaudi* or the *Encyclopaedia universalis* with the venerable *Encyclopaedia Britannica*! Perhaps ultimately we would arrive at something more like the spirit of d'Alembert's and Diderot's great *Encyclopédie*, which was also the offspring of a period of active engagement and transformation of the collective memory' (Le Goff, *History and memory*, p.96).

En conclusion, si l'hypertextualisation de l'*Encyclopédie* n'est probablement pas encore le moyen parfait de sa lecture, et le Web certainement pas celui ultime de savoir, il me semble, néanmoins, que les encyclopédistes ont trouvé un véhicule adéquat à la dissémination de leur pensée, la perception de leur doute quant à la possibilité de connaître et la saisie insensée de leur préhension d'un monde finalement mis en mouvement, dans un langage en images.

Appendice

A titre purement indicatif, voici la série des articles dans lesquels 'savoir' apparaît comme nom ou verbe. Ils restent naturellement listés par ordre alphabétique puisque l'engin de recherche lit l'*Encyclopédie* selon un ordre chronologique des volumes.

Ame	Envie
Ame des bêtes	Equation
Araignée	Errhins
Aristotélisme	Etherniteux
Artériotomie	Etonnement de sabot
Battre	Exposant
Bibliothèque	Ferrure
Capucins	Financier
Catalogue	Fistule
Champignon	Flatterie
Chenille	Foible
Chevreuil	Folie
C. Chesneau	Origine des Fontaines
Connoissance	Girofle
Cordeliers	Goût
Cornet	Hercule
Correct	Hermathène
Crise	Hippocratisme
C. Secondat	Histoire naturelle
Déshérence	Hypogastrique
Despotisme	Idole
Distribution	Impertinence
Docteur en Médecine	Imputation
Echecs	Intolérance
Edulcoration	Lettres
Effort	Licteur
Empirisme	Littérature
Encaustique	Maître en Chirurgie
Encyclopédie	Médecine

Mort
Nismes
Nofesch
Œconomie politique
Opérateur
Oreille
Palissades
Perroquet vert
Plantes
Plastique
Politesse
Polythéisme
Population
Pouls
Pythagorisme
Rapport
Recueil
Renommée
République d'Athènes
Richesse
Ridicule
Romane
Ryp̃
Salines
Samos
Santé

Savoir Vivre
Sculpture
Scyros
Sépulchre
Similitude
Société
Sommerset
Sot, fat
Subside
Suena
Suffolk
Sussex
Temple de la Gloire
Thyades
Tireur d'or
Tirinanxes
Trictrac
Troyes
Verrerie
Vingtième
Vœu conditionnel
West-Morland
Westminster
Wilton
Wolstrope

PATRICK COLEMAN

'Figure' in the *Encyclopédie*: discovery or discipline

By various means – ironic statements within articles, cross-references among articles, the juxtaposition of articles resulting from the choice of an alphabetical arrangement – the *Encyclopédie* invites us to read between and across the lines. We can distinguish three modes of such reading: the constructive, the critical, and the creative. Since knowledge is presented in a series of discrete articles organised alphabetically, the reader seeking a full understanding of a topic will have to piece it together from its presentation under various headings. Some topics, however, that must be included in the *Encyclopédie* for religious or political reasons yield no genuine knowledge at all, or only *préjugés* masked as knowledge. Since error cannot always be uncovered directly, the editors encourage readers to read ironically, and to follow cross-references to entries whose innocuous titles hide subversive arguments. Finally, the editors, and especially Diderot, see the *Encyclopédie* as more than a mere compilation of knowledge. The quotation from Horace on the title-page of the first volume:

> tantum series juncturaque pollet,
> tantum de medio sumptis accedit honoris![1]

suggests that the process of arrangement is itself a creative act to be admired. Readers who appreciate and imitate the editors' example may themselves arrive at new applications and even new discoveries.

Yet, while the possibilities opened up by these modes of reading are often celebrated, their limits have not been properly explored. It is assumed either that there are none, or that the reader will be guided by practical or philosophical concerns, which would curb any irresponsible flights of fancy. The first assumption reflects an idealised, ahistorical view of the work, while the second minimises the seductive power of the *Encyclopédie*'s ambitious presentation of all knowledge as a dynamic totality. Both these views, it must be said, are already present in the editors' programmatic

1. Horace, *Ars poetica*, l.242-43. In the translation of D. A. Russell, 'such is the force of arrangement and combination/such the splendour that commonplace words acquire' (*Ancient literary criticism: the principal texts in new translations*, Oxford 1972, p.285). Modern editions of Horace end the sentence with a period rather than an exclamation mark. Horace, it is true, boasted of using familiar linguistic elements so artfully as to make others believe they could do the same, and yet they would fail no matter how hard they tried. One assumes the encyclopedists, in borrowing the quotation, had rival writers and not their readers in mind.

statements, in which D'Alembert and Diderot legitimise the work as both a high philosophical and socially useful enterprise. Naturally enough, they downplay their own ideological agenda, as well as the possibility the work might be misread. But is it always obvious, as we explore different parts of the *Encyclopédie*, which of the three reading strategies we should properly adopt, or how far we should take it? How do we know when to read ironically, or when the creative, or even the constructive, connections we make are grounded in reality and not on arbitrary verbal associations?

If this question has not been asked more insistently, it is perhaps because we tend to think of the *Encyclopédie* in spatial terms. Partial readings (incomplete or tendentious) are in the end to be reconciled by reference to the encyclopedic order, which in turn rests on the ultimate unity of nature. Pursuing knowledge takes time, of course, and the *Encyclopédie* cannot be comprehended as a whole at any one moment, but this time is a purely abstract notion, merely a variable in the equation of the learning curve. But if the constructive mode of reading may imagined to proceed smoothly along this curve, the critical one surely does not. The relationship between two articles linked by a subversive *renvoi* is not one of complementarity within an ideal spatial order, but of disjunction. What emerges is not only the contradiction between the true and the false, but also the tension between what should and can be said at a specific historical moment. The reader's experience of following up such cross-references is also a temporal one in this more concrete sense, for beyond an increase in knowledge, the reader comes to appreciate the situation of that knowledge within an ongoing historical conflict. Furthermore, the text includes a concrete temporal dimension within its own structure. It is assumed that the subversive article will be read *after* the innocuous one, for otherwise much of the critical effect would be lost. To be sure, the official teaching will normally be encountered first, since it appears under the more obvious heading. But while different degrees of obviousness may correlate with different stages of knowledge as the encyclopedic order reconstructs them, they need not do so. As far as headwords are concerned, 'obviousness' does not mean self-evident, but rather expected; it is a function of contingent cultural circumstances. A similar point can be made about the creative dimension of reading. An unexpected connection is not necessarily a real discovery.

Nor is the problem of undisciplined reading a purely theoretical one. In the middle decades of the eighteenth century, French religious and secular authorities were concerned with a reading practice that was just as subversive in its own way as the one encouraged by the encyclopedists. This was the mode of biblical interpretation known as 'figurism', to distinguish it from the traditional forms of figural readings the Church had developed over the centuries. The primary concern of such readings had been to uncover the spiritual links between events in the Old Testament and Christ's advent in the New, and between sacred history and the salvation journey of contemporary Christians. The application of this method was governed by communally developed exegetical and ecclesiastical norms. Toward the end of the seventeenth century, however, some Jansenist writers, unjustly persecuted, as they believed, for their witness to the pure 'deposit' of apostolic faith by a blind or corrupted Church hierarchy, interpreted their suffering as an anticipation of the final vindication of the faithful in the last days. In connecting their experience in terms of the 'signs of the times' in biblical apocalyptic, they somewhat resembled the radical Reformers of the previous century, who also saw direct prophetic links between Biblical figures and contemporary events. Unlike their predecessors, however, the Jansenists did not break with the Catholic Church. On the contrary, they viewed themselves as a faithful remnant within it. They protested their general submission to papal authority while resisting the application of that authority in such matters as the compulsory *billets de confession* testifying to the penitent's acceptance of the anti-Jansenist papal bull *Unigenitus* (1713). Since the seventeenth century, the Jansenists had also differed with Rome's policy of discouraging translations and lay readings of the Bible, producing notable French versions and commentaries for private use. As the controversy developed, Jansenist polemicists like Jacques-Joseph Duguet proposed a method 'pour l'intelligence des Ecritures' that supported their position through 'figurist' readings that emphasised the contemporary relevance of the prophets warnings to the divided Israel and of the New Testament apocalypse.[2]

The controversy over the *billets* was particularly bitter in the 1750s, and the Jansenists attracted much sympathy from the public, indignant at seeing dying people used as pawns in a power struggle. Indeed, the conflict took on an explicitly political cast as an alliance developed between the Paris *parlement* and the Jansenists. The *parlement*, too, saw itself as the guardians of a *dépôt*, in this case the fundamental laws of the kingdom, and resented the monarch's efforts to impose its will unilaterally, as it did in insisting that *Unigenitus* become part of French law. Recent historical work by Catherine Maire and Dale Van Kley has now shown in detail how Jansenist figurist writing helped frame the political discourse of parlementary resistance to royal authority.[3] As in the relation between the Jansenists and the Church hierarchy, dissent was cast in terms of loyalty to a monarchy whose true character the dissenters were trying to restore. The ambiguity of this position made it difficult to convict the dissenters of subversion, and their resistance to arbitrary royal power won them considerable sympathy. But it also prevented the dissenters' resistance from taking what from the point of view of secular modernity we would call a 'progressive' cast. Thus, despite some affinities, the alliance between the *philosophes* of the *Encyclopédie* and the *parlementaires* was an occasional and uneasy one. Relations with

2. See Catherine Maire, *De la cause de Dieu à la cause de la nation: le jansénisme au XVIIIe siècle* (Paris 1998), esp. p.166f.

3. Maire, *De la cause de Dieu*; Dale Van Kley, *The Religious origins of the French Revolution: from Calvin to the Civil Constitution 1560-1791* (New Haven, Conn. 1996).

the Jansenists were more hostile. Eager to demonstrate their orthodoxy, the Jansenists vigorously attacked the encyclopedists, notably in the affair of the unfortunate abbé de Prades in 1752.

And yet, the *philosophes* retained considerable respect for the integrity and rigor of mainstream Jansenism, not only in the latter's conflict with the Jesuits, but, ironically, in matters of language and logic as well. For while one aspect of Jansenist thought culminated in the emotional intensities of figurism, another had produced the sober and rational linguistic analysis of Arnauld and Nicole. This 'Port-Royal' linguistics was itself a reaction against the more exuberant stylistics of the Baroque, including that associated with the Jesuits. Dumarsais, the leading grammarian of the *Encyclopédie* until his death in 1756, and the author of the article on 'figure' in rhetoric, was schooled in this tradition. In his treatise *Des tropes* Dumarsais sought to bring order to interpretation by defining the operation and appropriate use of linguistic figures. Dumarsais is celebrated today as the probable author of the boldly secular essay 'Le Philosophe', an abridged and less militant version of which appeared in the *Encyclopédie* as PHILOSOPHE.[4] Yet, in earlier years he had put his rhetorical expertise to use in religious-political polemics, deconstructing, somewhat in the fashion of Pascal's *Lettres provinciales*, the interpretative excesses of a Roman cardinal who opposed the claims of the Gallican Church. This is the 'disenchanted' side of Jansenism that unwittingly contributed to the rise of the French Enlightenment, such that Dumarsais is said to have described himself as a 'Jansenist atheist'.[5]

The relationship between Jansenism and *philosophie* still awaits a full investigation. This brief review should be enough to suggest, however, that in discussing methods of reading the *Encyclopédie*, we need to go beyond any simple contrast between freedom and reason, on the one hand, and authority and superstition on the other. Despite the many obvious differences between the *Encyclopédie* and the Bible, the controversy over the latter in the particular context of the French eighteenth century may help us perceive what is at stake in the former's attempt to encourage and to reconcile critical and creative forms of reading. For example, figurism may seen as an attempt to maintain, *in extremis*, the communal significance of Scriptures increasingly fragmented into a set of remote historical facts, on the one hand, and a set of abstract moral principles, on the other. As Hans Frei and others have shown, by the second half of the eighteenth

---

4. 'Le Philosophe' was published in a collection of short philosophical treatises entitled *Nouvelles Libertés de penser* (1743). For a comparative study of the different versions and adaptations of the work, see Herbert Dieckmann, *Le Philosophe: texts and interpretation* (Saint Louis, Mo. 1948).

5. J. S. Spink, 'Philosophical speculation and literary technique: the systematic context of Dumarsais's *Des tropes*', *Voltaire and his world: Studies presented to W. H. Barber*, ed. R. J. Howells, A. Mason, H. T. Mason and D. Williams (Oxford 1985), p.241-60. The title of Dumarsais's polemic is *Exposition de la doctrine de l'église gallicane par rapport aux prétentions de la cour de Rome*.

century a limited conception of biblical revelation as a series of abstract propositions behind the story had eclipsed the broader, pre-critical assumption that revelation had to be understood through the narrative and other symbolic forms of the story itself.[6] In part, this was the result of the development of historical and philological approaches to the text, as illustrated by Spinoza and Richard Simon, but an equally important cause was the predominance of philosophical apologetics since the early seventeenth century, in which narrative and other community-centred understandings of the Bible gave way to 'objective' arguments designed to convince sceptics of the existence of God and the truth of Christianity. In this context, references to the Bible concentrated on the historical 'evidence' of miracles worked and prophecies fulfilled.[7] In order to continue to claim probative value for typological figures within this context, however, these figures had to be isolated from their context within a particular kind of narrative, thus ironically reinforcing a purely historical-critical approach reading of the Bible which in turn further marginalised the book's significance as the expression and exploration of a community of faith.[8] What, then, might be involved in the *philosophes*' attempt to make the *Encyclopédie* an integrated work, such that readers will use it, not just as a source of information, but as a resource for the development of their own powers of understanding? Does the book become more or less universal, more or less empirical and rational in the process?

Another issue is the cultural position of the encyclopedists. Like the Jansenists, the *philosophes* occupy positions inside the society whose authority they question. The public to which they appealed was not a body outside, or separate from, the existing polity. In this sense they too rejected 'schism'. To the extent that the 'public' was identified with the 'nation', it was, on the contrary, the core element of that polity. More generally we need to see the *philosophes* as working within their culture, rather than merely enlightening it from above. It is not a matter of undermining their legitimacy as agents of change but of exploring the relationship between the inherited norms – the realm of the 'obvious' and the 'expected' – with and within which they work, and the rational principles, undetermined by context or previous commitment, to which they appeal.

The tension between intellectual activity as authorised by universally valid principles and as a process emerging from a situated community is

6. Hans W. Frei, *The Eclipse of biblical narrative: a study in eighteenth- and nineteenth-century hermeneutics* (New Haven, Conn. 1974).

7. See, among a number of historical and theological works, Alan C. Kors, *Atheism in France 1650-1729*, vol.i (Princeton, N.J. 1990); William L. Placher, *The Domestication of transcendence: how modern thinking about God went wrong* (Louisville, Ky. 1996); and Ephraim Radner, *The End of the Church: a pneumatology of Christian division in the west* (Grand Rapids, Mich. 1998).

8. The figurists' apocalyptic rhetoric, and the hysterical violence of the *convulsionnaires*, may be explained in part as an attempt to make this symbolic meaning 'real' again, distorted in its understanding of participation in prophetic narrative by the literalised perspective it sought to oppose.

an important aspect of Jansenism's relationship to the universal Church. It could not be dealt with explicitly, however, without calling into question ecclesiological principles fundamental to the self-understanding of French Catholics. Chief among these issues was one with important political implications: the position of the Gallican Church within the Roman communion. Was its autonomy limited to such issues as the procedure for the appointment of bishops and the official 'reception' by the *parlement* of Roman canons, or did it extend to theological issues as well? And did its autonomy really derive from that of the French king vis-à-vis the pope, or inhere in the local church considered in itself? Despite the acrimony of the debate over these issues, the parties involved avoided confronting the issues directly, fearing the possibility of schism or of open conflict between church and state. A similar, if more secularised, form of this ambiguity characterises the French Enlightenment as well, in which universalism coexists with an unreflective cultural francocentrism, and vigorous criticism of authority does not stifle enthusiasm for making the most of the instruments of state intervention to determine the course of progress. Nor, finally, are the *Encyclopédie* editors positioned in any simple way 'outside' the book of universal knowledge they present to their readers: by virtue of its scope, the work precedes and encompasses them as much as they dominate it.[9] To understand how the *Encyclopédie* is supposed to be read, we should look for texts that also reflect on the reading practices of the editors themselves.

One place to look is the large cluster of entries under the heading FIGURE, which discuss the various forms of figurative writing and reading. In addition to what they may tell us about the different modes of reading the *Encyclopédie* itself, a large cluster of entries under one headword, such as we find under FIGURE, reveals something of the editors' own activity, since the sequence of such entries is not determined by the arbitrary order of the alphabet, as the headwords themselves are, but by Diderot and D'Alembert themselves as they arrange the various contributions submitted to them and add their own. In addition, because the range of meanings of the French word 'figure' overlap closely with those of its English cognate, we can compare the order of entries in the *Encyclopédie*

---

9. This appears more clearly if we think of the *Encyclopédie*'s function as a dictionary offering precise definitions of words as well as things – an issue on which D'Alembert and Diderot disagreed. In her study of D'Alembert (whose article DICTIONNAIRE is less frequently read than Diderot's reply to it in ENCYCLOPÉDIE), Véronique Le Ru makes this crucial point. 'L'*Encyclopédie* vise à élargir la communauté des savants par l'institution d'une langue populaire, c'est-à-dire simple et rationnelle, composée de termes scientifiques ou techniques mais dûment définis à partir de termes vulgaires ou leurs dérivés. La théorie de la définition est donc la clé de voûte de toute l'entreprise encyclopédique, elle donne une langue commune aux savants et aux ignorants. Ainsi peut être constituée une communauté d'hommes dirigés par la raison, ou plus exactement par la langue de la raison [...]. Reste pourtant le problème du fondement de la théorie de la définition. Celle-ci suppose en effet l'accord des esprits sur le sens commun d'un petit nombre de mots primitifs et originaux. Autrement dit, la constitution d'une communauté de sens repose sur le postulat d'un sens commun fondé sur l'accord des esprits' (Véronique Le Ru, *Jean Le Rond d'Alembert philosophe*, Paris 1994, p.197).

with that in its British predecessor, Chambers' *Cyclopædia*. Here, perhaps, we may measure the integration of different areas of knowledge within the universal, progressive order of understanding figured – illustrated, suggested, anticipated – by the *Encyclopédie* itself.

The order of figures

As Diderot explains in his article ENCYCLOPÉDIE, the 'articles différents compris sous une même dénomination' constitute a specific kind of grouping whose shape needs to be thought out. And one element in this process is the relationship between 'simple' and 'figurative' uses of the term under consideration (v.641a):

Il y a un quatrième ordre moins général qu'aucun des précédents, c'est celui qui distribue convenablement plusieurs articles différents compris sous une même dénomination. Il paraît ici nécessaire de s'assujettir à la génération des idées, à l'analogie des matières, à leur enchaînement naturel, de passer du simple au figuré, etc. Il y a des termes solitaires qui sont propres à une seule science, et qui ne doivent donner aucune solicitude. Quant à ceux dont l'acception varie et qui appartiennent à plusieurs sciences et à plusieurs arts, il faut en former un petit système dont l'objet principal soit d'adoucir et de pallier autant qu'on le pourra la bizarrerie des disparates. Il faut en composer le tout le moins irrégulier et le moins décousu, et se laisser conduire tantôt par les rapports, quand il y en a de marqués, tantôt par l'importance des matières; et au défaut des rapports, par des tours originaux qui se présenteront d'autant plus fréquemment aux éditeurs qu'ils auront plus de génie, d'imagination et de connaissances. Il y a des matières qui ne se séparent point, telles que l'histoire sacrée et l'histoire profane; la théologie et la mythologie; l'histoire naturelle, la physique, la chimie et quelques arts, etc. La science étymologique, la connaissance historique des êtres et des noms fourniront aussi un grand nombre de vues différentes qu'on pourra toujours suivre sans crainte d'être embarrassé, obscur ou ridicule.

Diderot's concern to mitigate 'la bizarrerie des disparates' shows that in his view the *Encyclopédie* must not only illustrate an intellectual system but achieve the status of a truly integrated *work*, one in which the contingencies of composition are subsumed into an overall pattern. While his belief in the ultimate unity of nature provides a guarantee that in the end no *rapport* is a matter of chance, we see in this passage an interesting movement from an emphasis on the writer's subjection to already accepted understandings of the ways ideas and words are to be ordered, to a freer and more active discovery of relationships based on 'tours originaux'. Diderot preserves the objectivity of knowledge by suggesting that these figures 'se présenteront' of themselves, and the expression also echoes the *Encyclopédie*'s emphasis on the immediately graspable quality of enlightened understanding.[10]

---

10. For a discussion of this issue in connection with another important grouping of articles, see Patrick Coleman, 'The idea of character in the *Encyclopédie*', *Eighteenth-century studies* 13 (1979), p.21-47.

Yet, the last sentence of the paragraph offers a more pluralistic and prob-abilistic conception of encyclopedic organisation, at least at this level. Instead of the logical genesis of ideas, Diderot speaks of etymology and the 'connaissance historique des êtres et des noms' as the basis for overcoming 'bizarrerie'. The notion of 'tours originaux' also undermines the notion of an orderly progression from the 'simple' to the 'figuré'. Furthermore, the criterion of success is not the immediate apprehension of truth as such, but the avoidance of obscurity. While Diderot may be alluding here to the Car-tesian notion of clear and distinct ideas, clarity is to be judged in terms of the understanding of actual, not ideal readers. This focus on acceptance by the community of readers is also apparent in the shift away from the editors' genius and imagination to their ability to avoid embarrassment and ridi-cule – in other words, the reproach of bad taste. The editors must build on the readers' pre-existing sense of appropriate connections as well as on such *rapports* as are shown to them by the interpretation of nature itself. Sim-ilarly, in putting together a large-scale collaborative work, the editors cannot start entirely from scratch. They will inevitably build on what their contributors give them, as well as on models of organisation provided by predecessors such as Chambers.

Thus, the *Encyclopédie* will be a more impure work than Diderot's and D'Alembert's initial statements lead us to believe. This is not in itself some-thing to be regretted, for, in addition to making the work generally read-able, this impurity is also what allows it to play its critical role within its particular historical context. What is less clear is the extent to which the *Encyclopédie* does in fact think through the relationship between the situat-edness of readers' assumptions or expectations and the creative mode of reading it seeks to unleash.

A reader looking under FIGURISME for an explanation of that contro-versy finds only a short definition of intra-biblical typology, along with two cross-references: 'On a donné ce nom à l'opinion de ceux qui pensent que tous les événemens de l'ancien Testament sont autant de figures de des évé-nemens du nouveau. En ce sens les figures de l'ancien Testament seroient autant de prophéties. Voyez PROPHETIES; voyez aussi FIGURES (Théol.).'[11]

The article PROPHÉTIE (in the singular) would not appear until 1765 (in volume xiii), by which date the Jansenist controversy had largely died down.[12] The early reader of the *Encyclopédie* would therefore be able to go only to FIGURE in theology (again in the singular). This is a extended composite entry, consisting of a short piece translated from Chambers, a somewhat longer discussion of the rules 'pour l'intelligence du sens *figuré*

11. *Encyclopédie*, vi.784a. Unless otherwise noted, all references to *Encyclopédie* articles will be to this volume (published in October 1756), with reference to page and column. Mallet's article ECRITURE SAINTE also refers to PROPHETIES.
12. The expulsion of the Jesuits in 1762 played a large role in ending the long-running Jesuit-Jansenist feud, which had attained almost mythical status over the previous century.

des Ecritures' by Mallet, based, it is said, on the abbé de La Chambre,[13] and a much longer supplement 'sur la même matière' by Morellet. The peculiar structure of the article suggests the editors believed the subject required more clarification than was at first supplied, and from the insistence on rules we may infer an anxiety about undisciplined reading. It is interesting that the various parts of the article are not folded into a single discussion, so that the editors' intervention is made obvious. The reader may ask why it was necessary to add the supplementary entries: was it the complexity of subject-matter, or the pressure of external circumstances? Since matters of biblical interpretation had been extensively covered in Mallet's ECRI-TURE SAINTE in volume v,[14] and since further details on such a subject would not seem warranted by the constructive mission of the *Encyclopédie*, it seems reasonable to assume that Morellet's supplement serves a critical function, and one that had not been anticipated when the assignments for volume vi was initially distributed.[15]

Reading a composite entry of this kind has other results as well, for the separation of its three distinct parts blurs the boundary between this particular entry and the larger sequence of entries under FIGURE. The connection between the entry and its context is in fact made explicit by its opening sentence: 'FIGURE (Théolog.) est *aussi* un terme qui est en usage parmi les Théologiens' (my emphasis). Even if they have forgotten Dide-rot's remarks in ENCYCLOPÉDIE, readers are thus encouraged to explore the other articles under the headword FIGURE.

There are seventeen of these, followed by seven under FIGURE and two under FIGURER (see Appendix). The first entry refers to physics, where 'figure' means 'la forme extérieure des corps'. We move on to geometry, where D'Alembert distinguishes two meanings: 'un espace terminé de tous côtés', and 'la représentation faite sur le papier de l'objet d'un théorème [...] pour en rendre la démonstration ou la solution plus facile à concevoir'. Since the actual diagramming of geometry does not affect its conceptualisa-tion, the double meaning of 'figure' as object of analysis and as means of conveying that analysis is not considered to be problematic here. We move on to FIGURE DE LA TERRE, a long article by D'Alembert on recent efforts to determine more precisely the shape of the earth (749b-769b). Short entries follow on figures in astrology and geomancy. The entries on theological (that is, biblical) figures appear next. Then come two substan-tial essays on 'figure' in logic and metaphysics, defined first as a 'tour de mots & de pensées qui animent ou ornent le discours' by Jaucourt in an entry on their proper use in general speech (765a-766b), and then by Dumarsais, following Scaliger, as 'une disposition particulière d'un ou de

13. This is most likely François Ilharat de La Chambre (1698-1753), the author a number of theological works, including one supporting *Unigenitus*.
14. Among other articles, including Diderot's own BIBLE.
15. Since Mallet died in 1755, it may be that he was unable to expand on his original con-tribution.

plusieurs mots', in a long article on the different types of rhetorical figures, supplemented by a section on syllogisms (766b-772b). After this extended discussion come short, dictionary-like entries on 'figure' as a term of art in fortification, architecture, and ship-building, and then another long article, by Guillaume d'Abbès, referring to physiology, in which we are told that the term 'se prend pour le visage' (772b-774a). The piece focuses less on muscle movement as such than on standards of beauty, for the face 'est le siège principal de la beauté'. This article leads in turn to a more technical discussion by Watelet of FIGURE, *terme de peinture* (774b-780b), which is devoted to the anatomical knowledge needed by the painter to convey accurately facial expressions. Two short entries on 'figure' in textile making and heraldry (780b) conclude the series.[16]

If we compare the entries under FIGURE in the *Encyclopédie* with those in Chambers, we see that Diderot and D'Alembert relied heavily on their predecessor. Both works begin with physics and geometry, and the articles that follow are similar in number and range of topic. Indeed, it seems many of the briefer entries (on heraldry and fortification, for example) were simply adopted from the earlier work. There are, however, two interesting differences in the order of presentation. First, the entries on 'figure' as facial expression and painting are placed close to the end of the series, whereas in Chambers they followed immediately the entry on geometrical figures. Thus, instead of the discussion of figure as geometrical representation leading into another, more aesthetic, kind of representation, we go directly to D'Alembert's article on the physical shape of the earth. In that article, the question of whether we should picture the earth as a flattened or elongated sphere forms part of a detailed, technical account of scientific observation and calculation.

On the other hand, the entries on biblical figures, which appear at the end of Chambers' listing, are moved up to a central position. It may well be that the editors, by placing them immediately after geomancy, wanted to discredit the whole enterprise of figurative interpretation of the Bible. The linking word 'aussi' cited above is already found in Chambers: 'Figure is also used among divines'. But whereas in Chambers the 'also' referred, logically enough, to the entry on figures of speech, the 'aussi' in the *Encyclopédie* takes the reader back to what were called the 'prédictions chimériques' of geomancy.[17] On the other hand, the entries on biblical

16. FIGURE includes an article by D'Alembert on 'nombres figurés' in mathematics (781a-782b); an entry on 'pierres figurées' (whose shapes may be the result of chance or of fossilisation) by d'Holbach (782b-783a); a brief entry on 'sens figuré' in the Bible by Mallet (783a); an aesthetic assessment of 'style figuré' by Voltaire (783ab). Entries on 'figuré' as used in law (for diagrams), in music theory, and heraldry are followed by 'figurer' in musical and dance performance. 'Figurisme' appears two short entries later.

17. 'Fantastical divinations' in Chambers, from which the entry on geomancy was taken. Note also, however, that the *Encyclopédie*'s entry on figures in Scripture is no longer followed by an entry on 'profane figures' such as symbols and hieroglyphics. The influence of Masonry on Chambers' work may be detected in this association.

interpretation are no longer an afterthought in the overall sequence of entries. Instead, they now precede the articles on the figures of logic and rhetoric, and as one reads forward from Morellet's analysis of 'tours de mots' in the Bible to Jaucourt's history of figurative speech and on to Dumarsais's parsing of grammatical figures, one may be led to reflect on the relationship between these domains, and on the rules that govern them.

The other main difference, of course, is in the length of the entries. While the shorter, dictionary-like entries of the *Encyclopédie* resemble those of the *Cyclopædia*, the more truly encyclopedic ones are much longer. This distinction among the articles introduces an implicit hierarchy among them. That so much space is given to FIGURE DE LA TERRE in a work devoted to scientific advances (and on a topic to which D'Alembert made a significant mathematical contribution) is not surprising. But it is curious to see the sequence of entries conclude with two long articles on the human face. D'Abbès's entry on 'figure' in 'physiology' is really an essay on the widely varying standards of physical beauty applied to women in different countries. The reason for its inclusion is unclear, although it introduces a note of aesthetic appreciation and playfulness absent from both Dumarsais's approach to linguistic figures and from Watelet's much longer article on FIGURE, *terme de Peinture*, a sober treatise on the details of facial anatomy painters must learn in order to perfect their art. Watelet's entry is single-mindedly technical, and not linked to the preceding entry at all.[18] The same is true of the entries on rhetorical figures. The editors forge no link between Dumarsais's grammatical analysis, which is purely analytical in approach, and Jaucourt's reflections on the relationship between figurative speech and the historical stages of human development, on the one hand, and the passions of the individual soul, on the other. As with the articles on facial features, it is up to us to make what connection we will between them, and with the other entries in the series.

And yet, hints are not entirely absent. Jaucourt's essay concludes with a most peculiar word. After exhorting us to an 'emploi des figures bien ménagé', he writes (766b):

Je me contenterai seulement de remarquer que comme les *figures* signifient ordinairement avec les choses, les mouvements que nous ressentons en les recevant & en parlant [...]. Il est visible qu'il est ridicule de s'en servir dans les matières que l'on regarde d'un œil tranquille, & qui ne produisent aucun mouvement dans l'esprit; car puisque les figures expriment les mouvemens de notre ame, celles que l'on met dans les sujets où l'ame ne s'émeut point, sont des mouvemens contre nature, & des espèces de convulsions.

18. The article refers the reader to the plates, but none appear under this heading. One has to go to the plates under PEINTURE. See Richard Schwab, with the collaboration of Walter E. Rex, *Inventory of Diderot's Encyclopédie*, vii: *Inventory of the Plates, with a study of the contributors to the Encyclopédie by John Lough*, *SVEC* 223 (1984), p.287.

The reader of the 1750s, coming upon this last word, surely an unusual one in the context, could hardly fail to think here of the Jansenist *convulsionnaires*, who had caused so much trouble at the church of Saint-Médard in the 1730s. Their successors could still be found in various parts of Paris engaging in paroxistic rituals of pain to express their identification with Christ's suffering. In the eyes of Diderot and other *philosophes*, their behaviour was contrived and hysterical, governed more by the determination to fulfil prophecies than reflective of genuine passion. Without saying so directly, the *Encyclopédie* suggests that the interpretation of biblical figures needs to be prevented from leading to such phenomena.

According to Jaucourt, figurative language is appropriate if it faithfully represents the thing or emotion expressed and matches the level of intellectual development achieved by the community of speakers. It is understandable that men who are still 'grossiers' should use metaphors that stem from 'la grossièreté de la conception' [766a]), but in today's civilised world the norms of good taste should prevail: 'Ainsi le langage figuré n'est que le langage de la simple nature, appliqué aux circonstances où nous le devons parler' (766a). Or, as Voltaire puts it in FIGURE a few pages later, the *style figuré* designates 'les expressions métaphoriques qui figurent les choses dont on parle, & qui les défigurent quand les métaphores ne sont pas justes' (783a). We may ask, however, whether the judgement of appropriateness is to be made on the basis of knowledge one already possesses, or an assessment of the knowledge one acquires by working through the figurative statement itself. Another way of putting this is to ask to what extent the norms and expectations of readers today are themselves the reflection of a transitory stage in humanity's development, and can be tested through the exploration of figures, or permanent standards against which all figures are to be measured. Jaucourt does not address this question: while he does note that 'le langage figuré est proprement celui des prophètes' (765a), he does not view the primitive use of figures as a way of exploring the world on the way to understanding, but as the 'stérile & grossier' means of communication characteristic of primitive languages. This idea, that at a given time conventional language is insufficient to convey what its speakers are discovering, is absent from Jaucourt's discussion of figurative language in the present. The latter is dominated by norms of restraint, and is linked to emotion rather than knowledge: one should not say more than one feels. The shift is enabled by the ambiguity – one is tempted to say, the figurative potential – of Jaucourt's definition of figurative language as 'le langage de la simple nature'. As a stage of development, 'simple nature' grounds an historicising approach to figures; as a foundational philosophical norm, it makes what might be called a history of the present irrelevant.

The historical dimension is absent entirely from Dumarsais's long article on FIGURE, *terme de rhétorique, de Logique & de grammaire*. This is primarily a catalogue of different types of figure, in which the author shows how even the oddest figurative construction can be logically explained by being reduced 'à la forme de la proposition' (770a). For Dumarsais the use of figures for developing thought should be restricted to guided school assignments: 'Il faut laisser aux écoliers à faire des figures de commande.' Otherwise, they should be used with restraint: 'Les *figures* rendent le discours plus insinuant, plus agréable, plus vif, plus énergique, plus pathétique; mais elles doivent être rares & bien amenées. Les figures ne doivent être que l'effet du sentiment & des mouvemens naturels, & l'art n'y doit point paroître' (772a).

Neither Dumarsais nor Jaucourt believe it necessary to ask who should decide when these rules have been violated. Violations or excesses should be apparent to all those able to appreciate 'la simple nature', which presumably is everywhere manifest in a constant and reliable manner. There is thus no need to invoke a mediating authority to limit – or to foster – the use of figures. The 'convulsions' or 'mouvemens contre nature', as Jaucourt says, of those who inject figures (and the emotional resonance that accompanies them) into matters 'que l'on regarde d'un œil tranquille' can easily be recognised and dismissed. But what of figures in the Bible, a book from the past in which readers seek meaning for the present and inspiration for the future?

The first section of FIGURE (*Théolog.*), translated from Chambers, does not explicitly limit its application to inter-testamental relationships. The term designates 'les mystères qui nous sont représentés & annoncés d'une manière obscure sous de certains types ou de certains faits de l'ancien Testament. Voyez TYPE' (762a).[19] As in FIGURISME, however, the actual discussion avoids any mention of biblical figures as used for understanding the contemporary situation of the Church. The reason for this is not clear. Mallet's contribution consists entirely of six rules, drawn from the abbé de la Chambre, 'pour l'intelligence du sens figuré des Ecritures, que nous rappellerons ici, parce qu'il n'arrive que trop souvent qu'on se livre à cette opinion, que *tout est figure, sur-tout dans l'ancien Testament,* qu'on en abuse pour y voir des choses qui n'y furent jamais' (762a, italics in text). One should only look for a figurative sense when scriptural statements have no 'natural' relationship to the things they talk about. 'La simple force des expressions' is not sufficient justification for seeking a figural sense, since conferring rhetorical dignity on an object proves nothing by itself. On the other hand, one should look for other meanings 'lorsque le sens littéral renferme une doctrine qui met sur le compte de Dieu quelqu'imperfection ou quelqu'impiété'. Reprehensible human actions portrayed in the Bible are the least likely to contain a figural meaning and the crimes of biblical saints do not cease to be crimes even when they form part of a figural story. Furthermore, figural interpretation must not isolate what may be figured but rather remain grounded in the literal sense of passage as a whole: 'Il est faux que la *figure* disparaisse quelquefois entièrement, pour faire place à

---

19. As in Chambers, the *Encyclopédie* article preceding the one on geomancy is on astrological figures of the heavens, but there is no direct dismissal of their validity.

la chose figurée.' Most important are the fourth and fifth rules, which emphasise the importance of tradition and consensus in biblical interpretation (762a):

Quatrième règle. On ne doit admettre de figures & d'allégories dans l'Ecriture de l'ancien Testament, comme étant de l'intention du S. Esprit, que celles qui sont appuyées sur l'autorité de Jesus-Christ, sur celles des apôtres, ou sur celle d'une tradition constante et unanime de tous les siècles.

Cinquième règle. Il faut voir Jesus-Christ & les mystères de la nouvelle alliance dans l'ancien Testament, par-tout où les apôtres les ont vus; mais il faut ne les y voir qu'en la manière qu'ils les ont vus.

These rules are not new, going back indeed to Augustine's classic treatise *On Christian teaching*,[20] although in this context the rule about 'natural' meaning, which in Biblical exegesis is a hermeneutical concept, takes on the more rationalistic coloration of 'la simple nature' in Jaucourt's article.[21] Morellet's supplement to FIGURE, which is six times longer than Mallet's original article, develops this more rationalistic approach. It amplifies the warnings against unwarranted figural interpretation almost to the point of discrediting the procedure itself. Having already presented, in his article ECRITURE SAINTE, a general critique of the belief that 'il n'y a point de texte où Dieu n'ait voulu renfermer sous l'enveloppe de sens littéral, les vérités de la Morale, ou les événemens de la religion chrétienne' (762b), he focuses here on 'les causes qui ont amené l'usage abusif des explications figurées' and 'les inconvéniens qu'a entraînés cette méthode d'expliquer l'Ecriture'.

Morellet's critique goes much further than that of Mallet, since among the causes of abusive interpretation he lists the writers of the New Testament, whom he calls, with a note of disparagement, 'les premiers écrivains ecclesiastiques'. Other causes include 'la coutume des Juifs qui donnoient à l'Ecriture des explications spirituelles', the tendency of preachers to smuggle into biblical texts the moral or other lessons they want to teach, and 'l'opinion de l'inspiration rigoureuse de tous les mots, de toutes les syllabes de l'Ecriture & de tous les faits', which makes one look for hidden mysteries in every minute detail of the text. He gives as an example the determination to find spiritual meaning in the description of the materials and architecture of Noah's ark (763b).[22] Such interpretations are not only theologically unfounded, they reveal a lack of taste. Indeed, what clearly offends Morellet most (and here he invokes the authority of Claude Fleury's *Histoire ecclésiastique*) is 'le mauvais goût qui faisoit mépriser ce qui étoit simple et naturel, & la difficulté d'entendre la lettre de l'Ecriture, faute

---

20. Augustine, *On Christian teaching*, translated by R. P. H. Green (Oxford 1997); *De Doctrina christiana: a classic of western culture*, ed. Duane W. H. Arnold and Pamela Bright (Notre Dame, Ind. 1995).

21. Jaucourt, it may be noted, was himself a Protestant.

22. The reference given is to the Jesuit Athanasius Kircher's *De Mystico-allegorico-tropologica arcae expositione*, or *Arca Noë, in tres libros digesta* (1675).

de savoir les langues originales, je veux dire le grec et l'hébreu, & de connoître l'histoire & les mœurs de cette antiquité si reculée' (763a). This
blindness to the 'majestueuse simplicité des Ecritures' is one of the 'inconvéniens' Morellet sees in excessive figural interpretation, along with the
temptation to transform figures into dogma,[23] which leads to a reaction in
the opposite direction, as Socinians and other dissenters turn dogmas into
figures, denying real mysteries such as the Trinity.

Yet, while Morellet poses here as the defender of orthodoxy, he frames the
discussion in a way that encourages scepticism. By focusing on the techniques of interpretation themselves, and by lumping together allegorical
speculations and moral applications as equally extraneous and harmful distortions, Morellet is easily able to show how many figural interpretations
exceed the limits of the kind of plausibility that controls the tasteful
interpretation of a text. In fact, Morellet's article makes the reader wonder
whether it is legitimate ever to engage in figural interpretation. It is true
that at the end of his article he does give an example of an acceptable
interpretation. Referring to Abraham's two wives as figures of the two cove-
nants is appropriate, he says, following Fleury, because Saint Paul does so
explicitly (Gal. iv.24), and his text is no less inspired than that of Genesis to
which it refers (xvi.1-4), so that 'nous sommes également assurés de l'histoire et de son application' (765a).[24] Yet, Morellet's endorsement is under-
cut by his earlier sarcasm about the 'explications détournées' (762b) even of
'les écrivains du nouveau Testament'. Of course, he later express his gratitude God's Providence, that is, to the exclusive teaching authority given by
God to the Church, thanks to which 'cette prodigieuse quantité d'explications détournées' has not permeated Christian doctrine 'comme la cabale
des juifs dans leur théologie' (764a). How the Church does this, Morellet
does not say, either because we should take the Church's role as the guar-
dian of truth for granted or, more likely, because there is no basis for its
judgement other than an instrumental concern for order. Thus, as far as
biblical figures are concerned, right use is determined by institutional
regulation, on the one hand, and the good taste of the individual interpreter, on the other. If Morellet does not view these criteria as standing in
opposition to each other (as in earlier debates between Protestants and
Catholics), it is no doubt because he believes the whole debate to be irrelevant to the search for real knowledge. But the logic of his argument is that
there is no contradiction between these sources of authority because an
enlightened Church has left bad taste behind, and good taste is a universal
standard.

Whatever the case, the disciplining of the reader's use of biblical figures is
structurally similar to what we have seen in *Encyclopédie*'s discussion of

23. Morellet's example of this is the image of the two swords, used 'pour attribuer à
l'Eglise une autorité sur les souverains, même dans le temporel' (764a).
24. Fleury's 'histoire' may be read either as 'story' or as 'historical account'.

figures in the secular sphere. In neither domain, given the emphasis on restraint and abstract rationality, is there much room for using figurative connections as a discovery procedure, such as Diderot imagines in ENCYCLOPÉDIE. The critical aspect of the work is much in evidence in these articles, as is the constructive function. The effort to demystify the figural reading of the Bible by appealing to ahistorical rational standards and the determination to view readers' initiative in this case as a source of distortion only, and not of emancipatory interpretation, may also have prevented the encyclopedists from thinking through what a creative reading of the *Encyclopédie* might involve. Diderot's programmatic statements invite the making of creative connections across texts and disciplines as crucial to advancing knowledge beyond what today's scientific community can conceive, and in his dispute with D'Alembert Diderot recognises that such connections will necessarily exceed the limits of rational definition, but in trying to limit the consequences of figurative excess, the *Encyclopédie*, at least in this group of articles, limits the development of its own self-understanding.

Appendix

'Figure' in Chambers' *Cyclopaedia* (1741)
FIGURE, FIGURA, in physics
   in relation to the form of bodies
FIGURE is also applied to representations, or images of things
FIGURE in geometry
FIGURE, in conics
FIGURE of the diameter
FIGURE in painting and designing
FIGURES, in architecture and sculpture
FIGURE, in heraldry
FIGURES among the matters of defence
FIGURE of an eclipse
FIGURE, or delineation of the full moon
FIGURE, in astrology
FIGURE, in geomancy
FIGURE, in fortification
FIGURE, in dancing
FIGURE, in the manufactures
FIGURES, in arithmetic
FIGURE, in logic
FIGURE, in rhetoric (sentences, words, prosody)
FIGURE, in grammar
FIGURE is also used among divines, for the mysteries represented or delivered obscurely to us under certain types or actions in the Old Testament

FIGURE is also applied in a like sense to profane matters; as the emblems, enigma's [*sic*], fables [...] of the ancients.

'Figure' in the *Encyclopédie* (adapted from Schwab, *Inventory* iii)

FIGURE, Phys. .2
FIGURE, Géom. 1.0
FIGURE, Géom. .5
FIGURE, Arith.
FIGURE DE LA TERRE, Astron., Géog. Phys. & Méch. 24.7
FIGURE, Astrol. .1
FIGURE, Géomancie .1
FIGURE, Théol. 1.2
'A ces règles ...' 5.8
FIGURE, Log. Métaph. 2.8
FIGURE, Rhét. Logiq. & Gram. 11.8
FIGURE, Fortific. .1
FIGURE, Arch. & Sculpt. .2
FIGURE, FIGULES, ENFLECHURES, Mar.
FIGURE, Physiol. 3.1
FIGURE, Peint. 12.8
FIGURE, Ruban. .1
FIGURE, Blason

THOMAS DIPIERO

Bodies of knowledge

THE first entry under the *Encyclopédie* heading SIMPLE adj. (*Gramm.*) reads, simply: 'qu'on regarde comme sans composition, sans mélange' (xv.204). The example immediately following the word's definition offers an illustration of simplicity, but perhaps not the one we might expect for the definition proposed (xv.204):

Il a fait un raisonnement très simple, mais très fort quand il a dit: il y a environ douze cens ans qu'on a la petite vérole par toute la terre, & qu'elle est observée par tous les médecins du monde, parmi lesquels il n'y en a presque pas un qui assure l'avoir vue deux fois à la même personne; donc on n'a point deux fois la petite vérole.

Although one might well question the example's appropriateness to the definition – it is neither 'sans mélange' nor 'sans composition', given its at least partial syllogistic format – the above illustration of *simple* can help us understand a great deal about some of the eighteenth-century structures of knowledge that we can see at work in the *Encyclopédie*. Here we find reason, logic, the inferral of a general law from specific observations, and the application of all those things to material reality, in this case in the figure of the human body. And, while this particular example of 'un raisonnement simple' seems to apply almost randomly to illness and the human form, I intend to show that many encyclopedic models of knowing depended to a very great extent on existing conceptions of morphology as well as on what seemed natural and normal in human corporality.

Eighteenth-century conceptions of morphology relied heavily on established distinctions between the material and the abstract on the one hand, and the natural and the cultural on the other. I intend to show that the *Encyclopédie* and some other eighteenth-century works implicitly premise modes of thinking on the physical arrangement of human bodies, particularly as that arrangement correlates the social indicators commonly referred to as race and gender. Specifically, I plan to demonstrate that authors of *Encyclopédie* articles construed the human body as both an object and a mode of knowledge. The entry SIMPLE just cited contains the germ of such a construal, but we can find a more protracted illustration of the phenomenon in the entry ANTHROPOLOGIE (which, incidentally, is connected to SIMPLE through a *renvoi*). ANTHROPOLOGIE designates a theological concept that consists of a 'maniere de s'exprimer, par laquelle les écrivains sacrés attribuent à Dieu des parties, des actions ou des affections qui ne conviennent qu'aux hommes, & cela pour s'accommoder & se proportionner à la foiblesse de notre intelligence' (i.497).[1] By giving God a body, *anthropologie* materialises the abstract; by ascribing to God parts, *anthropologie* disarticulates that which is irreducibly unified, thus artificially dividing up a unity of being for the sole practical purpose of communicating a difficult theological concept. In fact, according to the author of the article the reasons for attributing to God body parts belonging more properly to human beings are purely heuristic: 'l'Esprit saint a seulement voulu nous faire entendre les choses ou les effets que Dieu opere comme s'il avoit des mains, des yeux, &c. sans que cela préjudicie à la simplicité de son être' (i.497). Not only is it the case that embodiment provides the physical means through which abstract ideas can be communicated, but the attendant division of the body into constituent parts throws into sharp relief the absolute and irreducible unity of the ideal that such materiality serves to convey. The body communicates information by providing the material means of conveyance, and it provides a template for the reception and organisation of the material conveyed.

From a rhetorical perspective the explanation of how *anthropologie* functions might amount to little more than prosopopoeia – in this case the literal giving of face (*les yeux*) to a purely spiritual being in order to help readers conceptualise and understand that being. However, I read the brief entry on *anthropologie* and its accompanying *renvoi* as illustrative of one of the fundamental currents constituting the *Encyclopédie*, one that might at first appear simply rhetorical but which is, as I will show, strategically epistemological. That epistemological strategy consists in modeling forms of knowledge on the material that conveys it, and in explicitly incarnating in human morphology the physical means of abstraction. Consequently, in encyclopedic modes of knowledge, reason and logic acquire a decidedly material orientation, while morphology abstracts social and ideological concerns.[2] Just as the 'anthropological' attribution of human body parts to God provides a vehicle for the transmission of ideas (even if it does violate the absolute integrity – simplicity – of God's being), the selection and description of morphological components in human beings betrays the ideological investments inhering in the particular social

1. A striking parallel formation occurs in the article ABSTRACTION: 'La Prose même, quoiqu'avec moins d'appareil que la Poësie, réalise, personifie ces êtres abstraits, & séduit également l'imagination [...]. Les Payens réalisoient l'amour, la discorde, la peur, le silence [...] &c. & en faisoient autant de divinités. Rien de plus ordinaire parmi nous que de réaliser un emploi, une charge, une dignité; nous personifions la raison, le goût, le génie, le naturel, les passions, l'humeur, le caractere, les vertus, les vices, l'esprit, le cœur, la fortune, le malheur, la réputation, la nature' (i.46).

2. In a similar fashion, in a study of Diderot's *Rêve de D'Alembert*, Michel Baridon has proposed the category 'imaginaire scientifique' to go along with 'imaginaire historique' and 'imaginaire politique' already in currency ('L'imaginaire scientifique et la voix humaine dans *Le Rêve de D'Alembert*', *L'Encyclopédie, Diderot, l'esthétique*, ed. Sylvain Auroux, Dominique Bourel and Charles Porset, Paris 1991).

abstractions underpinning the identification of specific parts in the first place. In short, what we see in *anthropologie* and its relationship to *simple* – and the phenomenon, as I will show, is by no means limited in the *Encyclo-pédie* to that conceptual pair – is a theory of signification that, oddly anticipating Saussure, not only postulates the necessity of both material and ideal components for the conveying of thought, but also recognises the social and political ramifications stemming from the conceptual disarticulation of a *simplicité* 'sans composition, sans mélange'.

In order to pursue the question of how bodies and modes of thinking inflected and articulated one another we need to consider what eighteenth-century thinkers took to be the natural or normal body, particularly in its demarcation into parts, as well as how they understood the stability or predictability of that body. Why do some bodies differ from others? Are there particular laws – such as the one gleaned in the example above positing that people can only get smallpox once because it was observed that no one got it twice – constituting the range of normal morphological variation? How might the laws specifying how bodies could appear relate to abstractions such as logic or reason, and furthermore, how did conceptions of law apply both to physical bodies as well as to taxonomic abstractions such as race and gender? David Hillman and Carla Mazzio have recently argued that concepts of bodily partitioning were especially fluid during the Enlightenment, but that sometimes the particular morphological partitioning people recognised seemed distinctly natural. They write that 'influential philosophers like Paracelsus and Van Helmont went so far as to argue that parts were individuated not only lexically and physiologically but also ontologically: to the isolated organs belonged what were termed *ideae singularum partium* – so that, for instance, there existed an *idea ocularis* in the eye, or an *idea sanguinis* in the heart – imparting integrity and spiritual significance to each part of the body.'[3] The idealisation of bodily functions implies on the one hand a natural necessity underlying the disarticulation of the unit into constituent elements. On the other hand, however, an abstract mode specifying a culturally recognised function divided the body into parts, and a way of thinking and a way of speaking thus compromised the body's *simplicité*. Consequently, articulation of the body brought about its disarticulation.

In general, what we see in encyclopedic discourse on knowing and the body is a tension between the concrete presence of the human form, which correlates its capacity to guarantee a certainty of knowledge, and a simultaneous variability of morphology that destabilises systems of classification. The intimate relationship between bodies and thinking arises in the very first pages of the *Encyclopédie*'s 'Discours préliminaire', where D'Alembert

3. See 'Introduction', *The Body in parts*, ed. David Hillman and Carla Mazzio (New York 1997), p.xviii.

rehearses the idea that human knowledge is either direct or reflected,[4] and that all direct knowledge comes from the senses: 'Toutes nos connoissances directes se réduisent à celles que nous recevons par les sens; d'où il s'ensuit que c'est à nos sensations que nous devons toutes nos idées' (i.ii). Averring that 'toute déduction qui a pour base des faits ou des vérités reconnues, est préférable à ce qui n'est appuyé que sur des hypothèses' (i.ii), D'Alembert goes on to remark that 'La premiere chose que nos sensations nous apprennent, & qui même n'en est pas distinguée, c'est notre existence; d'où il s'ensuit que nos premieres idées réfléchies doivent tomber sur nous' (i.ii). From the absolute inseparability of our existence from our senses it is only a short logical move to the concrete materiality of the body and its capacity to ground other modes of knowing: 'De tous les objets qui nous affectent par leur présence, notre propre corps est celui dont l'existence nous frappe le plus' (i.ii).[5] In effect, the opening pages of the 'Discours préliminaire' contribute a corporeal dimension to Cartesian notions of certainty, establishing a morphological baseline of conviction to complement the cognitive one. The 'Discours préliminaire' explicitly associates fundamental and parallel operations of the body and the mind, reminding us that 'comme il y a des regles pour les opérations de l'esprit ou de l'ame, il y en a aussi pour celles du corps' (i.xii).[6]

Unlike all other bodies in nature, however, that of the human being occupies the spiritual as well as the material realms. From a discussion in the 'Discours préliminaire' of the three general faculties governing classification in the *Encyclopédie* – reason, imagination, and memory – we move to an examination of how to order the diverse beings populating the universe. There we learn that the three branches of knowledge can be broken down further still: 'La distribution générale des êtres en spirituels & en matériels

4. 'On peut diviser toutes nos connoissances en directes & en réfléchies. Les directes sont celles que nous recevons immédiatement sans aucune opération de notre volonté; qui trouvant ouvertes, si on peut parler ainsi, toutes les portes de notre ame, y entrent sans résistance & sans effort. Les connoissances réfléchies sont celles que l'esprit acquiert en opérant sur les directes, en les unissant & en les combinant' (i.i-ii).

5. 'Nous connoissons d'abord que nous avons des sensations; nous savons ensuite que ces sensations ne dépendent pas de nous, & de-là nous pouvons conclure que nous n'en sommes donc pas la cause absolue, mais qu'il faut qu'il y ait d'autres causes qui les produisent; ainsi nous commençons à connoître que nous ne sommes pas les seules choses qui existent, mais qu'il y a encore d'autres êtres dans le monde conjointement avec nous, & nous jugeons que ces causes sont des corps réellement existans, semblables à ceux que nous imaginons' (CORPS, iv.261).

6. In the article ANATOMIE we discover a profound relationship between the materiality of the body and the most sublime of abstractions, that which unites the complexity of human parts with the simplicity of God: 'la connoissance du corps suppose celle d'un enchaînement si prodigieux de causes & d'effets, qu'aucun ne mene plus directement à la notion d'une intelligence toute sage & toute-puissante: elle est, pour ainsi-dire, le fondement de la Théologie naturelle' (i.410). As if to reinforce the postulate the human beings are composed of parts that the simplicity of God eschews, the article ANATOMIE reports that 'Le sujet de l'Anatomie, ou le corps, se divise en parties organiques, & en parties non organiques; en parties similaires, & en parties dissimilaires, spermatiques, &c.' (i.416).

fournit la sous-division des trois branches générales' (i.xvi). Finally, we can subdivide the spiritual and the earthly creatures (i.xvi):

A la tête des êtres spirituels est Dieu, qui doit tenir le premier rang par sa nature, & par le besoin que nous avons de le connoître. Au-dessous de cet Etre suprème sont les esprits créés, dont la révélation nous apprend l'existence. Ensuite vient l'homme, qui composé de deux principes, tient par son ame aux esprits, & par son corps au monde matériel; & enfin ce vaste Univers que nous appellons le Monde corporel ou la Nature.[7]

The system of classification proposed above varies little from the celebrated Great Chain of Being, which ranks all creatures along a continuous gradation from the most exalted to the most debased.[8] Also far from unprecedented is the suggestion that man occupies an undecidable spot between different orders of being: most contemporary commentators balked at putting human beings squarely into one or another category, and many placed them precisely at the demarcation proposed above between the two domains.[9] What interests me in the citation above is not so much the particular eighteenth-century manifestation of an ancient idea, however, but the very particular use to which that idea is put. In the example above, the human being in its corporeal and contemplative dimensions figures the very divisions of knowledge that the *Encyclopédie* takes to be fundamental.

7. In AME, the question arises concerning how many *substances universelles* exist: 'ceux qui en admettoient deux, les considéroient comme réunies & composant ensemble l'univers, précisément comme le corps & l'ame composent l'homme' (i.328).

8. Arthur O. Lovejoy has defined that gradation of creatures, 'every one of them differing from that immediately above and that immediately below it', as operating according to 'the "least possible" degree of difference' (*The Great Chain of Being*, Cambridge, Mass. 1936, p.59). In the *Encyclopédie*'s HISTOIRE NATURELLE a definition that seems to anticipate Lovejoy's appears: 'Les productions de la nature sont trop nombreuses & trop variées; la plûpart ne diffèrent entr'elles que par des nuances si peu sensibles, que l'on ne doit pas espérer de les peindre dans une phrase, ce protrait est le plus souvent infidele' (viii.226).

9. In the late seventeenth century Sir William Petty established a hierarchy separating God, man, and the 'holy Angells, Created Intelligences, and subtile materiall beings' (*The Petty papers*, New York 1927, p.21); he further elaborated two successions of animate beings, one with humans at the top, reigning over the animal world, and the other with humans at the bottom, beneath the celestial beings. Similarly, in 1714, Richard Blackmore mused upon the specific place in the Chain of Being that human beings held. A physician, Blackmore put humans in the natural order previously taken by animals. The result was a contiguity between people and animals that would later characterise most eighteenth-century anthropology: 'As Man, who approaches nearest to the lowest Class of Celestial Spirits (for we may justly suppose a Subordination in that excellent Order) being half Body and half Spirit, becomes the *Æquator*, that divides in the Middle the whole Creation, and distinguishes the corporeal from the Invisible Intellectual World, so the Ape or Monkey, that bears the greatest Similitude to Man, is the next Order of Animals below him' (*The Lay-Monastery*, London 1714, p.29). Further examples include James Burnett, who argued that man is 'rational, and he is irrational; he has intellect, and he has not intellect; he is a biped, and he is not a biped; he is a land-animal, and he is a water-animal [...]. In short, he appears to be placed on the confines betwixt different kinds of beings' (*Of the origin and progress of language*, 1773; Menston 1967, p.201-202).

The hierarchy of beings described above situates man in a well-established order, to be sure, but it also uses man not just as an *object*, but as a *mode* of knowledge. That is, the human being in its compositional complexity incarnates the hierarchical arrangement of faculties that the *Encyclopédie* prioritises (in hierarchies based largely upon their generative capacities) because it displays and deploys characteristics associated with those faculties, of course, but also because humans partake of both the abstract and the material worlds. Furthermore, put to the service of illustrating the *Encyclopédie*'s tripartite division of knowledge, man incarnates division itself, embodying, precisely as does the attribution of body parts to God in ANTHROPOLOGIE, an epistemological choice that functions heuristically to provide the physical conveyance of a purely abstract notion: 'Nous ignorons pourquoi l'Auteur célebre qui nous sert de guide dans cette distribution, a placé la nature avant l'homme dans son système; il semble au contraire que tout engage à placer l'homme sur le passage qui sépare Dieu & les esprits d'avec les corps' (i.xvii).[10] An equal dose of narcissism and humility no doubt accounts for why eighteenth-century thinkers did not place the human being directly in the middle of either the spiritual or the material world. In this particular encyclopedic discourse, however, man is not so much the object of knowledge as he is the embodiment of a problem or a conceptual knot, the unravelling of which might make possible insight into how encyclopedic bodies of knowledge functioned. Situated at the precise juncture where the spiritual joins the corporeal, man connects those irreconcilable realms. Significantly, he also keeps them apart. Bearing a striking resemblance to the dual nature of the signifier – whose materiality, Judith Butler has recently argued, must be contaminated by differentiating ideality and whose abstraction must also be compromised by the material means of conveyance – man in encyclopedic discourse is simultaneously matter and spirit, evolving and constant, body and mind.[11] Man presented to encyclopedists a very particular classificatory problem, because if he seemed able to *illustrate* the division of human faculties into the three principal parts the *Encyclopédie* vaunts, it was not clear that he could simultaneously be exhaustively *explained* by those parts.

10. In the article HOMME we read of man that 'Il est composé de deux substances, l'une qu'on appelle ame (Voyez l'article Ame), l'autre connue sous le nom de corps' (viii.256). A few lines later we find man situated more squarely into one of those two camps: 'L'homme ressemble aux animaux par ce qu'il a de matériel; & lorsqu'on se propose de le comprendre dans l'énumération de tous les êtres naturels, on est forcé de le mettre dans la classe des animaux' (viii.257).

11. Butler writes: 'The materiality of the signifier will signify only to the extent that it is impure, contaminated by the ideality of differentiating relations, the tacit structurings of a linguistic context that is illimitable in principle. Conversely, the signifier will work to the extent that it is also contaminated constitutively by the very materiality that the ideality of sense purports to overcome' (*Bodies that matter*, New York, N.Y. 1993, p.68).

Human beings as the embodiment of a problem or, to view the issue metaphorically, as the tightly wound threads of a rope that present as a single cord, are thus the 'anthropologie' of what I see to be one of the *Ency-clopédie*'s thorniest problems: given the epistemological move from geometric or mechanistic views of the universe to the more fluid and organic models rising to popularity beginning about the second quarter of the eighteenth century, do human beings belong to the natural order, or are they separate from it? Phrased another way, do contemplative and rational human beings belong to the same order as the plants, animals, and other objects they observe, and can the observers adequately account for their powers of observation and systematisation? To place the human being strictly within the schemes of classification that the *Encyclopédie* was supposed to develop failed to capture the very things – reason, imagination, memory – that allowed that being to classify in the first place. Conversely, to separate the human from other creatures or forms of being removes the human from the history and evolution that distinguished encyclopedic and other modes of eighteenth-century thought from the mechanistic theories that preceded it.[12]

Encyclopedists thus faced a knotty problem when they directed their observations onto human beings, because to use the human body to figure or 'anthropologise' how we know was necessarily to reify the ineluctably abstract. They renounced a degree of ideality for a measure of comprehension and communicability, and the body provided them a vehicle for abstraction. Nevertheless, the body on which they staked the stability of knowledge was itself profoundly variable. On the one hand the *Encyclopédie* abounds with entries and passages in articles that celebrate the mechanistic predictability of the human body, either by disposing people alongside animals in a single unified mechanism ('ce corps, ainsi que celui de tous les autres animaux, est une machine très-compliquée', HOMME, viii.261)[13] or by extolling the marvellously systematic nature of human machinery ('Le corps humain est une machine sujette aux lois de la Méchanique, de la Statique, de l'Hydraulique & de l'Optique; donc celui qui connoîtra le mieux la machine humaine, & qui ajoûtera à cette connoissance, celle des

12. In the article ABSTRACTION we find a brief passage on the interconnection between the material and the abstract in signification: 'A la vérité nous ne pouvons avoir de ces concepts à moins que quelque chose de réel ne nous donne lieu de nous les former: mais le mot qui exprime le concept, n'a pas hors de nous un exemplaire propre. Nous avons vû de l'or, & nous avons observé des montagnes; si ces deux représentations nous donnent lieu de nous former l'idée d'une montagne d'or, il ne s'ensuit nullement de cette image qu'il y ait une pareille montagne' (i.47).

13. See also the following passage in CORPS: 'Le corps humain étant considéré par rapport aux différentes motions volontaires qu'il est capable de représenter, est un assemblage d'un nombre infini de leviers tirés par des cordes; si on le considere par rapport aux mouvemens des fluides qu'il contient, c'est un autre assemblage d'une infinité de tubes & de machines hydrauliques; enfin si on le considere par rapport à la genération de ces mêmes fluides, c'est un autre assemblage d'instrumens & de vaisseaux chimiques, comme philtres, alembics, récipients, serpentines, &c.' (iv.264).

lois de la Méchanique, sera plus en état de s'assûrer par la pratique & les expériences [...] quand elles s'y dérangent' (ANATOMIE, i.410). On the other hand the *Encyclopédie* also betrays recognition that even highly regular mechanistic bodies require intervention, if only for the sorts of maintenance that the previous citation reveals. The 'Deuxième proposition' for the study of anatomy in the article ANATOMIE refers to some of the *dérangements* to which all bodies are subject, and those *dérangements* appear to derive from two principal sources in encyclopedic discourse. The first and conceptually simpler are those arising from the normal exercise of the body's functions. Thus, for example, in the article HOMME we read that 'il faut bien distinguer l'état de nature de l'état de société' (viii.260); that is because in *l'état de société* the exercising of particular culturally based functions has the effect of permanently altering the natural body practising them (viii.260):

Chaque art, chaque manœuvre, chaque action, exige des dispositions particulieres de membres, ou que la nature donne quelquefois, ou qui s'acquierent par l'habitude, mais toûjours aux dépens des proportions les plus régulieres & les plus belles. Il n'y a pas jusqu'au danseur, qui forcé de soûtenir tout le poids de son corps sur la pointe de son pié, n'eût à la longue cette partie défigurée aux yeux du statuaire, qui ne se proposeroit que de représenter un homme bien fait.

Recognising beyond the normal age- or illness-related breakdown of the body a modification resulting from culturally based use, encyclopedists determined that the most perfectly formed human that nature could create would no doubt be more or less inert: 'D'où il s'ensuit que l'homme de la nature, celui qu'elle se seroit complu à former de la maniere la plus parfaite, n'excelleroit peut-être en rien; & que l'imitateur de la nature en doit altérer toutes les proportions, selon l'état de la société dans lequel il le transporte' (HOMME, viii.260).

But would it be more appropriate to categorise human bodies modified in culturally regularised ways from their apparently original form as 'natural' or as 'social'? It seems that 'les proportions les plus régulieres & les plus belles' exist only when unchanged by activity sanctioned in a particular *état de société*.[14] The alteration of nature's beauty and regularity, however, extended well beyond individuals and sometimes characterised entire cultures, and thus the second source of anatomical *dérangement* as delineated in ANATOMIE consists of generalised corporeal modification. Many of the modifications proposed in this article remedy illness or injury – amputations, for example, are proposed in the 'Deuxième proposition' – but the study of anatomy, we are reminded, necessarily involves an epistemological dimension not always immediately apparent from simple examination of

---

14. The article HOMME describes a cultural practice that the author believed could well have long-term physiognomic repercussions: 'L'habitude de se remplir les narines de poussiere est si générale parmi nous, que je ne doute guere que si elle subsiste encore pendant quelques siecles, nos descendans ne naissent tous avec de gros nés difformes & évasés' (viii.260).

the body itself: 'la connoissance du corps suppose celle d'un enchaînement si prodigieux de causes & d'effets, qu'aucun ne mene plus directement à la notion d'une intelligence toute sage & toute-puissante: elle est, pour ainsi-dire, le fondement de la Théologie naturelle' (i.410). ANATOMIE introduces to the observation of material bodies the abstract and epistemologically contingent construction of cause and effect, and while the immediate application of those principles was designed to repair or otherwise rectify particular *dérangements*, the cross-cultural ramifications of applying notions of causality to the human body reveal not only that the natural body turned out to be European, as we will see, but also that the grounding of knowledge on the apparent stability of that body could actually be extraordinarily tenuous. Furthermore, the manners in which authors of *Encyclopédie* articles dealing with the human form chose to divide the body into parts or to attribute difference to some sort of causal structure reveal not only the taxonomic tensions they faced in attempting to classify human beings, but also the very particular admixture of material and abstract that seemed to define not only the human in general, but as we will see the European in particular.

One could cite myriad examples of the manners in which non-European bodies seemed to differ from the European variety. Here I might point out a fairly simple and straightforward example involving subjective notions of beauty offered up as objective realities: 'Les Cachemiriens sont beaux; le sang est encore plus beau en Géorgie qu'à Cachemire. Les femmes de Circassie sont renommées pour leurs charmes, & c'est à juste titre. Les Mingreliens ne le cedent en rien à ces peuples. Tous ces peuples sont blancs' (HUMAINE ESPÈCE, viii.346). The implicit comparison to the European body ('tous ces peuples sont blancs') makes that body the standard of comparison, but such comparisons to European touchstones also allowed for more abstract differentiations involving more general cultural phenomena.[15] For example, the same article describes the Senegalese: 'Ils sont tous fort noirs, bien proportionnés, d'une taille assez advantageuse [...]. Ils ont les mêmes idées de la beauté que nous; il leur faut de grands yeux, une petite bouche, des levres fines & un nez bien fait, mais la couleur très-noire & fort luisante. A cela près, leurs femmes sont belles, mais elles donnent cependant la préférance aux blancs' (viii.346). Even in vastly divergent geographic locales in which human morphology differs quite substantially from the European variety, ideas of beauty seem to remain remarkably consistent. More astonishing, however, is the fact that sexual desire achieves a universality so absolute and a standard of eroticisation so homogeneous that even people from non-European locales somehow appear to prefer European – white – bodies.[16]

15. Strikingly, the first phrase under the heading BLANC reads 'l'une des couleurs des corps naturels' (ii.269).
16. One finds the same notion of the universal appeal of European bodies in Buffon's *Histoire naturelle*: 'les sauvages du nord au-dessus des Esquimaux, sont donc tous des hommes de

Yet, if certain morphological features seemed simply to differ naturally from the European variety, others appear to have resulted from a specific cause. The earliest and most common application of causality to the human body comes from culturally specific ritual modification, which encyclopedists and others ascribed to the desire for distinction. In the article CIRCONCISION, for example, we read that 'la circoncision telle qu'on la recevait, avoit pour effet natural de distinguer les Juifs des autres peuples' (iii.460).[17] That article focuses on the diverse practices of circumcision found in different geographic locales as well as on the cultural compulsion to perform the operation exercised in various cultures: 'Il est certain que la pratique de la circoncision étoit fort différente chez les Juifs & chez les Egyptiens; les premiers la regardoient comme un devoir essentiel de religion & d'obligation étroite [...]; chez les autres, c'étoit une affaire d'usage, de propreté, de raison, de santé, même, selon quelques-uns, de nécessité physique' (iii.459). Different practices of morphological modification and different reasons for engaging in it produced culturally different bodies, and those bodies were subject to different laws as well. In fact, the *Encyclopédie* listed laws specifying bodily integrity or arrangement that distinguished people hierarchically: 'Enfin l'obligation de circoncire tous les mâles n'avoit jamais passé en loi générale chez les Egyptiens: S. Ambroise, Origene, S. Epiphane, & Josephe, attestent qu'il n'y avoit que les Prêtres, les Géometres, les Astronomes, les Astrologues, & les savans dans la langue hiéroglyphique, qui fussent astreints à cette cérémonie' (iii.459).

Articles in the *Encyclopédie* and in other eighteenth-century sources teem with evidence of ritual modification of the body to achieve cultural cohesiveness, but this is not the place to elaborate all of them. Here I would like to turn my attention to encyclopedic treatment of the people of colour encountered by travellers and naturalists in order to determine how physical modification seemed to produce generalised morphological difference – related to but not exhausted by what we term race or gender – that characterised an entire group. The article HUMAINE ESPÈCE, for

même espèce, puisqu'ils se ressemblent par la forme, par la taille, par la couleur, par les mœurs et même par la bizarrerie des coutumes. Celle d'offrir aux étrangers leurs femmes, et d'être fort flattés qu'on veuille bien en faire usage, peut venir de ce qu'ils connoissent leur propre difformité et la laideur de leurs femmes; ils trouvent apparemment moins laides celles que les étrangers n'ont pas dédaignées' (Georges-Louis Leclerc, comte de Buffon, *De l'homme*, Paris 1971, p.227).

17. The 'Discours préliminaire' provides speculative evidence that social groups sought to distinguish themselves through all sorts of means, including physical and social: 'Un des principaux fruits de l'étude des Empires & de leurs révolutions, est d'examiner comment les hommes, séparés pour ainsi dire en plusieurs grandes familles, ont formé diverses sociétés; comment ces différentes sociétés ont donné naissance aux différentes especes de gouvernemens; comment elles ont cherché à se distinguer les unes des autres, tant par les lois qu'elles se sont données, que par les signes particuliers que chacune a imaginées pour que ses membres communiquassent plus facilement entr'eux. Telle est la source de cette diversité de langues & de lois, qui est devenue pour notre malheur un objet considérable d'étude. Telle est encore l'origine de la politique' (i.xi).

example, postulates that 'le blanc paroît [...] être la couleur primitive de la nature, que le climat, la nourriture & les mœurs alterent, & font passer par le jaune & le brun, & conduisent au noir' (viii.347).[18] Perhaps the first thing we note here is that European observers considered themselves the natural or fundamental variety of human being, from which other manifestations somehow departed, a supposition that no doubt does not surprise. Closely connected to that assumption, however, is the postulate that something *caused* morphological difference. In that same article the notion of causality is explicitly invoked: 'la couleur dépend beaucoup du climat, sans en dépendre entierement. Il y a différentes causes qui doivent influer sur la couleur, & même sur la forme des traits; telles sont la nourriture & les mœurs' (viii.346).

A discourse of causality pervades most discussion of human variation in the *Encyclopédie*, whether such difference pertains to racial or sexual difference. 'Les Hottentots ne sont pas des Négres', we read in the beginning of the article HOTTENTOT, but they are not nevertheless black, 'quelque peine qu'ils se donnent pour le devenir' (viii.320). Similarly, in the article HUMAINE ESPÈCE we learn that 'les Hottentots ne sont pas des Negres, mais des Cafres, qui se noircissent avec des graisses & des couleurs' (viii.347).[19] Naturalists and other observers had argued since the seventeenth century that dark skins resulted from specific cultural practices, most often involving hygiene, and thus the idea that human complexion was fluid belongs to an existing and influential cultural tradition.[20] Although gross morphological difference constituted the most striking contrast for eighteenth-century observers,[21] almost as common in earlier writings on human variation were justifications for more minute variations such as facial features. Hence in the *Encyclopédie* the general category of skin colour correlates the specific features of the head and face; we read that

18. Cf. Buffon: 'Le blanc paroît donc être la couleur primitive de la nature, que le climat, la nourriture et les mœurs altèrent et changent même jusqu'au jaune, au brun ou au noir, et qui reparoît dans de certaines circonstances, mais avec une si grande altération qu'il ne ressemble point au blanc primitif, qui en effet a été dénaturé par les causes que nous venons d'indiquer' (p.304).

19. See also the article NEGRE, in which we learn that 'd'autres physiciens ont recherché avec beaucoup de soin la cause de la noirceur des negres' (xi.77).

20. The entry HUMAINE ESPÈCE begins: 'L'homme considéré comme un animal, offre trois sortes de variétés; l'une est celle de la couleur; la seconde est celle de la grandeur & de la forme; la troisieme est celle du naturel des différens peuples' (viii.344). The seventeenth-century traveller J. G. Grevenbroek maintained that the Hottentots' dark complexion resulted from cosmetics: 'In whiteness of soul they are superior to many of our countrymen, and in whiteness of body they are equal to some, and, in my judgment, would perhaps be so to all, if they cared for cleanliness. But as things are, what with fat and the scorching heat of the sun and the sharp pigment they put on their faces, they have grown dark and are of a swarthy brown colour' (*An Elegant and accurate account of the African race living round the Cape of Good Hope*, translated by B. Farrington, n.p. 1695, p.175).

21. In Buffon's monumental *Histoire naturelle* we read the following remark in the beginning of the section titled 'Variétés dans l'espèce humaine': 'La première et la plus remarquable de ces variétés est celle de la couleur' (p.223).

other modified forms of physiognomic modification contributed to forming the corporeal character of this group: 'Les Hottentots ont le nez fort plat & fort large; ils ne l'auroient cependant pas tel, si les meres ne se faisoient un devoir de le leur applatir peu de tems après leur naissance, parce qu'elles regardent un nez proéminent comme une difformité' (viii.320).

The introduction of causality into the domain of the ostensibly natural human body ascribes a symbolic dimension to the material universe. That is, just as the delineation of specific body parts revealed the cultural value placed on particular social functions, as we saw above, the identification of features different enough that they appear to have undergone some dramatic change reveals the cultural chauvinism behind the assumption of difference, a chauvinism that situates the observing culture's physiognomy as originary and itself underived. Furthermore, and perhaps more important, the identification of specific causal elements, necessarily limited to what is known and understood in the culture finding cause, casts the physical universe as an expression of that culture, and such identification in addition restricts what can be known of the universe to what is known in the observing culture. Thus, when encyclopedists and other eighteenth-century observers chose to view non-European features as *differing* from their own (and not simply *as different*), they attached to the materiality of the natural world their own symbolic and value structure.

We can glean something of the tenor of those structures when we look more closely at the physical features most often selected as different. If skin colour and facial features attracted observers' attention, what nevertheless appear to have been the most unusual of the Hottentots' features as described in the *Encyclopédie* are their genitals. Toward its beginning the HOTTENTOT article reports on the famous 'apron' of skin adorning the female genitals ('les femmes [...] ont la plûpart une espece d'excroissance, ou de peau dure & large qui leur croît au-dessus de l'os pubis, & qui descend jusqu'au milieu des cuisses en forme de tablier', viii.320), the characteristic perhaps most often noted by European travellers.[22] Little has been said, however, about the Hottentot men's genitals, although that anatomical feature attracted a tremendous amount of attention in seventeenth- and eighteenth-century travel and naturalist writings. The entry on Hottentots in the *Encyclopédie* continues the tradition of reporting on that group's

22. William Ten Rhyne wrote that the Hottentot women 'have this peculiarity to distinguish them from other races, that most of them have dactyliform appendages, always two in number, hanging down from their pudenda' (*A Short account of the Cape of Good Hope and of the Hottentots who inhabit that region*, 1686, in *The Early Cape Hottentots*, ed. I. Schapera, translated by I. Schapera and B. Farrington, Cape Town 1993, p.115). Olfert Dapper observed the same phenomenon, but wrote that 'the lining of the body appears to be loose, so that in certain places part of it dangles out' (*Kaffraria or Land of the Kafirs, also named Hottentots*, 1668, also in *The Early Cape Hottentots*, p.45). See also Sander Gilman's 'Black bodies, white bodies: toward an iconography of female sexuality in late nineteenth-century art, medicine, and literature', in *'Race', writing, and difference*, ed. Henry Louis Gates, Jr. (Chicago, Ill. 1985), p.223-61.

uncharacteristic generative organs; describing the Hottentot women's unusual genitals first, the article moves on to the men's (viii.320):

Tachard & Kolbe disent que les femmes naturelles du Cap sont sujettes à cette monstrueuse difformité, qu'elles découvrent à ceux qui ont assez de curiosité, ou d'intrépidité pour demander à la voir ou à la toucher. Les hommes de leur côté, sont tous, à ce qu'assurent les mêmes voyageurs, à demi-eunuques, non qu'ils naissent tels, mais parce qu'on leur ôte un testicule ordinairement à l'âge de huit ans, & quelquefois plus tard.

The women's monstrosity in this citation correlates the bizarre status of *demi-eunuque* ascribed to the men, but significantly their bodies naturally produced the unusual genital configuration observed, whereas the men deliberately modified their organs. The women's *monstrueuse difformité* thus seemed less troubling than the strange category *demi-eunuque* applied to the men, and as I will show in a moment, the men's genital modification made them into a very particular kind of monster for European observers, one that allowed Europeans the fiction of stability that their bodies and epistemologies seemed to allow. Although significant work has appeared on the category of monsters found in the *Encyclopédie* and in other, generally earlier works, in most cases the individuals as extraordinary human prodigies that filled that category quite unexpectedly appeared in their cultures.[23] Unlike human monstrosities that nature sometimes seemed to produce, however, the different cultural bodies described in the *Encyclopédie* enjoyed a regularising discursive tradition that established their difference as part of a particular mode of being – an *état de société*, in fact.

The discursive tradition surrounding the Hottentot practices described above goes at least as far back as 1636, when one William Ten Rhyne reported that all Hottentot males have a testicle removed at birth, presumably, he reports, so that they might be able to run faster. Toward the end of the seventeenth century, J. G. Grevenbroek compared that practice to Jewish circumcision rituals.[24] In 1719 Peter Kolb had provided perhaps

---

23. See in particular Jean-Louis Fischer's 'L'*Encyclopédie* présente-t-elle une pré-science des monstres?' Fischer argues that 'la période scientifique est celle où le monstre n'est plus ni 'en marge', ni un 'jeu' de la nature, mais un être correspondant à une autre normalité répondant aux lois 'biologiques' des êtres qui ont été définis comme normaux' (*Recherches sur Diderot et sur l'Encyclopédie* 16, 1994, p.136). Jean Ehrard has also looked at monsters in the *Encyclopédie*: 'il est paradoxal de voir nos encyclopédistes consacrer ici exactement autant de place à ces "écarts" qu'à la règle. Si fécond qu'ait pu être l'intérêt porté aux "monstres" par les naturalistes des Lumières, il ne peut faire oublier que l'univers des philosophes, celui de l'*Encyclopédie* elle-même, est le monde de Descartes et de Newton, un monde mécanisé, régi par des lois aussi immuables qu'universelles' ('L'arbre et le labyrinthe', *L'Encyclopédie, Diderot, l'esthétique*, ed. Sylvain Auroux, Dominique Bourel and Charles Porset, Paris 1991, p.233-34).

24. Of the Hottentot practice of removing one testicle from each male at birth, Grevenbroek writes: 'It must be supposed that it is from the Jews that the inhabitants of the remoter parts have learned the practice of circumcision, although it is a more serious operation with the Africans, involving the cutting away not only of the prepuce but of the skin right up to the base of the abdomen. From the Jews also the natives near us must have acquired the practice of removing the left testicle, if you will excuse the mention of it' (p.209).

the most lengthy and spectacular account of the Hottentots' ritual male genital mutilation, and in it the practitioner smeared sheep's fat all over the initiate and urinated on him when the operation was complete.[25] While the *Encyclopédie* provides a far more sober account of the ritual, that of Georges-Louis Leclerc, the comte de Buffon, arguably the eighteenth century's greatest naturalist, borrows directly from Kolb's account – to the point, in fact, of producing a largely word-for-word appropriation. Similarly, the unsigned HOTTENTOT entry in the *Encyclopédie* borrows liberally from Buffon's reports, including, once again, language that in many instances coincides directly with his.[26]

My point in invoking a trend of discursive appropriation concerning Hottentot men's genitals lies not in accusing writers of plagiarism, but in demonstrating that even in works as ostensibly dedicated to dispassionate empirical observation as Buffon's or the *Encyclopédie* we find continued mystification of morphology's significance, often in the guise of racial and sexual difference. That is, these writers invoke tradition and hearsay in the place of first-hand observation, thus further committing to the symbolic domain the ostensibly material certainty of physical bodies. And, while the very particular confrontation of the bodily markers of race and sex in the eighteenth century certainly warrants study,[27] here I am focusing on how encyclopedists' conceptions of difference produced a vector of variation away from a putatively stable European norm as well as an exceedingly problematic contamination of the heretofore separate physical and abstract realms. The word-for-word accounts of monstrous male mutilation reveal an almost poignant malaise on the part of the encyclopedists and those who partook of the same discursive tradition, a malaise concerning precisely what it takes to be male and what specifically distinguishes a European. Had such criteria been immediately and unambiguously accessible through empirical observation we would not expect to find attempts to locate cause for difference, because morphological composition would not have the *meaning* that it comes to have when specific privileged characteristics available in quantifiable terms – people can be whiter, for example, or

25. See Kolb, *The Present state of the Cape of Good Hope*, p.113-14.

26. The author of the *Encyclopédie* article never mentions Buffon by name, but toward the beginning of the entry he refers to him obliquely as 'l'auteur de *l'Histoire naturelle de l'homme*' (viii.320).

27. One might well begin with Londa Schiebinger's excellent *Nature's body*. Schiebinger argues that the Great Chain of Being was far more taxonomically problematic than many eighteenth-century scholars have admitted: 'Scientific racism depended on a chain of being or hierarchy of species in nature that was inherently unilinear and absolute. Scientific sexism, by contrast, depended on radical biological divergence. The theory of sexual complementarity attempted to extract males and females from competition with or hierarchy over each other by defining them as opposites, each perfect though radically different and for that reason suited to separate social spheres. Thus the notion of a single chain of being worked at odds with the revolutionary view of sexual difference which postulated a radical incommensurability between the sexes (of European descent)' (Boston, Mass. 1993, p.146).

more male – unpredictably adorn individuals.[28] Given the irresolution surrounding the place in nature that the human being occupied, encyclopedic
musings over morphological features that Europeans took to be *sans mélange*
or *sans composition* reveal that the defining characteristics of what constituted the male or the European were equally unclear.[29] Thus, by referring
to the Hottentots as both *demi-eunuques* and as somehow oddly inter-raced
('On pourroit les regarder dans la race des noirs comme une espece qui tend
à se rapprocher des blancs', viii.347),[30] *Encyclopédie* authors established
those people in an axial taxonomic position that privileged their own identities as European males as somehow unproblematically uncontaminated.

Encyclopedists who perpetuated the sensational stories of how some
other males differed from the European variety in effect unmanned those
males and in that gesture preserved the stability of their own taxonomic
designation 'man'. Since that designator referred to a socially and historically evolving entity that both was and was not continuous with the
natural order of earthly creatures, what was still open to question was the
delimitation of who and what belonged in that category. By casting racial
and sexual others as taxonomically the same as the European males directing the classification, but somehow quantitatively deficient in the manifestation of prized characteristics, *Encyclopédie* authors cast their own bodies as
hallmarks of morphological – and hence epistemological – stability. Hottentot men as *demi-eunuques* are somehow less than men, and hence they find
their place on the scale of nature's productions somewhere beneath European men. The anxiety over the stability of the designator 'man' hinged on
the reliability of what we now think of as racial and gender markers. (And
an especially poignant demonstration of the instability of that category
occurs at two points in the article FEMME: 'Tout le monde a entendu
parler d'une dissertation anonyme, où l'on prétend que les femmes ne font
point partie du genre humain, mulieres homines non esse', vi.470-71; and
'Toutes les femmes & filles sont quelquefois comprises sous le terme

---

28. And some people can be too white: 'Dans cet isthme qui sépare la mer du Nord avec la
mer Pacifique, on dit qu'on trouve des hommes plus blancs que tous ceux que nous connoissons: leurs cheveux seroient pris pour de la laine la plus blanche; leurs yeux trop foibles pour
la lumiere du jour, ne s'ouvrent que dans l'obscurité de la nuit: ils sont dans le genre des
hommes ce que sont parmi les oiseaux les chauve-souris & les hibous' (NÈGRE, xi.76).

29. In an argument also concerned with demonstrating the material dimensions of what
had been taken as purely abstract, Jacques Proust writes: 'ayant trouvé à partir des sciences
de la nature les éléments d'une science des mœurs, mais rien qui puisse fonder une morale
positive, Diderot, comme Rousseau, a cherché ce fondement du côté de la politique et du
droit. Mais, alors que Rousseau considère les rapports sociaux envisagés par le juriste et le
politique, comme de simples effets de l'*art*, résultant de conventions non nécessaires, Diderot
garde le souci d'accorder la politique et le droit avec les sciences de la nature, et considère que
l'institution sociale est comme inscrite dès l'origine dans la *nature* même de l'homme' (*Diderot
et l'Encyclopédie*, Paris 1962, p.304).

30. Buffon was equally explicit on this front: 'il est aisé de voir que les Hottentots ne sont
pas de vrais Nègres, mais des hommes qui, dans la race des noirs, commencent à se rapprocher du blanc' (p.286).

d'hommes', vi.475.) By maintaining the nebulous distinction between abstract ideological categories and materially based empirical ones, those who based the stability and certainty of knowledge on the self-presence of the human body caused preconceived notions of how a body ought to look and feel to inform what they saw in their observations, and at the same time they allowed the incarnate reality of flesh to overflow into variable abstractions such as gender, health or race. Revealing the extent to which taxonomic categories fail when human bodies and the abstract capacities normally associated with them interact, the author of the article NEGRE balks at classifying the inhabitants of the islands in the Indian Ocean (xi.76):

Si l'on parcouroit toutes ces îles, on trouveroit peut-être dans quelques-unes des habitans bien plus embarrassans pour nous que les noirs, auxquels nous aurions bien de la peine à refuser ou à donner le nom d'hommes. Les habitans des forêts de Bornéo dont parlent quelques voyageurs, si ressemblans d'ailleurs aux hommes, en pensent-ils moins pour avoir des queues de singes? Et ce qu'on n'a fait dépendre ni du blanc ni du noir dépendra-t-il du nombre des vertebres?

Delimiting the parameters of the human through selective reference to body parts allowed authors of *Encyclopédie* articles to speculate about the moral and intellectual qualities that they presumed correlated the morphologies they observed.

I pointed out above that the eighteenth-century conception of *anthropologie* was a theological trope that attributed to God human parts in order to make palatable to simple minds the radical indivisibility of God's being. The examples I have provided here illustrate how the apparent self-presence of the body's sensory perceptions correlated a sense of knowledge's stability, and how differing human physiognomies signalled philosophical and taxonomic problems that strictly speaking overflowed the materiality of the morphologies in question. To that end, bodies reify abstractions of European integrity either by correlating the certainty of what we know, or by illustrating, through their causal divergence from a tacitly acknowledged European norm, that the white male body is originary and integral. Bodies thus abstract not only particular ideological concerns such as those associated with the promulgation of a racial and sexual ideal type, but generalised epistemologies associated with the problematics of categorising and arranging on a scale the problematic human being. These bodies of knowledge advance European epistemologies and European physiognomy as enjoying the *simplicité* attributed to God and associated with the concept of *anthropologie*: composed of a radical indivisibility that is *sans mélange* and *sans composition*, encyclopedic knowledge and the bodies affiliated with it seem to present themselves simply as naturally given.

'Il est composé de deux substances', we read above in the article HOMME, 'l'une qu'on appelle ame, l'autre connue sous le nom de corps.' Encyclopedic investigations into the nature of knowledge and the knowledge of nature turned up a striking coincidence: those two pursuits converge on the same point, one at which the long-standing separation between mind and body loses its distinction. Reason and logic find their grounds not in some ultimate idealisation, then, but in physical bodies; and morphology's touchstone lies not in some fundamental materiality, but in social abstractions. It seems that the *Encyclopédie* understood that apparent contradiction all along – the author of the article NEGRE poses the apparently rhetorical question: 'Chaque peuple, chaque nation a sa forme comme sa langue; & la forme n'est elle pas une espece de langue elle-même, & celle de toutes qui se fait le mieux entendre?' (xi.76).[31] With an expressive capacity equal to that of discourse, bodies in encyclopedic investigations express the most abstract of ideals, and they achieve a level of comprehension exceeding that of the most inflected language.

31. Samuel Stanhope Smith wondered about a similar issue in his *Essay on the causes of the variety of complexion and figure in the human species*: 'If I have applied this term [habitual] to the colour of the skin, as well as to the features and form of the countenance and person, it is because I believe that the greater part of the varieties in the appearance of the human species may just be denominated habits of the body. Like other habits, they are created, not by great and sudden impressions of their causes, but by continual, and almost imperceptible touches. Of habits, both of mind, and of body, nations are susceptible as well as individuals' (p.29).

JULIE CANDLER HAYES

Translation (in)version
and the encyclopedic network

Les armes je célèbre et l'homme qui le premier des Troyennes rives
en Italie, par la fatalité fugitif, est venu au Lavinien
littoral; longtemps celui-là sur les terres jeté rejeté sur le flot
de toute la violence des suprêmes dieux, tant qu'à sévir persista
   Junon dans sa rancune,
durement eut aussi de la guerre à souffir, devant qu'il ne fondât
   la ville
et n'importât ses dieux dans le Latium; d'où la race Latine
et les Albains nos pères, d'où enfin de l'altière cité les murs –
   Rome.

Virgil, *L'Enéide*, translated by Pierre Klossowski

THE rise of historical translation studies in the past two decades has found
fertile territory in eighteenth-century France. Although France produced
no single monumental literary translation comparable in its lasting effects
to, say, Dryden's Virgil or Pope's Homer, the literary world was rich in
translations and in sophisticated reflection on the relation of languages
and literary traditions to one another, reflections that were influenced by
significant developments in the questions of 'philosophical grammar' that
occupied many of the *philosophes*. It was quite natural, given the discursive
fields in question, that, in addition to the many translators' prefaces, pedagogical manuals, and philosophical treatises on translation, historians of
translation should look to the *Encyclopédie* in their efforts to locate the
space of translation in the late Old Regime.

Those who did may have been somewhat disappointed. Translation does
not appear as an area of knowledge in the *Système figuré des connaissances*, and
the two articles manifestly dedicated to the subject, TRADUCTION,
VERSION by Nicolas Beauzée (vol.xvi; 1765) and TRADUCTION by
Marmontel (appearing in the fourth volume of the 1777 Supplément), do
not overwhelm by either their theoretical density or their originality,
although both certainly touch on a number of classical issues for
translators, such as freedom versus fidelity, or the question of whether or
not to make a translation sound as if it had originally been written in the
language of the translator. Furthermore, as one critic points out, it is very
difficult to know what status to assign the articles: to what extent do the
individual contributors Beauzée and Marmontel speak for themselves, to

what extent do they speak for a collective opinion? What authority do the *Encyclopédie* articles convey?[1] Critics who refer to these articles tend more often to set them in a wider textual context; that they are cited at all, indeed, testifies to the significance lent them by the cultural and intellectual prominence of the *Encyclopédie* itself.

But although the two articles are 'marginal' in numerous respects, one relegated to an obscure corner of the discussion on grammar, the other to the fourth volume of the supplements, it is certainly possible to explore in a more thorough way their connections to the larger encyclopedic enterprise, its driving preoccupations, its overriding structures. One can indeed *use* the *Encyclopédie* to broaden the discussion in and around translation in the mid-eighteenth century, to rediscover the shapes of ideas, the articulations and connections that have been reconceptualised in the intervening centuries. Of prime importance in such a task are the encyclopedic *renvois*, the cross-references, that help us reconstruct the conceptual fabric woven around a given topic. As Diderot pointed out in an oft-cited passage, the *renvois* had multiple functions: some were 'documentary' and served to complete information; some provided a critical counterpoint; others, more 'conjectural', were meant to spur new thoughts. As for Diderot's audience, so too for modern readers. On the one hand, the network constituted by cross-references and other connective devices helps us perform an 'archaeological' reading, mining the text for lost connections and taxonomies, correcting our understanding of historical phenomena; and on the other, the system continues to offer us connections and conjectures that can still prove productive, offering new approaches to perennial problems. The *Encyclopédie*'s emphasis on the relations among words and texts, via *renvois* and other citational structures, is one of its most powerful features. To what extent, and in what terms, was this reflection on relationality, on 'the structurality of the structure', thinkable or able to be articulated in eighteenth-century discourse?[2] There is no complete answer to such a question, of course: one could begin by pointing to Diderot's own writing, as well as to the discourse of 'systems' at large – but in fact the issues of linguistic and conceptual relationships, change, and difference were most dramatically foregrounded in the discourse of translation. Locating the space of translation within the *Encyclopédie*, then, becomes a method for reflecting on the greater project as well.

Situating translation in the multidimensional space of the *Encyclopédie* could potentially involve an examination of all the examples of contrastive syntax and lexicons in nearly all the articles dealing with language and

---

1. José Lambert, 'Le discours implicite sur la traduction dans l'*Encyclopédie*', in *La Traduction en France à l'âge classique*, ed. Michel Ballard and Lieven D'Hulst (Villeneuve d'Ascq 1996), p.101-19.

2. Contemporary readers have one striking reminder of the historicity of discourse in Beauzée's reprimand to Batteux for his incorrect, figurative use of the word 'structure' (INVERSION, viii.858).

grammar, as well as all the uses of translated text within thousands of articles. More realistically, the task should not only involve a reading of the most immediately relevant articles, but also take into account their citational networks: quotations, examples, and references to works beyond the *Encyclopédie*. Looking at these last, for example, José Lambert considers the use of classical and modern examples in Beauzée's and Marmontel's articles, and argues for a slight modernising trend in Marmontel. Given the nature of the encyclopedic project, however, there are other, 'material' relations linking article to article in the cross-references and the rubrics. Most of the commentators on Beauzée's article have noted that its four renvois to INVERSION, MÉTHODE, SUPPLÉMENT, and SYNEC-DOQUE (all by Beauzée) place it in the context of grammar and rhetoric; Marmontel's article refers to a single article, also by him, MOUVEMENS DU STYLE, which like his TRADUCTION is classified under the rubric of 'belles-lettres' and is also to be found in the *Supplément*. As a number of the other contributors to this volume observe in their articles, the networks of *renvois* can be profoundly revealing in themselves; connections laden with semantic import, they further the work of individual articles and bring unexpected – and unforeseeable – turns to the act of reading. Marmontel's one linked article has no cross-references. Much more complex is the case of TRADUCTION, VERSION. Let me take each of its cross references in turn.

INVERSION. A major article of which I will have more to say in a moment, INVERSION marks one of Beauzée's primary contributions to the debate on language and 'natural order'; despite its significant length (twenty-two columns), it has only four cross-references: HYPERBATE, SYNCHYSE, MÉTHODE, and IDIOTISME.[3] (INVERSION also discusses a number of contemporary interventions in the debate, especially those by Charles Batteux and his followers Pluche and Chompré; the 'anonymous' *Lettre sur les sourds et les muets* makes a brief appearance. The first two cross-references are to short articles on what Dumarsais termed 'figures de mots' or syntactical variants on natural order; IDIOTISME takes on the question of how usage specific to individual languages can be reconciled with the universalising claims of general grammar. None of these contains references to other articles. MÉTHODE, however, far surpasses the other three in length and complexity. As it is also one of the

---

3. I shall be referring to the author of all articles signed '(B.E.R.M.)' and its many variants as Nicolas Beauzée; a few articles signed '(E.R.M.)', are by Beauzée in collaboration with his colleague at the Ecole Royale Militaire, Jacques-Philippe Augustin Douchet, during the first year after Dumarsais's death in 1756. On the nature and extent of the collaboration, see Frank Kafker, *The Encyclopedists as individuals: a biographical dictionary of the authors of the Encyclopédie*, *SVEC* 257 (1988). For a list of the variants on (B.E.R.M.), including apparent typographical mistakes, see Richard Schwab *et al.*, *Inventory of Diderot's Encyclopédie*, *SVEC* 80, 83, 85, 91-93, 223 (1971-1984).

renvois in TRADUCTION, VERSION, let us consider its structure in some detail.

Beauzée's MÉTHODE refers to many articles.[4] Here, the word 'méthode' is understood in its pedagogical sense, with the particular application to the style of grammatical analysis recommended by Dumarsais and his successors. The article allows Beauzée to pick up the debate on inversion where he had left it in the earlier INVERSION. A major piece spanning twenty-six columns, it is also part of an important series of sub-articles under the same title that includes pieces by D'Alembert and de Jaucourt on logic, mathematics, taxonomy, and 'arts and sciences'. None of these approaches Beauzée's for length or complexity of cross-references, however. A particularly striking feature of Beauzée's cross-references, in addition to their sheer number (over fifty) is their repetition; many, such as GÉNITIF or INCIDENTE, appear two or three times. INVERSION is referred to seven times. (INVERSION, as noted above, also refers to MÉTHODE; and both are referred to in TRADUCTION, VERSION.) With only rare exceptions, Beauzée's *renvois* are to articles either by himself or by Dumarsais.

The other two cross-references contained in TRADUCTION, VERSION correspond to this pattern, but are shorter and simpler. SUPPLÉMENT *en Grammaire* and SYNECDOQUE, both by Beauzée (he notes that most of the latter is by Dumarsais, to which he has made occasional additions), offer references to articles by the two grammarians; these articles in turn refer to others by them (including the omnipresent MÉTHODE, INVERSION, and CONSTRUCTION, by Dumarsais).[5] The main features of Beauzée's cross-references, then, are repetition (references to the same article that appear more than once in a given article), recursion (articles that refer to other articles that refer either back to the first article, or to a third article that refers back to the first article),[6] and

---

4. Here is the list; all articles are by Beauzée (B.E.R.M. and variants) unless otherwise indicated (when MÉTHODE refers to articles more than once, I indicate this with 'x2', 'x3', etc.): ETUDE (Faiguet), LANGUE, INVERSION x7, GÉNITIF x2, RÉGIME x2, INCIDENTE (anon., but attributed to Beauzée by Kafker) x3, PRÉSENT, VERBE, EUPHONIE (Dumarsais) x2, SUJET, PARADIGME x2, CONCORDANCE (Dumarsais) x3, IDENTITÉ x2, VOCATIF, GENRE, PRONOM, INTERROGATIF x2, LETTRES, CONSONNE (Dumarsais), VOYELLE, HIATUS, MOT, TEMS, PARTICULE, FORMATION, AUXILIAIRE (Dumarsais), PROPOSITION, SYNTAXE, INFLEXION, PERSONNES, GENS (Jaucourt), MODES, DÉCLINAISON (Dumarsais), CONJUGAISON (Dumarsais), SUPERLATIF, INFINITIF, GÉRONDIF, MÉTAPLASME, TROPE (B.E.R.M., but composed of extended quotations from Dumarsais's *Des Tropes*), FIGURE (Dumarsais), SUBJONCTIF.

5. SUPPLÉMENT's *renvois*, by Beauzée unless otherwise noted: INTERROGATIF x2, RELATIF, and SUBJONCTIF; SYNECDOQUE sends us to MÉTONYMIE (excerpted from Dumarsais's *Des Tropes*) and TROPE (B.E.R.M., but includes numerous excerpts from *Des Tropes* to which Beauzée responds).

6. For example, as we have seen, TRADUCTION, VERSION refers to four articles, including MÉTHODE and INVERSION; INVERSION refers to MÉTHODE and other articles; MÉTHODE contains over 60 references to more than 40 different articles, including

authorial consistency (the vast majority of the articles referred to are either by Beauzée himself, with or without his collaborator Douchet, or by his predecessor Dumarsais). If one follows the network of *renvois* from TRA-DUCTION, VERSION to the fourth degree, one finds references to over 140 different articles, many of them occurring numerous times (CON-STRUCTION, INVERSION, and TEMS are referred to roughly a dozen times each). Given that Dumarsais is listed as the author of some 130 or so articles, and Beauzée with about the same number (even though he became the *Encyclopédie*'s official grammarian starting around the letter G), it is clear that even this brief excursus beginning with TRADUCTION, VERSION gives us a significant percentage of their contributions, especi-ally Beauzée's. So tightly knit together is the web of articles that one could almost speak of a grammatical encyclopedia within the *Encyclopédie*, whose connections to the work as a whole are less pronounced than its own internal structure.[7] Dumarsais makes it clear in the opening words to CONCORDANCE that he writes for a more specific audience than that of the *Encyclopédie* as a whole: 'Ce que je vais dire ici sur ce mot, & ce que je dis ailleurs sur quelques autres de même espèce, n'est que pour les per-sonnes pour qui ces mots ont été faits, & qui ont à enseigner ou à en étudier la valeur & l'usage; les autres feront mieux de passer à quelque article plus intéressant' (iii.821).

Reflection on the dual structure of the renvois as both 'outward' and 'inward' bound makes us aware that the *Encyclopédie* contains both more currents urging us in a specific direction, and more compartments prevent-ing us from making certain connections than we generally recognise. Everything is *not* connected to everything else; there are loops and dead-ends within the network. We should not focus on the cross-references to the exclusion of other 'hypertextual' features, however. The rubrics that indicate each article's relation to the encyclopedic Tree offer another device for relating article to article, for example, as is the practice of

---

INVERSION (seven times) and LANGUE, which itself refers twice to MÉTHODE, once to INVERSION, in addition to others.

7. There is no way to count *renvois* as such, of course, but the string search capabilities of ARTFL allowed me a simple experiment on references to selected articles. I queried the entire *Encyclopédie* for 'Voyez [name of article]', allowing a margin of up to six words between 'Voyez' and the title (since 'Voyez' can introduce a series of titles). The method is imperfect for a number of reasons, since some lists of articles contain more than six words, and not all renvois are introduced with the word 'Voyez'. Nevertheless, the results were inter-esting: twenty-five references to Dumarsais's CONSTRUCTION; thirty-four to Beauzée's LANGUE; twelve to GRAMMAIRE; eleven to INVERSION; only three to TRADUC-TION, VERSION (one of which is in Jaucourt's TRADUCTEUR, which immediately pre-cedes it). By way of comparison, two of the articles often considered to represent the heart of the enterprise appear to receive disproportionately few references: 'Voyez [D'Alembert's] DICTIONNAIRE' turns up nine occurrences; 'Voyez [Diderot's] ENCYCLOPÉDIE' turns up four. Only two articles refer to both of these seminal essays: the short and appropriately pithy FÉCONDITÉ, by Voltaire, and ÉVENEMENT, by Diderot.

grouping articles in multiple-authored series under a single headword. One could contrast the relative self-containment of the grammarians' articles with the open-ended proliferation of articles under the rubric 'Grammaire', which in addition to the essays on general grammar includes a myriad of short 'definitional' articles, many by Diderot, that further the *Encyclopédie*'s function as *dictionnaire*.[8] Thus despite the recursive, self-enclosed structure encoded by their authors, the entries on grammar are put in contact with a wider network, especially given the presence of compound rubrics such as 'Grammaire et morale', 'Grammaire et jurisprudence', or 'Grammaire et logique'. A number of the grammar articles fall into multi-authored series: Beauzée's MÉTHODE for example, or Dumarsais's CONSTRUCTION and FIGURE. The reader who comes upon one of these articles, as specialised as it may be, is confronted with another form of relationship generated by the multiple meanings of the term, the variety of language games in which it participates. Just as one of the recurring threads among the grammar entries is the subset of articles classified under 'Synonymes' – whose major thrust is to show that there are no perfect synonyms, that all words are distinguished by nuances – so too the multi-authored series point out the heterogeneity within single terms.

i. Translation and general grammar: Beauzée

To see translation as a sub-category of grammar is to confirm a shift in the conceptualisation of linguistic phenomena that had been taking place for over a century, removing translation from the sphere of 'éloquence' and rhetoric and bringing it into a more logically rigorous domain identified with the Port Royal intellectuals.[9] Dumarsais and Beauzée concretised the 'grammaticalisation' of rhetoric by setting their articles on the tropes under the rubric 'Grammaire'. As Daniel Droixhe has argued, however, the 'general grammar' of the Encyclopedists is no longer entirely that of Port Royal; though Dumarsais and Beauzée contest the work of the sensationists Condillac and Batteux, their work has nevertheless been inflected by some of the same underlying principles, in particular by an awareness of

---

8. See DICTIONNAIRE. See also Marie Leca-Tsiomis, *Ecrire l'Encyclopédie: Diderot: de l'usage des dictionnaires à la grammaire philosophique*, *SVEC* 375 (1999), an important study for setting lexicographical issues in the Encyclopédie in a broader philosophical context (as well as contrasting the *Encyclopédie*'s lexicon with other dictionaries). Leca-Tsiomis discusses the extreme mutability of the rubric 'Grammaire' and the different perspectives of Diderot and Beauzée (p.283-91).

9. In his study of seventeenth-century translator Perrot d'Ablancourt, Roger Zuber argues that the reign of 'eloquent' translations, the 'belles infidèles', declined after 1660 in the wake of demands for greater rigor and especially for codified 'rules' of translation emanating both from erudite circles and from the translators and intellectuals, and their sympathisers, associated with Port Royal. See *Les 'Belles infidèles' et la formation du goût classique*, 2nd edn (Paris 1995), p.130-61.

historical contingency.[10] Their 'secular' approach already marks an end to Port Royal's elegant logical abstractions that exist *sub specie aeternitatis*. As we have seen in the examination of the network of *renvois*, even the relatively homogeneous set of articles on grammar does not form a completely closed circuit; the discourse on translation highlights the inconsistencies.

As the renvois suggest, reflection on translation in the mid-eighteenth century was inescapably bound up in the 'inversion controversy' of the 1740s and 1750s. The debate on the 'natural order' of thought and whether or not French or any other language corresponded with it brings together many of the linguistic, epistemological, and national-cultural preoccupations of the era.[11] The inversion problem is, in many of its formulations, a translation problem. Translation appears not just in the relation between two languages, say French and Latin, but in the structure given to language itself and the mimetic processes in which language is bound up. For Charles Batteux, as well as for his opponents in the debate, language represents thought, which in turn represents the world, in what Sylvain Auroux has called the 'structure ternaire' of classical linguistics and epistemology. (D'Alembert, following Condillac, refers to chains of identical propositions as 'translations' of one another.)[12] In Batteux's account, language bears the imprint of the world in a concrete way. For him, translation is a form of mimesis, in which all terms of the equation are considered to be fungible equivalents. Translations can thus be considered as both materially and functionally equivalent to their originals. Beauzée complicates and intensifies the mimetic scenario. For him, *la parole* is also an 'image' of thought – but it is hardly a snapshot. Thought being 'indivisible', it can be articulated only through a process of analysis that breaks it into a sequence, 'figuring' it: 'La parole doit peindre la pensée & en être l'image; c'est une vérité unanimement reconnue. Mais la pensée est indivisible, & ne peut par conséquent être par elle-même l'objet immédiat d'aucune image; il faut nécessairement recourir à l'abstraction, & considérer l'une après l'autre les idées qui en sont l'objet & leurs relations; c'est donc l'analyse de la pensée qui seule peut être figurée pas la parole' (INVERSION, viii.854).

Language is thus always already a translation. Just as translations bear differing relationships to their originals, so, according to Beauzée, different

10. See Daniel Droixhe, *La Linguistique et l'appel de l'histoire (1600-1800)* (Geneva 1978), p.13-16. See also his sub-chapters on Beauzée (p.181-86) and on the inversion controversy (p.233-38).

11. The most extended account is Ulrich Ricken, *Grammaire et philosophie au siècle des Lumières* (Villeneuve d'Ascq 1978); see also his *Linguistics, anthropology and philosophy in the French Enlightenment: language theory and ideology*, trans. Robert E. Norton (London 1994), p.111-33; other useful analyses of the debate, with particular attention to Diderot's position, include Marian Hobson, 'La *Lettre sur les sourds et les muets* de Diderot: labyrinthe et langage', *Semiotica* 16, no. 4 (1976), p.291-327, and Gérard Genette, 'Bonnet blanc *versus* blanc bonnet', in *Mimologiques: voyages en Cratylie* (Paris 1976). Sylvain Auroux discusses the debate in numerous contexts throughout *La Sémiotique des encyclopédistes* (Paris 1979).

12. See Auroux on the 'hypothèse langage-traduction' (p.70).

languages figure thought in different ways. All languages are subject to the analytic process that sorts out the simultaneity of experience – and this 'ordre analytique' is nothing less than universal reason – but whereas some languages reproduce this order in their syntax, others do not. Borrowing terms from the abbé Girard, Beauzée calls the former *langues analogues*, and the latter, *langues transpositives* (INVERSION, viii.853). The latter, of which Latin becomes a prime example, are *langues à inversions*; others, character- ised like French by subject-verb-object syntax, follow *l'ordre naturel*.

'Translation', or the 'figuring' of one set of (logical) relations into another, thus becomes constitutive of language itself. Beauzée is corre- spondingly less interested in translation *per se* than in establishing a founda- tional link between grammar and the structures of thought. Literary translation is as divorced from this operation as rhetoric (understood by Beauzée as harmony, embellishment) is from grammar, which is entirely aimed at 'l'énonciation claire de la pensée' (INVERSION, viii.861).[13]

Even so, Beauzée's approach has implications for a broader theory of translation. The two hallmarks of eighteenth-century general grammar, the representativity of language and the universality of thought, support a view of language as a transparent vehicle enabling ideas to be transmitted from one linguistic system to another without either gain or loss. As Auroux puts it: 'le langage est l'expression de la pensée (hypothèse du langage-tra- duction), la pensée est universelle; l'universalité de la pensée est l'étalon de la correspondance *universelle* entre les langues [...]. Tant que l'arbitraire est réduit à la différence matérielle de ces signes, il n'y a aucun problème: pour traduire, il suffit de retourner à ce qu'ils désignent' (p.193). General grammar hence becomes the cornerstone for the continuation of the neo- classical 'French school' of translation in the eighteenth century: the extent to which French could be understood as the most able vehicle of pure thought assures the integrity of all translation into French, any differ- ences from the original being 'superficial' by definition. Indeed, the more an author's 'idea' had been distilled into French 'clarity', the better its instantiation in language – any language, including that of the original.[14]

It is Batteux's sensationist critique of general grammar and concomitant stand on translation that earned him his place in the history of linguistics as

13. In the final section of INVERSION, Beauzée attacks the translation methods espoused by Batteux's allies Pluche and Chompré, but this is translation as a pedagogical exercise for inculcating Latin grammar. Beauzée defends Dumarsais's method, which is expounded in the latter's article CONSTRUCTION and in his own MÉTHODE.

14. On the relationship between translation theory and general grammar, see Daniel Mercier, 'La problématique de l'équivalence des langues au XVIIᵉ et XVIIIᵉ siècles', in Ballard and D'Hulst, p.63-81. An earlier article by André Leclerc, while marred by odd mis- takes (referring to Beauzée's and Marmontel's articles on translation as if they were a single piece, and minimising the importance of translators' theoretical interventions throughout the period) nevertheless offers useful comments on eighteenth-century language theory and translation: 'Le problème de la traduction au siècle des Lumières: obstacles pratiques et limites théoriques', *TTR* 1 (1988), p.41-62.

well as the history of translation.[15] In his *Lettres sur la phrase française* (1748), expanded over the course of the inversion debate as the *Traité de la construction oratoire*, Batteux based language not on reason, but on another universal: *besoin* or *intérêt*. While similarly 'representational', Batteux's linguistic model differs from general grammar by shifting the object from the domain of logic and grammar to that of persuasion and affect. His account also has a distinctly organic tinge: 'Nous observons d'abord que les expressions sont aux pensées, ce que les pensées sont aux choses. Il y a entre elles une espece de génération, qui porte la ressemblance de proche en proche, depuis le principe jusqu'au dernier terme. Les choses font naître la pensée, & lui donnent sa configuration. La pensée à son tour produit l'expression.'[16] Batteux goes on to tell us that thought and its expression are 'images' of one another. Inversion occurs whenever one such 'image' fails to correspond to another: either when the 'order of thoughts' is different from the order of nature, or when the order of words is different from the order of thoughts (Batteux, iv.291-92). His interest lies in considering the latter eventuality (although Beauzée mocks both: INVERSION, viii.859). The order of nature, however, depends on the perspective of the observer, which is shaped by the *intérêt* of the individual. Batteux goes on to argue that the flexibility of Latin syntax makes it more apt to render the modulations of desire, which are distorted, or inverted, by the inflexible subject-verb-object order of French. Syntax is thus not a neutral expository device, but is instead invested with meaning. Batteux then proceeds to elaborate a series of principles for literary translation in which he offers suggestions on how to preserve as many of the original text's structures – expository, syntactical, and rhetorical – as possible.

These are the arguments that Beauzée is at pains to counter in INVERSION, which cites Batteux at length. He pokes fun at the idea of 'inversions' occurring within the process of the generation of ideas (viii.859):

Voilà sans doute la premiere fois que le terme d'inversion est employé pour marquer le dérangement dans les pensées par rapport à la réalité des choses, ou le défaut de conformité de la parole avec la pensée; mais il faut convenir alors que la grande source des inversions de la premiere espece est aux petites – maisons, & que celles de la seconde espece sont traitées trop cavalierement par les moralistes qui, sous le nom odieux de mensonges, les ont mises dans la classe des choses abominables.

---

15. See for example L. G. Kelly, who sees Batteux as an important forerunner of twentieth-century notions of formal structural equivalence: *The True interpreter: a history of translation in the West* (Oxford 1979), p.19, 157, 165-69. Batteux's eleven 'principles' (though not, usually, their full epistemological justification) are habitually included in anthologies of historical translation theory; for example *Anthologie de la manière de traduire: domaine français*, ed. Paul A. Horguelin (Montréal 1981), p.123-25.

16. Charles Batteux, *Cours de belles-lettres, ou principes de la littérature*, nouvelle édition, 4 vols (Paris 1763), iv.290.

He goes on to attack the universality of 'intérêt', citing the 'anonymous' author of the *Lettre sur les sourds et les muets*: ' "Ce qui sera inversion pour l'un, ne le sera pas pour l'autre" ' (viii.859; DPV iv.155). The quotation of Diderot here rings somewhat strangely. As numerous commentators have pointed out, while Diderot explicitly critiques Batteux in the *Lettre*, he points out from the start that he could just as easily have addressed himself to Dumarsais, Beauzée's mentor (DPV iv.134). Indeed, despite the momentary usefulness of the *Lettre* in his attack here on Batteux, Beauzée would in his later work combat the *Lettre* as energetically as he would the work of the other sensationists.

Despite the novelty and significance of his 'Principes de la traduction' in suggesting alternatives to the adaptative strategies of most French translators, Batteux hedges his proposals by returning to the notion that 'thought' and 'expressions' remain nonetheless separate, and that thoughts can pass unchanged through shifts in articulation: 'on lui [le traducteur] pardonnera les métamorphoses, pourvû qu'il conserve à la pensée le même corps et la même vie' (Batteux, iv.347). Even so, his emphasis on the meaningfulness of 'material' order, rather than disembodied, pre-linguistic logical relations, clearly opens the way to another concept of translation, in which the target language somehow shadows forth the 'goût de terroir' and unfamiliar rhythms of the source text.

Let us return to our original interrogation of TRADUCTION, VERSION. This is a 'grammatical' article of the 'synonym' species; like many other articles under the rubric 'Synonymes' it undertakes to distinguish the nuances of meaning held by Diderot and others – notably the abbé Girard, whose work on synonyms was a major source for the articles – to be among the principal indices of the richness and complexity of the French language. In the present case, Beauzée points out that although the two terms may at first appear synonyms, upon consideration of their 'idées accessoires', it becomes evident that the two participate in very different language games, and indeed that they point toward two different conceptions of translation. In the initial examples of usage, *version* is associated with scripture ('*la Version des septante, la Version vulgate*') and *traduction* with literary endeavours ('Vaugelas a fait une excellente *traduction* de Quint-Curce', xvi.510).

Beauzée deduces that *version* is more literal, closer to the source text, as well as to the 'construction analytique'; *traduction* is closer to the author's 'fond de pensée', and to the target language. This is somewhat paradoxical, as we shall see that 'ordre analytique' is far from what we would think of as word-for-word. *Version*, we are told, suggests respect for sacred texts, as when Saint Jerome brings Hebrew closer to us 'sous les simples apparences du latin dont il emprunte les mots' (xvi.510). *Version* thus foregrounds the mimetic effect of translation, representing another language; the other language's reality remains palpable through the word order, rather than specific lexical elements. Beauzée gives an example from the Vulgate (John i.19) of Saint Jerome's 'hebraicised' Latin: 'tu quis es?' He then offers a *version* ('qui es-tu?') and a *traduction* in indirect discourse ('pour savoir qui il étoit'). The question put to John the Baptist is a striking example in this context: the answer is simultaneously negative and annunciatory ('I am not the Christ') – not the logos but a sign pointing to the logos, as if it were a translation.

Version, however, is associated not only with sacred texts, but also with the learning of languages through school exercises. By painstakingly mastering *version*, students will gradually become both proficient in the second language and more adept in their own, until they are able to produce more fluent *traductions*. The two terms thus suggest not only different language games, but also a sequence: *traduction* presupposes a prior *version*. So far so good. But there is another step: 'La *version* littérale trouve ses lumieres dans la marche invariable de la construction analytique, qui lui sert à lui faire remarquer les idiotismes de la langue originale, & à lui en donner l'intelligence, en remplissant les vuides de l'ellipse, en supprimant les redondances du pléonasme, en ramenant à la rectitude de l'ordre naturel les écarts de la construction usuelle. *Voyez* Inversion, Méthode, Supplément, &c.' (xvi.511). So there is actually a preliminary operation, prior to the *version*, in which the original text's lacunae are filled, redundancies eliminated, inversions straightened out.

The three cross-references elaborate the point. INVERSION, of course, explains the concept of 'ordre analytique', as we have seen. MÉTHODE, among other things, details the school exercises recommended by Dumarsais, which include the process of 'rectifying' ('filling' and 'suppressing') the Latin text prior to carrying out the version.[17] SUPPLÉMENT drives home the point still further (xv.672, 673):

Quoique la pensée soit essentiellement une & indivisible; la parole ne peut en faire la peinture, qu'au moyen de la distinction des parties que l'analyse y envisage dans un ordre successif. Mais cette décomposition même oppose à l'activité de l'esprit qui pense, des embarras qui se renouvellent sans cesse, & donne à la curiosité agissante de ceux qui écoutent ou qui lisent un discours, des entraves sans fin. De là la nécessité générale de ne mettre dans chaque phrase que les mots qui y sont les plus nécessaires, & de supprimer les autres, tant pour aider l'activité de l'esprit, que pour se rapprocher le plus qu'il est possible, de l'unité indivisible de la pensée, dont la parole fait la peinture.

Ce n'est en effet qu'au moyen de ces supplémens, que les propositions elliptiques sont intelligibles; non qu'il soit nécessaire de les exprimer quand on parle, parce qu'alors il n'y auroit plus d'ellipse ni de propriété dans le langage; mais il est indispensable de les reconnoître & de les assigner, quand on étudie une langue étrangere, parce qu'il est impossible d'en concevoir le sens entier & d'en saisir toute l'énergie, si l'on ne va jusqu'à en approfondir la raison grammaticale.

This is a striking view of language: thought emerges from a whole, indivisible, prelinguistic state, only to enter language that is both lacunary

17. See the Daniel Mercier article cited above for a brief synopsis of how this process worked, p.71-72.

and redundant. One cannot but see a vision of the Fall here, a vision that comes into sharper focus in Dumarsais's article DÉCLINAISON (which may be reached from TRADUCTION, VERSION via MÉTHODE, as well as by less direct paths). Dumarsais too posits the indivisibility of the prelinguistic state ('Il n'y a alors dans la pensée ni sujet, ni attribut, ni nom, ni verbe', iv.694) from which we are drawn only when the need to communicate with others asserts itself. Or, as Dumarsais puts it, when we choose to 'faire passer notre esprit dans l'esprit des autres' and hence 'notre pensée [...] devient pour ainsi dire un corps', which is to say, a language, which is to say, elliptical. Understanding requires reestablishing the lost relations, which some languages indicate to us via word endings, *terminaisons*. The original term for these flexions, as Dumarsais explains it, embodies the process he has just described: 'Les autres terminaisons s'écartent, déclinent, tombent de cette première, & c'est de-là que vient le mot de *déclinaison* [...]: *declinare*, se détourner, s'écarter, s'éloigner de' (iv.695).

The task of Beauzée's translator begins to sound strangely like that of Walter Benjamin's: to grasp at the originary unity of language, to point the way to 'the predestined, hitherto inaccessible realm of reconciliation and fulfilment of languages'.[18] For Benjamin, the extent to which language deserts its ability to gesture toward higher meanings and instead speaks merely of 'things' reveals its post-Babelian, fallen state. Beauzée, too, is conscious of Babel as the metaphysical event making the divide between the ideal Adamic tongue and our present lacunary one. In his reading of the Babel story in the article LANGUE (reachable from TRADUCTION, VERSION via MÉTHODE and other ways) he is at pains to emphasise both the miraculous suddenness of the confusion of languages and the inevitable process of language change in a contingent, historical world.[19] But despite the logical and theological dilemmas posed by the story, Beauzée finds in *l'ordre analytique* a technique for revivifying pre-Babelian universal communicability: 'L'ordre analytique est donc le lien universel de la communicabilité de toutes les langues & du commerce de pensées, qui est l'ame de la société: c'est donc le terme où il faut réduire toutes les phrases d'une

---

18. Walter Benjamin, 'The task of the translator', trans. Harry Zohn, in *Illuminations*, ed. Hannah Arendt (New York 1968), p.75. On language, the Fall, and Babel, see also his 'On language as such and the language of Man', trans. Edmund Jephcott, in *Reflections*, ed. Peter Demetz (New York 1978), especially p.325-29.

19. See Droixhe, p.183-84. For a nuanced account of the cultural narratives brought to bear on the Babel story in the early modern period, see James J. Bono, *The Word of God and the languages of man: interpreting nature in early modern science and medicine* (Madison, Wis. 1995), especially p.48-84. Bono points out two important strains in the accounts of Babel: one in which the Adamic language, or traces of it, survives Babel in some discernable form; another in which all traces of the originary language are obliterated and human languages become purely conventional constructs. Despite their allegiance to the logical and scientific discourses that are enabled by the second strain, the echoes of Babel and a linguistic Fall in Dumarsais and Beauzée bespeak perhaps a residual attachment to the first strain, which derived its authority at least in part from Saint Augustine (Bono, p.62-63n.).

langue étrangere dans l'intelligence de laquelle on veut faire quelques progrès sûrs, raisonnés & approfondis' (LANGUE, ix.257-58).

As 'faire quelques progrès' reminds us, the reconstitution of analytic order in *version* remains a pedagogical exercise, not a literary technique. *Traduction*, on the other hand, is intended to render a 'thought' in the target language 'comme […] si on l'avoit conçue, sans la puiser dans la langue intermédiaire' (TRADUCTION, VERSION, xvi.511). One hears the echo of the driving trope of neo-classical translation, to make one's author 'speak' as if he were born into our language. Here, however, it is not 'words' that are being brought into our tongue, but 'thoughts' – and we are also reminded that for Beauzée and Dumarsais, translation has exactly the same structure as speech: in order to 'faire passer notre pensée dans l'esprit des autres […] notre pensée prend une nouvelle forme, & devient pour ainsi dire un corps divisible' – in words (Dumarsais, DÉCLINAISON, iv.694).

Curiously, in TRADUCTION, VERSION, Beauzée offers us only a negative illustration of translation ('repréhensible', he calls it) in La Bruyère's rendering of a short quotation from Cicero in the 'Discours sur Théophraste'. In the course of his critique, he demonstrates the Dumarsais 'method' of filling in Cicero's ellipses, prior to establishing his own more literary translation. This gesture prompts his article's remaining cross-references, which, as he indicates, are to articles containing similar critiques and explications of other translations. One is to MÉTHODE (the second reference in this relatively short article), where Beauzée completes the laborious unfolding of his critique of Chompré's rendering of Cicero that he began in INVERSION. The other *renvoi* is to SYNECDOQUE, where Beauzée turns his critical eye to a translation by Dumarsais of a passage in Horace (xv.751-52). SYNECDOQUE is actually largely by Dumarsais himself, with Beauzée's comments inserted in square brackets. Beauzée offers his critique as a form of homage: 'M. du Marsais est trop au-dessus des hommes ordinaires, pour qu'il ne soit pas permis de faire sur ses écrits quelques observations critiques […] je ne sais s'il n'est de mon devoir d'en remarquer les fautes'. The insertion completed, Beauzée emphasises the change of speakers with a parenthetical note: '(c'est M. du Marsais qui continue)'. The speech-like turn allows a momentary illusion of a conversational exchange with a Dumarsais returned from the dead.[20]

Having inserted his conversation with Dumarsais and Chompré into his article via the *renvois*, Beauzée proceeds to yield the floor entirely to another speaker, a somewhat surprising one in view of the acrimony of their debates elsewhere: Batteux. In one of the odder turns of TRADUCTION,

20. Such memorials are to be found elsewhere among the neo-classical translators, most notably in the case of Vaugelas's Quinte-Curce, the most famous translation of the age, laboriously edited and published by his friends after his death. See Pierre Du Ryer, preface to Claude Favre de Vaugelas, trans. *Quinte-Curce, De la vie et des actions d'Alexandre le Grand*, 2 vols (Paris 1653).

VERSION, the single longest statement describing the translator's work comes from the same text cited with such fierce opposition in INVER-SION. To be sure, the opening paragraphs of Batteux's 'Principes de tra-duction' raise general issues, not the specific techniques that cast their differend into sharp relief. Beauzée's manner of quotation, critiquing his allies and enlisting his opponents in support of his views (quoting Diderot against Batteux in INVERSION, or Pluche's account of Babel in LANGUE), point to a particularly pragmatic and tactical approach to reading, one in which contexts and overarching arguments matter less than particular discrete passages. To the extent that his citational practice can be taken as a kind of language, Beauzée is somewhat at odds with his own and Dumarsais's view that structures and logical relations convey meaning, rather than individual words. It is however in keeping with his earlier description of *version* and Saint Jerome's practice of putting Hebrew 'sous les simples apparences du latin dont il emprunt les mots': hence, a 'word-for-word' citational strategy, and one that is also closer to Batteux's contention that words signify, rather than syntax, and to his translating principles, which recommend imitating the word order of the original. Both translation and citation function in many respects like the *renvois* themselves: unpredictable and, while subject to some broad classifications, still evincing no grand plan and often indeterminate in their punctuality (are these *renvois* of concession or opposition?) even in a configuration as 'programmed' as the set of grammar articles, leaving the door open to readers' interpretations.

Let us take a final look at TRADUCTION, VERSION. Given that Beauzée has not held up a single example of a successful translation, it comes as no great surprise that in his conclusion he portrays the ideal translation as lost and inaccessible. Here he cites (in the untranslated original) Cicero's famous account of his translation of Demosthenes in *De optimo genere oratorum*. Beauzée laments: 'Qu'il est fâcheux que les révolutions des siècles nous aient dérobé les traductions que Cicéron avoit faites de grec en latin [...] elles seroient apparemment pour nous des modèles sûrs; & il ne s'agiroit que de les consulter avec intelligence pour *traduire* ensuite avec succès' (xvi.511). This passage from Cicero has often been regarded as the founding moment in Western translation theory: it is the passage upon which Saint Jerome drew in order to recommend translation 'not word for word, but sense for sense', and initiating the idealising or 'ascetic' mode, as Douglas Robinson has termed it, that in many ways reached its fullest articulation in the neo-classical translators. Such idealising abstractions have come under considerable suspicion in the present day in translation studies from critics such as Robinson, Antoine Berman, and Lawrence Venuti.[21] Their

21. See Douglas Robinson, *Translation and taboo* (DeKalb, Ill. 1996), p.97-107, etc. On the seventeenth- and eighteenth-century translators, see Lawrence Venuti, *The Translator's invisibility* (London 1995), p.43-98. Such critiques are important, but I hope to have shown in the present analysis that a more nuanced view is needed.

critique is of course part of a larger movement in many intellectual domains where, as mathematician Brian Rotman puts it, the 'principled forgetting' of 'embodied human agency' needs to be overcome through a salutary reinfusion of history and contingency.[22] Certainly the sensationist critique of general grammar by Batteux, Condillac, and Diderot – and of neo-classical translation by a generation of writers and readers more attuned to translations with foreign accents – has certain features in common with the contemporary critique, particularly with regard to the claim to take embodiment and historicity into account.[23] But, as we have seen, Beauzée's engagement with these issues is more complicated, and not at all immune to its own entanglements in history, contingency, and mate-riality. Writing in a language permeated with ellipsis, but that nevertheless gestures toward an ultimate, complete 'thought', Beauzée's apparent 'for-getting' of material language in the project of translating only meaning occurs within the context of a project deeply immersed in the nuts and bolts of language, *figures de mots* just as surely as *figures de pensée*. Beauzée does not deliberately engage with the tensions inherent in general grammar in the manner of Diderot, but those tensions are evident both within his text and in the manner of its insertion into the encyclopedic network.

If we turn from TRADUCTION, VERSION to the other immediately relevant articles on translation, we take immediate leave of the grammati-cal 'encyclopedia' within the *Encyclopédie*. Immediately preceding TRA-DUCTION, VERSION is Jaucourt's TRADUCTEUR, which places translation within the domain of *belles-lettres*, but has nothing particularly positive to say about translators. After emphasising the need for precision, de Jaucourt offers an analogy: 'On dit que M. de Sévigné comparoit les *tra-ducteurs* à des domestiques qui vont faire un message de la part de leur maître, & qui disent souvent le contraire de ce qu'on leur a ordonné' (xvi.510). Nearby, the anonymous TRANSLATION notes that the use of this term to refer to translation is obsolete, but nonetheless takes a parting shot at translators: 'Les Italiens disent proverbialement *traduttore, traditore*,

---

22. Brian Rotman, *Ad Infinitum – the ghost in Turing's machine: taking God out of mathematics and putting the body back in: an essay in corporeal semiotics* (Stanford, Cal.1993), p.35. As his title suggests, Rotman sets his critique of classical number theory in a much wider philosophical framework: 'Behind [...] refusals to allow any role to an embodied human agency in [...] pic-tures of numbers, one can discern a certain ideological profile, the sedimented numerical version of a hierarchy recurrent in Western culture that ranks soul over body, psyche over soma, mind over matter, spirit over flesh, thought over action, ideal over real, mental signi-fier over material signifier, and so on' (p.148).
23. On Diderot's relation to general grammar, see Daniel Brewer, 'Language and grammar: Diderot and the discourse of encyclopedism', *Eighteenth-century studies* 13 (1979), p.1-19. In her discussion of the *Lettre sur les sourds et les muets* Marian Hobson also reads Diderot as performing a 'dérapage' within the structures of classical representation theory ('Lettre', p.321). Even without a great deal of help from Diderot, however, I am arguing that we can discern, if not outright *dérapage*, at least a certain *glissement*, within what initially appears to be Beauzée's well-defended grammatical machine.

pour faire entendre que les traducteurs trahissent ou défigurent ordinairement leur original' (xvi.555). Jaucourt also wrote the series of articles
linked under the headword VERSION (*Critiq. sacrée*), as well as SEP-
TANTE (*Critiq. sacrée*). These refer in turn to the anonymous VULGATE
(*Théologie*). The VERSION series and VULGATE offer straightforward
historical accounts of different Bible translations, primarily ancient.
Luther's version is mentioned, as are Wycliffe's and Tyndale's, but although
a separate article discusses the King James version in some detail, the only
French translation mentioned is an obscure thirteenth-century version;
there is no discussion of the humanist, Protestant, or Jansenist French translations. SEPTANTE, interestingly, takes a sharply critical, even ironic,
look at the supposedly miraculous origin of the Septuagint as 'une pure
fable' (xv.68).

ii. Translation and literature: Marmontel

Ultimately, then, we must turn to Marmontel's TRADUCTION (*Belles-
lettres*) in the *Supplément*. According to the 'Avertissement', these volumes
provide updates and corrections to the earlier articles. Marmontel's contribution is highlighted in glowing terms:

La *Littérature* est de M. Marmontel, de l'Académie Françoise, & Historiographe de
France. Cette partie, si foible dans l'*Encyclopédie* (quelques articles exceptés, du
nombre desquels sont tous ceux que le même Auteur a donnés depuis la lettre *C*
jusqu'à la lettre *G*), reparoît ici sous la forme la plus intéressante. Un goût sur, une
critique sobre & judicieuse, des observations neuves, des traits piquans, des vues
fines ou profondes, une diction pure & élégante, voilà ce que le public attend. Le
nom de M. Marmontel annonce tout cela et davantage. L'attente du Public ne sera
point trompée.[24]

Although his articles appear with the long-established encyclopedic rubric
'Belles-lettres', the use of the more modern term 'Littérature' here marks a
significant shift in the discursive field. Up until now, none of the articles we
have examined, particularly those in the category of 'Belles-lettres', casts
the activity of translators in a positive light; even Beauzée, who sees translation as an extension of a larger psycho-linguistic process, suggests that
ultimately, good translation is well-nigh impossible. While conceding
many of the same points, however, Marmontel's article offers a somewhat
more sympathetic view, as well as a synthesis of much of the period's discussions of the topic.

He begins by signalling the diversity of that discussion:

Les opinions ne s'accordent pas sur l'espece de tâche que s'impose le traducteur, ni
sur l'espece de mérite que doit avoir la *traduction*. Les uns pensent que c'est une folie
que de vouloir assimiler deux langues dont le génie est différent; que le devoir du
traducteur est de se mettre à la place de son auteur autant qu'il est possible, de se

24. *Supplément*, i.iii.

remplir de son esprit, & de le faire s'exprimer dans la langue adoptive, comme il se fût exprimé lui-même s'il eût écrit dans cette langue. Les autres pensent que ce n'est pas assez; ils veulent retrouver dans la *traduction*, non-seulement le caractere de l'écrivain original, mais le génie de sa langue, &, s'il est permis de le dire, l'air du climat & le goût du terroir.[25]

The first group sees languages as fundamentally incompatible; translation can only be achieved via a form of metempsychosis ('se remplir de son esprit'), recalling the (neo)classical tradition of translation as somehow disembodied, a matter of thought rather than words, and via prosopopoeia ('le faire s'exprimer'), reminding us of the ways in which translation functions as a means to recuperate a lost past by giving voice to the dead.[26] Marmontel's second group, not satisfied with the disembodied 'caractère de l'écrivain', demands a closer approximation of the original's language, even 'le goût du terroir'.

Terroir: here Marmontel appears to be quoting D'Alembert's 'Observations sur l'art de traduire', published some years earlier, in which the latter recommends linguistic innovation and borrowings from the language of the original: 'Alors la traduction aura toutes les qualités qui doivent la rendre estimable: l'air facile & naturel, l'empreinte du génie de l'original, & en même tems ce goût du terroir que la teinture étrangère doit lui donner.'[27] This is the 'progressive' trend in eighteenth-century translation, heralded most notably by Pierre Le Tourneur and Jacques Delille, and foreshadowing the German Romantics' recommendation that the translator '[leave] the author in peace, as much as possible, and move the reader toward him'.[28] Here, Marmontel associates this style with 'les savans' and the former, with 'les gens du monde'. But he refuses to take sides: 'Chacun a raison dans son sens' (*Supp.*, iv.952).

Like many theoreticians of the period, Marmontel recommends a 'middle way', but charts his course not only between 'freedom' and 'servitude', but also between emphasising the author's 'thought' and emphasising the author's 'language'. Although Marmontel will claim that the translator's primary duty is 'de rendre la pensée', he spends more time in the course of his article qualifying the rhetorical and stylistic nuances expressed by the term 'harmonie'. In certain literary genres, language and thought cannot be conveniently divided: 'le caractère de la pensée tient plus à

25. *Supp.*, iv.952.

26. I develop this notion, particularly with regard to seventeenth-century French and British translators, in the larger project of which this is a part.

27. Jean Le Rond D'Alembert, 'Observations préliminaires sur l'art de traduire en général', in *Mélanges de littérature, d'histoire et de philosophie*, nouvelle édn, 3 vols (Amsterdam 1763), iii.19.

28. Friedrich Schleiermacher, 'On the different methods of translating' (excerpts), in *Translation / history / culture: a sourcebook*, ed. André Lefevere (London 1992), p.149. For an extended discussion of German translation theory, which constructed itself to a certain extent in response to French neo-classical theory, see Antoine Berman, *L'Epreuve de l'étranger* (Paris 1984).

l'expression' (*Supp.*, iv.953). The single cross-reference to Marmontel's article MOUVEMENS DE STYLE further underscores the point through its analysis of what might be called the psychosomatics of rhetoric, the link between literary style and the 'movements' of the soul. Style – crucial to the success of a translation – is a function of literary genre, and it is an issue of language, aesthetics, and audience, rather than abstract epistemological structures. The French translation of Locke, although by 'un homme médiocre' (Pierre Coste), is more successful than 'la prose si travaillée d'Ablancourt' for rendering 'la vigueur' of Tacitus.

Marmontel nods in the direction of the inversion controversy and, without making too much of it, takes both sides. First, he emphasises the centrality of *intérêt* in determining word order in 'des langues où l'inversion est libre', echoing Batteux; then he describes French as a language in which words must be arranged 'dans le même ordre que les idées se présentent à l'esprit', siding with Beauzée. Such carelessness appears to reflect disengagement from the debate more than anything else. It is not philosophical grammar that interests Marmontel, but literary style, language, and genre, and how they intersect, whether in 'la ligne droite de la phrase française' or 'l'espèce de labyrinthe de la période des anciens' (*Supp.*, iv.953).

Marmontel's own style is worth commenting on. The short excerpts cited hitherto do not begin to suggest the highly descriptive, metaphorical language of the essay. Marmontel is incapable of discussing style without drawing on analogies and metaphors: 'la légéreté, la gravité, enfin le tour, le mouvement, le coloris & l'harmonie' (*Supp.*, iv.953). In the final paragraphs, as he evokes the difficulty of the translator's task, the rarity of true talent, he turns to a series of comparisons. The first we have already seen (with a different attribution) in Jaucourt's TRADUCTEUR: 'Madame la Fayette comparoit un sot traducteur à un laquais que sa maîtresse envoie faire un compliment à quelqu'un. *Plus le compliment est délicat*, disoit-elle, *plus on est sûr que le laquais s'en tire mal*' (*Supp.*, iv.954). He then returns to the notion that some genres admit translation more easily than others, and that classical works of 'eloquence and reasoning' in prose 'peuvent passer dans toutes les langues sans trop souffrir d'altération, comme ces liqueurs pleines de force qui se transportent d'un monde à l'autre sans perdre de leur qualité, tandis que des vins délicats & fins ne peuvent changer de climat'.

But this comparison is immediately replaced with another:

Mais une image plus analogue fera mieux sentir ma pensée. On a dit de la *traduction* qu'elle étoit comme l'envers de la tapisserie. Cela suppose une industrie bien grossiere & bien mal-adroite. Faisons plus d'honneur au copiste, & accordons-lui en même tems l'adresse de bien saisir le trait & de bien placer les couleurs: s'il a le même assortiment de nuances que l'artiste original, il fera une copie exacte à laquelle on ne desirera que le premier feu du génie; mais s'il manque de demi-teintes, ou s'il ne sait pas les former du mêlange de ses couleurs, il ne donnera qu'une esquisse, d'autant plus éloignée de la beauté du tableau que celui-ci sera mieux peint & plus fini. Or la palette de l'orateur, de l'historien, du philosophe n'a guere, si j'ose le dire, que des couleurs entieres qui se retrouvent par tout. Celle du poëte est mille fois plus riche en couleurs; & ces couleurs sont variées & graduées à l'infini.[29]

These metaphors are themselves 'translations', carrying out the etymological relationship between the two terms. Lafayette's image of the translation as a 'sending' furthers this connection. Her vehicular metaphor contains other aspects: class status and concomitant mastery of language clearly enough – although there remains the central enigma: why would anyone send a lackey out with a 'delicate' compliment, if one were certain that he would acquit himself badly? To press the point in such a manner is to put oneself in the place of the lackey, who is incapable of appreciating the deftness of the turn. Marmontel pursues his thought that different sorts of writing are differently susceptible to translation by shifting to the image of different wines that do and don't travel well (maintaining the 'sending' analogy); his final paragraph takes up the topos of translation as the reverse side of a tapestry, but replaces it with the more nuanced metaphor of different artists' palettes. In both instances, he takes an earlier metaphor (the lackey, the tapestry) and replaces it with his own, echoing and updating them in a sense, as well as filling in distinctions that were originally missing. We are also reminded of the relation of the *Supplément* to the *Encyclopédie*, that of TRADUCTION (*Belles-Lettres*) to TRADUCTION, VERSION, and, in a broad sense, of the figural status of translation itself.

Something 'happens' in translation, just as, in Diderot's account of the poetic hieroglyph, something 'happens' in language. A material, linguistically embodied event, the hieroglyph is untranslatable, but nevertheless repeatable. Translations too, as Benjamin reminds us, are untranslatable, 'not because of any inherent difficulty, but because of the looseness with which meaning attaches to them' ('Task', p.81). The point being partly for Benjamin that to the extent to which language is merely vehicular, it is further removed from *die reine Sprache*, pure meaning. Even for Beauzée (as he quotes Batteux), translation's mimesis extends to far more than the conveyance of information: 'représenter dans une autre langue les choses, les pensées, les expressions, les tours, les tons d'un ouvrage; les choses telles qu'elles sont, sans rien ajoûter, ni retrancher, ni déplacer; les pensées dans leurs couleurs, leurs degrés, leurs nuances; les tours qui donnent le feu, l'esprit, la vie au discours; les expressions naturelles, figurées, fortes, riches, gratieuses, délicates, &c.' (xvi.511). Language here surpasses the merely vehicular; its matter and form produce consciousness and knowledge. Thus a seemingly technical discussion of contrastive syntax and translational strategy leads us to confront the central mission of the *Encyclopédie*, one might say its 'work': the production of knowledge.

The space of translation in the *Encyclopédie* is the space of knowledge; its mechanics are the mechanics of knowledge. Translation both transmits and

29. *Supp.*, iv.954.

produces knowledge, despite interruptions, noise, typos, misattributions (was it Sévigné or Lafayette who came up with the lackey analogy?), misunderstandings, disagreement, censorship. Such too was George Steiner's account of translation, set within his conviction of the world-disclosing capacities of language: 'Each different tongue offers its own denial of determinism. "The world", it says, "can be other." Ambiguity, polysemy, opaqueness, the violation of grammatical and logical sequences, reciprocal incomprehensions, the capacity to lie – these are not pathologies of language but the roots of its genius [...]. In one sense, each act of translation is an endeavour to abolish multiplicity and to bring different world-pictures back into perfect congruence. In another sense, it is an attempt to reinvent the shape of meaning, to find and justify an alternate statement.'[30] If, as has been argued, the *Encyclopédie* as a whole undercuts the neat universals, the identity logic, of general grammar, so too does translation, operating in an analogous way, from within the heart of general grammar. There is nothing neutral in the arrangement and transmission of knowledge, and nothing innocent in the work of translation.

Postscript

I began this essay by quoting the 1964 translation of the *Aeneid* by Pierre Klossowski, a project that even in the late twentieth century met with considerable controversy for its daring adherence to Latinate syntax.[31] For Klossowski what matters in Virgil is the 'physiognomy' of each line of verse, its ability not simply to recount, but to recreate an action: 'Ce sont les mots qui prennent une attitude, non pas le corps; qui se tissent, non pas les vêtements; qui scintillent, non pas les armures; qui grondent, non pas l'orage; qui menacent, non pas Junon; qui rient, non pas Cythérée; qui saignent, non pas les plaies.'[32] By taking the French language into places that Beauzée, Marmontel, and even Batteux and Diderot could have scarcely imagined, surely this translation also carries out the unfinished business of the inversion debate. 'Je reconnais les vestiges d'une ancienne flamme' (a verse cherished by Diderot): in the statements and counter-statements of Batteux, Beauzée, and their interlocutors, there arises an irresistible challenge, a question, about the limits of language that – like the *Encyclopédie* itself – asks succeeding generations to change their way of thinking.

30. George Steiner, *After Babel: aspects of language and translation*, 2nd edn (Oxford 1992), p.246.

31. See Antoine Berman, *La Traduction à la lettre ou l'auberge du lointain* (Paris 1999), p.115-42. Berman, whose work in many ways inspired the contemporary theoreticians of 'foreignising' translation, was needless to say a profound admirer of Klossowski's project.

32. Pierre Klossowski, translator's preface to *L'Enéide* (Paris 1989), p.xi.

CYNTHIA J. KOEPP

Making money: artisans and entrepreneurs in Diderot's *Encyclopédie*

By now it is commonplace to say that the *Encyclopédie*, by so thoroughly describing and illustrating the mechanical arts, bestowed a new dignity on craft and technology in the eighteenth century. This ambitious undertaking – with its countless entries carefully laying out the details of the arts and crafts both in text and in the magnificent plates – has led many to see the *Encyclopédie* as revolutionary: that its role in 'the promotion of the cause of the artisan and his art was outstanding'.[1] As a noted biographer of Diderot observed:

Diderot always respected craftsmanship, and although he sometimes spoke disdainfully or despairingly of 'the people' and employed the word in much the same sense that we now give to 'the masses', he never spoke disparagingly of the artisan or his social usefulness. It was this attitude, faithfully reflected in a thousand places in the *Encyclopédie*, that made the work so revolutionary. New values were here being set forth and admired, the dignity of just plain work was being extolled.[2]

Other scholars have echoed these claims. One author suggests that Diderot's primary goal was simply to ensure that the mechanical arts be recognised as just as important as the liberal arts: to insist that 'not only artisans but the whole of society had suffered from the invidious distinctions between the mechanical and liberal arts.'[3] Another notes that by 'discussing the techniques of carpenters, instrument makers, and other artisans with the same serious tone as the ideas of Bacon, Locke, Bayle, or Newton', Diderot and his collaborators 'bestowed a new dignity on work as such and on an important segment of French society'.[4] Other writers focus on Diderot's concern for the people hurt by 'the prejudice which caused the manual trades to be regarded as unworthy'[5] and insist that his purpose was 'to gain respect for those who traditionally had been disrespected', namely artisans and craftsmen.[6] Some scholars point to 'utility', a growing

    1. Robert Shackleton, 'The Enlightenment and the artisan', *SVEC* 190 (1980), p.5.
    2. Arthur M. Wilson, *Diderot* (Oxford 1972), p.136-37.
    3. William H. Sewell, Jr., *Work and revolution in France: the language of labor from the Old Regime to 1848* (Cambridge 1980), p.65.
    4. *The Encyclopedia: selections*, ed. and translated by Stephen Gendzier (New York 1967), p.xv.
    5. F. G. Healy, 'The Enlightenment view of "homo faber" ', *SVEC* 25 (1963), p.837-59, esp. p.854-59.
    6. Clinio L. Duetti, 'Work noble and ignoble: an introduction to the history of the modern idea of work' (doctoral dissertation, University of Wisconsin, 1954), p.88.

praise and recognition of the useful, which came to include workers (at least when they were actually working).[7] More general interpretations suggest that Enlightenment thinkers advanced the idea that 'labor should be exalted as an essential foundation of human happiness rather than despised as a stigma of baseness and sin'. Nowhere was this idea allegedly 'more prominent than in the pages of the *Encyclopédie*'.[8]

It is not difficult to find passages in this monumental text that substantiate these familiar interpretations. In a number of key entries the editors do seem to advance a new social and economic order: by speaking up for those who work with their hands, while at the same time criticising elites for their laziness, their useless pastimes, and their mistaken disdain for the mechanical arts. In the 'Prospectus' and 'Discours préliminaire', for example, Diderot and D'Alembert underscore their commitment to improving attitudes toward workers, as they credit themselves for being the first who actually went into the workshops and talked to the craftsmen themselves, and for including a huge number of engraved plates illustrating mechanical processes, machines, and tools in their massive tomes.[9] Indeed the editors' own pronouncements about what they were doing may have acted as blinders on later readers and scholars, who consistently find a celebration of the artisan in the *Encyclopédie*, despite what I would call 'dissonances' or counter-tendencies in its depiction of the world of work.[10]

Yet the *Encyclopédie* could well have seemed revolutionary in a number of ways, at least to some readers. Unlike earlier 'dictionnaires encyclopédiques' devoted entirely to specific topics, the aim of the *Encyclopédie* was more ambitious: to try to make what was known on every topic accessible to the educated Frenchman.[11] To achieve that goal meant including a lot of information about very humble activities of many different kinds of artisans. Furthermore, unlike traditional jurists' texts that typically presented all society in terms of carefully delineated hierarchies within the

---

7. See Harry C. Payne, *The Philosophes and the people* (Princeton 1976), esp. ch.3.

8. Sewell, *Work and revolution*, p.64-65.

9. In a forthcoming article entitled 'Anticipating the *Encyclopédie*: artisans and the mechanical arts in Pluche's *Le Spectacle de la nature*' I discuss the striking similarities between Pluche's long-ignored best-seller and Diderot's original 'Prospectus'. Almost twenty years before Diderot, Pluche was publishing descriptions of the various arts and crafts, illustrating them with technical plates, and writing about the advantages of going directly into the workshops and speaking with artisans face to face. There is evidence that Diderot knew these volumes well. Dennis Trinkle makes the same point briefly in 'Noël-Antoine Pluche's *Le Spectacle de la nature*: an encyclopaedic best seller', *SVEC* 358 (1997), p.93-134, esp. p.116.

10. For an extremely valuable discussion about how the *Encyclopédie* represents knowledge – and what that representation says about work, utility, and technology – see Daniel Brewer, *The Discourse of Enlightenment in eighteenth-century France: Diderot and the art of philosophizing* (Cambridge 1993), esp. ch.1.

11. As Diderot explains, 'En effet, le but d'une *Encyclopédie* est de rassembler les connoissances éparses sur la surface de la terre; d'en exposer le système général aux hommes avec qui nous vivons, & de le transmettre aux hommes qui viendront après nous; afin que les travaux des siècles passés n'aient pas été des travaux inutiles pour les siecles qui succéderont' (ENCYCLOPÉDIE, v.635).

three estates (with much detail devoted to the clergy and nobility, and almost none to the third estate and its activities),[12] the *Encyclopédie* paints a society that looks quite different. Work and workers often dominate its pages and plates. One can read more about the production of iron ore than about coats of arms, and more on the herring trade than on heraldry. Fifty-one pages discuss the art of carpentry in the article CHARPENTERIE, while in CHASSE one finds only thirty-one pages devoted to that noble privilege. And thanks to its arrangement by alphabetical order rather than by social hierarchy, in the *Encyclopédie* MENDIANT precedes NOBLESSE and CHAIRCUITIER comes before CLERC.

It is difficult to assess what effects those differences might have had on readers. The sheer number of pages and plates devoted to crafts and technology might have altered the way readers thought about workers and their contributions to society. First, however, we need to remember that the compiling of information (even that about crafts and technology) is not a neutral or transparent exercise, nor is the act of reading itself. The *Encyclopédie* (despite its stated goal to give all knowledge to everyone) shapes the information it offers – sometimes in ways that differ from the stated intentions of its creators. Editors had to choose what to include and omit. General statements from the editors ostensibly defending the dignity of artisans, for example, were printed alongside articles on other topics – on particular crafts and industries, on guilds, finance, and the economy, for example – that sometimes depicted workers in more problematic ways.

How, then, are we to sort out these seemingly contradictory commentaries on work and workers? Do the articles in the *Encyclopédie* express an implicit ideology of work that upholds the dignity of artisans (as many twentieth-century scholars have maintained), or is something else going on? Who are the ideal or intended readers of these articles? How might they have read the *Encyclopédie*, especially the more technical entries on the arts and crafts, on guilds, on the economy? Or better yet, how might they have 'used' this information, and to what purposes? To try to answer these questions, we must turn to the articles themselves.

One place to begin is with the early texts in the first volume where the editors announce their guiding principles – where passages from the original 'Prospectus', the 'Discours préliminaire', and the entry ART seem to affirm the importance of artisans. Yet I would suggest that even these familiar passages are not unambiguous. For example, how is one to interpret Diderot's ostensible effort to gain esteem for the mechanical arts in his article ART when he writes (i.714):

En examinant les productions des arts on s'est apperçu que les uns étoient plus l'ouvrage de l'esprit que de la main, et qu'au contraire d'autres étoient plus

---

12. See, for example, Charles Loyseau, *Traité des ordres simples dignitez* (Chasteaudun 1610), who devotes ninety-four pages to the first and second estates, and a mere eleven to the third, despite the fact that the first two estates comprised about 4% of the whole society.

l'ouvrage de la main que de l'esprit. Telle est en partie l'origine de la prééminence que l'on a accordée à certains arts sur d'autres, et de la distributions qu'on a faite des arts en arts libéraux et en arts méchaniques. Cette distinction, quoique bien fondée, a produit un mauvais effet, en avilissant des gens très estimables et très utiles.

Here Diderot accepts the fundamental dichotomy between liberal and mechanical arts (mind versus body) but not its consequences. He insists that these people are deserving of respect because of their usefulness to society – despite the fact that they work with their hands.[13] Similarly, in the 'Discours préliminaire' D'Alembert invokes utility in his defence of the manual arts when he writes: 'Cependant l'avantage que les Arts libéraux ont sur les Arts méchaniques, par le travail que les premiers exigent de l'esprit, & par la difficulté d'y exceller, est suffisament compensé par l'utilité bien supérieure que les derniers nous procurent pour la plûpart' (i.xiii). Again, this newly expressed respect for manual labour derives from the usefulness of the arts and crafts rather than anything intrinsically of value in the manual skills themselves.

According to the editors, not only are the mechanical arts more useful than the liberal arts, but it is also the responsibility of the latter to raise the esteem owed to the manual arts. Defining his own role in the process, Diderot argues:

Rendons enfin aux Artistes la justice qui leur est dûe [...]. C'est aux Arts libéraux à tirer les Arts méchaniques de l'avilissement où le préjugé les a tenus si long-tems; c'est à la protection des rois à les garantir d'une indigence où ils languissent encore. Les Artisans se sont crus méprisables, parce qu'on les a méprisés; apprenons-leur à mieux penser d'eux-mêmes: c'est le seul moyen d'en obtenir des productions plus parfaites.[14]

Although Diderot's aim here may be to elevate opinions toward the manual arts and increase workers' self-esteem, his text equivocates nonetheless. One might ask, for example, how the liberal arts could bring about these changes in attitude? Or why, if the mechanical arts are so important, do they need justification and support from those who eschew manual labour? Furthermore, in this passage Diderot suggests that current artisans are letting their crafts 'languish', hardly a ringing endorsement of their practices or work ethic. But these are minor considerations when we are faced with the last sentence, which I would argue is central to Diderot's project. Why do we need to have artisans think better of themselves? Because that is 'le seul moyen d'en obtenir des productions plus parfaites'.

---

13. To be fair, in the same passage Diderot condemns those who suggest that experiments and working with material objects are beneath the dignity of the human spirit, and he criticises the prejudices of 'orgueilleux raisonneurs & de contemplateurs inutiles & [...] de petits tyrans ignorans, oisifs & dédaigneux' who abound in cities and countryside. A more positive evaluation of work does exist in the *Encyclopédie*, but we must further explore its precise grounding. We should not ignore the more critical, pejorative, and even repressive depictions of work and workers also found within its pages.

14. ART, i.717.

Thus his primary interest is not to gain unqualified respect for persons, or for the dignity of manual work itself. Rather, he wishes to perfect products and enhance productivity.

Many other passages in the *Encyclopédie* also express a concern about the need to increase productivity. The article FÊTES DES CHRÉTIENS, for example, urges a reduction in the number of holidays in order to multiply the number of working days, for consequently 'on multipliroit à proportion toutes les espèces de biens'.[15] Of course it is probably advantageous to the entire society, and not necessarily inimical to the interest of the workers themselves, that they produce more and better goods. And increasing one's productivity could help raise one's self-esteem. But something else is at stake. To put the stress on workers' utility (and a utility based solely on productivity) is to conceive of workers as means merely, without ends of their own. Often Diderot finds more praise for the machines and tools he describes than for the human beings who operate them. The entry BAS (where Diderot discusses the wondrous stocking-weaving machine) is a case in point.[16] Thus we must consider some further implications of Diderot's praise of workers' utility.

i. Oxen and eagles

Daniel Mornet once wrote that Diderot sought to 'former des hommes plus utiles et non pas plus réfléchis',[17] and eighteenth-century debates on popular education demonstrate that Diderot was not alone in this view. Historian Harvey Chisick cites numerous eighteenth-century writers who questioned the wisdom of extending education to the lower classes, fearing the consequences if workers were to recognise their miserable condition. He suggests that Diderot's claim that universities should be open to all did not imply offering higher learning to the lower classes, 'for this would have deprived society of the artisans and peasants upon which it depended'.[18]

Various entries in the *Encyclopédie* support that opinion. For example, referring to the lower classes, the author of the entry HONNÊTE warns:

15. FÊTES DES CHRÉTIENS, vi.565. For more articles encouraging productivity, see below, footnotes 64-68.

16. See Jacques Proust, 'L'article "Bas" de Diderot', in *Langue et langages de Leibniz à l'Encyclopédie*, ed. Michèle Duchet and Michèle Jalley (Paris 1977), p.245-71. See also Paolo Quintili, 'Machines et "métamachines": le rêve de l'industrie mécanisée dans *l'Encyclopédie*', in *La Matière de l'homme dans l'Encyclopédie*, ed. Sylviane Coppola and Anne-Marie Chouillet (Paris 1998), p.247-74, where the author suggests that the article INDUSTRIE (by Quesnay and Jaucourt) expresses a utopian optimism about machines replacing human workers, in particular that 'métamachines' alone could make other machines.

17. Daniel Mornet, *Les Origines intellectuelles de la Révolution française* (Paris 1954), p.421.

18. Harvey Chisick, *The Limits of reform in the Enlightenment: attitudes toward the education of the lower classes in eighteenth-century France* (Princeton 1981), p.147. Marcel Grandière makes similar observations in *L'Idéal pédagogique en France au dix-huitième siècle*, *SVEC* 361 (1998), esp. p.289-96.

'Si vous métamorphosez vos taureaux en aigles, comment traceront-ils vos sillons?'[19] Editors worried about who would remain to labour in the fields or the manufactories if there were genuine opportunities for higher education and careers for people at the lower ends of society? Philosophes in general argued that peasants, artisans, and the *marginaux* should receive only the most minimal education, which would make them more inured to the hardships of manual labour and low wages. Striking his own blow against social mobility, Diderot wrote that 'rien n'est plus funeste à la société que ce dédain des pères pour leur profession et que ces émigrations insensées d'un état dans un autre'. Although Diderot himself was the son of a modest provincial artisan, he did not facilitate such 'emigrations' by encouraging the lower classes to study.[20]

This apparent desire to exclude the lower classes from anything more than the most rudimentary primary education, coupled with praise of worker utility, already sets up a certain tension in the encyclopedic depiction of the world of work. But there is much more going on. The editors also included articles that severely criticised the church and the nobility, that advocated a more liberal economy and urged abolition of the guilds, and that offered an immense amount of practical information on the crafts, technology, and financial matters. Indeed, the knowledge and opinions expressed in a wide variety of articles – when taken together – seem to advance a new ideology: a social division of labour that moves far beyond the somewhat clumsy categories of the three orders and corporate society inherited from feudal times. One might call it an 'alphabetical order', for a new world in which sophisticated skills of literacy would be one key to progress, profit, and success. But it is an ideology rife with contradictions. It put unproductive nobles and clergy on the defensive to be sure. But it also ensured that for those workers who are 'useful' but basically 'analphabètes', the *Encyclopédie* (and hence the new hegemony) would be inaccessible, for to understand its discourse would require much more than simply knowing the order of the alphabet.

ii. The reader as entrepreneur

Yet there would be one type of reader, rather close to the world of work but not himself a manual labourer, who could read, understand, use, and profit from many of these articles – especially the technical ones. The *Encyclopédie* could provide a potential entrepreneur the information needed to set up a workshop or manufactory, furnish it with exactly the right tools and machines, determine in advance how much everything would cost, and know which workers to hire, how much to pay them, and how to police

---

19. HONNÊTE (*Morale*), viii.287.
20. Denis Diderot, 'Plan d'une université pour le gouvernement de Russie', in *Œuvres complètes de Diderot*, 20 vols, ed. J. Assézat (Paris 1875-1877), iii.527.

them. If we keep that reader in mind, then the more equivocal picture of workers that emerges from the various entries begins to make sense.

Let us consider the description under the entry METIER, for example, where the author again appeals to the superior utility of the artisan, but not unambiguously. In an effort to gain respect for the crafts, the editors explain the division of labour, but at the same time tacitly remind us why manual labour is denigrated in the first place:

On donne ce nom à toute profession qui exige l'emploi des bras, et qui se borne à un certain nombre d'opérations méchaniques, qui ont pour but un même ouvrage, que l'ouvrier répéte sans-cesse. Je ne sais pourquoi on a attaché une idée vile à ce mot; c'est des métiers que nous tenons toutes les choses nécessaires à la vie [...]. Je laisse à ceux qui ont quelque principe d'équité, à juger si c'est raison ou préjugé qui nous fait regarder d'un œil si dédaigneux des hommes si essentiels. Le poëte, le philosophe, l'orateur, le ministre, le guerrier, le héro, seroient tout nuds, et manqueroient du pain sans cet artisan, l'objet de son mépris cruel.[21]

Here the author seems to urge respect for the manual arts, again by virtue of their superior usefulness to all of us. But again the place of the worker is less clear. The general description of the craftsman's routine makes him sound like a mindless automaton, for his job requires the use of his hands and is limited to a certain number of mechanical operations that produce the same piece of work, made over and over again ad infinitum.[22] Is this an activity deserving of 'dignity' and 'respect'? That the artisan mechanically produces the goods that we all need saves the other members of society from these deadening, repetitive menial tasks – and allows them to pursue liberal, intellectual endeavours and other more profitable activities. At best the editors are not calling for respect, but simple gratitude.

Far from celebrating workers, entries describing specific crafts often reinforce the idea of worker as automaton or worse. In the discussion of the pin factory, for example, we find descriptions of men who strike the hammer seventy times a minute and women who can fill papers with pins at a rate of 48,000 per day (for which they received 4 sols).[23] Or consider Diderot's own article, FORGE, which singles out the *marteleur* as key to the operation, while other workers are simply 'comme les bras qu'il fait mouvoir'.[24] The incredibly long and detailed article FER-BLANC similarly describes the menial and routine tasks involved in tin-plating: men dipping sheet after sheet of iron into barrels, and women scouring 500 to 600 tin-plated iron sheets in a day.[25] In ARDOISE we read about miners bent over from carrying 200 pounds of slate on their backs, as they

21. METIER (*Gram.*), x.483.
22. William H. Sewell Jr makes a similar observation in *Work and revolution*, p.68-69.
23. ÉPINGLIER, xxi, text accompanying plates.
24. FORGE (*Arts mechaniq.*), vii.136.
25. FER-BLANC, xxi, text accompanying plates on *Métallurgie*.

feel their way through dark underground passageways without the aid of candles;[26] the entry FOURREUR *ou* PELLETIER describes workers standing naked to the waist in barrels, kneading soaking pelts with their bare feet hour after hour.[27] Far from advancing the dignity of workers, these descriptions underscore the indignities and mindlessness of actual work processes – and would seem unlikely to attract readers of the *Encyclopédie* to take up these activities.

In fact a number of articles go beyond describing work processes to complain about the character of workers themselves, perhaps to alert the potential entrepreneur to the challenges at the workplace. Some entries make it clear certain workers will require domestication or surveillance of sorts. Under FORGE Diderot warns that the *marteleur* will need to maintain 'le bon ordre & une sévère discipline dans son attelier', because workers' vices emerge when they are far from home.[28] The author of ALSACE, discussing the various attempts to mine in that area, advises that proprietors never contract to pay workers in a lump sum for a job because then 'les ouvriers [...] ruinent nécessairement les Entrepreneurs, & empêchent la continuation des ouvrages; les galeries étant mal entretenues, les décombres mal nettoyées, & le filon tout-à-fait abandonné, quand il importeroit d'en chercher la suite'.[29] The author of the entry on fur preparation includes remedies for moments when the 'negligence des ouvriers' threatens to ruin a pelt.[30] The extremely detailed entry LAINE warns that proprietors of wool manufactories need to protect themselves against 'un grand nombre de supercheries fraudeuleuses' committed by workers and merchants at every stage in the process. Among his many recommendations, the author suggests determining carefully in advance both the weight and length of the standard skein when setting a price; otherwise workers will skimp on the wool and 'l'ouvrage sera foible & défectueux'.[31] Similarly, under GALE Diderot talks about various holes and imperfections in ribbons that result from 'le mauvais travail ou le négligence de l'ouvrier'.[32]

Further evidence of pejorative or cynical views of work and workers abounds in the descriptions of food trades. In the entry BOUCHER, for example, Diderot warns that butchers are 'gens violens, indisciplinables', and especially threatening and prone to revolt: 'Comme il est impossible de s'assûrer particulièrement de leur fidelité, il me semble que la bonne politique consiste à les diviser: pour cet effet, ils ne devroient point former de communauté, & il devroit être libre à tout particulier de vendre en étal

---

26. ARDOISE, xxiii, text accompanying plates on *Minéralogie, Ardoiserie de la Meuse*.
27. FOURREUR *ou* PELLETIER, vii.254-55.
28. FORGE, vii.136.
29. ALSACE, i.301.
30. FOURREUR *ou* PELLETIER, vii.256.
31. LAINE (*Economie rustique & Manufactures*), ix.183.
32. GALE (*Rubannier*), vii.433.

de la viande & du pain.'[33] By abolishing their guilds, Diderot curtails not only the butchers' potential political threat, but also their economic strength, for then anyone could set up a butcher's stall. This warning about the dangers of allowing butchers to remain in groups and their potential for violence would likely have left readers with the impression that butchers are dangerous and undisciplined, not skilled cutters of meat deserving respect.

Other food entries also depict workers in unflattering ways, placing special stress on the potential for fraud. In BOULANGER Diderot warns readers about bakers who sell at false weights, whereas his article CHAIRCUITIER dwells upon the deception and abuse found among pork butchers, concluding: 'C'est donc aux particuliers à se pourvoir contre cette fraude, en examinant eux-mêmes cette marchandise.'[34] Nowhere does Diderot praise the *charcutier* for his skill; he seems to deserve no sense of pride from his delectable creations. Rather, the *charcutier* is to be scorned, distrusted, and reported to police if spoiled meat should leave his stall.[35] These are just a few examples – drawn from crafts as different as mining, textiles, and food production – that depict workers in ways that question their character and skill. And most of these entries are attributed to Diderot himself.

Yet two articles that come soon after CHAIRCUITIER provide remarkable examples of a more optimistic view of work and technology, one that stands out all the more thanks to the curious juxtapositions always possible in arrangements by alphabetical order. In the first, CHAISE DE POSTE, Diderot describes a small two-wheeled carriage: 'C'est une voiture commode, légère & difficile à renverser, dans laquelle on peut faire en diligence de très-grands voyages [...]. La CHAISE DE POSTE considérée comme une machine, est certainement une des plus utiles & des plus composées que nous ayons; le tems & l'industrie des ouvriers l'ont portée à un degré de perfection auquel il n'est presque plus possible d'ajoûter.'[36] Diderot ends the account by referring the reader to a detailed engraving of this outstanding carriage.

The second article, CHAMOISEUR, also by Diderot, deserves attention too, for it fills four folio pages with extremely specific instructions on the art of preparing fine leather, concluding: 'Nous avons exposé l'art de Mégisserie et de Chamoiserie avec la derniere exactitude; on peut s'en rapporter en sûreté à ce que nous en venons de dire.'[37] In this latter entry the stated

33. BOUCHER (*Police anc. & mod. & Art*). ii.351-52.

34. CHAIRCUITIER (*Arts & métiers*), iii.12.

35. Obviously, if no contaminated or underweight food is sold, all society is better served, those at the bottom as well as at the top. The point is, rather, where is the careful description of the trade of butcher that Diderot implicitly promised?

36. CHAISE DE POSTE (*Sellier*), iii.60.

37. CHAMOISEUR, iii.74. Sometimes the information in the *Encyclopédie* proved very useful indeed. Arthur Wilson recounts an anecdote from the memoirs of Baron de Tott who in 1773 was asked by the Ottoman Sultan to help build up the Turkish artillery. Although the Baron had never designed or made a canon in his life, with the help of Diderot's article on

intentions of the encyclopedists indeed seem to be served: an enterprising person with this information could understand (and perhaps put into operation) the processes necessary for the production of high-quality leather.

The faith in humanity's ability to progress in science and industry so simply expressed in the CHAISE DE POSTE and CHAMOISEUR entries is thus characteristic of a kind of optimism found in some of the more technical or highly refined mechanical arts described in the *Encyclopédie* – an optimism or generosity that stands in stark contrast to many other entries concerning trades and industries. Painstaking details on rope-making, on locks or on the production of mirrors can be and have been read as testimony to the editors' belief in humanity's ability to perfect itself. The aim of my argument has not been to document further this justification and praise of the manufacturing process (other historians I have cited have found much evidence of that), but rather to investigate the dissonances in the pronouncements on workers and their crafts that become visible when placed within the larger context of the encyclopedists' general goals and implicit ideology.

iii. Telling secrets, or translating the 'world of work'

Let us continue to imagine that the editors included extensive technical information about the crafts not simply to inform readers in an abstract way, but actually to be used and useful. Then we can better understand why they often express frustrations about language. Their translation project would continually face a major obstacle: the practical, physical, and often unarticulated knowledge of workers themselves. On the one hand, corporations often tried to keep their techniques and ingredients secret.[38] On the other, many of the technical processes and tools were difficult to describe accurately in prose. In the 'Prospectus' Diderot suggested that artisans lacked sufficient practice. They had written and read so little about the mechanical arts that it rendered the crafts 'difficiles à expliquer d'une manière intelligible'. However, since a picture has always allegedly been worth a thousand words, the editors' remedy was to introduce the now famous engravings that would try to compensate for some of the failings of language. After all, Diderot wrote, nothing is so fruitless as to make great efforts at explaining extensively without drawings when 'un coup d'œil sur l'objet ou sur sa représentation en dit plus qu'une page de discours'.[39] Of course many of the illustrations in the *Encyclopédie* would be far

---

boring machines (ALÉSOIR) and several other relevant treatises, he succeeded in his task. See Arthur Wilson, *Diderot*, p.136.

38. For an interesting discussion of trade secrets among hat makers, see Michael Sonenscher, *The Hatters of eighteenth-century France* (Berkeley 1987), ch.6.

39. 'Discours préliminaire', i.xxxix-xl.

from simple, for one should also not underestimate the difficulties of illustrating technical crafts or of describing them in prose.

To translate real work into words, the encyclopedists had to subject to critical scrutiny the everyday gestures of workers, whose lack of consciousness about their craft over the years had resulted (according to the editors) in a stultifying technological lethargy. This meant that a major source of information and expertise would be the 'doer' himself, the individual craftsman. Indeed, Diderot, contrasting his encyclopedia with others he deemed less successful, describes with great pride how his writers went directly into the workshops for their information:

On s'est adressé aux plus habiles de Paris & du Royaume; on s'est donné la peine d'aller dans leurs atteliers, de les interroger, d'écrire sous leur dictée, de développer leurs pensées, d'en tirer les termes propres à leurs professions [...] & (précaution presque indispensable) de rectifier dans le longs & fréquens entretiens [...] ce que d'autres avoient imparfaitement, obscurement, & quelquefois infidelement expliqué.[40]

The status of the artisan still suffers from a certain real ambivalence. To be sure, the writers have gone to the workshops and talked with the craftspeople, but afterward they have had to sort out with experts all the conflicting opinions, misinformation, and obscure terminology offered by these unreliable, yet indispensable sources. Unfortunately for the editors, few artisans were 'gens de lettres' to whom editors could turn for accurate information. In fact, most craftsmen seemed not up to the task of explaining their trade to outsiders, for they had never pondered the meaning of what they had always done. As Diderot says in the article CHARPENTE *ou* CHARPENTERIE, 'il seroit à desirer que quelques-uns de ces habiles maîtres écrivissent sur cette matière d'un manière satisfaisant'.[41] Yet social reality dictates that most of the artisans will be inarticulate concerning their manual skills for 'la plupart de ceux qui exercent les Arts méchaniques, ne les ont embrassés que par nécessité, & n'operent que par instinct'.[42]

Here other subtle traces of the classical notion of work surface: the shamefulness of being chained to labour by sheer necessity, of subservience to a body whose activities are instinctive rather than intellectual. The indictment against illiterate workers continues, however, as Diderot laments, 'A peine entre mille en trouve-t-on une douzaine en état de s'exprimer avec quelque clarté sur les instrumens qu'ils employent & sur les ouvrages qu'ils fabriquent.' It is not surprising, then, that for Diderot,

---

40. 'Discours préliminaire', i.xxxix.

41. CHARPENTE *ou* CHARPENTERIE, iii.214.

42. 'Discours préliminaire', i.xxxix. Earlier I referred to the editors' desire to translate an 'illiterate world of work' into the *Encyclopédie*. I will soon discuss a conflict between the literate and official dominant culture on the one hand and a non-literate popular/work culture on the other. I do not wish to imply that during the Old Regime all workers are 'illiterate' or 'non-literate'. Rather, my point is that in the world of work literacy does not play the same role that it does in the dominant elite culture.

in 'un attelier c'est le moment qui parle, and non l'artiste'.[43] And when he discusses the language of the craftspeople – their jargons, inaccuracies, and disputes – one gets the sense that Diderot may in fact prefer his artisans mute.

Throughout the 'Discours préliminaire' the editors insist upon an encyclopedia bound by order, hierarchy, theory, and empirical observation: a tree of knowledge without any missing branches. Editors also want work processes to be orderly, uniform, and rationalised so that readers can understand them and perhaps even put them into practice. However, in specific articles the languages of the mechanical arts often confound the editors' aims by resisting simple, orderly classification. Like the workers themselves, who constantly posed the threat of insubordination and fraud, their jargons would not easily be domesticated. As Diderot describes it:

> Il y a des outils qui ont plusieurs noms différens; d'autres n'ont au contraire que le nom générique, *engin, machine*, sans aucune addition qui les spécifie: quelque fois la moindre petite différence suffit aux Artistes pour abandonner le nom générique & inventer des noms particuliers; d'autres fois, un outil singulier par sa forme & son usage, ou n'a point de nom, ou porte le nom d'un autre outil avec lequel il n'a rien de commun.[44]

Thus Diderot bemoans the lack of order and system in the languages of the mechanical arts. It is not hard to understand his frustration. Take his article FRAISE, for example, which demonstrates just the sort of problem he is confronting. Diderot discovers that 'fraise' has at least forty-two meanings – not including the fruit – and many of them refer to different tools in various trades.[45] In response to such illogical confusion, he advances a 'rational' way to repair the situation. He hopes that 'un bon Logicien à qui les Arts seroient familiers, entreprît des elemens de la *grammaire des Arts*. Le premier pas qu'il auroit à faire, ce seroit de fixer la valuer des correlatifs, *grand, gros, moyens, mince, epais, foible, petit, leger, pesant*, &c' and then to convince the artisans to adopt his recommendations. Language would become rational, uniform, and predictable. His second task would be to 'déterminer sur la différence & sur la ressemblance des formes & des usages d'un instrument & d'un autre instrument, d'une manœuvre & une autre manœuvre, quand il faudroit leur laisser un même nom & leur donner des noms différens.' Confusion would be eliminated for the reader, for there would be only one word for each unique process and each tool. Diderot concludes: 'C'est le défaut de définitions exactes, & la multitude, & non la diversité des mouvemens dans les manœuvres qui rendent les choses des *Arts* difficiles à dire clairement.'[46]

---

43. 'Discours préliminaire', i.xxxix.
44. ART, i.716.
45. FRAISE, vii.276. Among its many uses, 'fraise' was a term employed by clockmakers, woodworkers and gold platers referring to a kind of nail, a drill, a ratchet, a cogwheel and a collar.
46. ART, i.716.

Diderot's impatience with the language of the mechanical arts, however, stands as a further symptom of his distrust of artisans, his condemnation of the corporations, and his larger ideological goals. He ignores the corporation as a potential 'ordering mechanism', one that could in theory further his desire for 'true principles' and a uniform vocabulary, and instead vents his resentment against worker secrecy and ignorance. His complaints about artisans using too many words, or too few, and about their inexact terminology and confusion reveal more than just a desire for a rational, precise, unchanging language of description. What seems to be happening is a tacit move, underneath the rhetoric, to prise the vocabulary of the manual arts away from the domain of the workers, to change it, to bring it under control, and finally to create a new language describing the processes of the mechanical arts available to 'all'.

The irony, of course, is that it is quite likely that once a craft was defined by scientific canons and described in exact theoretical prose, the artisans themselves would be unable to understand it. The 'avertissement' to the 1781 edition of the *Encyclopédie*, trying to justify why its editors had decided not to include the expensive illustrative plates, states that when the engraving of a silk weavers' workshop was taken back to a workshop in Lyon, the silk weavers did not even recognise it as illustrating their own craft.[47] Nor could they likely have identified or comprehended the prose articles that 'scientifically' described their activities either. In this case the 'order' of the *Encyclopédie* would serve to defuse even the possibility of worker self-consciousness, while at the same time making it easier for a potential entrepreneur to imagine how to outfit a manufactory, manage its employees, and make a profit.

Just as the discourse of the *Encyclopédie* was accessible to one group while excluding another, so too the jargon and vocabulary of any specific craft functions as an ideological barrier. Its impenetrability defends its practitioners from the outside, not only making it difficult for the uninitiated to classify or understand, but excluding them from participation. In the corporations and *compagnonnages*, work secrets were maintained and protected in part by means of language comprehensible only to those on the inside. One goal of the encyclopedists was thus to expose those secrets, 'to crack the code' so to speak, for certain of its readers.

The language of the crafts developed over time, partly by accident no doubt, partly to serve the needs of the craftsman. In daily practice it made little difference whether the artisans in the workshop referred to a specific tool as a 'thingamajig' or a 'two-hole punch' as long as all understood the message. To someone committed to the project of a rational and economically efficient organisation of the mechanical arts, however, this sort of inexactitude meant only frustration, since it put up just one more

---

47. *Encyclopédie, ou dictionnaire raisonné* (Lausanne, Geneva 1781), i.lxxxv.

obstacle to 'progress', an obstacle perhaps more or less self-consciously imposed by workers themselves.

In the 'avertissement' to the third volume of the *Encyclopédie*, editors reiterate both their optimism and the problems they faced in their efforts to translate and rationalise the world of the arts and crafts. Again, they depict the artisan as little more than an automaton, working by instinct and blind practice, cut off from the light of reason in his cave, his skill in his hands but not in his mind: 'Les arts, ces momens précieux de l'industrie humaine, auront plus à craindre de se perdre dans l'oubli; les faits ne seront plus ensevelis dans les atteliers & dans les mains des Artistes; ils seront dévoilés au Philosophe, & la réflexion pourra enfin éclairer & simplifier une pratique aveugle.'[48] A similar exhortation in the article ART invites craftsmen 'à prendre de leur côté conseil des Savans, & à ne pas laisser périr avec eux les découvertes qu'ils feront. Qu'ils sachent que c'est se rendre coupable d'un larcin envers la société, que de renfermer un secret utile.'[49] Here artisans who guard their work secrets (or perhaps are simply unable to articulate them satisfactorily) are little better than common criminals.[50]

The assault on corporations is even more visible in the article COMMU-NAUTÉ. After relating a traumatic event from 1404 in Flanders, where 'les ouvriers de Louvain égorgerent leurs magistrats', the author implicitly defends a liberal economy while arguing that guild members reside totally outside the commonweal:

En effet ces *communautés* ont des lois particulieres, qui sont presque toutes opposées au bien général [...]. La premiere & la plus dangereuse, est celle qui fait des barrieres à l'industrie, en multipliant les frais & les formalités des réceptions. Dans quelques *communautés* [...] on ne voit qu'un monopole contraire aux lois de la raison & de l'état, une occasion prochaine de manquer à celles de la conscience &

---

48. 'Avertissement', iii.v-vi. One might well guess the problems that arise when philosophers go into the ateliers to rationalise the descriptions and theories of the arts and crafts. Steven L. Kaplan describes just this sort of encounter between a miller named Buquet and two scientists, Parmentier and Cadet de Vaux, who, armed with theory, chemistry, and scientific discourse, aimed to improve the practice of milling. Buquet, with years of experience, skill, and a certain critical knowledge of his own, bitterly resented the elites' arrogance toward practising millers and their refusal to acknowledge the worth of his particular expertise and insights. See Kaplan, *Provisioning Paris: merchants and millers in the grain and flour trade during the eighteenth century* (Ithaca 1984), ch.11.

49. ART, i.717. See a similar observation made in a speech to the Academy of Besançon on 15 November 1757 on the occasion of the reception of a new member to the group: 'En un mot, tous ceux qui peuvent faire des découvertes avantageuses soit en inventant, soit en perfectionnant, doivent les répandre à la société, sans quoy leurs productions sont vaines, et ils ne sont pas Citoyens' (Fonds de l'Académie de Besançon, Bibliothèque municipal de Besançon, vol.vi, f.146).

50. When discussing 'fondeurs', Diderot complains that they fear competition and 'sont ordinairement fort mystérieux sur les ouvrages; par-là ils obvient aux questions qu'ils ne peuvent résoudre [...]. Il est étonnant qu'on ne se soit pas encore avisé d'établir une école de fondeurs.' See FORGE, vii.136.

de la Religion [...] L'abus n'est pas qu'il y ait des *communautés*, mais qu'elles soient indifférentes sur le progrès des Arts mêmes dont elles s'occupent.[51]

This entry suggests in very strong language that members of some corporations act outside the bounds of conventional society, subverting law and religion, interfering with liberty, sharing neither in a commonwealth of ideals nor in a commitment to improve the very crafts they practised.[52]

The same concerns are expressed in somewhat less pejorative tones in the entry BOTANIQUE, which discusses the ignorance and lack of initiative among rural folks. Far from mincing words, the author describes a 'charrue' as 'une machine grossière abandonnée a des mains qui le sont encore plus'. He complains that the current plow is no better than that of the ancient Greeks and Romans, for it has been abandoned to rural folks who do things the way they always have. He notes a similar problem with the informal ways agricultural knowledge get passed on from generation to generation without the benefit of scientific method or analysis: 'Les gens de la campagne ont sur ce sujet une sorte de tradition, qu'ils ont reçûe de leurs peres, & qu'ils transmettent à leurs enfans. Ils supposent chacun dans leur canton, sans aucune connoissance de cause [...] que tel ou tel terrain convient ou ne convient pas à telle ou telle plante. Ces préjugés bien ou mal fondés, passent sans aucun examen.'[53] In these examples the encyclopedists are concerned that as a result of this informal (or even secretive) transmission of practice, not only will useful knowledge be forgotten, but also mistaken beliefs might be preserved in its place – hence denying both the possibility of rational organisation and improvement over time. The *Encyclopédie*, then, offers itself as the antidote to the classic fear of literate cultures: that all knowledge not preserved in print is destined to be lost or never even 'discovered'.

51. COMMUNAUTÉ (*Jurispr.*), iii.724. The entry discussing masters is also extremely critical of the guilds, as it begins: 'Nous montrerons même que rien ne contribue davantage à fomenter l'ignorance, la mauvaise foi, la paresse, dans les différentes professions' (MAÎTRISES (*Arts, Commerce, Politique*), ix.911). For more on debates about the guilds, see Steven L. Kaplan, *La Fin des corporations* (Paris 2001), esp. ch.1.

52. One should remember that there was enormous variation in the guilds. In some corporations, the popular culture of work belonged more or less exclusively to the *compagnons*; in others, the masters shared in it. In some, the masters identified more nearly with (for lack of a better word) official culture.

53. BOTANIQUE, ii.343. An interesting new monograph on paper-making shows in great detail the efforts of mill owners to break the shackles of 'blind routine' and custom as practised by their workers, as they tried to run their establishment with 'efficiency and the spirit of innovation' and gain control over the journeymen's skill. See Leonard N. Rosenband, *Papermaking in eighteenth-century France: management, labor, and revolution at the Montgolfier mill, 1761-1805* (Baltimore 2000), p.x-xi.

iv. Making money

If we were to ask the question 'what use could some readers make of the *Encyclopédie*', one answer would certainly be to make money – at least if they had some to begin with. If an ideal reader felt any improprieties about amassing a profit or the indignities of managing a manufactory, a number of articles in the *Encyclopédie* would help dispel those fears. The entry FORTUNE, for example, clearly advanced the notion that among the honest means to make money, at the top 'on doit placer le Commerce [...]. Cette une étrange barbarie dans nos mœurs, & en même tems une contradiction ridicule, que le commerce, c'est-à-dire la manière la plus noble de s'enrichir, soit regardé par les nobles avec mépris, & qu'il serve néanmoins à acheter la noblesse.'[54] On the other hand, the entry CHASSE severely criticised nobles for one of their favourite leisurely pastimes, while articles on FAINEANTISE, PARESSE, and OISIVETÉ pointed out that there was nothing honourable or noble about idleness – that even the wealthy had a duty to be engaged in useful work.

In addition, a number of articles addressed general theoretical questions, often defending various versions of physiocracy and economic liberalism.[55] Authors such as François Quesnay, Faiguet de Villeneuve, and the chevalier de Jaucourt advocated for efficiency, improved machines and technology, and a strict division of labour, suggesting that high productivity and progress would be more likely to follow from policies encouraging free trade and an end to the guilds.[56] If any single aspect of the treatment of the arts and crafts stands out, it is the editors' preference for large scale operations. Many long articles describe vast enterprises of the most basic industries: glass-making, paper manufacturing, iron and steel production, porcelain manufacturing, and mining and metal works of various kinds – all accompanied with impressive plates and numerous pages of description.

In one of the longest entries, the author of ARDOISE articulates what he sees as the goal of the *Encyclopédie*. He explains why he discussed much more than just the actual processes of slate-mining and production: 'Je n'ai point cru devoir me borner au détail de l'art; je suis aussi entré dans celui de la police du travail, parce que le but du Dictionnaire encyclopédique est

---

54. FORTUNE, s.m. (*Morale*), vii.205.

55. Like their equivocations about workers, the enlighteners did not unambiguously embrace a liberal economy, for they recognised the way guilds provided a certain measure of social control. I investigate discourse reflecting those reservations in 'Before liberty: the ideology of work, taste, and the social order', in *Naissances des libertés économiques: liberté du travail et liberté d'entreprendres: le décret d'Allard et le loi Le Chapelier*, ed. Alain Plessis (Paris 1993).

56. The importance of the *Encyclopédie* in advancing new thinking about the economy – in particular physiocracy – cannot be overstated. Quesnay's first published articles appeared there in 1758 (FERMIER and GRAIN); other authors followed suite. By articulating positions on freeing the grain trade, on prices, markets, import duties, and other aspects of the economy, these various entries helped define economics as a science and brought all these topics into political debate. See Catherine Larrère, *L'Invention de l'économie au XVIIIe: du droit naturel à la physiocratie* (Paris 1992), esp. ch.5.

d'étendre non-seulement les arts, mais encore le commerce, & que c'est de l'ordre & de l'économie que dépend ordinairement le succès des grandes entreprises.'[57] Here the author seems to reveal an implicit ideological goal of the *Encyclopédie*. He has laid out the details of the craft and how to police the work, with the hope of encouraging large-scale industry and an expanding commerce. He clearly imagined the *Encyclopédie* as a 'how-to' book, at least for some readers.

Many other authors follow the example of ARDOISE, doing much more than simply describing a particular trade or industry. They also give investment advice and discuss various ways to enhance productivity and increase profits. Their remarks seem to speak to one version of an 'ideal' reader: someone with money to invest, and literate enough to find in the *Encyclopédie* much useful and practical information about running a business and keeping workers under control. The entry ÉPINGLIER, for example, not only provides great detail on the processes and equipment used in making pins, it also reveals valuable information about every level and type of worker needed in the shop – from the men who start the process by cutting wire all the way to the women and children who push pins into paper for sale. The author tells how much to pay for each type of work, which workers should furnish their own tools, and how much work one could expect them to accomplish in a minute, an hour, and a day.[58]

Perhaps even more helpful for those considering taking up this business, the author includes a chart showing the actual expenses of production: what it costs to produce pins of various sizes, what they sell for, and the resulting profit. In case the reader missed the point, he notes that from the chart one can see 'que les marchands gagnent plus sur les grosses épingles'. He concludes by calculating one more bit of crucial information: the total cost to fit out a pin factory adds up to 380 livres.[59]

Diderot's thirty-three page article FORGE similarly speaks to a potential proprietor of a mine and foundry operation, seemingly with the goal to convince some enterprising persons to consider investing their time, talent, and money in this essential operation. Diderot begins rhetorically, first by bemoaning the fact that 'les fourneaux & les *forges* sont pour la plûpart à la disposition d'ouvriers ignorans'. He acknowledges traditional prejudices against something as lowly as iron, and he makes a case for its singular importance: 'Le fer remue la terre; il ferme nos habitations; il nous défend; il nous orne: il est cependant assez commun de trouver des gens qui regardent d'un air dédaigneux le fer & le manufacturier.'[60] Next he discusses the personal qualities a proprietor would need to establish a successful ironworks: discretion, honour, good credit rating, good reputation, calm temperament, and managerial skills, among others.

57. ARDOISE, xxiii, text accompanying plates.
58. ÉPINGLIER, xxi, text accompanying plates.
59. ÉPINGLIER, xxi, text accompanying plates.
60. FORGE, vii.135.

At this point in the article, the implicit ideology of the *Encyclopédie* again becomes visible, thanks to Diderot's use of direct address. In FORGE he is clearly not talking to armchair literati when he makes the following query: 'Vous proposez-vous, de bâtir, acheter, ou prendre à bail une forge? Combinez votre santé, votre argent, avec la connoissance du terrain, des héritages voisins, du cours d'eau, des bois, des mines, de la qualité du fer, du débit: voilà le premier pas.' What follows is an even more detailed description on what a successful undertaking will require: extensive information on hiring workers, on investments and keeping accounts, on dealing with merchants and suppliers, where to locate mines, the importance of nearby forests for fuel, drilling procedures, scientific information on the composition of soils, and so on.[61]

Articulating what will become a commonplace in the nineteenth century, Diderot even warns that success or failure of this undertaking will depend greatly on the proprietor's wife and her ability to provide him the refuge of the bourgeois home: 'Si le paix & l'ordre ne regnent pas dans l'interieur de la maison, il est impossible de réussir. La paix demande de bonnes mœurs, de la douceur, de la simplicité, de l'ordre, de l'intelligence, du travail, du bon exemple.' The manager of a successful ironworks will need a tranquil home – a moral and orderly retreat – so that all his energies can be directed toward the operations at the forge.[62]

A number of authors offer advice on how to increase production and profit, while complaining about the inefficiencies of workers and traditional methods. The entry BONNETERIE notes the huge piles of scraps of gauze lost on the shop floor, suggesting that they might be valuable in papermaking: 'j'invite les fabriquans de papier à en faire l'essai. Si cet essai réussissoit, il y auroit un gain considérable à faire pour les premiers entrepreneurs.'[63] The article INDUSTRIE points out the economic advantage of reducing the number of hands employed, especially by replacing people with watermills and wind mills, or other machines.[64] The author of MANUFACTURE DES GLACES talks about his many experiments with soda, altering the placement of various basins, changing the flow of air – anything that could help improve efficiency: 'Cette methode me donna une économie réelle sur tous les objects, puisque je fis plus de besogne avec les mêmes ouvriers, avec le même feu, & dans le même tems.'[65] In the end he claimed to have saved money both on wages and on wood.

---

61. FORGE, vii.134-68. Diderot provides cross references in this article for those who feel they need yet more information on hiring special key workers for the forge: 'Comment juger de leurs talens, si on ignore le travail du charbon, de la fonte, & du fer? Voyez les articles FER & CHARBON' (vii.135).
62. FORGE, vii.135.
63. BONNETERIE, ii.327.
64. INDUSTRIE (*Droit polit. & Commerce.*), viii.694.
65. MANUFACTURE DES GLACES, xxi, text accompanying plates.

Sometimes authors offer observations about making wise investments; many recommend locating new manufactories near sources of water and forests that would provide power, fuel, and transportation, thus saving time and money. They also typically stress the importance of continuous work, thereby striking a blow against age-old traditions of workers' holidays, custom, Saint-Mondays, worker rites, and seasonal exigencies that interfered with regular hours.[66] The entry discussing the details of tin-plating operation, for example, gives detailed day-by-day instructions (starting on 1 January) on how to begin operations in a plant that will plate 1800 sheets of iron every working day all year round.[67] In FONDERIE d'Holbach suggests verifying that one's sources of water will not freeze in winter, otherwise 'on est obligé de cesser le travail'. To avoid that problem, he recommends locating the foundry near hot springs. The same entry alerts readers that a new entrepreneur should not take on too much, but should only build a foundry proportional to the size of the mine to be exploited: 'Cet avis, quelque peu important qu'il paroisse, est bon à suivre, sur-tout en France, où l'on n'est que trop disposé à faire dans les commencemens d'un établissement, de grandes dépenses, sans être assûré si le succès répondra aux espérances qu'on a formées.'[68] Here d'Holbach alerts readers not to be so ambitious that their new enterprises end in bankruptcy.

To help avoid such financial difficulties, the *Encyclopédie* provides even more direct practical instruction. The article INTÉRÊT, for example, offers readers myriad complicated formulas on how to figure simple and compound interest on loans and investments so that they can better assess their chances of economic success. The entry also spells out various laws regarding interest, concluding with an argument justifying setting the rate at 5 per cent.[69] The eight-page entry LIVRE begins: 'LIVRE, un terme de Commerce, signifie les différens registres dans lesquels les marchands tiennent leurs comptes.' What follows are comprehensive instructions on book-keeping, with details for specific situations: current accounts, orders, commissions, expenses, accounts by the month, incoming and outgoing goods, and so forth. Even more striking, in the middle of pages 614-15 (volume nine) are printed two huge sample pages from two different types of account books, followed by explicit directions. This entry concludes with a discussion of the French monetary unit *livre*, and lists equivalent currencies of other countries.[70]

66. For more on the incredible array of custom and rituals that defined daily life for workers in the *compagnonnages* see Cynthia M. Truant, *The Rites of labor: brotherhoods of compagnonnage in old and new regime France* (Ithaca 1994).
67. FER-BLANC, xxi, text accompanying plates on *Métallurgie*.
68. FONDERIE, vii.79.
69. INTÉRÊT, viii.819.
70. LIVRE (*un terme de Commerce*), ix.611-18. For a fascinating discussion of the great interest in accounting and bookkeeping in England, in both literary and commercial realms, see Rebecca E. Conner, '"Can you apply arithmetick to everything?" *Moll Flanders*, William

These examples and the many others mentioned above suggest that the audience to whom these articles are addressed is not the artisans themselves who (expertly or instinctively) practice their trades, but rather the literate bourgeois reader of a particular type. He is the audience for whom practical financial and investment details should be available, for whom the workers' language must be expropriated and rationalised, for whom details on work processes, tools, and machines must be laid out. All this is not so that he can learn to do a craft himself, but so that he can learn how to manage the work, bring the workers under control, and make a profit.

v. Conclusion

One view of the Enlightenment has described it as 'an attempt to substitute empirical knowledge for traditional practice and belief',[71] and the *Encyclopédie* furnishes ample support for this claim, although how exactly one is to interpret the motivations for substitution is still an open question. Much scholarship has emphasised the progressive, optimistic, rational sides of this effort, and yet its more repressive aspects should not be overlooked.

The attempt to 'translate' the entire sphere of the mechanical arts into the *Encyclopédie* highlights the confrontation between an oral, practical, physical, and sometimes inefficient world of work and a dominant literate culture trying to make it rational and productive. There are a number of ways to discuss this confrontation. One might compare coarse, obscure or colourful jargons of workers with Diderot's goal of a clear, simple, prescriptive language for the manual arts. Work itself seems to have remained something of a bulwark of popular culture in the eighteenth century, thanks to the workers' trade secrets, private languages, and the intricate hierarchies, rivalries, rites, rituals, symbols, and myths found among various occupational groups. Those who worked spent so much time at it, and so much of their lives even outside the work place revolved around matters concerned with work, that we might speak of a popular culture of work in opposition to authority or society at large.

At the same time there is a specific desire on the part of the dominant, elite culture to control language and discourse: in our case, the editors of the *Encyclopédie* expropriating and transforming work techniques. By exposing and altering the secrets of the crafts, the editors sought to undermine the authority of specialised artisans. Their formerly unique talents, knowledge, and abilities became dispensable once the techniques were

Petty, and social accounting', *Studies in eighteenth-century culture* 27 (1998), p.169-94. The author notes that double-entry bookkeeping seemed to be particularly difficult to understand. See also Mary Poovey, *A History of the modern fact: problems in the sciences of wealth and society* (Chicago 1998), especially ch.2 where Poovey argues that systematic representations of double-entry bookkeeping both challenged traditional status hierarchies and contributed substantially to producing new kinds of theoretical knowledge in seventeenth-century England.

71. Norman Hampson, *A Cultural history of the Enlightenment* (New York 1968), p.86.

available in print to 'all', that is, to anyone who could understand the discursive order of the *Encyclopédie*. Thanks to the careful description of any specific craft, whatever esteem artisans might have deserved as a result of their possessing particular knowledge no longer seems compelling. As Diderot expressed it, 'il suffit d'avoir décrit exactement un art tel qu'il se practique dans un lieu, & tel qu'il se peut practiquer par-tout'.[72]

The art of the crafts also seems to be losing out to a rational, efficient means of organising the manufacturing processes that demands a strict division of labour:[73] 'Lorsqu'une manufacture est nombreuse, chaque opération occupe un homme différent. Tel ouvrier ne fait et ne fera de sa vie qu'une seule et unique chose; tel autre, une autre chose: d'où il arrive que chacune s'exécute bien et promptement, et que l'ouvrage le mieux fait est encore celui qu'on a à meilleur marché.'[74] This projection seems to ensure that workers will become almost robots, going through a few simple motions over and over again to ensure productivity and a good price. Early in the 'Discours préliminaire' D'Alembert provides us with a comment on the sort of men who work in crafts and the kind of work they do all day: 'Les arts méchaniques dépendans d'une opération manuelle, & asservis, qu'on me permette ce terme à une espece de routine, ont été abandonnés à ceux d'entre les hommes que les préjugés ont placés dans la classe la plus inferieure' (i.xiii). One might reasonably expect the continuation of this statement (appearing as it does at the beginning of volume i) to predict that when the mechanical arts finally get the respect they deserve, life at the bottom will not seem so lowly. But the insistence upon a strict division of labour in the passage cited above makes it likely that, in the interests of productivity and progress, the lowest classes of workers will find more occasions to spend their workdays in blind practice and deadening routine.

More optimistic views about the Enlightenment suggest that during the eighteenth century an awareness of society's dependence upon 'homo faber' led to a new respect and dignity for the mechanical arts and for those who performed them.[75] There is little doubt that the editors of the *Encyclopédie* recognised the growing importance of work and suspected what a force industry and manufacturing could eventually become in France, as their many envious comparisons to England and Holland's successful commercial ventures indicate. And although we find ample lip service paid to fears of losing art and trade secrets 'ensevelis dans les atteliers', it is more likely that the encyclopedists' real aim was to gain some powerful say over

72. CHAMOISEUR, iii.74.
73. See Sewell, *Work and revolution*, p.21-25, for an interesting discussion of 'art'. If we accept Sewell's argument that art in the eighteenth century meant rules, order, discipline and proof of human skill and intelligence, then the rationalisation of the manufacturing process may simply be its logical extension. But we should remember that a sophisticated machine may both testify to the intelligence of its designer and simultaneously reinforce the mindlessness of those needed to operate it.
74. ART, i.717.
75. See Healy, 'The Enlightenment view of "homo faber" '.

the uses to which those techniques and trade secrets were put. True, the incredibly detailed description of rope making presents readers with the information necessary to produce their own rope.[76] But more important, it represents the work process in such a way as to encourage one to imagine how to control, dominate, and regulate rope manufacturing more efficiently.

What then is the place of work in the *Encyclopédie*? The care and attention devoted to the technical aspects of many of the mechanical arts indicate their great importance in eighteenth-century French society, and that careful treatment could be construed as implying a positive evaluation of the manual arts, as many scholars have suggested. But D'Alembert's hierarchical design put work at the bottom, reaffirming and perhaps reinforcing traditional prejudices that dictated that the third estate carry the burden of labour for the society as a whole. The messages in the individual alphabetically arranged articles are more equivocal. The length of many of the technical entries testifies to their perceived importance; positive views of the mechanical arts stress their complexities, their technology, their usefulness, and their role in human and material progress. Yet rather than any simply valorisation of the manual arts, of labour or of workers themselves, the articles are replete with traces of more classical (albeit sometimes veiled) notions of work: as vile, as thwarting attempts at virtue, as implying subservience to instincts and to necessity. That some people build and operate technology in society saves everyone else from having to perform menial tasks and allows them to pursue liberal, intellectual endeavours and profitable enterprise. There is a residual attitude here, comprising both the positive and negative utility of work. Work keeps people tied down; it is a kind of drudgery or even punishment. But by having a whole class of people engaged in manual labour, others are able to escape into a world of leisure, thought, philosophy, and art – not to mention wealth, privilege, and power.

Throughout the *Encyclopédie* one finds traces of a confrontation between a literate culture and a non-literate one, a confrontation undertaken throughout the West and whenever ignorance and irregularity obstructed the coming of a new order, but a confrontation that the encyclopedists pursued with particular relish and to particular effect. To the extent that workers were perceived as marginal and disruptive, their private languages, their corporate groups, their manual skills, their rites and rituals served to insulate them somewhat from the dominant official culture. This rendered them culturally self-sufficient and provided some small defence against the kinds of economic movements transforming industry in the eighteenth century, in others words allowing them a source of autonomous power. What we have in a number of the articles in the *Encyclopédie* is a subtle and comprehensive expropriation of that nonliterate

76. CORDERIE, iv.215-38.

knowledge and hence power by the literate culture: an attempt, largely successful, to remove the inefficient and inarticulate world of work from the
hands and mouths of the workers and to place it in printed form before the
eyes of an enlightened 'management' whose ordered purposes it would
serve.

ROBERT MORRISSEY

The *Encyclopédie*: monument for a nation

THE identification of the nation with universal values is arguably one of the most fundamental tenets of French self-perception.[1] It is widely accepted that this self-representation emerged in the course of the Revolution, the dynamics of which thrust France into nationhood while at the same time projecting the universal values of the Enlightenment onto France redefined as a nation. According to this vision, revolutionary ideals steeped in Enlightenment principles informed the uses and abuses of the emerging French nation-state. This interpretation would seem to imply a pre-eminent role for the *philosophes* in shaping and even fomenting the Revolution.[2] Yet, while the *philosophes* articulated a clear and passionate attachment to the universal, their position concerning the nation was less apparent and simply more difficult to document and understand. Other currents openly contesting the absolute monarchy demonstrated a more marked investment in the concept of nation. Thus, in aristocratic, parliamentary and other, more republican strains of opposition to absolutism, one finds a substantial body of thought devoted to the question of collectivities – peoples, 'nations' – in their historical evolution and, in particular, to the French 'national' past.[3] With the notable exception of Montesquieu, the *philosophes*, when reflecting on the collective, seem preoccupied rather with general, more conceptual and more universal categories like society or what was coming to be designated as 'civilisation'.[4]

1. This essay was first presented in a series of public seminars at the Ecole des Hautes Etudes en Sciences Sociales in March and April 1998.
2. For an excellent overview of the question, see Roger Chartier, *The Cultural origins of the French Revolution*, translated by Lydia G. Cochrane (Durham, N.C. 1991). For long, a direct relation was assumed between Enlightenment thought and the Revolution ('C'est la faute à Voltaire; c'est la faute à Rousseau'). Studies of the last twenty years or so have, on the contrary, to a great extent accorded diminished importance to the *philosophes* and have looked away from the rarefied world of ideas to more material, structural, and social causes. See also the recent reflections on the subject by Jean M. Goulemot, 'Histoire littéraire et histoire des idées du XVIIIe siècle à l'épreuve de la Révolution', *Modern language notes* 114 (1999), p.629-46.
3. See Keith Baker, *Inventing the French Revolution: essays on French political culture in the eighteenth century* (Cambridge 1990); Lionel Gossman, *Medievalism and the ideologies of the Enlightenment: the world and work of La Curne de Sainte-Palaye* (Baltimore, Md. 1968); Georges Benrekassa, *La Politique et sa mémoire: le politique et l'historique dans la pensée des Lumières* (Paris 1983); Blandine Barret-Kriegel, *La République incertaine* (Paris 1988); and for a larger overview, Jürgen Voss, *Das Mittelalter im historischen Denken Frankreichs: Untersuchungen zur Geschichte des Mittelalterbewertung von der zweiten Hälfte des 16. bis zur Mitte des 19. Jahrhunderts* (Munich 1972).
4. See Keith Baker, 'Enlightenment and the institution of society: notes for a conceptual history', in *Main trends in cultural history: ten essays*, ed. Willem Melching and Wyger Velema

143

Recent work has begun to explore what might be called proto-nationalist formulations in Enlightenment thought as expressed, for example, in Voltaire's zealously patriotic stance and in his praise of military glory in the context of the Seven Years War.[5] The rise of the cult of specifically French *grands hommes* promoted by figures such as Diderot and the extensive debate on patriotism spurred in part by the abbé Coyer's *Dissertation sur le vieux mot de 'Patrie'* testify to the existence of not only strong patriotic sentiments, but also a need to reflect on the name and nature of the object of attachment.[6] Was it the king and the realm (*royaume*)? Was it the *patrie*? Or was it the *nation*? There is no doubt that expressions of a deep attachment to France, a fervent *sentiment national*, can be traced back to the very beginnings of France – from the Middle Ages onward.[7] However, with perhaps the significant exception of thinkers such as François Hotman and Etienne Pasquier during the Religious Wars, there was little debate and discussion concerning the very nature of the object of attachment. One might see it as a general consensus that permitted, indeed encouraged, various expressions of love for France, which remained unencumbered by any perceived need to reflect on how to classify and designate the collective entity; there was, so to speak, no gap between the *Royaume de France* and *la France* that needed to be bridged or explored by conscious reflection. This state of affairs has clearly changed by the time the abbé Coyer writes in the middle of the eighteenth century:

> On dit donc aujourd'hui *le Royaume, l'Etat, la France,* & jamais *la Patrie.* Je demande d'abord lequel de ces quatre termes flatte plus l'oreille & le cœur. *La France* ne présente à l'esprit qu'une portion de la terre divisée en tant de provinces, arrosée de tant de fleuves. *L'Etat* ne dit autre chose qu'une société d'hommes qui vivent sous un gouvernement quelconque, heureux ou malheureux. *Royaume* signifie (je ne dirai pas ce que disoient ces républicains outrés, qui firent anciennement tant de bruit dans le monde par leurs victoires & leurs vertus) un tyran & des esclaves; disons mieux qu'eux, un Roi & des Sujets. Mais la *patrie* qui vient du mot *pater*, exprime un père et des enfans.[8]

Plainly, the designation of the collectivity is up for grabs here. France as a geographical entity is an empty, unpeopled space; as a State it is without

(Amsterdam 1994), p.95-120; Daniel Gordon, *Citizens without sovereignty: equality and sociability in French thought, 1670-1789* (Princeton, N.J. 1994), especially ch.2, 'The Language of sociability', p.43-85.

5. See John Iverson, *Voltaire's heroes: violence and politics in the age of Enlightenment* (Ph.D. Thesis, University of Chicago, 1998) and a recent general study by David A. Bell, published while this article was in the press, *The Cult of the nation in France: inventing nationalism 1680-1800* (Cambridge, Mass. 2001).

6. Jean-Claude Bonnet, *Naissance du Panthéon, essai sur le culte des grands hommes* (Paris 1998) ('L'Esprit de la cité', ch.8-9); Gabriel-François Coyer, *Dissertations pour être lues: la première, sur le vieux mot de 'patrie'; la seconde, sur la nature du 'peuple'* (The Hague 1755).

7. See Bernard Guenée, 'Etat et nation en France au moyen âge', in *Politique et histoire au moyen âge: recueil d'articles sur l'histoire politique et l'historiographie médiévale (1956-1981)* (Paris 1981), p.151-64.

8. Coyer, p.13-14.

warmth or affective charge; as a realm it is inhabited, even in the best of worlds, by a king and his subjects and – with the pointed reference to tyrants and slaves – implies a submission inspiring more passive obedience to the person of the king than active participation in the collective enterprise. Only when conceived of as a *patrie* does France acquire the dynamics of a collectivity with the emotional solidarity of a family. 'Ce qui nous manque, c'est de penser en commun', states Coyer in the same essay as he lays out a programme of redefinition: we need to think of France not as a realm but as a *patrie* (p.31). Striking in its absence from Coyer's list of possible appellations is the term *nation*, which had already acquired a strong polemical valence through its use by such political theorists and activists as the aristocrat Henri de Boulainvilliers and the parliamentarian Louis Adrien Le Paige.[9]

The problems of definition and designation are central to Enlightenment thought, and no enterprise demonstrates a more acute and articulate awareness of the strategic importance of language than Diderot's and D'Alembert's *Encyclopédie*:

L'art de bien définir est-il un art si commun? Ne sommes nous pas tous, plus ou moins, dans le cas même des enfans, qui appliquent avec une extrême précision, une infinité de termes à la place desquels il leur seroit absolument impossible de substituer la vraie collection de qualités ou d'idées qu'ils représentent? [...] Il n'y a que la méditation la plus profonde & l'étendue de connoissances la plus surprenante qui puissent nous conduire sûrement.[10]

For the encyclopedists, 'perfectionner les signes', that is, assuring a right relation between words and things, opens the path to understanding and transforming the world. The editors tout their authors for getting out of the dusty offices and quiet retreats of the bookish world and into the real one where men and women live and work. One might expect, then, that in their supposed peregrinations these reworkers of words would come into contact with the political circles where the very definition of the collective entity 'France' is being so hotly contested. Indeed, the most assiduous of them all, the chevalier de Jaucourt, draws heavily on Coyer, explaining that, while in the previous century Colbert had confused *patrie* and *royaume*, 'un moderne mieux instruit, a mis au jour une dissertation sur ce mot, dans laquelle il a fixé avec tant de goût & de vérité, la signification de ce terme, sa nature, & l'idée qu'on doit s'en faire, que j'aurois tort de ne pas embellir, disons plutôt ne pas former mon article des réflexions de cet écrivain' (PATRIE, xii.178). Most striking is the article's conclusion with its depiction of Trajan who is clearly designated to play the role of the heroic counter-example against which to measure the abuses of the

9. See Harold Ellis, *Boulainvilliers and the French monarchy: aristocratic politics in early eighteenth-century France* (Ithaca, N.Y. 1988); and Keith Baker, *Inventing the Revolution*, ch.2, 'Memory and practice: politics and the representation of the past in eighteenth-century France', p.31-58.
10. ENCYCLOPÉDIE, v.365.

current absolutist regime. Lowering taxes and helping the poor, he strove to avoid excessive economic inequality, he worked tirelessly for people's happiness, and he brought abundance, joy, order, and justice to the Empire. Trajan's door was always open; he recognised that he too was subject to the law of the land, and he restored the Senate to its former splendour and authority. In governing, he sought so selflessly to serve the collective good that mothers rejoiced in giving children to the *patrie* of which he was loudly acclaimed the father.[11] Thus the article PATRIE, with its classic anti-absolutist portrait, seeks to reinforce the value of the term *patrie* at the expense of that of *royaume* by exploiting the gap between the two (as well, of course, as that separating antiquity from modernity). The term is all the more powerful in that it can apply to collective entities with many different forms of government and that it is independent of king as well of religion. Its strong affective charge calls out for loyalty, selflessness, and defence. The declaration of 'la patrie en danger' in 1792 testifies to the mobilising force the term acquired.[12]

While the term *patrie*, like that of *peuple*, is certainly one of the major contenders in the terminological struggle to undo the identification between the collective entity of France and a particular type of government, that is, the monarchy, none was to equal the fortune of *nation*. Yet, as we have seen, Coyer studiously omits the term from his list, and, if one consults the articles NATION and FRANCE in the *Encyclopédie*, one finds little that would indicate its centrality or polemical force. In the article NATION, two brief paragraphs summarily define the notion in a very conventional manner with an opening sentence similar to one we might expect to find today: 'mot collectif dont on fait usage pour exprimer une quantité considérable de peuple, qui habite une certaine étendue de pays, renfermée dans de certaines limites, & qui obeit au même gouvernement'. The second paragraph alludes to a very different dimension, one that we might find singularly 'politically incorrect', that of national character, but contains nothing going beyond well-established stereotypes: 'Chaque nation a son caractere particulier: c'est une espece de proverbe que de dire, leger comme un françois, jaloux comme un italien, grave comme un espagnol, méchant comme un anglois, fier comme un écossais, ivrogne comme un allemand, paresseux comme un irlandois, fourbe comme un grec'. In fact, the two paragraphs contradict one another in at least one aspect. For in the list of nations illustrating various national temperaments some entities figure, such as Italy and Germany, that are not united under a single government (*'obéit au même gouvernement'*). This oversight would seem to imply a kind of automatic assumption that cultural and geographical coherence of nations correspond to political boundaries. In any case, to all appearances

---

11. *Encyclopédie*, xii.180; see Coyer, p.25-26.

12. Voir Philippe Contamine, 'Mourir pour la patrie, X[e]-XXe siècle', in *Les Lieux de mémoire*, II: *La Nation*, vol.iii, ed. Pierre Nora (Paris 1986), p.11-23.

this is a hastily written article drawing upon standard material and composed without much thought.[13]

If, on the other hand, we look to the article on France to see how it is described, the results do not appear, at first glance, to be much more encouraging. It too is a very short article composed in this case of only five paragraphs. It opens with a geographical description and briefly evokes the country's climate, natural resources, and some of its institutions, including a few lines outlining the rise of the monarchy. The remainder of the article, however, is much more critical and political in nature and clearly indicates that France is definitely not what it should be. For some nine centuries, the article notes, the French lived in a lethargic state of disorder and ignorance, distinguishing themselves above all by their absence of participation in the great discoveries of the ages. While other peoples were inventing printing presses, gunpowder, mirrors, telescopes, and compasses, or exploring the circulatory system, the laws of gravity, and the New World, the French were off tilting in jousting matches. Only fleetingly, during the reign of Louis XIV and under the guidance of Colbert, did France awaken and show Europe, through the development of the arts and sciences as well as commerce and navigation, that 'la nation françoise est propre à tout'. But the brief optimistic interlude quickly yields to another volley of strident criticisms: Paris is a pit and the provinces are plagued by a declining population living in miserable poverty. The article concludes by stating that the underlying causes of this disgraceful situation are not hard to find and, in a consummate ideological use of cross-references, advises the reader to consult the articles on taxes (IMPÔT) and tolerance. Far from being in any way exemplary, France is depicted as a country divided between rich and poor which squanders its wealth and natural resources. Only the reference to a 'nation françoise [...] propre à se porter à tout' would indicate that France, here explicitly designated as a nation, has the capability of redefining itself. Further, by affirming, with accompanying cross-references, that

13. The dictionary of the Académie provides a similar definition in the 1694 and 1718 editions. Only in its 1740 edition did it take note of the absence of correspondence between political and cultural boundaries: 'NATION Se dit aussi des habitants d'un mesme pays, encore qu'ils ne vivent pas sous les mesmes Loix: Ainsi quoique l'Italie soit partagée en divers Estats et en divers Gouvernements, on ne laisse pas de dire *La nation Italienne*. Et la mesme chose se peut dire des pays qui sont sujets à divers Princes.' It is significant that the *Encyclopédie* does not incorporate this correction into its definition. Michel Le Guern reviews the various definitions of the Academy in 'Le mot *nation* dans les six premières éditions du *Dictionnaire de l'Académie*', in Sylvianne Rémi-Giraud and Pierre Rétat, *Les Mots de la nation* (Lyon 1998), p.161-67. The importance of the 'character' element for the notion of *nation* is such that it merits its own article, CARACTERE DES NATIONS: 'Le caractere d'une nation consiste dans une certaine disposition habituelle de l'ame, qui est plus commune chez une nation que chez une autre, quoique cette disposition ne se rencontre pas dans tous les membres qui composent la nation: ainsi le caractere des François est la légereté, la gaieté, la sociabilité, l'amour de leurs rois & de la monarchie même, &c.' In addition to the two paragraphs described here, the article in the *Encyclopédie* contains four more short paragraphs devoted to the *nations* in the universities, particularly the University of Paris. While they are related to the question of place of origin, they do not directly concern us here.

the reasons for the current state of affairs are not difficult to find, the article suggests that the *Encyclopédie* itself contains the reasons and remedies necessary for the work of redefinition.

The idea that France should reform and redefine itself in accordance with the material provided by the *Encyclopédie* is, of course, consistent with the universalist goals of the work. However, the limited space accorded to the articles NATION and FRANCE would seem to imply that the question as such is not central for the encyclopedists. France is one case among many, and devoting too much space to any one country would compromise the goals and image of the work as a universal encyclopedia. Diderot affirms the essentially cosmopolitan nature of the *Encyclopédie* when he declares that 'un dictionnaire universel & raisonné est destiné à l'instruction générale & permanente de l'espèce humaine'. It represents the work of a group of authors 'liés seulement par l'intérêt général du genre humain et par un sentiment de bienveillance réciproque' (v.646, 636). His ideal editor 'considérera [...] le monde comme son école, & le Genre humain comme son pupille', and his ideal author would be 'ferme, instruit, honnête, véridique, d'*aucun pays*, d'*aucune secte*, d'*aucun état*' (v.648-49). From this point of view, the more general and abstract concept of society discussed by historians Keith Baker, Daniel Gordon, and others would seem more in harmony with the encyclopedic project as Diderot defines it.[14] Indeed, the force of concepts like 'society' and 'humanity' lies in their ability to provide a finality, a 'raison d'être' which transcends all particular interests without being swept up in the other-worldliness of what Voltaire would categorise as 'métaphysico-théologico-cosmologico-nigologie'.[15]

If, from the point of view of its cosmopolitan goals, the actual country from which the universal *Encyclopédie* emanates would seem nothing more than an accident and the concept of nation too tainted by connotations of national character as well as of cultural and geographical specificity, it is also true that there are, inherent in the undertaking, many elements that might lead us to question this preliminary conclusion. Foremost among these is, of course, the fact that the work is a dictionary of the French language. Further, in spite of its brevity, the article on France forcefully condemns France as it was and is while suggesting what it might be. Thus, even though the realm of France has spent too much time in jousting matches, the 'nation française' could be – and for a brief moment showed itself to be – 'propre à se porter à tout'. The formulation is interesting because it implies that, properly guided as happened under Colbert's stewardship, *la nation française* could have a kind of universal vocation similar to that of the *Encyclopédie* itself. This parallel between the

14. See Keith Baker, 'Enlightenment and the institution of society', p.95-120. See also Daniel Gordon, *Citizens without sovereignty*; Marcel Gauchet, *Le Désenchantement du monde* (Paris 1985); and David Avron Bell, *The Cult of the nation in France: inventing nationalism, 1680-1800*.

15. *Candide*, in *Contes en vers et en prose*, ed. S. Menant (Paris 1992), p.231.

Encyclopédie and the French nation is richly suggestive and raises the question of France's place in this work that sees itself both as a repository of all human knowledge and a vehicle for progress serving humanity as a whole. While the article implies no incompatibility between monarchical absolutism and the ideal of national self-fulfilment – on the contrary – it does designate France specifically as a nation and leads one to reflect on the status of the term 'nation' in the *Encyclopédie* as well as on its use in this vast work for designating France. These questions are all the more intriguing in that, affirmations to the contrary not withstanding, the *Encyclopédie* is a polyphonic work integrating voices from many different ideological quarters, from the most traditional savants to the most radical *philosophes*. In the light of this diversity, one may wonder whether any general conclusions may be reached concerning these issues.

Until recently it would have been difficult to pursue these lines of research. The absence of a central, key article or set of articles made locating occurrences of terms such as 'nation' or 'France' extremely time-consuming, difficult and, considering the very hypothetical nature of the question and the uncertainties surrounding the possible results, a 'high-risk' operation at best. The introduction of an electronic edition of the *Encyclopédie* now makes possible other, more 'transversal' readings of the work, while at the same time raising interesting methodological issues. Going beyond articles bearing an explicit reference to France in the title, an initial query concerning the term 'France' reveals that it occurs some 8300 times, more than any other European country. It is followed by England (3910; *Angleterre* as well as *Grande Bretagne*), Italy (3464), Spain (2738), Germany (2641) and Greece (1790), with other countries far behind.[16] Thus on the level of explicit references in the text, France occupies a preponderant place in the *Encyclopédie*. While this position is not surprising given that it is, after all, a dictionary of the French language, nevertheless the frequency of occurrence underscores the dominance of the French presence in relation to other countries and thereby serves as a forceful reminder of the underlying tension between the *Encyclopédie*'s universal vocation and its mission with respect to the French language, between the generality of its message and the particularity of its linguistic vehicle. As Jaucourt points out in his article LANGUE, a language represents 'la totalité des usages propres à *une nation* pour exprimer ses pensées par la voix'. Looked at from this point of view, the 'voice' of the *Encyclopédie universelle* is that of the French nation. At the same time, the *Encyclopédie* is itself reworking the French language to adapt it to the universal perspective espoused by its editors. Thus the tension inherent in the double mission of the work – a universal encyclopedia as well as a dictionary of a specific, national

16. For example, Holland (995), Poland (779) and Russia (381). These figures are taken from the ARTFL electronic *Encyclopédie* in its current state. Since the initial entry there has been no systematic effort to correct data entry errors.

language – reveals itself to be a vector for establishing a reciprocal relationship between cosmopolitan universality and French national particularity as 'voiced' in its language.

As for the term 'nation(s)', it occurs 3646 times. Like the word 'peuple(s)' (9858 occurrences), it is often used to designate populations having the same 'birth' in the sense of being rooted in a place of birth or origin. Thus, for example, the *Cosaques* are defined as a 'nation située aux confins de la Pologne, de la Russie, de la Tartarie, & de la Turquie, comme les CARIPOUS sont un *peuple* de l'Amérique méridionale'. However *peuple*, unlike *nation*, can refer to a class: the *peuple* as opposed to the aristocracy or the bourgeoisie. In his article on the subject, Jaucourt takes note of the multiple layers and shifting nature of the term when he states: 'Nom collectif difficile à définir parce qu'on s'en forme des idées différentes dans les divers lieux, dans les divers tems, & selon la nature des gouvernemens [...]. Autrefois le peuple étoit l'état général de la nation, simplement opposé à celui des grands & des nobles', but now it is limited to workers and peasants (*ouvriers, laboureurs*). In sum, *peuple* can refer to part of a nation divided, as it were, as well as to the whole. For its part, *patrie* shows up 1255 times with particularly strong affective connotations generally linked to patriotic sentiments. *Nation*, on the other hand, turns out to be a more neutral manner of designating collectivities having the geographical, cultural and – at least potentially – political coherence to be a sovereign state.[17] While any full treatment of the subject would require analysis of all the major competing terms – *nation, peuple, patrie, royaume* – I will limit myself here to a discussion of *nation*, most notably as related to France. This, in turn, will perhaps shed further light on the place of France itself in relation to the general, universal project of the *Encyclopédie*. I have examined all the occurrences of the substantive 'nation(s)' as well as the adjectival forms of the word (*national/aux/ ale/ales*). They fall into three general categories: one such category could be described as geo-cultural; another is political in nature; and the third relates to economic issues.

As a point of departure, the paratextual elements – the 'Epître dédicatoire', the 'Discours préliminaire' and the 'Avertissements' – together with the article ENCYCLOPÉDIE constitute particularly fertile ground because of their strategic importance in defining the *Encyclopédie*, its mission, and its relationship to France in the particular context of the 1750s and 1760s. Indeed, a curious use of the term is to be found at the very beginning of the *Encyclopédie*. In the open letter that D'Alembert and Diderot address to the comte d'Argenson appealing for his protection and

---

17. As already mentioned, nations such as Italy or Germany were not sovereign states. The same can be said for the many tribes and ethnic groups described as nations in the *Encyclopédie*.

assuring him that by giving it, he will insure himself a glorious reputation amongst future generations, the editors stress the disinterested nature of their praise of the minister, but also their own power and authority. The minister's reputation and popularity at home and abroad, in the present as well as in the future, depends on the community of philosophers:

L'autorité suffit à un Ministre pour lui attirer l'hommage aveugle & suspect des Courtisans; mais elle ne peut rien sur le suffrage du Public, des Etrangers, & de la Postérité. C'est à la nation éclairée des Gens de Lettres, & sur-tout à la nation libre & desintéressée des Philosophes, que Vous devez, MONSEIGNEUR, l'estime générale, si flateuse pour qui sait penser, parce qu'on ne l'obtient que de ceux qui pensent.[18]

While only metaphorical, the idea that the *philosophes* constitute a *nation* is nonetheless somewhat surprising. Clearly the authors are transposing the notion of a Republic of Letters into that of a 'nation' of men of letters and philosophers. Their freedom and disinterestedness gives them great sway over enlightened public opinion. Yet the choice of metaphor reveals the importance and stature the term *nation* has acquired.[19]

The 'Discours préliminaire' confirms the importance of the notion and the term both directly and indirectly. While from a general point of view, the *Encyclopédie* may well wish to speak to (and for) all of humanity, when it comes to measuring the progress of philosophy, D'Alembert chooses the nation as the significant context. According to him, while arts and letters have progressed measurably since the Renaissance, the same cannot be said for philosophy, 'du moins dans chaque nation prise en corps' (i.xxiii). There is then a relative imbalance among nations in the quality of philosophic discourse. As compared to France, 'la Nation [anglaise] considère [ses Savants ...], elle les respecte même; & cette espece de récompense, supérieure à toutes les autres, est sans doute le moyen le plus sûr de faire fleurir les Sciences et les Arts' (i.xxxiii). The fundamental nature of relations between nations is agonistic. But competition also means emulation, and it is in France's national interest to equal or better the English by honouring its 'grands hommes', that is, those whose role is precisely that of rising above the national character, while the lot of '*les gens médiocres*' is to follow that of their nation. But the question remains as to the language in which these outstanding individuals should express their thoughts. D'Alembert explains that the triumph of the vernacular over Latin serves the goals of universality in that, on the national level – in principle at least – the

18. 'Epître dédicatoire'.

19. In the 1718 and 1740 editions of the *Dictionnaire de l'Académie*, the definitions contain a pejorative use of the term: 'Il se dit odieusement et par mespris, des personnes d'une certaine profession, d'une certain condition', and gives as examples: 'La nation des Pedants est une estrange nation, une nation incommode, c'est une meschante nation que les Laquais.' This usage disappears from the dictionary after the 1740 edition. Diderot's and D'Alembert's is indicative of the positive valence the term has acquired. See Le Guern, 'Le mot *nation*', p.163.

ideas are more accessible to all members of the community. Given the dominant position French achieved in Europe, it might have served as the best vehicle of expression on a broader scale. However, here too the principle of competition and emulation was maintained and led to a problem 'que nous aurions bien dû prévoir' (i.xxx):

> Les Savans des autres nations à qui nous avons donné l'exemple ont crû avec raison qu'ils écriroient encore mieux dans leur Langue que dans la nôtre. L'Angleterre nous a donc imité; l'Allemagne, où le Latin sembloit s'être réfugié, commence insensiblement à en perdre l'usage: je ne doute pas qu'elle ne soit bien-tôt suivie par les Suédois, les Danois, & les Russiens.

The very spread of enlightened thinking threatens to transform Europe into a tower of Babel in which the clarity of universal reason is obscured by the veils of national languages for the simple reason that 'les philosophes, comme les autres Ecrivains, veulent être lûs, & sur-tout de leur nation' (i.xxx). The fundamental tension once again becomes apparent: philosophical thought is anchored, so to speak, in the nation which also constitutes the principal public to which it addresses itself, but its goal is to rise above the nation and national character in order to attain and explore the higher reaches of universality.

This tension between the universal and the national structures the rhetoric of the 'Discours préliminaire' and is of strategic importance in that it allows D'Alembert to pit France against its political rival England in a race where France's handicaps are many: 'En effet notre nation, singulierement avide de nouveautés dans les matieres de goût, est au contraire en matiere de Science très-attachée aux opinions anciennes.' France's devotion to Descartes has transformed itself into a kind of national point of honour and become 'la honte de la philosophie' (i.xxix). Then there is the 'character' issue of France's '*légèreté*'. The very trait that worked to France's advantage in an era of taste when arts and manners were of primary importance has become an obstacle to its success in an age of philosophy. In fact France is now threatened by an excessive refinement of taste. Seen in this light, the challenge is a national one, and the 'Discours préliminaire' argues for making philosophy a national priority. The *Encyclopédie* is taking up the challenge by working to make France rise above its national character and serve all of humanity in the new age of philosophy.

This rhetoric emphasising the reciprocity between France and the *Encyclopédie* does not, of course, develop in a vacuum; it is very much motivated by prevailing politics and circumstances. While appealing to humanity as a whole is perhaps gratifying on many levels, the editors clearly understand how important government protection is to their success. The crisis of 1752 only serves to heighten their sense of fragility. The concrete effect of the *arrêt du conseil* does little more than delay the appearance of the third volume, but it certainly makes Diderot and D'Alembert aware of how vulnerable they are and elicits from them a set of strategic responses to parry the attacks by their enemies.[20] Most notable among these responses are their efforts to reinforce the rhetoric of the nation by insisting on the importance of the ties between the nation and the *Encyclopédie* and by highlighting foreign competition, above all that of England. We have already seen how the editors stressed their influence over the public in the 'Epître dédicatoire'. The third volume, the first to appear after the crisis of 1752, opens with a veritable manifesto justifying the project of the *Encyclopédie*. The 'Avertissement' does much more than appeal for the protection of the monarchy; it strategically deploys the notion of *nation* as a transcendent entity constituting a fundamental value and a finality unto itself. 'L'empressement que l'on a témoigné pour la continuation de ce Dictionnaire est le seul motif qui ait pû nous déterminer à le reprendre', states D'Alembert before going on to define the source of this enthusiasm: 'Le Gouvernement a parû desirer qu'une entreprise de cette nature ne fut point abandonnée; & *la Nation a usé du droit qu'elle avoit* de l'exiger de nous' (my italics). Having established a clear distinction between government and nation and affirmed that it is public opinion, the *'confiance publique'* that incites them to continue working, the encyclopedist discusses their decision and, in so doing, amply develops the effect and the content of the nation's exercise of its 'right':

Les circonstances nous y engagent, l'Encyclopédie le demande, la reconnoissance nous y oblige. Puissions-nous, en nous montrant tels que nous sommes, intéresser nos concitoyens en notre faveur! Leur *volonté* a eu sur nous d'autant plus de pouvoir, qu'en s'opposant à notre retraite, ils sembloient en approuver les motifs. Sans une *autorité* si respectable, les ennemis de cet Ouvrage seroient parvenus facilement à nous faire rompre des liens dont nous sentions tout le poids, mais dont nous n'avions pû prévoir tout le danger.

The nation acquires the power to confer a fundamental legitimacy and constitutes an effective force against the enemies of the *Encyclopédie*. In pursuing their work, the encyclopedists are doing nothing less than accomplishing their patriotic duty: 'Incapables de manquer à notre patrie, *qui est le seul objet dont l'expérience & la Philosophie ne nous ayent pas détachés* [...] nous serons [...] [h]eureux, si par notre ardeur & nos soins, nous pouvions engager tous les gens de lettres à contribuer à la perfection de cet Ouvrage, *la nation à le protéger, & les autres à le laisser faire.'*

The term *patrie* underscores the sentimental attachment to the nation which becomes the only object to which their experience and philosophy, with its universal goals and implications, have not shaken their devotion. The nation is the collective entity that survives philosophical doubt and the betrayals of daily experience. But who are *'les autres'* referred to in this passage? D'Alembert suggests that those who do not adhere to the project of the *Encyclopédie* are not part of the nation. From there to declaring the

---

20. On the possibility of pursuing publication outside France, see Jacques Proust, *Diderot et l'Encyclopédie* (Paris 1962), p.72-77.

philosophes martyrs for the cause, there is only a small step that D'Alembert does not hesitate to take: 'Nous nous trouvons, pour ainsi dire, au commencement d'un nouvel ordre de choses, nous sommes très-résolus de tout sacrifier désormais au bien de l'Encyclopédie.' The 'Avertissement' describes a clear reciprocal relationship between the nation and the *Encyclopédie*, with the nation taking on the role of the defender of the work and the universal perspective it espouses.

Denouncing the *Encyclopédie* for being a vehicle of the *philosophes*' ideas was one tactic employed by its enemies; another consisted in decrying its lack of originality and its incoherences. To respond to this challenge, D'Alembert, while stating that he is anything but a chauvinist, nevertheless notes that the original project of translating Chamber's *Cyclopedia* had been conceived by '*un Anglais*' with the help of '*un Allemand*'. Further, he points out that Chambers had himself heavily drawn on '*Dictionnaires françois*' and that, while Chambers does not cite his sources, 'l'*Encyclopédie françoise*' does its best to do so. The moral superiority of the 'French encyclopedia' over its English rival is clear; the encyclopedists are, in a sense, restoring to France what Chambers had taken without proper acknowledgement.

These polemical manoeuverings are doubtless a product of the crisis of 1752, but it is significant that in such a context the encyclopedists opt for the language and set of arguments they deem will have the greatest impact. For this, they choose to appeal to the authority of the nation rather than that of the monarchy and to evoke a foreign adversary. By the will of the Nation and in competition with a foreign adversary, the French *Encyclopédie* positions itself aggressively both as an achievement of national solidarity and as a means of assuring that France will fulfil the promise of the 'nation of *philosophes*'.

These arguments give fuller meaning to the words of Diderot, when, in the article ENCYCLOPÉDIE, he reflects with a more than a wisp of sadness on the transient nature of the project he has undertaken: 'Mais ce qui donnera à l'ouvrage l'air suranné, & le jettera dans le mépris, c'est surtout la révolution qui se fera dans l'esprit des hommes, & dans le caractere national.' By the very goals the encyclopedia sets for itself, it is, in a sense, striving for its own obsolescence. But particularly intriguing in Diderot's formulation is the juxtaposition of the universal ('*l'esprit des hommes*') and the national ('*le caractère national*'). In this passage the fundamental difference seems to lie in the distinction between *esprit* and *caractère*. The movement from the minds of men to national temperament implies a shift from the abstract generalisation concerning the intellect of humankind to the cultural reality of the nation. While the way of reasoning can be modified in humanity conceived of as the sum of all individuals, the way of being in the world has to be considered from the perspective of insertion in society. The nation reveals itself to be the compelling instantiation of civil society. A revolution in the national character implies not simply a reform of laws and institutions, but a transformation in the collective psychology and way of being together.

A similar juxtaposition occurs in the famous passage in the same article in which Diderot continues his reflection on the constraints and limits imposed by the passage of time.

Dans un vocabulaire, dans un dictionnaire universel & raisonné, dans tout ouvrage destiné à l'instruction générale des hommes, il faut donc commencer par envisager son objet sous les faces les plus étendues, connoître l'*esprit de sa nation*, en pressentir la pente, le gagner de vîtesse, ensorte qu'il ne laisse pas votre travail en arriere; mais qu'au contraire il le rencontre en avant; se résoudre à ne travailler que pour les générations suivantes, parce que le moment où nous existons passe, & qu'à peine une grande entreprise sera-t-elle achevée, que la génération présente ne sera plus. Mais pour être plus longtems utile & nouveau, en devançant de plus loin l'*esprit national* qui marche sans cesse, il faut abreger la durée du travail, en multipliant le nombre des collegues.[21]

The opening clause affirms the universal mission of the work and seems to echo other passages from the same article describing the *Encyclopédie* as an 'ouvrage composé par des philosophes, & adressé à tous les hommes & à tous les tems' or defining 'un dictionnaire universel & raisonné' as being for 'l'instruction générale & permanente de l'espece humaine'. Yet the rest of the passage seems to abandon the more general and abstract perspective in favour of a particularly national one. The encyclopedist needs to under-stand the spirit of the nation, its temperament and mindset, in order to anticipate its evolution. Although the *Encyclopédie* is, so to speak, doomed to become obsolete, it should struggle to prolong its useful life as much as possible. While on an abstract level the encyclopedia seeks universality and immortality, when confronted with the contingencies of time and politics, it is forced to situate itself on another plane. In some sense the choice lies between the ideal and the real, between the abstract and the concrete, a choice inscribed in the initial project of a comprehensive dictionary of the sciences, arts, and trades, and one that goes to the very heart of the *philo-sophes'* mission. As we have seen, when threatened by politics the encyclope-dists appeal to the nation. Now, when confronting the more existential and inexorable menace of time, seen not as the promise of unlimited progress of humanity but as the necessary movement toward their own irrelevance and obsolescence, the editors turn not to abstractions such as humanity or society in general but to the collective entity of the nation. It is as if the notion of nation represented a satisfactory middle ground between abstract, universal entities such as 'humanity' or 'society' and other, more concrete entities that reveal themselves to be unacceptable because they are too limited in scale or represent particular forms of government (such as monarchy or realm). 'Nation' is a neutral term in that it can be applied to countries with any and all forms of government. It suggests a social

21. ENCYCLOPÉDIE, v.637.

solidarity and organisation of a scale that allows for the deployment of the discourse of universality, while at the same having the existential reality that encourages the development of concrete strategies. Traditional classifications of 'national temperament' imply a certain sense of critical (and even ironic) distance that allows for judgements on the entity as a whole and designates a kind of collective psychology. Not only is nation an intuitively 'real' object, it is also free of the strong affective charge of *patrie*, and is closer in nature to objects of knowledge than to objects of unreasoned affection. Endowed with these traits, the notion of 'nation' as it functions in the *Encyclopédie* reveals itself to have profound affinities with the ideology of the Enlightenment.

By juxtaposing the universal and the national, Diderot and D'Alembert are making of the later a privileged place for achieving goals formulated in terms of the former. Seen in this light, the relationship between the particularity of a dictionary of the French language and the universal mission of instructing the human race becomes clearer: 'La langue d'un peuple donne son vocabulaire, & le vocabulaire est une table assez fidele de toutes les connoissances de ce peuple: sur la seule comparaison du vocabulaire d'une nation en différens tems, on se formeroit une idée de ses progrès.' From this point of view, France has an indisputable advantage:

Il me paroît démontré que l'esprit humain a fait plus de progrès chez un des peuples que chez l'autre. On ne sait pas encore, ce me semble, combien la langue est une image rigoureuse & fidele de l'exercice de la raison. Quelle prodigieuse supériorité une nation acquiert sur une autre, sur-tout dans les sciences abstraites & les Beaux-Arts, par cette seule différence! & à quelle distance les Anglois sont encore de nous par la considération seule que notre langue est faite, & qu'ils ne songent pas encore à former la leur! C'est de la perfection de l'idiome que dépendent & l'exactitude dans les sciences rigoureuses, & le goût dans les Beaux-Arts, & par conséquent l'immortalité des ouvrages en ce genre.[22]

Whatever problems might plague France, the state of its language makes French the right choice for a truly universal encyclopedia. In the race for enlightenment, France has in its language a distinct advantage over its principal rival, England. This linguistic advantage reflects a larger one, for, in as much as language is 'une image rigoureuse & fidele de l'exercice de la raison', France is positioned at the forefront of the philosophical revolution based on the universal truths and values that will eventually transform all of humanity. But it is important to note to what extent Diderot dematerialises the image of France in these passages. This France is one of literature and abstract reasoning. The *Encyclopédie* will, of course, play a crucial role in perfecting the idiom, in moving it from a kind of instinctive genius to the plane of the philosophic project. 'Le génie ne connoît point les regles; cependant il ne s'en écarte jamais dans ses succès. La Philosophie ne connoît que les regles fondées dans la nature des êtres, qui est immuable &

22. ENCYCLOPÉDIE, v.638.

éternelle. C'est au siecle passé à fournir des exemples; c'est à notre siecle à prescrire les regles.' Thanks to the *Encyclopédie*, itself a concrete manifestation of a broader philosophical movement, the coming of enlightenment will occur first in a France destined to become the philosophical beacon among nations.

To this idealisation of France in the name of universal goals that lie beyond its particularity corresponds a very different orientation that tends to give France a central place in the more concrete world of everyday objects and practices. Besides the 'enlightened' dematerialisation of France constructed largely, but by no means exclusively, in the paratextual and metatextual elements of the *Encyclopédie*, there is another, much less ideologically marked orientation toward a constant materialisation of France, to which references are legion in this dictionary of sciences, arts, and trades. They manifest themselves in the 13,500 occurrences of the terms *France, françois, françoise(s)* in 5000 of the 45,000 main articles.[23] They are found in descriptions of institutions (the *parlements*, the university, the Estates) and their procedures and activities. They turn up in descriptions of mores and in reflections on daily life that use France as a primary reference point.

BUFFET, s. f. (*terme d'Architecture*) c'étoit chez les anciens de petits appartemens séparés du reste de la salle, pour y ranger la porcelaine, les vases; & en France dans les derniers siecles, les buffets se mettoient dans les salles à manger, & servoient autant pour y dresser les choses utiles pour le service de la table, que pour y étaler la richesse & la magnificence des princes ou des particuliers qui donnoient des festins. Aujourd'hui dans les maisons de quelqu'importance, on place les buffets dans des pieces séparées.

The buffet is, practically from the outset, placed in a French perspective that expands outwards and becomes subtly more general as the author moves into the contemporary period while at the same time dropping clear markers of national specificity. Thus, the houses of a certain importance that the author evokes are delocalised, so to speak, and the subjects positioning the furniture are introduced by the general, indefinite pronoun *on*.

The geography of France is well represented in the *Encyclopédie*. More than 25% of the occurrences of the term 'France' are to be found in entries whose subject is classified as 'geography'. France affirms its presence in articles on its rivers and plains, on its cities as well as on its architecture. In the Blondel's article CHAPELLE, defined as 'la partie d'une église consacrée à quelque dévotion particuliere', one finds: 'L'on voit en France de ces [chapelles] placées avec trop de négligence, contre toute idée de bienséance. Dans le nombre de celles qui méritent quelque considération, & qui font partie de la magnificence de nos palais, celles du château de Fresne, de Choisi, & de Sceaux, tiennent le premier rang, après celles de Versailles &

23. These numbers are to be taken only as indicative; they include, for example, occurrences of the proper names *François* and *Françoise*.

de Fontainebleau, &c.' After the initial reference to France criticising the often too casual placement of chapels comes a short list of more positive examples, all in France and attached to 'our' magnificent palaces. Throughout the *Encyclopédie*, the use of the personal pronoun *nous* and the possessive adjectives *notre* and *nos* reinforces the status of France as the fundamental point of reference.

These allusions sometimes take the form of praise, as in the article DÉCORATION, where France is cited as a model for all nations:

La décoration intérieure a pour objet la magnificence des appartemens. Cette partie de l'Architecture est sans contredit celle qui, après la distribution, fait le plus d'honneur à la France; & on peut avancer qu'à l'exception de quelques ornemens peut-être trop frivoles que nos sculpteurs ont introduits dans leurs décorations, il n'est point de nation, sans excepter l'Italie, qui entende aussi-bien cette partie que nous.

Often, on the other hand, these references to France carry condemnations and criticisms. Nevertheless, be it to praise or to condemn, these allusions signal the prominent place of France and strengthen its position in the *Encyclopédie*. Take, for example, the way D'Alembert criticises French education in his article COLLEGE:

Au reste, si l'éducation de la jeunesse est négligée, ne nous en prenons qu'à nous-mêmes, & au peu de considération que nous témoignons à ceux qui s'en chargent; c'est le fruit de cet esprit de futilité qui regne dans notre nation, & qui absorbe, pour ainsi dire, tout le reste. En France on sait peu de gré à quelqu'un de remplir les devoirs de son état; on aime mieux qu'il soit frivole.

The collective subject here is 'we' French, and D'Alembert invokes the frivolous temperament that reigns in 'our nation' in order to criticise French education, the aims of which should, but do not, correspond to the *philosophes'* programme. The *topos* of the French national character constitutes one of the principal axes along which a host of articles praise, condemn or simply describe the state of affairs in France. Positively it is often expressed in terms of sociability or gaiety; the negative side of the coin is formulated in terms of frivolity. It constitutes the point of departure for Voltaire's famous article FRANÇOIS and resurfaces in articles on a range of subjects, from gallantry and taste to music, architecture, theatre, and even military arts.

Far from embracing uniquely the position of the *philosophes*, these articles represent a broad spectrum of ideological positions. Thus, while in the paratext the editors successfully position the *Encyclopédie* as a forward looking work at the avant-garde of contemporary thought, the reality of the work taken as a whole is, as we know, very different. Many of the entries are tradition bound and happy to be so. The legends of the extensive set of plates on heraldry, for example, often refer to France. From the point of view of the presence of France in the *Encyclopédie*, articles, composed from very different, at times incompatible, ideological positions, work harmoniously together to reinforce its position and assure its prominence in a work that defines itself not only as a philosophical enterprise, but also a national monument.

If references to France place it at the 'centre' of the *Encyclopédie*, the use of the word 'nation' designates the so-named collective entities as the strategically privileged arena for implementing universal values and endeavours. This tendency manifests itself in often unexpected contexts, and one way to understand its importance is through comparison with other definitions. Take, for example, the definition of word *'illustre'* in the *Dictionnaire de l'Académie* (1694): '*Illustre.* adj. de tout genre. Esclatant, celebre par le merite, par la noblesse, ou par quelque autre chose de loüable & d'extraordinaire. *Un homme illustre. les hommes illustres de Plutarque. une race illustre. une maison, une famille illustre. il s'est rendu illustre par ses grandes actions, par sa vertu, par ses ouvrages'.* Fame is defined in terms of the action or quality that leads to celebrity. The definition can be characterised as universal in the sense that fame develops not in relation to any specific collectivity, but rather in terms of an abstraction which could be understood as mankind (*l'homme en général*). Such is not the case in the anonymous article on the subject in the *Encyclopédie*: 'ILLUSTRE, ILLUSTRATION, S'ILLUSTRER (*Gramm.*) un homme illustre est celui *qui a mérité l'estime & la considération générale de sa nation, par quelque qualité excellente.* On peut naître d'une maison illustre, & n'être qu'un homme ordinaire, & réciproquement. Plutarque a écrit la vie des hommes illustres, grecs & romains'.[24] In this entry, fame is defined above all in terms of the nation. Like the philosophers writing to be read in their own nations and the editors of the *Encyclopédie* acting in response to the citizens of their nation exercising their 'right' to demand the completion of the *Dictionnaire raisonné des arts, des sciences et des métiers,* those who acquire fame do so in the context of the nation. This type of transformation in which what could be considered a universal value or truth is placed in the context of the nation crops in up several significant contexts concerning the economy.

Such is the case for the noun *journalier,* for which the Académie furnishes the following meaning: 'Quelquefois il signifie, Un homme travaillant à la journée, & alors il est substantif. *C'est un pauvre journalier. le roolle* [*sic*] *des journaliers. payer des journaliers.'*[25] Turning to the *Encyclopédie,* one finds an article written by Diderot. 'JOURNALIER; s. m. (*Gramm.*) ouvrier qui travaille de ses mains, & qu'on paye au jour la journée. Cette espece d'hommes forment la plus grande partie d'une nation; c'est son sort qu'un bon gouvernement doit avoir principalement en vûe. Si le journalier est misérable, la nation est misérable.' The same phenomenon occurs in the anonymously composed discussion of *laboureurs* (ix.148):

24. There are three articles on the word 'illustre': CELEBRE, ILLUSTRE, FAMEUX, RENOMME; ILLUSTRE, ILLUSTRATION; ILLUSTRE.
25. Antoine Furetière's *Dictionnaire universel* gives the following definition: 'se dit en quelques endroits, d'un ouvrier qui travaille à la journée'.

LABOUREUR, s. m. (*Econom. rustiq.*) Ce n'est point cet homme de peine, ce mercenaire qui panse les chevaux ou les bœufs, & qui conduit la charrue. On ignore ce qu'est cet état, & encore plus ce qu'il doit être, si l'on y attache des idées de grossiereté, d'indigence & de mépris. Malheur au pays où il seroit vrai que le laboureur est un homme pauvre: ce ne pourroit être que dans une nation qui le seroit elle-même, & chez laquelle une décadence progressive se feroit bientôt sentir par les plus funestes effets [...]. La richesse plus ou moins grande des laboureurs peut être un thermometre fort exact de la prospérité d'une nation qui a un grand territoire.

The status of the farmer differs markedly from that of the day labourer, but both articles have recourse to the nation as the touchstone of value. In each case, the author casts a critical gaze on the scandalous situation of these categories of workers, as it exists in France, with the clear implication that the country should implement reforms to remedy the problem. The argument is formulated not in terms of humankind or society in general, but in relation to the well-being of the nation. It is universal in that it concerns all nations, whatever form of government they might be under: 'Cette espèce d'hommes forment la plus grande partie d'une nation [...]. La richesse plus ou moins grande des laboureurs peut être un thermometre fort exact de la prospérité d'une nation qui a un grand territoire' (ix.148). In both cases the reference to France is apparent to the reader, but each preserves its general formulation. France would thus be a particular case, or, perhaps we should say *the* case par excellence. These articles illustrate in a striking manner how the universal is conceived in terms of the national. Behind this nationalisation of the universal looms the image of France as the principal illustration, be it as example or counter example. In a wide range of areas, the nation has become the fundamental collective entity for conceptualising and describing the general welfare. No article explains more fully the dynamics behind this evolution than Rousseau's article ECONOMIE (v.341):

Il semble que le sentiment de l'humanité s'évapore & s'affoiblisse en s'étendant sur toute la terre, & que nous ne saurions être touchés des calamités de la Tartarie ou du Japon, comme de celles d'un peuple européen. Il faut en quelque maniere borner & comprimer l'intérêt & la commisération pour lui donner de l'activité. Or comme ce penchant en nous ne peut être utile qu'à ceux avec qui nous avons à vivre, il est bon que l'humanité concentrée entre les concitoyens, prenne en eux une nouvelle force par l'habitude de se voir, & par l'intérêt commun qui les réunit. Il est certain que les plus grands prodiges de vertu ont été produits par l'amour de la patrie: ce sentiment doux & vif qui joint la force de l'amour propre à toute la beauté de la vertu, lui donne une énergie qui sans la défigurer, en fait la plus héroïque de toutes les passions.

Once again Rousseau strikes the limits of Enlightenment thought, and in so doing he goes to the heart of a fundamental paradox at work in the *Encyclopédie*. While formulating its scope and principles on the level of humankind and universality, the *Dictionnaire raisonné* nevertheless returns constantly to the national as the collective entity in which functions an effective sentiment of human solidarity and interest. With its underlying attachment to place, its historical application to a collective way of being or temperament, its connotations of cultural unity, and its 'political' neutrality freeing it from attachment to any particular form of government, the term nation itself acquires a universal value ideal for designating the domain for implementing in the real world the ideals espoused by the editors. France's place in the *Encyclopédie*'s world of nations is a privileged one for it is the nation of reference. Far from detracting from its position, the ideological diversity of the authors works hand in hand with the fundamental paradox to strengthen France's place in this massive dictionary. Through a mixture of interest, passion, and principle, the *Encyclopédie* establishes itself as a national monument and places France in the universalist perspective of its editors. France becomes the *Encyclopédie*'s leading candidate for rising to the challenge posed by the work itself and leading the world of nations into the age of philosophy.

PIERRE SAINT-AMAND

Les progrès de la civilité dans l'*Encyclopédie*

LE 'Discours préliminaire' de l'*Encyclopédie* de D'Alembert ne considère que l'aventure intellectuelle humaine; elle ne touche que superficiellement à l'histoire sociologique; elle offre une spéculation minimale de la genèse de la culture. L'objet du 'Discours' comme celui de l'*Encyclopédie* essentiellement, est de considérer 'les progrès de l'esprit' (i.xix). D'Alembert offre une origine utilitariste à la société humaine, dégagée du sensationnisme (i.iii):

à peine commençons-nous à parcourir ces objets [extérieurs], que nous découvrons parmi eux un grand nombre d'êtres qui nous paraissent entièrement semblables à nous, c'est-à-dire dont la forme est toute pareille à la nôtre, et qui autant que nous en pouvons juger au premier coup d'œil, semblent avoir les mêmes perceptions que nous: tout nous porte donc à penser qu'ils ont aussi les mêmes besoins que nous éprouvons, et par conséquent le même intérêt à les satisfaire; d'où il résulte que nous devons trouver beaucoup d'avantage à nous unir avec eux pour démêler dans la nature ce qui peut nous conserver ou nous nuire.

La genèse sociale coïncide avec l'invention des langues. La communication sociale est à penser avant tout comme communication des idées. Les notions juridiques et métaphysiques découleront de ce premier commerce. D'Alembert examine également le vivre-ensemble sous l'angle des passions, ce qui le mène à distinguer l'éloquence comme une des branches essentielles de la connaissance humaine et l'histoire comme effort de projection dominatrice des hommes à la fois sur le passé et l'avenir (i.x).

Si j'évoque ce parcours du 'Discours préliminaire', c'est pour considérer un autre domaine de l'*Encyclopédie*, celui des mœurs et de leur évolution. Y a-t-il un progrès des mœurs comparable à celui de l'esprit? Et comment se traduirait cette évolution? Nous pensons ici au fameux 'progrès de la civilisation' étudié par le sociologue Norbert Elias et dont les manifestations dans les sociétés occidentales sont les mutations pacifiques du comportement des hommes qui vont s'accomplir dans l'étiquette, le savoir-vivre, bref la civilité. Elias isole cette dynamique particulière de la civilité, en fait son essence: 'L'observation minutieuse des différences hiérarchiques sera, dorénavant – au moins en France – le critère même de la politesse, la condition *sine qua non* de la "civilité".' Aristocrates et intellectuels bourgeois entretiennent des rapports mondains, mais le tact exige de respecter les différences d'état et d'en tenir compte dans les relations sociales.[1]

---

1. Norbert Elias, *La Civilisation des mœurs*, tr. Pierre Kamnitzer (Paris 1973), p.107.

La référence éliasienne servira ici de guide à la vérification, à partir d'une série d'articles de l'*Encyclopédie*, de la façon dont se trouve pensée la hiérarchie, à l'ombre de l'appareil étatique de l'Ancien Régime. Quoique engagés dans un débat intellectuel, nous savons que les encyclopédistes n'ont pas cessé de s'engager dans la poursuite d'une réforme sociale et politique, qui concerne toutes les institutions qui structurent et symbolisent l'ancienne société. Le 'progrès de l'esprit' entrevu par D'Alembert ne pourra être assuré, nous le savons rétrospectivement, que par un progrès qui affecte toute la communauté humaine, celui des mœurs. Ce combat de l'esprit, constamment brandi en avant, ne cessera de façon souvent secrète, en sourdine (si on reprend ici la lettre de la pensée de Diderot dans l'article ENCYCLOPÉDIE), de construire l'avancée politique. Il faudra suivre, à partir d'un jeu d'articles et de l'écho stratégique qu'ils entretiennent entre eux, dans le paysage des renvois, comment se construit cette machine d'opposition et de réfutation des préjugés nationaux qu'envisageait Diderot dans le fameux article.[2] Les encyclopédistes sont eux-mêmes, pour la plupart, ces 'intellectuels bourgeois' dont parle Elias mais qui pousseront la civilité au-delà du rapport conservateur et accommodateur de tact et de respect avec leurs partenaires aristocrates pour repenser de fond en comble l'arbitraire de la pesante hiérarchie.

Un des lieux pour débuter l'examen de cette question dans l'*Encyclopédie* est l'article CIVILITÉ, POLITESSE, AFFABILITÉ, signé par Louis de Jaucourt, à partir duquel nous partirons pour essayer d'analyser cette perspective (iii.497). Si Jaucourt considère ensemble civilité et politesse, c'est en fait pour dévaloriser la politesse. Il s'agit de l'accaparement de certaines règles par une classe sociale, la cour. La politesse est avant tout cérémonie. L'effort que fait Jaucourt est de donner un fondement anthropologique à la civilité, comme pratique de distinction entre les hommes, comme obligation de porter du respect à autrui. En fait, il s'agit pour lui de trouver un fondement politique et juridique à la notion. On peut voir que Jaucourt vise à asseoir la civilité dans le droit naturel, qu'elle soit une pratique valable 'pour le plus grand nombre de citoyens'. Plutôt que la pratique arbitraire et exclusive d'une classe, il essaye de l'envisager comme guidée par la raison, par un 'sentiment intérieur': 'La civilité [...] a un prix réel; regardée comme un empressement de porter du respect et des égards aux autres, par un sentiment intérieur conforme à la raison, c'est une pratique de droit naturel, d'autant plus louable qu'elle est libre et bien fondée.'

Comment faire de la civilité, non plus seulement l'apanage artificiel de quelques hommes mais l'artefact symbolique de l'humain, une inclination profonde, dictée par le sentiment d'autrui. Jaucourt évoque Sparte et la

---

2. ENCYCLOPÉDIE, v.635-48. Je me permets de renvoyer à mon analyse de la stratégie des renvois telle qu'elle est pensée par Diderot dans mon livre *Diderot, le labyrinthe de la relation* (Paris 1984), p.71-73. On devrait reprendre ici les mots fabuleux de Diderot, indiquant l'avantage des renvois polémiques: 'L'ouvrage entier en recevrait une force interne et une utilité secrète, dont les effets sourds seraient nécessairement sensibles avec le temps.'

Chine où la civilité s'est répandue au plus grand nombre, à la faveur de lois bien intériorisées imposant la réciprocité, la 'dépendance' des uns aux autres. Les règles de la civilité, ajoute-t-il, y ont trouvé 'la plus grande étendue'.

Il faut voir dans le texte de Jaucourt et son rejet de la politesse plus qu'une simple critique, une dénonciation des usages mondains, mais l'établissement d'une notion à répercussion juridique. L'évocation du texte de Montesquieu, *De l'esprit des lois*, dans l'article de Jaucourt est en ce sens bien choisi tout autant que les références à d'autres cultures (la Chine, Lacédémone). Jaucourt universalise le principe de civilité plutôt que d'en faire la chasse gardée des cours européennes.

Roger Chartier, dans un texte décisif sur la généalogie et les avatars de la notion de civilité, avait déjà montré comment la distinction opérée par Jaucourt entre civilité et politesse, distinction s'étayant sur le texte de Montesquieu, gagne en fait le siècle. La réhabilitation de la notion de civilité prend alors une dimension éthique: la civilité devient pratique morale. C'est bien le sens de la différenciation effectuée selon lui par l'*Esprit des lois*. Chartier précise ainsi son propos: 'Le texte de Montesquieu désigne donc avec acuité l'espace social dans lequel s'inscrit la civilité: le resserrement des dépendances entre les hommes, lié à la différenciation accrue entre les hommes [...] [la civilité] garantit des relations sociales disciplinées et soustraites à la violence ou à la corruption.'[3]

On peut dire que la réévaluation de Jaucourt situe la question de la civilité au cœur d'une crise de la considération qui atteint l'Ancien Régime, dans l'attente de son dépassement. Un réseau d'articles dans l'*Encyclopédie* témoigne du même glissement des notions, d'un attachement à de nouvelles valeurs. Le rééquilibrage éthico-juridique de la civilité se répercute dans l'ensemble des articles qui analysent l'appareil des égards dûs à autrui. En effet, l'*Encyclopédie* se révèle le terrain fertile d'une remise en cause des notions traditionnelles de respect et de considération, celles appartenant à la société hiérarchique d'Ancien Régime. L'historien Alan Forrest nous rappelait ainsi les valeurs de la sociabilité de la France du dix-huitième siècle: 'le respect du statut légal, le maintien des ordres et des états, l'honneur surtout, exprimé dans le devoir du service à la fois civique et militaire. La société était fondée sur le respect de l'ordre social existant, ce qui nécessitait une inégalité essentielle entre les hommes, reconnue par l'Etat et renforcée par le système judiciaire.'[4]

Sans aucune surprise, les collaborateurs de l'*Encyclopédie* tiennent à inscrire un changement dans cette perspective, ils enregistrent les modifications de la notion. Jaucourt, dans l'article RESPECT (*Société civile.*), voit déjà l'arbitraire de la notion associée à 'la supériorité du rang' (xiv.181). Il

3. Roger Chartier, 'Distinction et divulgation: la civilité et ses livres', *Lectures et lecteurs dans la France d'Ancien Régime* (Paris 1987), p.73.
4. Alan Forrest, 'Respect et reconnaissance dans la France révolutionnaire' in *La Considération*, éd. C. Haroche et J.-C. Vatin (Paris 1998), p.59.

prône plutôt celle du mérite qui ne s'appuie pas sur des 'marques extérieu-res' mais sur les valeurs de la 'personne': 'Rien de si triste qu'un grand sei-gneur sans vertus, accablé d'honneurs et de respects, à qui l'on fait sentir à tous moments, qu'on ne les rend, qu'on ne les doit qu'à sa naissance, à sa dignité, et qu'on ne doit rien à sa personne.'

Quand Duclos rédige l'article ETIQUETTE (*Histoire mod.*), qu'il définit comme ce 'cérémonial [...] qui règle les devoirs à l'égard des rangs, des places et des dignités', il évoque un rituel arbitraire, artificiel, établi à défaut de la sanction du vrai mérite. Si l'étiquette garantit l'ordre social, Duclos est conscient cependant des inégalités et des abus exprimés par ces formes de la vieille hiérarchie:

> comme la noblesse et plusieurs autres distinctions sont devenues héréditaires; qu'il est arrivé que des enfants n'ont pas eu le mérite de leurs pères; qu'il y a eu nécessai-rement dans la distribution des places, des abus qu'il n'est pas toujours possible de prévenir ou de réparer, il a été nécessaire de ne pas laisser les particuliers juges des égards qu'ils voudraient avoir, et des devoirs qu'ils auraient à rendre, la philosophie même, et par conséquent la justice, ont obligé d'établir des règles de subordination.

Ces marques extérieures peuvent devenir excessives et Duclos met bien en garde que 'l'étiquette s'étend à mesure que le mérite diminue' (vi.58).

La quête d'une reconnaissance générale se poursuit parallèlement dans d'autres articles qui dénoncent les fondements de la considération dans l'ancienne société. Dans l'article CONSIDÉRATION, rédigé cette fois par D'Alembert, l'auteur revoit l'ensemble des notions de sociabilité tels qu''égards', 'respect', 'déférence', et met en garde le lecteur ainsi: 'Il ne faut point, dit un auteur moderne, confondre la considération avec la réputa-tion: celle-ci est en général le fruit des talents ou du savoir-faire; celle-là est attachée à la place, au crédit, aux richesses, ou en général au besoin qu'on a de ceux à qui on l'accorde' (iv.43). L'article RÉPUTATION (*Morale*) conti-nue l'esprit du texte de D'Alembert, essayant de définir plus avant la répu-tation, et donnant au mot une contextualisation morale (xiv.161-62). Il va plus loin que D'Alembert et appuie la notion sur la raison. La réputation est obligation; elle n'a de sens que dans un horizon d'universalité. La quête de réputation est en fait fondée sur un sentiment naturel: 'ce serait aller contre la raison qui nous oblige d'avoir égard à ce qu'approuvent les hommes, ou à ce qu'ils improuvent le plus universellement et le plus constamment'.

Le désir de réputation obéit en effet à une mécanique particulière. Il est lié à la reconnaissance de l'estime. Or ce sentiment transcende l'univers des hommes. Il s'agit d'un sentiment moral quasi divin qui s'impose malgré l'aléa de l'humain et de la temporalité. En effet, l'estime d'autrui est tou-jours relayée par une estime supérieure. Celle-ci est hors d'atteinte de la particularité et de la fragilité des hommes. Suivons bien l'argument de l'article:

> [Les hommes] méconnaissent quelque fois la vertu; mais ils sont obligés souvent de la reconnaître; et alors ils ne manquent point de l'honorer: être donc insensible, par

cet endroit, à l'honneur, je veux dire à l'estime, à l'approbation et au témoignage que la connaissance des hommes rend à la vertu, ce serait l'être en quelque sorte à la vertu même, qui y serait intéressée.

La vertu est la référence universelle. Elle fait le poids de l'unanimité du jugement des hommes. On comprend pourquoi l'auteur peut conclure:

L'estime des hommes en particulier étant plus subordonnée à leur imagination qu'à la Providence, nous la devons compter pour peu de chose ou pour rien; c'est-à-dire que nous devons toujours la mériter, sans nous soucier de l'obtenir: la mériter par notre vertu, qui contribue à notre bonheur et à celui des autres; nous soucier peu de l'obtenir, par une noble égalité d'âme qui nous mette au-dessus de l'inconstance et de la vanité particulière des hommes. Recherchons l'approbation d'une conscience éclairée, que la haine et la calomnie ne peuvent nous enlever, par préférence à l'estime des autres hommes qui suit tôt ou tard la vertu.

Comme on le voit, le texte opère une série de glissements: de l'honneur à l'estime à la vertu. Il faut donc regarder ces notions de plus près. Examinons d'abord l'article ESTIME (*Droit natur.*), écrit par Jaucourt (v.1003-5). Le Chevalier reconnaît tout de suite le piège de l'estime, en particulier celui de l'estime de distinction. Comment en effet assumer que des hommes naturellement égaux dans l'état de nature reconnaissent la supériorité d'un autre? Qu'est-ce qui peut justifier cette posture d'abaissement? Tout de suite est rejeté ce que le philosophe considère 'hors de nous': 'la noblesse, les biens, les dignités, les honneurs'. Il y a aussi l'estime accordée par le souverain qui distribue les dignités. Mais Jaucourt conclut que la véritable estime 'ne s'accorde qu'au mérite'. Citant tout de suite La Bruyère pour expliquer le penchant des hommes pour l'estime imposée – celle qu'accordent 'les éminentes dignités et les grands titres' – Jaucourt se conforte encore une fois finalement dans le mérite de la *personne*. Le Chevalier cite à l'appui Montaigne, enlevant un à un ses simulacres au mannequin de l'homme: 'Il le faut juger par lui-même, non par ses atours; et comme le remarque très plaisamment un ancien, savez-vous pourquoi vous l'estimez grand? vous y comptez la hauteur de ses patins; la base n'est pas de la statue. Mesurez-le sans ses échasses; qu'il mette à part ses richesses et honneurs, qu'il se présente en chemise.'

Dans l'article MÉRITE (*Droit nat.*), Jaucourt finit par placer cette notion sous l'égide du droit naturel (x.388). C'est pour lui une 'qualité qui donne droit de prétendre à l'approbation, à l'estime et à la bienveillance de nos supérieurs ou de nos égaux et aux avantages qui en ont une suite'. Evitant de nouveau le mérite immédiat que peut accorder la naissance et les richesses, Jaucourt cherche un autre fondement transcendant au mérite. C'est la vertu qui apparaît à l'horizon de sa pensée. De même, il cherche la rationalité et l'universalité du jugement d'estime:

nous sommes faits de telle manière que la perfection et l'ordre nous plaisent par eux-mêmes, et que l'imperfection, le désordre et tout ce qui y a rapport nous déplaît naturellement. En conséquence nous reconnaissons que ceux qui répondant à leur destination font ce qu'ils doivent et contribuent au bien du système de l'humanité, sont dignes de notre approbation, de notre estime et de notre bienveillance; qu'ils peuvent raisonnablement exiger de nous ces sentiments, et qu'ils ont quelque droit aux effets qui en sont les suites naturelles.

La notion d'honneur, clef de voûte de la symbolique sociale de l'Ancien Régime, doit finalement dans ce contexte perdre son sens. L'auteur de l'article HONNEUR (*Morale*), Saint-Lambert, retrace une généalogie de l'honneur dans les sociétés et sa corruption (viii.288-90). L'honneur se civilise mais jusque dans les abus. Il s'annule par exemple dans la distinction donnée à la naissance, aux emplois ou aux richesses. L'honneur se dégrade en 'honneurs', en distinction arbitraires et imméritées. L'honneur, que considère l'encyclopédiste, le véritable, va devoir 's'épurer'. Il est en effet disjoint des préjugés de classe. Il devient la 'vertu' du citoyen: 'la conscience de son amour pour ses devoirs, pour les principes de la vertu et le témoignage qu'il se rend à lui-même et qu'il attend des autres, qu'il remplit ses devoirs, et qu'il sait les principes'.

Diderot est sensible à cette modification des notions que nous avançons ici. S'il n'est l'auteur d'aucun article sur cette question, on peut dire que son fameux dialogue, *Le Neveu de Rameau*, témoigne de cette crise de la considération sous l'Ancien Régime et que son texte fournit une étonnante peinture de la crise des divisions dans l'ancienne société. C'est en tout cas l'honneur, comme moteur de la société hiérarchique, que le texte de Diderot met très tôt à l'épreuve. Il est de ces 'vieux propos qui ne signifient rien'.[5] Dans *Le Neveu*, la considération telle qu'elle est instituée dans les mœurs est menacée. La déférence, les égards pivotent vers le négatif. Devant un philosophe qui incarne encore la civilité, Diderot place un personnage insensible à la considération respectueuse. Le vagabond de Diderot conteste le système des égards par rapport à ses trois exigences traditionnelles: l'âge, le mérite et plus généralement la dignité.

Le texte de Diderot est surtout une attaque contre le mérite des grands hommes. Les qualifications qui pouvaient justifier leur imitation, l'obligation donc de les suivre, ont perdu leur prestige. Ainsi: 'On loue la vertu; mais on la hait; mais on la fuit; mais elle gèle de froid.' L'idée d'un sentiment éthique de vénération sombre dans son impossibilité: 'La vertu se fait respecter; et le respect est incommode.'[6] Le texte de Diderot laisse plutôt la place à la souffrance, au ressentiment devant l'inégalité des talents et des mérites arbitraires. Le Neveu déplore: 'Je me rappelais un tas de coquins, qui ne m'allaient pas à la cheville et qui regorgeaient de richesses. J'étais en surtout de baracan, et ils étaient couverts de velours; ils s'appuyaient sur la canne à pomme d'or et en bec de corbin [...]. Qu'étaient-ce pourtant? La plupart de misérables croque-notes; aujourd'hui ce sont des espèces de seigneurs.'[7]

---

5. Diderot, *Le Neveu de Rameau*, DPV xii.93.
6. *Le Neveu*, p.119.
7. *Le Neveu*, p.94-95.

Mais, dans l'esprit cynique du Neveu, la mort rééquilibre les inégalités. Tous les états s'abaissent devant cette inévitable échéance, l'identique néant, destin commun de l'humanité. Ainsi la mort rend vaine toute cérémonie: 'Le mort n'entend pas sonner les cloches. C'est en vain que cent prêtres s'égosillent pour lui; qu'il est précédé et suivi d'une longue file de torches ardentes; son âme ne marche pas à côté du maître des cérémonies. Pourrir sous du marbre, pourrir sous la terre, c'est toujours pourrir.'[8] L'article SOCIÉTÉ de l'*Encyclopédie* en arrive au même constat. Il rappelle d'abord que 'l'égalité de nature entre les hommes est un principe que nous ne devons jamais perdre de vue' et continue sur cette remarque (xv.253):

quelque inégalité que semble mettre entre eux [les hommes] la différence des conditions, elle n'a été introduite que pour les faire mieux arriver, selon leur état présent, tous à leur fin commune, qui est d'être heureux autant que le comporte cette vie mortelle; encore cette différence qui paraît bien mince à des yeux philosophiques, est-elle d'une courte durée. Il n'y a qu'un pas de la vie à la mort, et la mort met au même terme ce qu'il y a de plus élevé et de plus brillant, avec ce qui est plus bas et de plus obscur parmi les hommes.

Le collaborateur de Diderot, D'Alembert, a aussi laissé sur ces questions un texte important, un *Essai sur la société des gens de lettres et des grands*. En abordant le problème de la renommée littéraire, D'Alembert y fait des réflexions générales sur la considération et la réputation. D'Alembert commence par admettre que les hommes sont égaux par le droit de la nature, mais il considère trois inégalités sociales, trois ordres des distinctions: celles des talents, de la naissance et de la fortune. Il déplore particulièrement une forme de distinction, la considération, qui s'appuie sur les critères du rang et de la fortune. Dans la société hiérarchique qu'analyse D'Alembert, les talents sont la dernière des distinctions. Lorsque le collaborateur de Diderot recommande aux gens de lettres le commerce des grands, il distingue particulièrement ceux qui sont capables d'égalité:

Il est si vrai que la considération tient beaucoup plus à l'état qu'aux talents, que de deux hommes de lettres même, celui qui est le plus sot et le plus riche est ordinairement celui à qui on marque le plus d'égards. Si les talents sont justement choqués de ce partage, c'est à eux seuls qu'ils doivent s'en prendre; qu'ils cessent de prodiguer leurs hommages à des gens qui croient les honorer d'un regard, et qui semblent les avertir par les démonstrations de leur politesse même qu'elle est un acte de bienveillance plutôt que de justice; qu'ils cessent de rechercher la société des grands malgré les dégoûts visibles ou secrets qu'ils y rencontrent, d'ignorer les avantages que la supériorité du génie donne sur les autres hommes, de se prosterner enfin aux genoux de ceux qui devraient être à leurs pieds.[9]

En fait, les talents ne trouveront leur reconnaissance que dans un autre système de distinction: l'estime. Ce critère de distinction rend seul justice à la personne.

8. *Le Neveu*, p.97.
9. D'Alembert, 'Essai sur la société des gens de lettres et des grands', in *Œuvres complètes* (Paris 1822), iv.355.

L'éloignement de ces notions attachées aux références de l'ancienne société vont conduire à la complète reformulation de la civilité à l'époque républicaine. Roger Chartier montrait comment dans le *Dictionnaire d'éducation* de Pierre-Louis Lacretelle, publié dans le quatrième tome de l'*Encyclopédie méthodique* de Panckoucke, la civilité est désormais 'tenue pour une disposition de l'esprit et du cœur', une 'vertu qui est la première et la plus charmante de toutes les vertus sociales'.[10] Il explique: 'Détachée du réseau d'obligations et d'interdits qui le caractérisait, la civilité est ainsi identifiée à une vertu majeure, garante et émanation de toutes les autres puisqu'elle suppose le respect d'autrui, la bienveillance, la modestie, la bienfaisance.'[11] C'est encore la fameuse vertu, cette valeur transcendante qu'on trouvait au centre de la réflexion de Jaucourt, qui devient la substance de la nouvelle civilité: 'c'est une vertu qui établit entre les hommes un commerce doux, honnête'.[12] La notion en tout cas est, à ce stade, parfaitement révolutionnée. Elle se veut étrangère au cérémonial aristocratique. La civilité républicaine n'est plus comme son ancêtre défunt différenciatrice et hiérarchisante. Elle est au contraire égalitaire, morale et naturelle. Chartier peut citer la *Civilité républicaine* de Chemin qui indique cette transformation dans les critères de l'estime: 'Du temps où les hommes ne s'estimaient et n'étaient estimés que suivant leur puissance, leur rang ou leurs richesses, il fallait beaucoup d'études pour savoir toutes les nuances d'égards et de politesse à observer en société. Aujourd'hui, il n'est plus qu'une règle à suivre dans le commerce de la vie, c'est d'être avec tous libre, modeste, ferme et loyal.'[13] La civilité retrouve en même temps toute sa signification politique. Elle oriente dans une même entreprise, sous le regard du droit, la nouvelle communauté des hommes. Elle fait du respect de toute personne, la tâche altière du désir de vivre-ensemble.

On pourrait s'accommoder ici de l'argument de Charles Taylor et dire que les philosophes de l'*Encyclopédie* tracent le chemin qui va inaugurer une autre politique de la reconnaissance. On s'éloigne en effet de l'univers inégalitaire des 'dignités', celui des places et des rangs, pour s'approcher d'un autre univers, plus démocratique, celui de la 'dignité', de l'estime de la personne, de la reconnaissance individuelle.[14]

L'*Encyclopédie* participe ainsi à la réévaluation égalitaire que Daniel Gordon a retrouvée tout au long de la période pré-révolutionnaire et qui émane du camp de certains salonniers et des philosophes. Dans une analyse controversée, l'historien s'en prend à ce qu'il entend comme l'imposition malencontreuse du concept éliasien de civilité, c'est-à-dire l'équation de civilité et de hiérarchie. Il montre, à travers de nombreux exemples au

---

10. Chartier, 'Distinction et divulgation', p.75.
11. Chartier, 'Distinction et divulgation', p.75.
12. Chartier, 'Distinction et divulgation', p.77.
13. Chartier, 'Distinction et divulgation', p.77.
14. Voir Charles Taylor, 'The Need for recognition' in *The Ethics of authenticity* (Cambridge, Mass. 1991), p.43-53.

dix-septième siècle (le chevalier de Méré, Jean-Baptiste Morvan de Belle-garde, François de Caillières), que le modèle sociologique éliasien, asymé-trique, n'est pas unique et qu'il peut être à l'époque contrasté à un autre dont l'inclination est plutôt la réciprocité, l'interaction égalitaire. C'est cette civilité-là, conçue comme un 'égalitarisme prérévolutionnaire', quoique limitée au champ conversationnel, que Gordon voit, plus tard, comme le fondement actif de la philosophie des Lumières, la source des nouvelles valeurs qui commandent l'idéal politique de la société.[15] Les juristes du projet encyclopédique ouvrent la première page d'un débat sur la civilité qui la détourne vers le juridique, l'ancrant dans la question du droit naturel et dans le champ de la moralité. Les interprètes d'Elias conti-nueront sa réflexion dans la même direction, sur l'implication de la civilité dans la question du droit, celui de chacun dans les sociétés démocratiques égalitaires. Le fameux 'tact' qu'Elias évoquait comme la ressource essen-tielle des liens aristocratiques peut devenir pour un sociologue comme Georg Simmel, au contraire, comme ce qui trace 'la limite qu'exige le droit d'autrui'.[16]

Il faudrait conclure, comme pour fermer la boucle ouverte avec l'article CIVILITÉ, et relire l'article SOCIABILITÉ du chevalier de Jaucourt. Examinant cette 'disposition' universelle de l'humain, Jaucourt affirme tout simplement que: 'La raison nous dit que des créatures du même rang, de la même espèce, nées avec les mêmes facultés, pour vivre ensemble et pour participer aux mêmes avantages, ont en général un droit égal et commun. Nous sommes donc obligés de nous regarder comme naturelle-ment égaux, et de nous traiter comme tels' (xv.251). L'obligation, on le voit, a perdu définitivement sa nuance ancienne de subordination; elle est au contraire affirmation d'égalité, le souhait d'un même partage des avan-tages. Le *Dictionnaire* de Diderot et D'Alembert est donc à ajouter au nombre de ces œuvres qui offrent un modèle alternatif, transformateur à la civilité aristocratique, ne confondant plus distinction et hiérarchie. En ce sens, la mouvance encyclopédiste vise, sur ce chapitre particulier des mœurs, au-delà de l'un des buts fixés par les créateurs de l'*Encyclopédie*, celui de 'changer la façon commune de penser', elle veut changer la façon de vivre en commun.

15. Daniel Gordon, *Citizens without sovereignty: equality and sociability in French thought 1670-1789* (Princeton, N.J. 1994), ch.3, p.86-128. Gordon malheureusement semble errer sur la question de l'antipathie d'Elias pour la France. Le contraire serait plutôt vrai. Sur la franco-philie d'Elias, voir *Norbert Elias par lui-même* (Paris 1991), p.74-76.

16. Cité par Claudine Haroche in 'Egards, respect, considération: les formes du souci de l'autre', *Magazine littéraire* 345 (1996), p.36.

PHILIP STEWART

The *Encyclopédie* on-line

IT would have seemed unimaginable to the creators of the *Encyclopédie* that the hindrance posed by the alphabet could one day prove surmountable. And indeed such a development is possible only thanks to a quantum leap on a technological level quite beyond the Enlightenment's model of robots as purely mechanical contrivances. The computer makes possible an entirely new use of the *Encyclopédie* that in many ways flattens earlier obstacles, in particular the fragmentation of blocks of related subject matter into disparate articles, necessarily entailed by the principle of alphabetical ordering. This was an issue on which they had much reflected, as is shown by a lengthy discussion of its implications in Diderot's article ENCYCLOPÉDIE.

The alphabetical model had been used by Moréri in his *Grand Dictionnaire historique* (1674), by Bayle in his *Dictionnaire historique et critique* (1696-1697), then in Chambers' *Cyclopædia* (1728) and many other reference books. The alphabet is of course not a way of knowing things, it is just a way of ordering them. It is not even an organisation, but rather a dispersal of arbitrary frag-ments. Nevertheless, it permits locating what one is seeking so long as one knows where to look. In this respect, as a writing tool adapted to a new use, it is a sort of primitive technology for data storage. The *Encyclopédie* is, as its title says, a *dictionnaire raisonné*; and as D'Alembert states in its *Discours pré-liminaire*, the double title corresponds to the work's dual purpose (i.i):

[C]omme *Encyclopédie*, il doit exposer autant qu'il est possible, l'ordre et l'enchaîne-ment des connaissances humaines; comme *Dictionnaire raisonné des Sciences, des Arts & des Métiers*, il doit contenir sur chaque Science & sur chaque Art, soit libéral, soit mécanique, les principes généraux qui en sont la base, & les détails les plus essen-tiels, qui en font le corps & la substance.

Now these purportedly complementary goals are more in conflict than D'Alembert allows, since the fragmentation imposed by a comprehensive list of articles necessarily compromises the aim of cohesive exposition.

A partial remedy, as Diderot points out in a well-known passage of the article ENCYCLOPÉDIE, was the extensive use of cross-references or *renvois* to link disparate articles thematically; they are, he asserts, '[la] partie de l'ordre encyclopédique la plus importante' (v.642). (Diderot's article is indeed like a long series of variations on the theme of tension between *ordre* and *désordre* – two words that frequently appear.) Whereas an alphabetical order disperses knowledge, the tree of knowledge will provide a structure for bringing it back together again, and in its application the commanding notion will be *subject* and not *article*.

There were early attempts to compensate for what was perceived as an imbalance in favour of the dictionary over the linkages. Pierre Mouchon's two-volume *Table analytique et raisonnée des matières* of 1780 is still a dictionary, although a comprehensive one that compiles the cross-references and thus provides a valuable, flexible means of access to a range of appropriate headings. The *Encyclopédie méthodique*, on the other hand, takes essentially the same seventeen volumes of text as the original *Encyclopédie* but totally reorganises it in terms of subject matter.

These problems and their developing solutions continue to be much studied. Indeed, it has long been recognised that there are two basic ways to envision an encyclopedia: it can be a synthesis of related subject matters, like the various Pléiade volumes entitled *Encyclopédie* of this or that; or it can be alphabetical, as most other things calling themselves 'Encyclopedias' have been, from the *Britannica* to the *Grand Larousse*. The current *Universalis*, with its 'Thesaurus' or expansive index that refers back to the 'Corpus', represents an attempt to combine traditional encyclopedia and *table analytique et raisonnée*.

In any case, the structure of the *Encyclopédie* was in some ways an impediment to its use, and this inherent limitation applies to its accessibility to researchers as well. Very few people since 1765 have actually read the whole thing, and one cannot undertake to do so for every topic whose depths one may wish to plumb. Although it was a great boon to *Encyclopédie* studies when the affordable (if microscopic) Pergamon Press reprint became available in 1969[1] (not to mention some other extremely useful reprints of the plates),[2] we had nothing better for research purposes – aside from the obvious and unquestionably essential synthetic studies, especially those of Jacques Proust[3] – than the Mouchon *Table* until 1971-1972 when the Voltaire Foundation published Richard Schwab's six-volume *Inventory of Diderot's Encyclopédie*.[4]

The *Encyclopédie* being still largely uncharted at the time, Schwab had begun by detailing the contributions of Jaucourt and in the process establishing the major role he had played in the later volumes, largely taking

1. This edition in five folio volumes including plates and *Supplément* is in fact still in print.

2. *Diderot Encyclopedia: the complete illustrations, 1762-1777*, 5 vols (New York 1978); *L'Univers de l'Encyclopédie* (Paris 1964).

3. *Diderot et l'Encyclopédie* (Paris 1962), *L'Encyclopédie* (Paris 1965), and *Marges d'une utopie: pour une lecture critique des planches de l'Encyclopédie* (Cognac 1985).

4. Richard N. Schwab, Walter E. Rex and John Lough, *Inventory of Diderot's Encyclopédie*, *SVEC* 80, 83, 85, 91, 92, 93 (1971-1972); these were complemented in 1984 by a seventh volume (223), an equally valuable index of the plates.

over from Diderot.[5] Patient and meticulous collations of various copies of the *Encyclopédie*, principally those in various libraries of the University of California, led Schwab to the conclusion that there were five printings of the 'original' edition and that many of them were mislabelled even in the collections of the most famous libraries. In the process, he also discovered the numerous amended pages or 'cancels' that often rendered even copies of the same printing non-identical. The introduction which he wrote in collaboration with Walter E. Rex is a marvellous story of literary sleuthing as well as a synthesis of all the discoveries.

Schwab's *Inventory* was much more than an exhaustive list, though it was that. It also collated a good deal of additional information that was precious to anyone who did not have an *Encyclopédie* at hand, and even those few who did: volume number, signature, subdivisions of the topic, and length of the articles. It also provided up-to-date information on attribution where the signature did not suffice, which was very often indeed. As such, the *Inventory* constituted a dramatically new means of access: it made possible some assessment of the treatment that could be found on any subject, and its exact location in the volumes, in advance of a trip down to the rare book room where they usually had to be called up one at a time.

For the information we seek within the covers of the *Encyclopédie* is not the same as that sought by its contemporary readers. They too were, of course, looking for a variety of things, ranging from immediate personal needs – Diderot himself gives such an example: 'il était tourmenté par des crampes, et il n'eut rien de plus pressé que de lire l'article *crampe*' (ENCY-CLOPÉDIE, v.644) – to the state of the art in fledgling sciences and a plethora of applied domains, or evidence to adduce in arguments against their adversaries. Therefore they needed to know where to find things. The advantage of the way subject matter was carved up, at the obvious price of synthesis, was, as Diderot put it, to 'reserver à chacun l'honneur de son travail, et au lecteur la commodité de ne consulter que l'endroit d'un article dont il a besoin'. From there, the reader could ascend via cross-references a ladder of increasing abstraction until reaching finally 'la science des axiomes ou de ces propositions que leur simplicité, leur universalité, leur évidence, rendent indémontrables' (v.642).

The *Encyclopédie*'s polemical force no longer operates on us in the same way, since we are more interested in historicising the debates in which it participated than in re-enacting them. To us the *Encyclopédie* is an archive of potential information as it is embedded in a social and intellectual process. It is all the same a mine of such extraordinary complexity that our ability to exploit it thoroughly has been quite limited. There are of course many kinds of use one may wish to make of such a resource.

5. In the words of Walter E. Rex, 'It is difficult to recall what a mass of unknowns the *Encyclopédie* still was in the '50s: Schwab's discovery was a first bridge over a very large gulf.' The author gratefully acknowledges the information received about this work from Mr Rex by personal communication.

Sometimes the author's identity, when it can be ascertained, is a central concern, either for isolating his particular contribution or for discerning the various voices that intervene in a given subject area. It will not do, when sorting out vast and varied matters such as economics, for instance, to lump the whole *Encyclopédie* together as a monolith, for it contains within its pages the full range of debate in a given historical dimension. At other times the amalgamation of the encyclopedists' expressed positions can construct a group portrait of sorts[6] that potentially has its own kind of historical value – when considering, for instance, the validity of purportedly shared positions and values, and in what ways it might or might not be valid to identify the Enlightenment with the encylopedists. To read the text now is to read it without any sense of immediacy, in an effort to make historical sense of its discourse, whatever the particular focus of the enquiry may be.

The practical reader of the mid-eighteenth century had no imperative need to locate every occurrence of a word, curious though he or she may have been to discover where intriguing morsels might be tucked away. And for some purposes our own interest may be directed principally towards the most obvious headword(s) and perhaps just a handful of *renvois*. Even an index, however, is of limited assistance when the information we need might be located at what one might call the sub-article level. That is, the topic one wishes to pursue may not have a separate heading of its own; and in such a case, ascertaining whether it is touched upon elsewhere is largely a matter of luck and – though perhaps educated – guesswork. Disseminating subject matter throughout the volumes is one of the explicit intentions of the *Encyclopédie*. An index alone will not help us find things in unexpected places. Yet placing things in unexpected places was precisely one of the *Encyclopédie*'s occasionally wilful strategies. Thus the ocular reader can *never* be sure all the essential data has been located, that something fairly crucial has not been overlooked in some out-of-the-way place. Only exhaustive word-searches can open up the text entirely, and these have never been possible until now.

Such thoroughness may be particularly useful when trying to ferret out the pre-disciplinary configuration of what were then emerging fields of enquiry. The terminology of emotions, somewhat explored later in this article, is a good example, since modern psychological vocabulary is based on a plethora of terms invented at the time its diagnostic structure was later mapped out, to which was subsequently added, notably, a large supplement of terms of Freudian inspiration. Almost none of the first group, and none of the latter, will be found in the *Encyclopédie*, not even terms like *dépression* (a technical, surgical term only). Moreover, *âme* then occupied a good part of the territory of what we now think of as the conscious subject.

---

6. For example Frank Kafker's *The Encyclopedists as a group: a collective biography of the authors of the 'Encyclopédie'*, *SVEC* 345 (1996).

To begin with one term that had a wide use in the eighteenth century, we find that *mélancolie* is 'un délire particulier, roulant sur un ou deux objets déterminément, sans fièvre ni fureur, en quoi elle diffère de la manie et de la phrénésie. Ce délire est joint le plus souvent à une tristesse insurmontable, à une humeur sombre, à la misanthropie, à un penchant décidé pour la solitude' (MELANCHOLIE, x.308). These other terms used to frame the definition provide other paths to follow: PHRÉNÉSIE will further lead to the articles DÉLIRE and DÉMENCE, etc. MANIE will suggest others going in the direction of severe pathology: 'assez souvent ce délire est furieux, avec audace, colère, et alors il mérite plus rigoureusement le nom de *manie*; s'il est doux, tranquille, simplement ridicule, on doit plutôt l'appeler *folie*, *imbécillité*. Voyez *ces mots*' (x.31).

But one would still risk missing a good deal. There are 71 occurrences of *phrénésie* and 53 of *démence*, and most of them are not in the articles by those names. It might be important to know what is said about *phrénésie* in AEROPHOBIE, BAIN, CORYBANTISME, DÉLITESCENCE, IDIOPATHIQUE, INFLAMMATOIRES, SAIGNÉE, SUICIDE, SYMPATHIE, and even PARAPHRÉNÉSIE (9 occurrences). There are 353 occurrences of *délire* in a plethora of articles ranging from ALEXIPHARMAQUES to ZONES GLACIALES, and the five occurrences of *démence* in CURATEUR or the four in STUPIDITÉ might prove essential. One might not suspect that, because *démence* unlike some related terms also has a legal application, it turns up in articles like EXHÉRÉDATION DES ASCENDANS, FRÈRE, SUBSTITUTION EXEMPLAIRE, and even PARLEMENT À AMIENS. While all those usages *may* be consistent with the parameters supplied under the main headword, they may also contain significant extensions and additional contexts for understanding the concept.

For this reason, the on-line data base created under the aegis of ARTFL[7] is in the process of wholly revolutionising the possibilities for any kind of research that makes use of the *Encyclopédie*. It permits not only the random recovery of any segment of the text, but also the searching of headwords sorted by entry, author, classification or part of speech, and occurrences (singly or in combination) of words or phrases anywhere in the text. This on-line *Encyclopédie* happily includes both the supplements and the textual explanations that accompany the plates. One can also call up a list of articles in order of number of occurrences of the term being searched, thus focusing one's attention on those that are its preponderant sources.

---

7. American and French Research on the Treasury of the French Language, a collaboration between the CNRS (Centre National de la Recherche Scientifique) and the University of Chicago, and attached to INALF (Institut National de la Langue Française); the French version of this on-line resource is called Frantext. For a history of the project see Robert Morrissey, John Iverson and Mark Olsen, 'L'*Encyclopédie* de Diderot sur Internet', *RDE* 25 (1998), p.163-68.

The computer's edge is not just that it is fast; it is that it does not read the way we do – which is to say in plodding, linear fashion. The price of this difference is that it reads without comprehension, which we must supply. Where the alphabet scatters, the computer is able to reassemble. On the other hand, a machine-encoded text does not *organise* anything; that is why its active memory is referred to as 'random access'. To the computer, the *Encyclopédie* is just a gigantic, haphazard pile of words, which it can go find in any order we ask it to. In being subjected to the computer's operations, the *Encyclopédie* utterly ceases to shape knowledge; it is just a haystack out of which the computer can extract needles. The on-line *Encyclopédie* is not even the 'labyrinth' to which Diderot likened the original version (ENCYCLOPÉDIE); it is the scattered remnants of a big bang.

So now the question becomes: what *kind* of information do we seek from the *Encyclopédie*? Words, of course, and sometimes words in combinations – the very kinds of searches we have already come to value in the general ARTFL (in France, Frantext) database. Even to locate obscure information by article name alone one needed a hunch and the help of an index; to some degree, this applies even to an *encyclopédie méthodique*, which will still contain unpredictable occurrences of a given subject outside the main article heading. To find them in a database, one needs no such hunch. But one must apply judgement to the information accessed. There is no logic to a computer printout; although intelligent things can be done with it, it is nothing but a list – raw data. In the next stage, however, it can help us reassemble the pieces we need to work with.

The cross-referencing scheme (*renvois*) built into the *Encyclopédie* itself, of course, provides multi-forking paths. Although they are deliberate, however, they are not necessarily methodical in their ramifications, and for good reason: their extensions increase exponentially so that there would be no possible means for even the authors and editors to keep track of them all. At the third or fourth level they can well link an article – and perhaps only remotely by that point – with hundreds of others. What the word search can follow is not a path at all, or at least not one expressly carved out; it is a hidden lexical network that may or may not lead to concepts closely related to a particular line of research.

There is no predicting how fecund the *renvoi* trail will be. There are no cross-references at all to be found in Jaucourt's entry entitled SENTIMENT, AVIS, OPINION. A separate entry, SENTIMENT INTIME, points to an extremely limited range, just three references in all even when taken to the third level (the cross-reference here is symbolised by >):

SENTIMENT INTIME > EVIDENCE > SENSATIONS
SENTIMENT INTIME > SENS COMMUN

On the other hand, the occasional expandability of *renvois* is illustrated by the fact that – still in the same semantic field – the article

SENSIBILITÉ, SENTIMENT by Fouquet contains nine cross-references, and thus in germ, pursued to the next level, the astounding total of 197:

ÂME >	AME DES BESTES, CENTRE OVALE, CERVEAU, CERVELET, ENTONNOIR, GLANDE PINEALE, IMMATÉRIALISME, MOELLE, SPINOSISME, SPIRITUALITÉ, TARENTULE (11).
SECRÉTION(S) >	DIGESTION, GLANDES, POULS, REIN (4).
POULS >	ARTERES, BLANCHE, CIRCULATION, CŒUR, CRISE, CROCHE, DIASTOLE, DOUBLE-CROCHE, ECONOMIE ANIMALE, FIEVRE, INFLAMMATION, INFLAMMATOIRE, NOIRE, OBSERVATEUR, PULSATION, RHYTHME, SPASME, SYTOLE (18).
INFLAMMATION >	CHALEUR, EPAISSISSEMENT, ERESIPELE, IRRITABILITÉ, PLÉTHORE, RARÉFACTION, SENSIBILITÉ (7).
HEMORRHOÏDES >	CANCER, FISTULE À L'ANUS, FLUX HEMORRHOIDAL, SANGSUE (4).
AIR >	ACIDE, ADHERENCE, ALTERATION, ANIMAL, ANTIMOINE, ARQUEBUSE-À-VENT, ATMOSPHERE, ATTRACTION, BALANCE, BAROMETRE, CIRCULATION, COHÉSION, COLCOTHAR, CONDENSATION, CORRUPTION, CUIVRE, DENSITÉ, DIGESTOIRE, DILATATION, DISSOLUTION, ELASTICITÉ, ELÉMENT, EMANATION, EOLIPILE, ETHER, EXHALAISON, FER, FERMENTAITON, FEU, FLAMME, FLUIDE, FONTAINE, GRAVITÉ, HUMIDITÉ, HYGROMETRE, LABYRINTHE, MACHINE PNEUMATIQUE, MAGNÉTISME, MANOMETRE, MÉTÉORE, MILIEU, MINE, MONTAGNE, NITRE, OPTIQUE, OR, OSCILLATION, OUÏE, PESANTEUR, PIERRE, PLANTE, PNEUMATIQUE, POMPE, PUTRÉFACTION, RARÉFACTION, REACTION, RÉFRACTION, REPULSION,

	RESPIRATION, ROUILLE, SANG, SEL, SON, SOUFRE, TARTRE, TERRE, TERRESTRE, THERMOMETRE, TONNERRE, TRANSPIRATION, TREMBLEMENT, VAPEUR, VÉGÉTAL, VÉGÉTATION, VENT, VENTILATEUR, VERD-DE-GRIS, VIBRATION, VOLATIL, VOLATILISATION, VOLCAN, VUIDE (82).
LAIT >	BEURRE, COAGULATION, CONCOMBRE, CORRECTIF, DIGESTION, DISTILLATION, DOUX, ENFANT, FERMENTATION, FIEVRE MILIAIRE, FROMAGE, MALADIES, MANUEL CHIMIQUE, MÉDICAMENT, MIXTION, MUQUEUX, NOURRICE, PETIT-LAIT, PRESURE, RAFINAGE DU SUCRE, RAFINERIE, REGIME, SEL VOLATIL, SUCRE, SUCRE DE LAIT, VUIDANGES (26).
INFLUENCE DES ASTRES >	ACRIMONIE, AIR, APHORISMES, ATMOSPHERE, AUTOMNE, CABALE, CHALEUR, COMETE, CRISE, EPAISSISSEMENT, ETÉ, FERMENTATION, FEU, FIEVRE INTERMITTENTE, FROID, HYVER, JOUR, LUMIERE, MANIE, MERCURE, NUIT, PRINTEMS, PURGATIFS, SAIGNÉE, SAISONS, SEL, SOLEIL, SOUFRE (28).
CLIMAT >	CHALEUR, CRISE, EAU, ENDEMIQUE, GLACE, HEURE, MALADIES ENDEMIQUES, METHODE CURATIVE, MOIS, PARALLELE, PASSION, RÉFRACTION, RÉGIME, SAISON, SOL, TERRE, TYPE (17).

At this point, were this a research project, it would already have become almost unmanageable, not just because of quantity but because of semantic dispersal. Had the editors had in hand at one time the whole work, they could of course have made certain cross-references more systematic, but in fact this would not have sufficed to create a completely ordered system, for the inevitably exponential structure of cross-references makes them inherently beyond control.

But the important point to be made about electronic searching is that it in no way disables the cross-reference system; the computer *also* finds the cross-references. Using it, both systems operate complementarily and should be utilised in informed conjunction with each other. In order to research treatment of questions of emotion, for example, one will find, under EMOTION, an article a mere two lines long. Under PASSION, on the other hand, there are several headings:

PASSIONS (*Philos. Logique, Morale*)
PASSION DE JESUS-CHRIST (*Critique sacrée*)
PASSIONS, *dans l'Eloquence*
PASSIONS, *en Poésie*
PASSION (*Méd. Hyg. Pathol. Thér.*)
PASSION (*Peint.*)
PASSION (*Médecine*)
PASSION, *en Blason*
PASSION DE JESUS-CHRIST, *ordre de la* (*Histoire mod.*)
PASSION, *cloux de la* (*Blason*)
PASSIONS, *terme de Peintres-Doreurs*
PASSIONNER, PASSIONNÉ (*Gram.*)

In addition to these, the headword search on-line will yield:

COMPASSION (*Morale*)
FLEUR DE LA PASSION
MYSTERES DE LA PASSION (*Théat. françois*)
SEMAINE DE LA PASSION
TÉNEBRES DE LA PASSION (*Critiq. sacrée*)

– which may or may not be pertinent to what one is looking for. Going straight to the articles under *sentiment*, one will find the following entries:

SENTIMENT, AVIS, OPINION
SENTIMENT INTIME
SENTIMENS, EN POESIE
SENTIMENT D'EPÉE, SENTIR L'EPÉE (*Escrime*)
SENTIMENT (*Vénerie*)

By conventional means, one would quickly eliminate the last three by scanning the articles themselves, finding at least a useful starting point. The data base, however, will also, for *sentiment*, turn up SENSIBILITÉ, SENTI-MENT (*Médecine*), which may be equally important. And would one think to test RESSENTIMENT et PRESSENTIMENT as well? Now it happens that these are the titles of two fairly short articles classified as grammatical; but there is also PRESSENTIMENT (*Phil.*), a quite substantial article almost two columns in length. Intuition has heretofore been our only available tool for locating all pertinent connections when, as in these examples, both index and cross-reference systems will to some extent fail.

Suppose that my interest in animations leads me to inquire how much attention the *Encyclopédie*'s authors collectively paid to Vaucanson and his celebrated robots. In the first place, one will not find an entry for 'Vaucanson', not because he is insufficiently important but because of a general policy that refers, as far as headwords are concerned, only to schools of thought. There is no 'Aristote' or 'Platon' but there is ARISTOTÉLISME and PLATONISME. Similarly, there is no 'Newton', but NEWTONIA-NISME. Though Newton is a very important presence in the *Encyclopédie*, the form that presence takes is theoretical and is focused on the name given to the philosophy he founded. Nevertheless, most occurrences of his name occur not under NEWTONIANISME but under WOLSTROPE, the name of his birthplace.[8] Twenty of the fifty-one occurrences of Shake-spear(e)'s name (usually without the final 'e') are to be found in STRAT-FORD OU STRETFORD.

Therefore I might try AUTOMATE, an article bearing the signature of D'Alembert. It indeed mentions Vaucanson's flute player, referring the reader to the article ANDROÏDE for further information, and extensively describes two others robots: a tambourine player, and Vaucanson's famous duck. Yet Vaucanson's name is mentioned only once, so it might be missed by quick ocular scanning. Other cross-references in the article are HORLOGE, MONTRE, PENDULE, and RESSORT.

Although such a yield may satisfy the researcher's main purpose, it would certainly miss allusions to Vaucanson, which the on-line database can now supply, in such perhaps unsuspected locations as AIGUILLE, ASPLE, BOBINE, CARILLON, FIL, FINANCES, INDUSTRIE, MAGIE, NEUCHÂTEL, PONT MILITAIRE, SOIE, and VOIX – not to mention the text corresponding to the plates for TAPISSERIE DE BASSE LISSE and SOIERIE. Several of these occurrences have to do with Vau-canson's role in the design of weaving machinery, another dimension of his fame which one might otherwise have overlooked. And even if one somehow noticed that there was a second, revised version of the article ASPLE on a separate sheet – this would depend on where it happened to have been inserted in the particular copy of the *Encyclopédie* consulted – its signifi-cance would never be grasped without the additional information that now leaps to hand. In fact, Vaucanson had so protested over the article ASPLE (because an invention of his appeared to be attributed to someone else as well) that the editors not only profusely apologised but agreed to distribute a replacement page. All this is revealed in the 'Avertissement des éditeurs' of volume two: 'nous sommes convenus de réformer cet article, et de distribuer avec le second volume la feuille corrigée' (ii.ii).

On another level, the word *automate* is to be found in an almost wholly separate set of articles: ÂME DES BÊTES, ANDROÏDE, BÊTE, BON-SENS, CARTÉSIANISME, CÉLIBAT, CHIRURGIEN, DIGESTEUR (as a cross-reference), ENCYCLOPÉDIE, FORTUIT, INSTINCT, LEIBNITZIANISME, LIBERTÉ, OPERATEUR, PLATONISME, PYTHAGORISME, SCHOLASTIQUES, TOLÉRANCE. As one can suspect from such a constellation, these articles have little to do with machines per se, and in such philosophical contexts the reference to

8. Morrissey *et al.*, p.167.

automata is largely metaphorical. Indeed one can virtually guess, even without looking it up, the polemical charge the word *automate* might have in an article such as TOLÉRANCE.

It is hard to imagine any subject mentioned in the *Encyclopédie* for which a word search would not be potentially revealing. In the course of preparing a paper on French protestantism, I checked allusions (of which there are twenty-five) to the Huguenots. Only three of these, however, are in the article HUGUENOT. Other occurrences have rather specific related contexts one might anticipate (FRONDE, LIGUE, PAU, ROUEN, POLITIQUES, RELIGION, and just possibly PARPAILLOTS); but no one, probably, would independently think to look under the entries ESTIME, MARIAGES PAR PAROLES DE PRÉSENT, PÉTARD, QUARTENIER, SEIZE, SOEST, VERS COUPES, or WIGHS, where other occurrences are to be found. A *huguenotte*, on the other hand, turns out to be a kind of earthenware pot.

Similarly, a researcher interested in saltpetre would easily locate, even in a pre-computer age, the rather substantial article (SALPETRE, five columns) under that heading, and perhaps the numerous plates on its manufacture and refinement. Given the principal use of saltpetre, one might possibly think to look also in such articles as AMORCE, ARTIFICE, BRÛLOT, FEU D'ARTIFICE, POUDRE À CANON, if not so obviously in chemically related articles such as ACIDE, ANTIMOINE, BALLE À FEU, ECUME DE NITRE. And one would have no chance at all of locating the rest of the 170 occurrences of the word in the articles COULER, CUITE, EMBAUMEMENT, SOIE, and so on.

It goes without saying that so much information can sometimes be too much information; it is available, and the rest is up to the researcher to decide. A person writing a dissertation on the *Encyclopédie*'s representation of protestantism would be prudent to check every single occurrence of *huguenot*,[9] but on the other hand such exhaustiveness for another purpose might be a waste of time: the most scrupulous form of research would be unlikely to be able to take stock of all 3490 occurrences of *religion*. The headwords of the articles listed are of course an indication of whether the reference is going to lead in a useful direction, and in any case checking the hypertext context on-line is much more quickly done than opening the physical volume even if available.

Statistically, since it is such a large corpus and one not chosen for its specifically literary (or other) bias, the *Encyclopédie* might also serve to provide certain comparative indices both for lexicographical research and for aspects of intellectual or cultural history. The theoretical and ideological importance of Newton (780 mentions) is not surprising, nor his

9. He or she would be prudent also to pursue synonyms: there are 52 occurrences of *protestant* (many, however, being verbal participles), and in addition 78 occurrences of *réformée*, many of which also refer to protestantism.

ascendancy over Descartes (at 501); more so is to find Locke (at 116) no more preponderant than Copernicus (113). On the literary side, consider the obvious stature, measured by such criteria, of Voltaire (308 mentions); yet a staggering gap still appears to separate him from Racine (3240 mentions), except that the latter figure refers most often to a common noun. It is certain that a number of the 87 hits for *pascal* relate to Easter, and those that really refer to Blaise Pascal are much more oriented toward mathematics than to the *Pensées*. 'Rousseau' comes in respectably at 116 mentions, the great majority of which are to Jean-Baptiste Rousseau, not Jean-Jacques; the handful of allusions to him usually qualify him specifically as 'Rousseau de Genève'.

Limitations

With this kind of search facility, one must always be mindful of morphological variations so as not to miss potentially significant occurrences. A search for *inoculation* turns up only 27 occurrences. In order to include both plurals and verbal forms it is more productive to search for INOCUL* (in DOS wild-card language; in ARTFL it is coded 'inocul.*'), which yields 135 hits.

Also beware miskeyed words. The data base was entered by hand, because scanning techniques available are not sufficiently reliable for eighteenth-century typography. This fact necessarily entails some misreadings by the key operators, especially *f* for long *s*, or vice versa: this chance mistake will result in the omission of many potentially important occurrences from the reference list of words containing those letters. Diderot's article ENCYCLOPÉDIE contains the word *articles* for *artistes* (v.636), which shows that compound misconstruals also occur. Also common are slight misreadings of Latin. The present instance of the on-line *Encyclopédie* is a work in progress, the asymptote of which is the perfectly keyed text, reproducing the original exactly, and which by progressive correction will be approached.

But the same caveat applies to any variations of spelling, of which there are assuredly many. Even the 3490 instances of *religion* could well be missing a few more where the word has been accidentally mis-entered. Variations in proper names can be just as troublesome. Lurking behind the 25 occurrences of 'Galilée' are an additional two spelled 'Galilee' and 'Galileo' – and maybe others. The huge representation of 'Newton' in the *Encyclopédie* needs to be supplemented with the ten occurrences of 'Neuton'; similarly, there are 45 occurrences of *newtonien(s)* – conflating substantive and adjective – but also three of *neutonien(s)*.

A computer is a pure literalist; it cannot find, and therefore cannot compile, without special tools, varied spellings of the same word. That is why all eighteenth-century spellings had to have been normalised for input into the main *Trésor de la langue française* database, for which the data would otherwise have been unreliable. The present manual transcription can be controlled by use of the pixel page images also available on-line; but until there is a third version which will be a complete text normalised on standard spellings of the year 2000, one will always have to look for variant forms and, to that degree, the ARTFL *Encyclopédie* project will not yet be a complete tool. But what looks extraordinary today will look ordinary tomorrow: the *Encyclopédie* will have soon mushroomed into an entirely different kind of work from what it was when Jacques Proust and Richard Schwab tackled it.[10]

10. Another version, available on four CD-ROMs from Redon, offers similar but not identical tools: the ARTFL and Redon versions are best used in combination.

DOWNING A. THOMAS

Taste, commonality and musical imagination in the *Encyclopédie*

THE French eighteenth century, which has long been known for its 'all-pervasive philosophic and critical spirit', was as fascinated with irrationality as it was with reason.[1] The *Encyclopédie*, with its multi-faceted critical perspectives, testifies to this fact, as we see in Diderot's attempt to question the boundary separating humans from animals in the article ANIMAL, or Voltaire's article IMAGINATION, documenting the importance of involuntary processes and outside influences on thought: 'comment se peut-il faire qu'un peu d'une certaine liqueur [le vin] qui empêchera de faire un calcul, donnera des idées brillantes' (viii.562)? For all the emphasis they placed on reason, Enlightenment writers were nonetheless immensely intrigued by that which escapes its grasp. For many reasons, however, twentieth-century scholarship tended to ignore this aspect of the eighteenth century.[2] During the late 1980s and throughout the 1990s eighteenth-century studies on the American continent relied particularly heavily on the conception of the public sphere that Jürgen Habermas developed during the early 1960s but which was widely disseminated in the English-speaking world only over the past two decades. In Habermas's original account, the bourgeois public sphere emerges from the experience of reading novels, or more precisely from reading practices in which

---

1. *The Age of Enlightenment*, ed. O. E. Fellows and N. L. Torrey (New York 1942), p.1.

2. Peter Gay's contributions to eighteenth-century studies, to take one highly influential example, were implicitly grounded in the conviction that Enlightenment reason was a necessary antidote to twentieth-century experience. Though he refrained from elaborating on this connection, Gay made it clear that such a connection could be made: 'if there is an age that desperately needs the humane aims and the critical methods of the Enlightenment, it is certainly our age' (Peter Gay, *The Enlightenment: an interpretation: the science of freedom*, New York 1969, p.xi). In their *Dialektik der Aufklärung*, first published in 1944, Max Horkheimer and Theodor W. Adorno were notable exceptions to the general tendency to see Enlightenment as a simple synonym for reason. For Horkheimer and Adorno, Enlightenment feeds on and becomes myth just as it dispels myth. See their *Dialectic of Enlightenment*, translated by J. Cumming (1972; New York 1991), p.11-12. For an analysis of the 'dark side' of Enlightenment as seen by twentieth-century philosophers and critics, see Julie Candler Hayes, *Reading the French Enlightenment: system and subversion* (Cambridge 1999), p. 3-21. My own concern does not lie in examining or characterising Enlightenment as 'rational' or 'irrational', but rather in exploring the interest eighteenth-century writers expressed in processes and areas of inquiry in which reason had little or no hold.

performative or 'audience-centred' models of subjectivity were cultivated.[3] Yet rather than underscore the projected *Intimität* that is at the heart of Habermas's conception, scholarship inspired by Habermas has largely centred on the rational debate and open exchange of ideas, taking place in salons and coffee houses, and through which the eighteenth-century public sphere was shaped. As a result, the most identifiable tendency in eighteenth-century studies in America has continued to focus almost exclusively on the category of reason. Dena Goodman, for example, has argued that in contrast to the 'mere civility' of previous generations a 'polite sociability' came to be identified with the eighteenth-century salonnières and fostered the free exchange of ideas, giving a new identity to the seventeenth-century Republic of Letters.[4] Scholars like Goodman have reconsidered in compelling ways earlier views of the salons, those who frequented and hosted them, and their contributions to the development of the public sphere. Others, inspired by the pioneering work of Robert Darnton, have turned their attention to changes in print culture and its impact on the public sphere.[5] In most cases, whatever the merits of current trends in public-sphere scholarship (and there are many), the exclusive focus on forms of rationality has tended to marginalise or overshadow the eighteenth-century fascination with the 'irrational' basis of a common or shared existence.[6]

The contested notion of shared values and exchange of ideas on which the public sphere is based, moreover, has been at the centre of recent debates on 'difference' and the highly charged identity politics that emerged from it, both inside and outside the Academy. Specific groups have appealed to a basic, shared identity that they feel distinguishes them from others, whereas traditional humanists extended a commonality to humanity as a whole. K. Anthony Appiah remarks that 'now you could be [attacked as] an essentialist both for saying that people were different and for saying

---

3. See Jürgen Habermas, *The Structural transformation of the public sphere*, translated by T. Burger (Cambridge, Mass. 1989), p.27-30. Regarding the development of the forms of subjectivity on which the emergence of the public sphere depended, Habermas notes that 'the empathetic reader repeated within himself the private relationships displayed before him in literature; from his experience of real familiarity (*Intimität*), he gave life to the fictional one, and in the latter he prepared himself for the former' (p.50-51). This text was originally published as *Strukturwandel der Öffentlichkeit: Untersuchungen zu einer Kategorie der bürgerlichen Gesellschaft* (Neuwied 1962).

4. Dena Goodman, *The Republic of letters: a cultural history of the French Enlightenment* (Ithaca, N.Y. 1994), p.5.

5. See the recent contributions to *The Darnton debate: books and revolution in the eighteenth century*, ed. H. T. Mason (1998; Oxford 1999). See also Lucien Febvre and H.-J. Martin, *The Coming of the book: the impact of printing, 1450-1800*, ed. G. Nowell-Smith and D. Wooton, translated by D. Gerard (London 1984); and Elizabeth L. Eisenstein, *Print culture and Enlightenment thought* (Chapel Hill, N.C. 1986).

6. There are, of course, some salient exceptions to this tendency in eighteenth-century studies. See, for example, Elena Russo, 'The Self, real and imaginary: social sentiment in Marivaux and Hume', *Yale French studies* 92 (1997), p.126-48.

that they were the same'.[7] The divisive issue of sameness and difference – the question of a shared humanity – is therefore still very much with us today and has informed to a greater or lesser degree modern scholarship on the eighteenth-century public sphere.

Like the notion of identity, the question of 'taste' has been considered as either primarily inclusive or exclusive at various points in its conceptual history, either bringing people together through their common ability to feel or separating them through forms of distinction. Taste was an important component of early-modern views of a common humanity, defined as an ability to sense beauty which, like its object – *le beau* – often appeared 'indéfinissable' to eighteenth-century commentators. In some measure because of this elusiveness, it produced veritable floods of ink.[8] What follows is an investigation into taste as a shared but non-rational aspect of a common humanity. I have taken the *Encyclopédie* as an ideal site to engage in such an inquiry for two interrelated reasons. First, the *Encyclopédie* was written and compiled at a time when the concept of taste was undergoing important changes. Second, the project was defined from the beginning in D'Alembert's 'Discours préliminaire' both as a collective undertaking, and therefore indicative of the eighteenth-century public sphere, and as a work centred around the concept of 'man', of a common humanity which the *Encyclopédie* would in some measure seek to represent.

Taste took an important conceptual turn in the early modern period. By the mid-sixteenth century, the meaning of the term *le goût* was uncoupled from the purely physiological meaning; it came to refer specifically to artistic works only in the mid-seventeenth century. During the eighteenth century, the concept of taste was closely linked to the development of aesthetics and therefore came into contact with new concepts of feeling, its potential for refinement, its distinctiveness as a mode of knowledge, and its moral value. In the essays collected in his *Characteristics of men, manners, opinions, times* (1711), Shaftesbury posited a connection between human beings – a moral conscience that correlates with an inborn sense of discrimination. For Shaftesbury, taste – understood as the ability to distinguish between the beautiful and the plain – coincided absolutely with virtue.[9] Summing up this neoclassical perspective on taste, Charles Batteux wrote that 'il est un bon Goût, qui est seul bon'. 'Notre ame',

7. K. Anthony Appiah, 'Battle of the bien-pensant', *The New York review of books* 47, no.7 (27 April 2000), p.42.

8. On taste as 'indéfinissable', see, for example, Louis Charpentier, *Causes de la décadence du goût sur le théâtre* (Paris 1768), ii.131. The idea of a common humanity was of course essential to much political philosophy of the period. On the impact of this philosophy on the *Encyclopédie* particularly, see Jacques Proust, *Diderot et l'Encyclopédie* (Paris 1967), p.408-16. For a more general overview of sociability in eighteenth-century France, see Daniel Gordon, *Citizens without sovereignty: equality and sociability in French thought, 1670-1789* (Princeton, N.J. 1994).

9. See Anthony Ashley Cooper, Earl of Shaftesbury, *Characteristics of men, manners, opinions, times*, ed. P. Eyres (Oxford 1999). See in particular the essay, 'An Inquiry concerning virtue or merit', originally published in 1699 and later included in the *Characteristics*. See also Barbara

Batteux continued, 'est faite pour connoître le vrai, & pour aimer le bon: & comme il y a une proportion naturelle entre elle & ces objets, elle ne peut se refuser à leur impression.'[10] L'abbé Dubos made pleasure the central criteria of judgement, dissociating taste from the normative rules of art. Yet Shaftesbury's universalism is nonetheless still present in the 'sixième sens' Dubos posited, a form of sentiment shared by all: 'tous les hommes, à l'aide du sentiment intérieur qui est en eux, connaissent sans savoir les règles si les productions des arts sont de bons ou de mauvais ouvrages'.[11] As the conviction behind the unbroken synchronisation of taste and virtue came to be questioned, perhaps in part because Lockian sensationism could be understood to imply an inherent disjunction rather than a continuity between individuals, the universal basis of taste had to be reevaluated. For Hume, though he conceded that a standard must exist somewhere, taste was predicated on regularities in manners and the repeated, public display of preferences.[12]

When Barnabé Farmian de Rozoi wrote in 1766 that 'le Goût n'est plus, parmi nous, qu'une affaire de mode, & que les principes les plus respectables ne sont plus que des problêmes que chacun résout selon ses caprices & ses préventions', he articulated an understanding of taste very close to our own.[13] The absolute aplomb with which Rozoi made his claim, however, was extremely uncharacteristic of eighteenth-century writers who fretted endlessly over the shared value of taste. If taste is taken as a model for the definitive immanence and isolation of subjectivity, as Rozoi appears to view it, however flirtatiously given the context of his poem, then the question of a common sense or shared sensibility remains in abeyance. Kant's solution to the problem – perhaps more appropriately described as a shutting down of the problem – was to make aesthetic judgements proceed *as if* they were made from the perspective of a (lost) *sensus communis*. Yet, as many commentators have pointed out, given that taste for Kant is autonomous and indeterminant, it is difficult to see how a hypothetical or lost *sensus communis* would shore up the shared moral and/or cognitive dimensions of taste so crucial to eighteenth-century anthropology and aesthetics.[14] Understood as embracing the problem of the singularity or

M. Benedict, *Framing feeling: sentiment and style in English prose fiction, 1745-1800* (New York 1994), p.2-3.

10. Charles Batteux, *Les Beaux Arts réduits à un même principe* (1773; Geneva 1969), p.77, 83.

11. Jean-Baptiste Dubos, *Réflexions critiques sur la poésie et sur la peinture*, pref. by Etienne Wolff (Paris 1993), p.277, 278.

12. 'We are more pleased, in the course of our reading, with pictures and characters that resemble objects which are found in our own age and country, than with those which describe a different set of customs' (David Hume, *Of the Standard of taste and other essays*, ed. J. W. Lenz, Indianapolis, Ind. and New York 1965, p.20).

13. Barnabé Farmian de Rozoi, *Les Sens, poème en six chants* (Londres 1766), p.i-ij.

14. Immanuel Kant, *Critique of judgment*, translated by W. S. Pluhar (Indianapolis, Ind. 1987), p.89. For one recent discussion of the difficulties associated with taste in Kant, see Gérard Genette, *L'Œuvre de l'art: la relation esthétique* (Paris 1997), p.84-85. See also J. M. Bernstein, *The Fate of art: aesthetic alienation from Kant to Derrida and Adorno* (University Park, Pa.

commonality of feeling, the question of taste has continued to haunt contemporary theory as one of the most acute and problematic issues of aesthetic modernity. In his discussion of the history of taste and aesthetics in the twentieth century, for example, Luc Ferry has referred to modern art as 'un prolongement de soi, une sorte de carte de visite particulièrement élaborée' – indicative, in other words, of the isolation of the individual in the twentieth century, and of the thorough disjunction between artist and spectator.[15]

It would be beyond the scope of this essay to examine in its every detail the highly charged question of the generality and particularity of feeling implicit in the notion of taste, or the full gamut of the problems and virtues of aesthetic commonality that emerged in relation to taste. Beginning with the articles specifically devoted to *le goût,* I wish to provide an overview of the issues raised by the changing concept of taste as it entered into the web of knowledge that constitutes the *Encyclopédie* (1751-1772) and its *Supplément* (1776-1777). In the mid-eighteenth century, the notion of taste was connected to areas of knowledge as diverse as physiology, *belles-lettres,* moral philosophy, and the emergent field of aesthetics. The first part of the essay, devoted to the articles on taste published in the seventh volume of the *Encyclopédie,* will explore how the question of taste may have served as a locus for concerns about forms of common human feeling or understanding in light of the contemporary development of empiricist discourse. The second part will focus on several of the articles Jean-Jacques Rousseau wrote for his *Dictionnaire de musique,* many of which were included in the *Supplément à l'Encyclopédie.* Rousseau's articles revisit the question of commonality of feeling raised in the articles from the *Encyclopédie* specifically devoted to taste. The new possibilities opened up by philosophy on the one hand and music theory on the other led to questions about the objective, conventional, or subjective bases of our experience of art objects. Christopher Norris has argued that in the eighteenth century 'music becomes something more than a source of aesthetically appealing images and metaphors. It assumes the central role in a new way of thinking about language, art and representation whose effects reach far beyond the discourse of art

---

1992). For Bernstein, Kant's aesthetics is a 'memorial aesthetics': 'in making aesthetic judgements we judge things "as if" from the perspective of our lost common sense, a common sense that may never have existed [... and which is] both presupposed in the judgement of taste and yet to be obtained. [...] As remembered/presupposed, common sense is constitutive of the judgement of taste; as not existent, it is regulative. Hence the answer to Kant's remarkable and curious question: is common sense, the necessary condition for the possibility of judgements of taste, constitutive or regulative?; the answer is both. Of course, if a common sense did exist, then Kant's moral theory would become redundant; alternatively, if Kant took common sense as regulative, then the disinterestedness of aesthetic judgement would have been infringed upon' (p.60).

15. Luc Ferry, *Homo aestheticus: l'invention du goût à l'âge démocratique* (Paris 1990), p.23.

criticism.'[16] Rousseau's complex and sometimes contradictory positions in the music articles shed light on a burgeoning aesthetic discourse during the second half of the eighteenth century.

As might be expected in a work as heterogeneous as the *Encyclopédie*, the cluster of articles on *le goût* is varied and sometimes incongruous. The series begins with the Chevalier de Jaucourt's article on the physiological meaning of the term. The broader sense of the term, which the *Encyclopédie* placed in its *système des connaissances humaines* under the rubrics of grammar, literature, and philosophy, is succinctly addressed by Voltaire. Following Voltaire's article two further discussions of taste were interpolated: the first is a fairly extensive essay on taste which Montesquieu had offered D'Alembert in lieu of the articles on democracy and despotism that the editor had requested of him;[17] the second is D'Alembert's 1757 address to the Académie française, originally entitled 'Réflexions sur l'usage et sur l'abus de la philosophie dans les matières de goût'. Three extremely brief additions follow D'Alembert's contribution: Blondel contributed two short paragraphs on taste in architecture (GOÛT, *en Architecture*); the second, by Rousseau (GOÛT DU CHANT, *en musique*), is a technical explanation of the practice of non-notated ornamentation in song; finally, Paul Landois provided a cursory treatment of taste in painting – 'GOÛT, se dit *en Peinture*, du caractere particulier qui regne dans un tableau par rapport au choix des objets qui sont représentés & à la façon dont ils y sont rendus' (vii.770).

Jaucourt outlined the physiological processes involved in taste, and explained the reasons behind the differences that exist in taste, varying from one person to another but also from one moment to the next. The variations we witness, he argued, are due to disparate physical conditions that affect the mechanism of taste: 'le vin du Rhin', for example, 'si agréable aux adultes, irrite les jeunes enfans à cause de la délicatesse de leurs nerfs' (vii.760). Jaucourt noted the extension of the physiological term to refer to all experiences in which sensation is involved: 'Le *goût* en général est le mouvement d'un organe qui jouït de son objet, & qui en sent toute la bonté; c'est pourquoi le *goût* est de toutes les sensations: on a du *goût* pour la Musique & pour la Peinture, comme pour les ragoûts, quand l'organe de ces sensations savoure, pour ainsi dire, ces objets' (vii.758). Taste in its extended sense, then, depends on the organs of its experience – the eyes and ears in painting and music, for instance – just as physiological taste, according to Jaucourt, depends on the bodily system composed of the mouth, esophagus, and stomach.

Moving into what we would call aesthetics, but what the *Encyclopédie* classified under literature and philosophy, Voltaire reiterated and

16. Christopher Norris, *What's wrong with postmodernism* (New York 1990), p.219. Alain Cernuschi's *Penser la musique dans l'Encyclopédie* (Paris 2000) appeared too late to be taken into account in this essay.

17. See Montesquieu, *Essai sur le goût*, ed. C.-J. Beyer (Geneva 1967), p.12.

expanded the parallel Jaucourt had established between physiological taste and taste in the arts. For Voltaire, taste is 'le sentiment des beautés & des défauts dans tous les arts: c'est un discernement prompt comme celui de la langue & du palais, & qui prévient comme lui la réflexion; il est comme lui sensible & voluptueux à l'égard du bon; il rejette comme lui le mauvais avec soulevement; il est souvent, comme lui, incertain & égaré, ignorant même si ce qu'on lui présente doit lui plaire, & ayant quelquefois besoin comme lui d'habitude pour se former' (vii.761). Physiological taste and taste in the arts part ways at this point in the article, however. Voltaire claimed that taste in the arts requires more cultivation than physiological taste and that 'le *goût* [dans les arts] se forme insensiblement dans une nation qui n'en avoit pas' (vii.761). He remarked that the oft-repeated phrase, 'il ne faut point disputer des *goûts*', is perfectly correct when it is a question of physiological taste, but quite false when art is the object of judgements of taste. Whereas the former is dependent on the particular physical state of a food substance and on the proper functioning of the individual's organ of taste, which may vary from person to person or from moment to moment in the same person, as Jaucourt had noted, the latter has a fixed object, 'la belle nature', which never changes: 'comme ils [les arts] ont des beautés réelles, il y a un bon *goût* qui les discerne, & un mauvais *goût* qui les ignore' (vii.761). Our taste, our ability to bring judgements to bear on beauty, may be 'incertain & égaré'. 'La belle nature', however, remains a fixed point of reference; and our taste should be calibrated on its unwavering mark.

In Batteux's magisterial treatise, *Les Beaux Arts réduits à un même principe*, first published in 1746, or just a few years before the first volumes of the *Encyclopédie* appeared, judgements of taste were similarly located under the aegis of 'la belle Nature'. Taste was the ability in the perceiving subject to feel the objective validity of the imitative arts with respect to 'la belle Nature', which always remained their object – the ability, in other words, to 'sentir le bon, le mauvais, le médiocre, & de les distinguer avec certitude'.[18] This ability, which both Batteux and Voltaire saw in taste, made possible objective claims to good and bad taste: if two claims to taste consider 'le même objet & que l'un l'approuve & l'autre le condamne; il y en aura un des deux qui sera mauvais'.[19] Batteux further specified that taste joins the feeling of the perceiving subject – his or her 'sentiment' – with the objective qualities that gave rise to it:

elle [la belle Nature] doit nous flatter du côté de l'esprit, en nous offrant des objets parfaits en eux-mêmes, qui etendent & perfectionnent nos idées: c'est le beau. Elle doit flatter notre cœur en nous montrant dans ces mêmes objets des intérêts qui nous soient chers, qui tiennent à la conservation ou à la perfection de notre être, qui nous fassent sentir agréablement notre propre existence: c'est le bon.[20]

18. Batteux, *Les Beaux Arts*, p.80.
19. Batteux, *Les Beaux Arts*, p.133.
20. Batteux, *Les Beaux Arts*, p.81, 110.

Both interested and disinterested, both *esprit* and *sentiment*, taste is Janus-like in its affinities. The perfection of the object is perceived by the mind and becomes an object of contemplative pleasure, 'sans intérêt', simply by virtue of its perfection.[21] Yet because we are drawn into a relation with these objects through identification or repulsion, taste is also grounded in sentiment and self-interest, *l'amour propre.*[22]

Montesquieu's essay on taste, published posthumously and placed directly after Voltaire's article by the editors of the *Encyclopédie*, reiterated the distinctions between the interested and disinterested aspects of taste that Batteux had outlined in his treatise, turning this distinction, however, into evidence of the thoroughly relational or contingent nature of taste. Montesquieu argued that 'ce sont ces différens plaisirs de notre ame qui forment les objets du *goût* [...]. Par exemple, lorsque nous trouvons du plaisir à voir une chose avec une utilité pour nous, nous disons qu'elle est *bonne*; lorsque nous trouvons du plaisir à la voir, sans que nous y démêlions une utilité présente, nous l'appellons *belle*' (vii.762). The error of the ancients, Montesquieu remarked, was to regard all judgements of taste – 'le beau, le bon, l'agréable, le naïf, le délicat, le tendre, le gracieux, le je ne sais quoi, le noble, le grand, le sublime, le majestueux, &c.' – as referring to 'des qualités positives' which belonged to the objects to which these judgements refer, rather than being the reflection of a particular relationship to these objects. 'Les sources du beau, du bon, de l'agréable, &c.', he concluded, 'sont donc dans nous-mêmes' (vii.762). There was therefore a decided shift in emphasis in Montesquieu's perspective on taste, from the object – *la belle Nature* – to our relationship to objects in general.

Montesquieu distinguished 'le *goût* naturel & le *goût* acquis', and remarked on their complementarity. The first issues from the natural dispositions of the soul toward qualities such as variety and symmetry, the second from attitudes it has acquired as a result of education and exposure to society. Though he did not ground his discussion of taste in a concept of *la belle Nature* as had Batteux and Voltaire, Montesquieu nonetheless retained the concept of a fixed nature ('le *goût* naturel'), since taste remains rooted in an invariable humanity. The possibility of rendering positive judgements of taste was therefore left intact. Because of the ways in which it engages our natural dispositions, Montesquieu noted by way of example, Greek architecture is extremely pleasing because it appears uniform and yet offers an appropriate dose of variety. The gothic, however, because its tendency toward variety is excessive, 'est une espece d'énigme pour l'œil qui le voit, & l'ame est embarrassée, comme quand on lui présente un poëme obscur' (vii.763-64). For Montesquieu, taste is based on perhaps hidden but nonetheless universal regularities, and is more or less well-developed in given individuals: 'c'est une application prompte & exquise des regles même que

---

21. Batteux, *Les Beaux Arts*, p.118.
22. Batteux, *Les Beaux Arts*, p.104.

l'on ne connoît pas' (vii.762). Montesquieu was nonetheless more willing than either Voltaire or Batteux to allow the object qua object – '[ses] qualités positives' – to retreat as the measure of taste. This shift away from the object could be said to point to the impact and development of sensationism and the epistemological adjustments it fostered in eighteenth-century thought.

The discourse D'Alembert presented at the Académie française on 14 March 1757 was placed directly after Montesquieu's essay. A polemical defence of 'l'esprit philosophique' against 'l'ignorance ou l'envie', its essential claim is that philosophy can deliver us from the slavery of the 'faux principes de *goût*', the products of ignorance, which will always tend to constrict 'les bornes de l'art [et] prescrira des limites à nos plaisirs' (vii.769). Philosophy will provide us with the correct principles of taste. Taste is not arbitrary, but 'est donc fondé sur des principes incontestables; & ce qui en est une suite nécessaire, il ne doit point y avoir d'ouvrage de l'art dont on ne puisse juger en y appliquant ces principes', which remain to be identified. Because these critera are grounded in our pleasure or 'ennui' in contemplating works of art, D'Alembert agreed with Montesquieu that they are to be discovered in our relations to objects rather than within the objects themselves (vii.768). However, D'Alembert's article appears not to be concerned with taste per se, but rather with taste as a new front for the philosophical project: 'un des avantages de la Philosophie appliquée aux matieres de *goût*, est de nous guérir ou de nous garantir de la superstition littéraire' (vii.768). It is therefore less interesting as a commentary on taste than as a polemical piece.

If we reconsider the group of articles dealing with *le goût*, scrutinising each author's assessment of the shared aspects of taste – DuBos's reference to a sixth sense, or Shaftesbury's postulate of the equivalence of taste with virtue – it is clear that society is an important factor in the development of taste. For Voltaire some societies were better than others at the task of affirming and developing the natural attention human beings give to the qualities of art objects. Because it is cultivated in society, taste can be perfected over time: for example, 'Regnier fut goûté des François avant que Boileau parût.' On the contrary, if perfection has already been reached, if the artists of a given culture have already managed to capture 'la belle nature', taste may degenerate when these same artists, now fearful of being labelled as imitators, 'cherchent des routes écartées'. Voltaire concluded his article, specifically mentioning 'les Asiatiques', with a comparison between European and non-European cultures: 'il est de vastes pays où le *goût* n'est jamais parvenu; ce sont ceux où la société ne s'est point perfectionnée [...]. Quand il y a peu de société, l'esprit est retréci, sa pointe s'émousse, il n'a pas dequoi se former le *goût*' (vii.761). For Voltaire, it is only within society that individual dispositions to pleasure are confronted with a shared moral framework and sets of values – with 'les liens du sang & de la naissance', as society is defined in the *Encyclopédie* (xv.252) – which allow it to emerge as a collective judgement. It is this process of exchange among like men and women that produces 'les esprits bien faits' able to discern 'les beautés réelles' (vii.761).

Though Montesquieu's article on taste did not place great emphasis on the collective aspects of taste, in *De l'esprit des lois* he had argued that taste was moulded by 'la société des femmes' and explicitly connected *le goût* with an awareness of others: 'plus les peuples se communiquent, plus ils changent aisément de manières, parce que chacun est plus un spectacle pour un autre; on voit mieux les singularités des individus. Le climat qui fait qu'une nation aime à se communiquer, fait aussi qu'elle aime à changer; et ce qui fait qu'une nation aime à changer, fait aussi qu'elle se forme le goût.'[23] Montesquieu remarked on the connection between increased sociability and the refinement of taste: 'l'envie de plaire plus que les autres établit les parures [...]. on augmente sans cesse les branches de son commerce'. Social values and aristocratic standards of decorum were thus built into the notion of taste, even if, for Montesquieu, salon culture 'gâte les mœurs' to the same degree that it forms taste.[24] Voltaire identified a closed circle of European nations as the only ones in which sociability was sufficiently developed to shape taste: 'le *goût* n'a été le partage que de quelques peuples de l'Europe' (vii.761). In his contribution on taste, D'Alembert remarked on the need for a specifically philosophical outlook in matters of taste and an exchange of ideas among like thinkers: 'le même esprit philosophique qui nous oblige, faute de lumieres suffisantes, de suspendre à chaque instant nos pas dans l'étude de la nature & des objets qui sont hors de nous, doit au contraire dans tout ce qui est l'objet du *goût*, nous porter à la discussion' (vii.768). Certain conceptions of society and sociability – whether Eurocentric, aristocratic, philosophic or some combination thereof – were therefore explicit components of the concept of taste as it was constructed in the *Encyclopédie*. Various forms of publicness, in other words, were as crucial to the flowering of taste as it was to them.

The encyclopedists, however, never understood taste as utterly conventional, as a product of the negotiations for visibility and influence that occur within given communities, as we tend to view it today. In the eighteenth century, it is always assumed that taste fundamentally derives from the immanent experience of the subject, from the essentially private feeling of individuals. Montesquieu insisted on the interiority of taste, which is grounded in the pleasures of 'notre être' or 'l'âme' as it is moved by its perception of order, variety, symmetry, contrast, surprise, and so on (vii.762-65). D'Alembert followed Montesquieu in this regard, insisting that the basis for taste is 'uniquement & entierement en nous' (vii.768). Taste is first and foremost a private mechanism; only subsequently is it exposed to public scrutiny in order to be refined and confirmed. Just as

23. Montesquieu, *Œuvres complètes*, ed. R. Caillois, 2 vols (Paris 1951), ii.560.
24. Montesquieu, *Œuvres complètes*, ii.560.

D'Alembert's overall epistemology was private, based on 'un petit nombre de sensations [à] l'origine de nos connoissances', his understanding of taste was equally grounded in the immanence of feeling (vii.768). Likewise, as much as Voltaire insisted on its social cultivation and validation, at its core taste is for him a natural 'sentiment' or 'discernement' that attaches to 'les beautés réelles' of aesthetic objects. For the authors of the articles on taste as a group, taste was the mechanism that links the feeling and judgement of individuals to the natural and objective beauty of objects. Indeed, Batteux's description of the pre-existing harmony of the aesthetic relation of subject to object elided the social realm entirely: 'dans ce qui concerne le Goût, c'est notre cœur qui nous mene presque sans nous: & rien n'est si aisé que d'aimer ce qui est fait pour être aimé'.[25] Similarly, Montesquieu referred to taste as 'l'avantage de découvrir avec finesse & avec promptitude la mesure du plaisir que chaque chose doit donner aux hommes' (vii.762). As important as certain conceptions of society were for their understanding of taste – many of which reveal implicit exclusions, such as Voltaire's focus on 'l'homme de *goût*, le connoisseur' and his explicit dismissal of 'les Asiatiques' whose society remained underdeveloped – taste was always understood as corollary to a private epistemology.[26] Instead of being consubstantial with certain forms of publicness or understood as a social or ideological construction, as modern thinkers such as Pierre Bourdieu have characterised it, taste in the eighteenth century was concomitant with an epistemology in which taste was to sentiment as knowledge was to sensation. 'Choisir selon ses goûts', for Bourdieu, 'c'est opérer le *repérage* de biens objectivement accordés à sa position [sociale].'[27] For Bourdieu, taste is a product of education and functions as a class marker. For Voltaire, in contrast, taste pertains to an intimate connection between the individual soul, albeit that of the 'cultured' individual, and the beauty of objects.

Even the encyclopedists' notion of *habitude*, which at first glance might be understood to refer to socially determined practices and choices (as in Bourdieu's conception of *habitus*), underscores instead the essentially private function of taste. For the encyclopedists under discussion here, *habitude* did not necessarily involve convention but rather described the relationship between the subject and the accumulation of his or her

---

25. Batteux, *Les Beaux Arts*, p.83.
26. I borrow the idea of a private epistemology from Ian Hacking. See his 'How, why, when, and where did language go public?', *Common knowledge* 1 (1992), p.74-91.
27. Pierre Bourdieu, *La Distinction: critique sociale du jugement* (Paris 1979), p.258. Bourdieu writes: 'l'idéologie du goût naturel tire ses apparences et son efficacité de ce que, comme toutes les stratégies idéologiques qui s'engendrent dans la lutte des classes quotidienne, elle *naturalise* des différences réelles, convertissant en différences de nature des différences dans les modes d'acquisition de la culture' (p.73). Bourdieu connects – erronéement in my view – the emergence of a concern with form above representation in modern, post-impressionist art with the increasingly prevalent function of good taste as a 'pure' class marker, as no longer concerned with ethical or other content (p.iv-viii).

individual experiences of the world.[28] In his discussion of the development of taste in a given individual, Voltaire argued that 'ce n'est qu'avec de l'habitude & des réflexions qu'il [un jeune homme sensible] parvient à sentir tout-d'un-coup avec plaisir ce qu'il ne démêloit pas auparavant' (vii.761). In order to bring home the point that taste is not a matter of social convention ('opinion') but rather is based on the natural conformity of our senses to objects of beauty, D'Alembert imagined a tone-deaf composer who, wrongheadedly, 'pour prouver que le plaisir de la mélodie est un plaisir d'opinion, dénatureroit un air fort agréable en transposant au hasard les sons dont il est composé'. The true *philosophe*, D'Alembert continued, would examine carefully that which should be attributed to nature and that which is the result of convention: 'il ne confondra point le plaisir d'habitude avec celui que est purement arbitraire & d'opinion; distinction qu'on n'a peut-être pas assez faite en cette matiere' (vii.768). *L'habitude*, then, insofar as this reading of taste is concerned, was not understood as socially determined, but was founded instead on *la Nature*. And *la Nature*, in matters of taste, referred to the necessary meeting of the faculties of the individual and the natural beauty of objects.

In his article BEAU, Diderot rested many of his arguments on similar assumptions. Though twenty-first-century readers might tend to place the notions of taste and of beauty in different conceptual universes, because we take the former to be sustained largely by social forces whereas we identify the latter with subjective experience, for eighteenth-century writers the distinction does not appear to have been so dramatic. Diderot first considered problems with other philosophers' conceptions of beauty. Discussing Francis Hutcheson's *An Inquiry into the original of our ideas of beauty and virtue*, first published in 1725, Diderot argued that Hutcheson creates a fundamentally tautological description of beauty: 'M. Hutcheson entend par *beau*, ce qui est fait pour être saisi par le sens interne du *beau*' (ii.170). In his discussion of Hutcheson, Diderot sent the reader, with a *renvoi*, to the articles on taste. In their views of beauty, taste, and pleasure, Diderot concluded, Hutcheson and his followers 's'efforcent d'établir la nécessité *du sens interne du beau*: mais ils ne parviennent qu'à démontrer qu'il y a quelque chose d'obscur & d'impénétrable dans le plaisir que le *beau* nous cause' (ii.171). Another problem to which Diderot alluded, not without a measure of humor, is that the difficulty in defining beauty had resulted in a proliferation of philosophical categories and subcategories of beauty: he mentioned Hutcheson's relative and absolute beauty; and described P. Yves Marie André's 'beau essentiel', 'beau naturel', and 'beau artificiel', the latter

---

28. It is intriguing, however, to note that in *De l'esprit des lois* Montesquieu argued that taste rested on vanity. Opposing the positive effects of vanity with the negative effects of pride, he noted 'les biens sans nombre qui résultent de la vanité: de là le luxe, l'industrie, les arts, les modes, la politesse, le goût' (Montesquieu, *Œuvres complètes*, ii.560-61). Montesquieu therefore found vanity productive. Bourdieu, in contrast, critiques taste as a form of class-based *vanité*.

bifurcating further into 'un *beau de génie*, un *beau de goût*, & un *beau de pur caprice*', each of which carries its own tortuous explanation and justification (ii.172-74). Diderot also rejected Shaftesbury's equation of beauty and usefulness. Making disinterestedness a key to the distinctiveness of the appreciation of beauty, as Kant would many years later, Diderot argued that 'nous admirons souvent des formes sans que la notion de l'utile nous y porte. Quand le propriétaire d'un cheval ne le trouveroit jamais *beau* que quand il compare la forme de cet animal au service qu'il prétend en tirer; il n'en est pas de même du passant à qui il n'appartient pas' (ii.175).

The definition of beauty Diderot presented in his article elegantly characterises as beautiful 'tout ce qui contient en soi de quoi réveiller dans mon entendement l'idée de rapports' (ii.176). Diderot's understanding of the beautiful avoided the pitfalls he had outlined in Hutcheson, André, Batteux, and Shaftesbury, by shifting the emphasis from a nearly exclusive focus on the object, what Batteux called 'la belle nature', to the human act of perception. However, objectivity in no way disappeared in Diderot's conception. While discussing the problems in Christian Wolff's analysis of the question, for example, he strongly affirmed the objective beauty of aesthetic objects, noting that 'le philosophe Leibnitien [Wolff] [...] semble prétendre d'abord qu'une chose est *belle*, parce qu'elle nous plait; au lieu qu'elle ne nous plaît que parce qu'elle est *belle*' (ii.170). In his own definition, Diderot understood beauty as the encounter between the objective qualities of objects, which are incontrovertible, and our perception of relationships, which can vary: 'que je pense ou ne pense point à la façade du Louvre [...] qu'il y eût des hommes ou, qu'il n'y en eût point, elle n'en seroit pas moins *belle*, mais seulement pour des êtres possibles constitués de corps & d'esprit comme nous; car pour d'autres, elle pourroit n'être ni *belle* ni *laide*, ou même être *laide*' (ii.176). A verifiable relation exists between the given parameters of our perception and the configurations of objects.

When we turn to the collective dimension of aesthetic judgements, it is clear that Diderot's examination of beauty depends on assumptions similar to those of D'Alembert. Like his fellow editor, in the early 1750s Diderot relied on an empiricist epistemology for which the isolated individual is the locus of judgements of beauty. As D'Alembert had done at greater length in the 'Discours préliminaire', in the article on beauty Diderot briefly outlined the origin and development of knowledge through sensation: 'nous naissons avec la faculté de sentir & de penser [...]. Nous naissons avec des besoins' (ii.175). The final pages of the article are devoted to explaining why aesthetic judgements vary, given the common origin of sensation and thought. Differences in education, morality, social factors, and physical infirmity are accidents in his scheme, all subsumed under the fundamental and universal ability of the mind to perceive relationships. Voltaire's understanding of the real beauty of a given object relied on 'les esprits bien faits' (vii.761). By claiming that 'il n'y a peut-être pas deux hommes sur toute la terre, qui apperçoivent exactement les mêmes rapports dans un même objet, & qui le jugent *beau* au même degré', Diderot success-fully undermined many of the presuppositions behind Voltaire's assump-tion of a coterie of aristocratic 'esprits bien faits' (ii.180-81). As Diderot disrupted Voltaire's assumption of a common humanity, he found a new common principle in 'la perception des rapports', radicalising and formalis-ing the empirical framework he shared with D'Alembert. Aesthetic judge-ments based on a 'beau réel' varied insofar as the particularities of perception varied; yet they rested on the same principle of perceived relationships (ii.176). Diderot had crafted an exceptionally elegant defi-nition of beauty. Some readers of the *Encyclopédie* may have wondered, however, what exactly was shared, other than an abstract principle of sub-jective perception, in this conception of *le beau*.[29]

Eighteenth-century writers viewed taste as a nearly instantaneous and irrational affinity between a perceiving subject and an object worthy of his or her attention. From a certain perspective, therefore, taste was fully com-patible with an emerging aesthetics, as the field developed into the 1770s and beyond, since aesthetics was based on sensation and feeling. No article devoted to 'aesthetics' was included in the volumes of the *Encyclopédie*; however, one does appear in the *Supplément*, drawn from Johann Georg Sulzer's *Allgemeine Theorie der schönen Künste* (1771-74). The article ESTHE-TIQUE notes that it is '[un] terme nouveau, inventé pour désigner une science qui n'a été réduite en forme que depuis peu d'années' (ii.872). Sulzer defined aesthetics as 'la philosophie des beaux-arts, ou la science de déduire de la nature du goût la théorie générale, & les regles fondamentales des beaux-arts. Ce mot est pris du terme grec αισθυσις, qui signifie le senti-ment. Ainsi l'*esthétique* est proprement la science des sentimens. Le grand but des beaux-arts est d'exciter un vif sentiment du vrai & du bon' (*Supp.*, ii.872). In Sulzer's definition, aesthetics is derived from taste which is grounded, in turn, on sensation. Because the fine arts give us pleasure or displeasure, Sulzer argued, 'il faut donc que leur théorie soit fondée sur celle des sentimens, & des notions confuses que nous acquerrons à l'aide des sens' (*Supp.*, ii.872). Sulzer's article on taste (*Geschmack*), which was not included in the *Supplément*, made sensation the primary operator of taste: 'taste is really nothing other than the capacity to sense beauty [...] [which] flatters our imagination by presenting itself in an attractive, pleas-ing form'.[30] Though he noted that aesthetics is still in its infancy and that 'il faut donc ranger l'*esthétique* au nombre des sciences philosophiques qui sont encore très-imparfaites', Sulzer regarded its principles as simple, unproble-matic, and driven by precise goals (*Supp.*, ii.873):

---

29. In a chapter devoted to the *Salons*, Daniel Brewer notes that the abstractness of this approach 'falls apart' when it is applied practically (*The Discourse of Enlightenment in eight-eenth-century France*, Cambridge 1993, p.145).

30. Johann Georg Sulzer, *Allgemeine Theorie der schönen Künste*, in *Aesthetics and the art of musical composition in the German Enlightenment*, ed. N. K. Baker and T. Christensen (Cambridge 1995), p.48.

La psychologie enseigne l'origine des sentimens, & explique ce qui les rend agréables ou désagréables. La solution générales de ces problêmes, fournit deux ou trois théorêmes qui sont les principes de l'*esthétique*; à l'aide de ces principes on détermine d'un côté la nature des objets *esthétiques*, & de l'autre la loi selon laquelle ces objets agissent sur l'ame, comme aussi la disposition [où] l'esprit doit être pour recevoir leur impression. Tout cela peut être réduit à un petit nombre de propositions pratiques, qui suffiront à un bon génie, pour le diriger dans l'exécution des ouvrages de son art.

For Sulzer, as aesthetics evolved, it would be able to derive specific principles from the nature of beauty and the effects it produces in the spectator. These principles could then be applied to the creation of art works. The entire edifice rests on an empirical epistemology of sensation and feeling, which Sulzer called 'la psychologie', connecting sensation to truth ('le vrai' and 'le bon') through the experience of beauty.

A perceptible shift in the understanding of aesthetic pleasure can be detected in discussions of taste, one which had moved away from *le goût* as a quasi-aristocratic faculty, founded on a courtly *je-ne-sais-quoi*. This shift was already present to some extent in the *Encyclopédie*. In his article on aesthetics in the *Supplément* Sulzer revealed a tendency towards a science of sentiment, and towards taste as an element in an equation leading to the perfection of the process of artistic creation. Whereas Batteux and Voltaire had placed first emphasis on the qualities of ideal objects, Sulzer began with psychology. Rousseau's articles touching upon the question of taste, though hardly exemplary of any general consensus on the matter, offer an interesting case study of a different tendency – one that emphasised sensibility and feeling as forms of shared intersubjective community. Because the articles on music Rousseau contributed to the *Encyclopédie* were rewritten for his *Dictionnaire de musique*, many of which were included in the *Supplément*, they offer a convenient measure of the development of his thinking in this area. One important facet of this development involves a move to preserve the inscrutable quality of taste in music, its peculiar immediacy, and its implicit commonality, from what Rousseau undoubtedly perceived as the encroachment of an ever-expanding and naively empiricist or materialist discourse, in particular that of Rameau.

In the early 1750s, with the repercussions from the *Querelle des bouffons* at a peak, music was perceived as an area in which commonality was an unusually problematic, and indeed hotly debated, issue. In many contributions to the *Querelle*, a sense of lost commonality was expressed in the assertion that French and Italian music, then divorced from each other, had once derived from a single *goût*. Rousseau argued in the *Lettre sur la musique fran-çoise* that 'il n'y a eu pendant long-tems qu'un[e] même Musique en France et en Italie'.[31] Pellegrin, on the other side of the house, claimed that musical taste had been universal in the seventeenth century: 'une preuve que le goût

31. Jean-Jacques Rousseau, *Œuvres complètes*, ed. B. Gagnebin and M. Raymond, 5 vols (Paris 1959-1995), v.308.

& le caractere de la Musique étoit universel du tems de Mr de Lully, c'est qu'il n'auroit jamais pû suivre le goût François, s'il ne l'avoit apporté du berceau'.[32] In yet another view of the problems surrounding taste, Grimm noted that there was a point at which universal responses fractured into specific, national tastes. Everyone can agree that harmonic sounds are pleasurable, Grimm wrote; national tastes, however, are related to the character of the language and are modulated by sociability.[33]

Begun in the *Encyclopédie* in several articles by D'Alembert and continued in the *Supplément* in articles drawn from Rousseau's *Dictionnaire*, a debate arose concerning the explanations Rameau had advanced for musical plea-sure. This debated centred on Rameau's theories of the *corps sonore* and on the relationship that pertains between the complex configurations of musical objects and our perception of them. The notion of taste might be construed as having provided opportunities for the emerging field of aes-thetics, as I suggested above, because of its reliance on the empirical ground of immediate experience. Yet it was precisely this grounding that led to a shift, particularly evident in Rousseau's thinking, from the largely object-centred discourse on taste of the early eighteenth century (the rem-nants of which were still present to some extent in the *Encyclopédie*) to a con-ception of the aesthetic experience that gives more space to imagination. Even in the more radical formulations of the *Encyclopédie*, the ability of taste to provide a foundation for commonality was jeopardised by its monadic empiricism. In the *Supplément*, in contrast, the connection to others was formulated, in the margins of an aging discourse of taste, on the imagination. In the articles drawn from the *Dictionnaire de musique*, Rousseau's discussion placed itself in strong opposition to the empiricism of Rameau and his populariser, D'Alembert.

In the articles on musical topics he had composed for the *Encyclopédie*, D'Alembert made a strong bid for the promise music offered the philoso-pher as an art based on natural principles. In the 'Discours préliminaire' D'Alembert argued that our understanding and use of music could develop further if music were to take advantage of the insights of the new empirical philosophy (i.xii):

La Musique [...] est devenue peu-à-peu une espece de discours ou même de langue, par laquelle on exprime les différens sentimens de l'ame, ou plûtôt ses différentes passions: mais pourquoi réduire cette expression aux passions seules, & ne pas l'étendre, autant qu'il est possible, jusqu'aux sensations mêmes? Quoique les per-ceptions que nous recevons par divers organes different entr'elles autant que leurs objets, on peut néanmoins les comparer sous un autre point de vûe qui leur est commun, c'est-à-dire, par la situation de plaisir ou de trouble où elles mettent notre ame.

---

32. Simon Joseph Pellegrin, *Dissertation sur la musique françoise et italienne*, in *La Querelle des bouffons*, ed. D. Launay, 3 vols (Geneva 1973), iii.1671.

33. Friedrich Melchior, Freiherr von Grimm, *Lettre sur Omphale*, in Launay, *Querelle*, i.37.

Articulating his music theory with the sensationist epistemology that he expounded elsewhere in the 'Discours préliminaire' where he traced the origin of all ideas to sensations, D'Alembert suggested that music could express the full gamut of feeling – a kind of keyboard to our myriad pleasures and pains – rather than remain confined within the traditional categories of the passions.[34] These possibilities would be 'saisies par l'homme de génie, senties par l'homme de goût, apperçûes par l'homme d'esprit' (i.xii).

In his popularisation and limited critique of the music theory of Jean-Philippe Rameau, D'Alembert objected that the rules of harmony as a whole cannot truly be said to derive from the resonance of the *corps sonore*, as Rameau had argued. In the article FONDAMENTAL, he rejected the claim that 'l'accompagnement représente le corps sonore': 'M. Rameau a déduit sans doute avec vraissemblance de la résonnance du corps sonore, les principales regles de l'harmonie; mais la plûpart de ces regles sont uniquement l'ouvrage de la réflexion [...] & nullement l'ouvrage de la nature' (vii.59). D'Alembert emphasised experience: 'l'oreille est ici le vrai juge, ou plûtôt le seul' (vii.58); 'car encore une fois l'expérience est ici le grand juge' (vii.59). Here, as in the 'Discours préliminaire', he speculated on the possibility of entire ranges of new chords that could be identified as pleasurable and therefore accepted as belonging to the *basse fondamentale*, an implicit bass line consisting of chord roots occurring in a succession of harmonies, which he calls 'la vraie boussole de l'oreille dans le chant de notre gamme, & le guide secret qui nous suggere ce chant' (vii.60).[35] For D'Alembert, the ear should guide theory, not the reverse. In seeming contradiction with Diderot's definition of *le beau*, D'Alembert asserted that 'la considération des rapports est tout-à-fait illusoire pour rendre raison du plaisir que nous font les accords consonans' (vii.62). Rousseau had made precisely the same claim in volume four of the *Encyclopédie*, in the article CONSONANCE. Referring to Diderot as 'un écrivain judicieux', Rousseau nonetheless regarded with suspicion the claim that the simplicity of ratios was the key to musical pleasure, the claim Diderot had made in the first of his *Mémoires sur différents sujets de mathématiques* and that he made again, in somewhat different form, in the article BEAU.[36] In the former text, Diderot argued that 'le plaisir musical consiste dans la perception des rapports des sons. D'où il s'ensuit évidemment qu'il sera d'autant plus difficile de juger d'une pièce de musique qu'elle sera plus chargée de ces rapports et que ces

---

34. Michael O'Dea has characterised this distinction by noting that sensations 'differ from passions by being reponses to natural occurences rather than to situations arising in human relations' (Michael O'Dea, *Jean-Jacques Rousseau: music, illusion and desire*, New York 1995, p.48).

35. For a detailed examination of D'Alembert's relationship to Rameau's theory, see Thomas Christensen, *Rameau and musical thought in the Enlightenment* (Cambridge 1993), p.252-90.

36. The *Supplément* retained this conception of musical pleasure in Sulzer's article on CONSONNANCE (ii.554).

rapports seront plus éloignés.'[37] Rousseau suggested that this hypothesis is 'vraissemblable', but that 'il ne la faut pas regarder comme démontrée' (iv.51). Taking the examples of the minor third and the diminished third, Rousseau pursued his argument (iv.51):

comment il se peut faire que deux sons, dont l'un fait 5 vibrations pendant que l'autre en fait 6, produisent une *consonnance* agréable, & que deux sons, dont l'un fait 6 vibrations pendant que l'autre en fait 7, produisent une si affreuse dissonnance. Quoi, dans l'un de ces rapports les vibrations s'accordent de six en six, & mon oreille est charmée; dans l'autre elles s'accordent de sept en sept, & mon oreille est écorchée? Il y a plus, & je demande encore comment il se fait qu'après cette premiere dissonnance la dureté des accords n'augmente pas à mesure que les rapports des vibrations qui les forment deviennent plus composés.

The various degrees of complexity exhibited by the ratios determining musical intervals, in other words, do not match our perception of their consonance and dissonance. Rousseau was thus politely but firmly sceptical with regard to Diderot's theory of *rapports* in the articles he composed in 1749 for the *Encyclopédie*.[38]

Though Rousseau did not elaborate on the reasons we find certain intervals more pleasurable than others, in the articles from the *Dictionnaire de musique* that were included in the *Supplément* he shifts to an anthropological approach to music in order to account for our reactions to it. Frédéric de Castillon, the academician responsible for the music articles of the *Supplément*, began the article MUSIQUE with two key paragraphs from Rousseau's article of the same name in the *Dictionnaire*. These paragraphs incorporate pivotal elements of Rousseau's thinking as it developed from the mid-1750s on. Rousseau proposed a strong distinction between two types of music: 'naturelle' and 'imitative' (*Supp.*, iii.982). Natural music, 'bornée au seul physique', gives sensual pleasure: 'telle est la *musique* des chansons, des hymnes, des cantiques, de tous les chants qui ne sont que des combinaisons de Sons Mélodieux, & en général toute *musique* qui n'est qu'harmonieuse' (*Supp.*, iii.982).[39] In contrast to natural music, the effects

---

37. Denis Diderot, *Mémoires sur différents sujets de mathématiques*, DPV ii.236.

38. The absence of references to works by Diderot beyond the early 1750s in this essay is not intended to imply that Diderot did not move away the positions he took in the first volumes of the *Encyclopédie*. In his discussion of the *Salons*, for example, Daniel Brewer has explored the ways in which Diderot questioned the ability of the theoretical idiom to provide an account of 'what [he] seems able to sense only in terms of nongeneralisable particularity' (Brewer, *The Discourse of Enlightenment*, p.145). Given the modest scope of this essay, I have generally limited my references to arguments from the *Encyclopédie* that are pursued in the *Supplément*. For many reasons, Diderot apparently did not participate in the *Supplément* project. See Kathleen Hardesty, *The Supplément to the Encyclopédie* (The Hague 1977), p.7-10.

39. In this context, the terms 'mélodieux' and 'harmonieux' appear, unusually in Rousseau's writings, as synonymous: both refer in this instance to the pleasure of the ear. Castillon's additions to Rousseau's original article aim to attenuate Rousseau's formulations, proposing a compromise reuniting natural and imitative music and suggesting various changes to French prosody to make French music more appealing.

of imitative music, according to Rousseau, run deeper. Linked to language, imitative music is moving precisely because it enters into an imaginary realm of human relations: 'par des inflexions vives accentuées, &, pour ainsi dire, parlantes, exprime toutes les passions, peint tous les tableaux, rend tous les objets [...] & porte ainsi jusqu'au cœur de l'homme des sentimens propres à l'émouvoir' (*Supp.*, iii.982). Imitative music, 'cette *musique* vraiment lyrique & théâtrale', was the basis of the poems of antiquity and the source of the astonishing effects that Greek historians describe. The passage borrowed from Rousseau's *Dictionnaire* concludes: 'tant qu'on cherchera des effets moraux dans la seule physique des sons, on ne les y trouvera point, & l'on raisonnera sans s'entendre' (*Supp.*, iii.982).

Rousseau's division of music into 'naturelle' and 'imitative', not present as such in articles he contributed to the *Encyclopédie*, contained an implicit critique of those who based aesthetic response on empirical matters, from Rameau's proposal of the *corps sonore* as the basis of musical pleasure to Diderot's early consideration of *rapports*. His thinking is even clearer in a passage from the *Dictionnaire* in the article MUSIQUE, which was not included in the *Supplément* but is worth quoting at length. Rousseau offered an example to bolster his argument that the physical action of sounds was not the cause of the effects music has on the listener:

J'ai ajoûté dans la même Planche [la Planche N] le célèbre *Rans-des-Vaches*, cet Air si chéri des Suisses qu'il fut défendu sous peine de mort de le jouer dans leurs Troupes, parce qu'il faisoit fondre en larmes, déserter ou mourir ceux qui l'entendoient, tant il excitoit en eux l'ardent desir de revoir leur pays. On chercheroit en vain dans cet Air les accens énergiques capables de produire de si étonnans effets. Ces effets, qui n'ont aucun lieu sur les étrangers, ne viennent que de l'habitude, des souvenirs, de mille circonstances qui, retracées par cet Air à ceux qui l'entendent, et leur rappellant leur pays, leurs anciens plaisirs, leur jeunesse, et toutes leurs façons de vivre, excitent en eux une douleur amère d'avoir perdu tout cela. La *Musique* alors n'agit point précisément comme *Musique*, mais comme signe mémoratif. Cet Air, quoique toujours le même, ne produit plus aujourd'hui les mêmes effets qu'il produisoit ci-devant sur les Suisses; parce qu'ayant perdu le goût de leur première simplicité, ils ne la regrettent plus quand on la leur rappelle.[40]

The moral dimension Rousseau sought to make part of his music theory – moral effects he was convinced were lost to his contemporaries – could not abide an aesthetics based on taste understood as a physical rapport. The taste to which Rousseau refered above was embedded in personal and cultural meanings which were triggered in the imagination by a particular music.

The article GOÛT, one of two included in the *Supplément*, also taken from Rousseau's *Dictionnaire* (the other article, by Albrecht von Haller, concerns the physiological dimensions of taste), appears at first glance to hark

---

40. Rousseau, *Œuvres complètes*, v.924.

back to more traditional conceptions.[41] For Rousseau, the paradox of taste lies in its indeterminacy and failure to obey any discernible rules (*Supp.*, iii.247):

il y a dans la mélodie des chants plus agréables que d'autres, quoiqu'également bien modulés. Il y a dans l'harmonie des choses d'effet & des choses sans effet, toutes également régulieres [...]. De ces manieres, les unes plaisent plus que les autres; & loin de les pouvoir soumettre aux regles, on ne peut pas même les déterminer. Lecteur, rendez-moi raison de ces différences, & je vous dirai ce que c'est que le *goût*.[42]

Rousseau distinguishes between two kinds of taste. On the one hand there is each person's individual taste, improperly referred to as 'le goût', which differs from person to person and which derives 'tantôt de la différente disposition des organes [...] tantôt du caractère particulier de chaque homme [...] tantôt de la diversité d'âge ou de sexe' (*Supp.*, iii.248). Because these differences are anchored in the isolated characters or dispositions of individuals, there can be no disputing about this kind of taste. On the other hand, there is 'un goût général sur lequel tous les gens bien organisés s'accordent' – taste proper (*Supp.*, iii.248). Rousseau's reference to 'tous les gens bien organisés' is distinct from Voltaire's assumption in the *Encyclopédie* that taste belongs to 'les esprits bien faits' (vii:761). Unlike Voltaire's criterion, which points to a courtly or aristocratic identity of distinction, Rousseau's definition refers to the ordinary health of mind and body. For Rousseau, judgements of taste cannot rely on the rules of art or on reason. Rousseau does insist that taste is grounded in nature, in 'l'ordre des beautés naturelles' (*Supp.*, iii.248). However, he concludes his analysis on a somewhat different note. Returning to the quarrels that opposed French and Italian music beginning in the 1750s, Rousseau remarks that since 'nature' is not available as a reliable point of reference ('les préjugés de l'habitude ou de l'éducation changent souvent, par des conventions arbitraires, l'ordre des beautés naturelles'), the only way to resolve the conflict between the two camps is by a show of hands: 'je ne vois guere d'autre moyen de terminer la dispute que celui de compter les voix' (*Supp.*, iii.248). By turning to a pragmatic solution, one that assumes the social determination of

41. Michael O'Dea has remarked on the incompatibility between the category of taste and the emotional identification that is central to Rousseau's later writings on musical experience. O'Dea considers the article on taste as an anomaly, given the general thrust of these later writings, noting that 'many of the formulations to be found in the article *Goût* could have come from any of a hundred more conventional pens than Rousseau's' (*Jean-Jacques Rousseau*, p.66).

42. The first paragraph of the *Dictionnaire* article, the only part of the article not included in the *Supplément*, elegantly outlines a relatively orthodox understanding of taste: 'de tous les dons naturels le *Goût* est celui qui se sent le mieux et qui s'explique le moins; il ne seroit pas ce qu'il est, si l'on pouvoit le définir: car il juge des objets sur lesquels le jugement n'a plus de prise, et sert, si j'ose parler ainsi, de lunettes à la raison' (*Œuvres complètes*, v.841).

judgements of taste, Rousseau placed in abeyance the discourse on taste outlined in the early volumes of the *Encyclopédie*. Rousseau's solution to the dispute between French and Italian music unquestionably assumes that nature is, or was at one time, somewhere present; yet it remains inaccessible. The only resolution to the conflict, therefore, is to rely on a pragmatic, social determination of values. Rousseau's conclusion reveals the foundation of the rational public sphere I described at the beginning of this essay. While he maintains that there is something called 'good taste' which relies on a fundamental or essential beauty, because the latter is not necessarily accessible to us taste remains indeterminate and undecidable. Rousseau indicates that beauty does exist and that all human beings have an equal potential to experience it; yet he argues in the end that making one's voice heard was the only way to decide the matter of taste since the aesthetic community he imagined did not yet exist.

From the *Encyclopédie* to the *Supplément*, the notion of taste undergoes a discernable shift from the aristocratic ability, based on a *je-ne-sais-quoi*, to detect the objective beauty that belongs to objects, towards a hypothetical, shared intersubjective assessment based on an inaccessible 'nature'. Of course, a plurality of voices is at work within both texts. Rousseau's basic difference with respect to Sulzer, for example, lies in his rejection of the idea that taste is compatible with rules. For Sulzer taste provides aesthetics with both the general theory of the fine arts and their essential rules. In contrast, Rousseau sees a fundamental disjunction between the inexplicable nature of taste, on the one hand, and theory or rules, on the other.

From another angle, it cannot be denied that, to a great extent, a more fundamental continuity remains in force from the *Encyclopédie* to the *Supplément*. From Voltaire's article on taste in the *Encyclopédie* to Rousseau's contributions to the *Supplément*, aesthetic value is predicated on an assumed continuum between the production and consumption of beauty. In the article on taste from the *Supplément*, Rousseau notes that 'le génie crée, mais le *goût* choisit' (*Supp.*, iii.248). Similarly, Rousseau defined SENSIBI-LITÉ, sending the reader of the *Supplément* back his article on taste, as the 'disposition de l'ame qui inspire au compositeur les idées vives dont il a besoin; à l'exécutant, la vive expression de ces mêmes idées; & à l'auditeur, la vive impression des beautés & des défauts de la musique qu'on lui fait entendre' (*Supp.*, iv.779). These were precisely the categories invoked by D'Alembert in the 'Discours préliminaire' with respect to the new possibilities he imagined for musical art: these possibilities would be 'saisies par l'homme de génie, senties par l'homme de goût, apperçûes par l'homme d'esprit' (i.xii). A larger whole – an aesthetic continuum – ensures the integrity and unimpeded concord of the acts of creation, execution, and reception. Diderot's extreme position with respect to this continuum in the posthumously published *Le Neveu de Rameau* – a position Hegel would exploit in his *Phänomenologie des Geistes* (1807) – is evident in the split between the nephew's exquisite taste and his absolute inability to create.[43] Surely not incidentally, *Le Neveu de Rameau* raised the spectre of this split through music. Rousseau's innovation, from the *Encyclopédie* to the *Supplément*, consists in the hesitation he felt with respect to the assurances of D'Alembert's empiricism, which was grounded in Rameau's theories. Instead of responding to the difficulties he saw in the empiricist position by positing a radical split between artist and spectator, as Diderot did in the *Neveu*, Rousseau projected hypothetical aesthetic communities which would rely on a shared imagination.

However, for Rousseau the kind of community to which the Rans-des-Vaches testified was no longer possible and a renewed aesthetic community appeared as yet unattainable, though perhaps ideally present in the effect of the operatic air.[44] Whereas a materialist thinker such as Helvétius saw laws and education as the solution to the split between individual and society, Rousseau saw the solution as deriving from a fundamental, yet either inaccessible or suspended, spontaneous identification and *pitié*.[45] Thus, in the article on taste, the only solution to the quandary of taste that Rousseau could imagine in the present was a pragmatic show of hands.

Eighteenth-century discourse on taste comes to a halt with Kant's *Kritik der Urteilskraft* (1790). What Rousseau had formulated as imagination, Kant would later theorise as a hypothetical, but lost connection to others – a hypothetical *sensus communis*. However, whereas most eighteenth-century views of taste, including Rousseau's, depended on forms of *sensibilité*, engagement or interest to provide a shared moral foundation, the only way for Kant to justify the commonality of his concept of taste was to evacuate interest entirely, to extract taste from 'sensible charm', placing it instead on the 'supersensible substrate of humanity'.[46] Here, we are far

43. As Giorgio Agamben has written, 'precisely because he knows what is substantial only under the guise of duality and alienation, Rameau's nephew on the one hand is capable of *judging* it (and his language is in fact brilliant with intelligence) but on the other hand has lost the ability to *grasp* it: his consciousness is radical inconsistency, his fullness is absolute lack' (*The Man without content*, translated by G. Albert, Stanford, Calif. 1999, p.26).

44. 'Un *Air* savant et agréable, un *Air* trouvé par le Génie et composé par le Goût, est le chef-d'œuvre de la Musique' (Rousseau, *Œuvres complètes*, v.640). The air that can unite both intellect and pleasure, the incalculable inspiration of the artist and the shared cultural codes of good taste, is for Rousseau the finest accomplishment of music.

45. For an excellent discussion of identification in Rousseau, see Pierre Force, 'Self-Love, identification, and the origin of political economy', *Yale French studies* 92 (1997), p.46-64.

46. Kant, *Critique of judgment*, p.230, 213. Kant defines a judgement of taste as 'based on a concept (the concept of a general basis of nature's subjective purposiveness for our power of judgment), but this concept does not allow us to cognise and prove anything concerning the object because it is intrinsically indeterminable and inadequate for cognition; and yet this same concept does make the judgment of taste valid for everyone, because (though each person's judgment is singular and directly accompanies his intuition) the basis that determines the judgment lies, perhaps, in the concept of what may be considered the supersensible substrate of humanity' (p.213).

from the conceptions outlined in the *Encyclopédie* and its *Supplément*. As Adorno has characterised Kant's view of the supersensible, 'aesthetic feeling is not the feeling that is aroused: It is astonishment vis-à-vis what is beheld rather than vis-à-vis what it is about; it is a being overwhelmed by what is aconceptual and yet determinate, not the subjective affect released.'[47]

Reflecting an ongoing suspicion of these claims, many commentators and critics have found aesthetics to be a suspect form of activity. On the one hand, for Bourdieu, taste is a form of distinction and exclusion. On the other, as Christopher Norris has put it, the illusion of 'aesthetic ideology', as identified by Theodor Adorno and Paul de Man, 'promises to reconcile subject and object, mind and nature, concepts and sensuous intuitions' – illusory promises.[48] For our modernity, beauty is considered to be bereft of truth because art as an object of taste is placed outside the guideposts of truth and morality.[49] As the *Encyclopédie* and the *Supplément* attest, eighteenth-century perspectives, although quite distinct from those of modernity, nonetheless reveal the problematic nature of taste within an empiricist or sensationist framework. Eighteenth-century writers relentlessly sought in taste a point of connection between the singular feeling of the individual and shared values and purposes. Must we be suspicious of the universalism of eighteenth-century ambitions with respect to taste and beauty? Perhaps so, when we are faced with Enlightenment aesthetic systems that would derive a series of precepts for beauty from an empirical psychology of taste. However, it would be unwise to dismiss as part and parcel of 'aesthetic ideology' the more modest intersubjective ambitions of many eighteenth-century reflections on taste and aesthetics. 'What happens when there is no immortal realm behind the beautiful person or thing is just what happens when there *is* an immortal realm behind the beautiful person or thing', writes Elaine Scarry from a decidedly modern perspective – 'the perceiver is led to a more capacious regard for the world.'[50] And this more capacious regard for the world, which necessarily involves others, was precisely the object of the *Encyclopédie*.

47. Theodor W. Adorno, *Aesthetic theory*, ed. G. Adorno and R. Tiedemann, ed. and translated by R. Hullot-Kentor (Minneapolis, Minn. 1997), p.164.
48. Christopher Norris, *Paul de Man* (New York 1988), p.149.
49. Bernstein, *The Fate of art*, p.4.
50. Elaine Scarry, *On beauty and being just* (Princeton, N.J. 1999), p.47-48.

ANN-MARIE THORNTON

Translating the garden: references to Philip Miller's *The Gardener's dictionary* in the *Encyclopédie* of Diderot and D'Alembert

THE present study aims to examine the eighty-five *Encyclopédie* articles that refer to the celebrated English gardener Philip Miller (1691-1771). These articles shed new light upon the reception of Miller's influential *The Gardener's dictionary* in eighteenth-century France, and exemplify the role of source material in the construction and communication of knowledge in the *Encyclopédie*. Miller's *The Gardener's and florist's dictionary* was published in 1724.[1] The work was replaced in 1731 by a folio volume entitled *The Gardener's dictionary*,[2] of which a second little-altered edition appeared in 1733 followed by *An appendix to The Gardener's dictionary*, which Miller intended his readers to insert into their copies of the work, in 1735. A third edition of the dictionary was published in 1737, and in 1739 *The Second volume of The Gardener's dictionary*, which incorporated the appendix, completed the first three editions of the work.[3] *The Gardener's dictionary* was highly successful: by the mid-1730s it was 'more generally consulted than any other book on the subject'.[4] Miller overcame his deference to earlier purchasers and published four more editions of the work, the fourth in 1743, the sixth in 1752, the seventh in 1759, and the eighth in 1768.[5] A fifth London edition of 1747 has been recorded but not yet located.[6] In view of the obvious success of *The Gardener's dictionary*, it is surprising that no separate French translation appeared until 'shortly after 1775', when *Le Grand Dictionnaire des jardiniers* was published by the Librairie encyclopédique in Paris.[7] Although this French version had the merit of being based upon GD68 which adopted Lin-

---

1. This dictionary, which was published in 2 vols in 8°, will henceforth be referred to as GFD24.

2. The first edition of *The Gardener's dictionary* will henceforth be referred to as GD31.

3. *The Second volume* will henceforth be referred to as GD39.

4. 'Preface', GD39.

5. The sixth, seventh, and eighth editions will henceforth be referred to as GD52, GD59, and GD68. GD59 was originally published in 112 numbers from 1756 to 1759.

6. Blanche Henrey, *British botanical and horticultural literature before 1800*, 2nd edn (Oxford 1999), iii.90.

7. Frans A. Stafleu and Richard S. Cowan, *Taxonomic literature: a selective guide to botanical publications and collections*, 2nd edn, 7 vols (Utrecht 1976-1988), iii (1981), n° 6050. A number of translated extracts of *The Gardener's dictionary* also appeared from 1768.

naean indices, Miller's dictionary had been translated far earlier in Holland and Germany.[8] The eighty-five *Encyclopédie* articles that cite Miller demonstrate that *The Gardener's dictionary* became known to French readers far earlier than has hitherto been supposed.

The usefulness of these articles as a means of cross-cultural exchange depends upon their status as translations of Miller's text. Translation was a chief means by which botanical and horticultural knowledge was disseminated throughout Europe in the eighteenth century, when a broad range of scientific literature was translated with speed and accuracy, often by specialists who enriched their translations with accounts of new observations and experiments. In 1764 Miller produced a revised English version of Henri-Louis Duhamel Du Monceau's *Eléments d'agriculture*.[9] Translation was also central to the construction of knowledge in the *Encyclopédie*. Diderot established clear guidelines for his contributors concerning the correct use of source material, with particular reference to translated sources. Diderot was sensitive to this issue because Le Breton had advertised the *Encyclopédie* as 'traduit de l'Anglois d'Ephraim Chambres' in his 'Prospectus' of 1745. Diderot consistently contrived to modify his readers' perception of the *Encyclopédie* as a direct translation of Chambers' *Cyclopaedia*. His 'Prospectus' of November 1750 promoted the work as 'recueilli des meilleurs auteurs et particulièrement des dictionnaires anglois de Chambers, d'Harris, de Dyche'. When volume i appeared on 28 June 1751, all reference to Chambers had disappeared from the title-page.

Diderot clearly intended the *Encyclopédie* to be more than a straightforward translation. In his 'Prospectus' he admitted to having 'des raisons particulieres de peser le mérite' of the *Cyclopaedia* (i.xxxv). His critique centred on the issues of compilation and translation. Diderot charged Chambers with having compiled the greater part of his dictionary from French sources. Were Diderot to offer an accurate translation of the *Cyclopaedia*, he would disappoint and deceive his *French* public, 'à qui on n'eût présenté sous un titre fastueux & nouveau, que des richesses qu'il possédoit depuis longtems' (i.xxxv). Diderot wished to counter the commonly held view that compilation, particularly from reference works, was unavoidable in the construction of an encyclopedia. In his 'Prospectus' he detailed the measures he had taken to avoid being dubbed a mere compiler.[10] In the belief that incomplete knowledge of a broad range of subjects prompted editors to compile, he had distributed the *Encyclopédie* articles to over 139 identified contributors according to their particular fields of interest.[11]

---

8. *Groot en algemeen kruidkundig, hoveniers, en bloemisten woorden boek*, 2 vols (Leiden 1745); *Das englische Gartenbuch*, translated by G. L. Huth, 3 vols in folio (Nuremberg 1750-1758).

9. Miller's translation was published as *The Elements of agriculture*, 2 vols (London 1764), from Duhamel Du Monceau, *Eléments d'agriculture* (Paris 1762).

10. Cf. Edme Mallet's comment that 'La plûpart des Lexicographes ne sont que des *compilateurs*', in COMPILATEUR (*Belles-Lettres*.), iii.762.

11. Diderot admitted that this process had begun before he became chief editor (i.xxxv).

These specialists were to evince a reasoned response to their source material. They would not need to supplement their knowledge by drawing indiscriminately from other authors but would rather assess previous contributions in order to expose unreliable sources and ensure that past errors were not perpetuated. The principles of their sciences would be established only from outstanding authors prized for their clarity and precision whose principles would be reinforced with reference to 'des autorités constamment reçûes' (i.xxxvii). Contributors would not merely refer the reader to given sources but would cite them accurately within the body of their articles.

Diderot accepted that his authors found it expedient to work from translations of Chambers rather than to begin afresh (i.xxxvi). However, they were to read the *Cyclopaedia* with the circumspection that they applied to any source, particularly in view of the clear deficiencies of the work. The contributors would at various times abridge, correct or make essential additions to Chambers' articles in order to complete the encyclopedic order. Diderot believed that this methodical approach would provide each contributor with a solid foundation upon which to add 'des connoissances puisées dans son propre fonds' (i.xxxv-vi). He thereby hoped to distinguish the *Encyclopédie* both from Chambers' *Cyclopaedia* and from the recent Italian translation of the work.[12] Diderot intended the *Encyclopédie* to make an original contribution to scholarship which would be hailed by posterity as specifically French.

Diderot's response to Chambers' *Cyclopaedia* and his advice on the proper use of source material have a direct bearing upon the eighty-five *Encyclopédie* articles that refer to another contemporary English work of reference, *The Gardener's dictionary*. According to Diderot's recommendations, one would expect the five authors of these articles to be specialists in their subject areas, to consult Miller as an established authority in preference to Chambers, to evaluate *The Gardener's dictionary* against other sources, and to translate accurately within the body of their articles only those aspects of Miller's work that they deemed pertinent, thereby evincing 'l'exactitude & le discernement, pour ne présenter au lecteur que des choses dignes de son attention'.[13] They might variously abridge, correct or expand Miller's text with their own comments and original contributions, and would refer to the most recent editions of *The Gardener's dictionary*. The eighty-five articles are grouped under one or more of the subject headings of botany, natural history, gardening, exotic botany, agriculture, flower gardening, and medical matter. The articles and their references to Miller are not derived from Chambers' *Cyclopaedia*, in which there are no citations of *The Gardener's dictionary* prior to the supplement of 1753 which includes an extract from

---

12. *Dizionario universale delle arti e delle scienze*, 9 vols in 4° (Venice 1748-1749).
13. COMPILATEUR, iii.762.

GD31 on the raising of cypresses.[14] The authors prefer to consult *The Gardener's dictionary* as an authoritative source for their articles.

Miller was an ideal point of reference for the encyclopedists because he was both a gardener and a writer.[15] As a gardener, he had acquired practical skills in all of the subjects treated by the contributors: he worked in his father's market garden and nursery at Deptford before establishing his own florist's business at St George's Fields in Pimlico, and in 1722 he was appointed curator of the Physic Garden of the London Apothecaries at Chelsea, which had been founded in 1673 to grow and catalogue medicinal plants, and participate in the global exchange of roots and seeds.[16] Miller was thus qualified as a market gardener, nurseryman, florist, herbalist, and plant collector. By January 1751 Miller had been curator of the Chelsea Physic Garden for almost thirty years and the botanic garden had become the most richly stocked in the world.[17] Due to the seed consignments sent by the Pennsylvanian collector John Bartram,[18] it contained the American maples, oaks, and pines that Miller described in *The Gardener's dictionary*, much to the delight of Pierre Daubenton. Crucially for the encyclopedists, Miller combined specialist knowledge with the ability to write clearly on all aspects of botany and horticulture.[19] *The Gardener's dictionary* contained 'descriptions, classifications and histories of plants as well as notes on cultivation and pertinent criticism of agricultural methods', and its dictionary format made this material readily accessible, particularly from 1752, when the work was arranged in a single alphabetical sequence; and at a time when garden literature generally failed to keep pace with garden practice, Miller strove to correct and enlarge his dictionary with descriptions of new plants, many of which he had raised, and of new horticultural practices, some of which he had pioneered.[20] William T. Stearn posits a conceptual link between the *Encyclopédie* and *The Gardener's dictionary* when he describes the latter as 'an expression in horticultural terms of the encyclopaedic spirit of the eighteenth century which also animated such very different men as Chambers, Zedler, Robert James, Pivati, Linnaeus and Diderot'.[21] It is thus singularly appropriate that the five contributors should have turned to Miller for guidance.

14. Chambers concentrates on the medicinal properties of plants rather than on their descriptions. He explains a number of garden features but describes few trees.

15. 'Miller', in Anthony Huxley, Mark Griffiths and Margot Levy (eds), *The New Royal Horticultural Society dictionary of gardening*, 4 vols (London 1992), iii.239.

16. 'Chelsea Physic Garden', F. Nigel Hepper, in Geoffrey and Susan Jellicoe, Patrick Goode and Michael Lancaster (eds), *The Oxford Companion to gardens* (Oxford 1991), p.110.

17. 'Miller', Hazel Le Rougetel, in *The Oxford Companion to gardens*, p.374.

18. 'Bartram', Sandra Raphael, in *The Oxford Companion to gardens*, p.40.

19. Cf. Diderot's acknowledgement in the 'Prospectus' of the difficulty of finding experienced artists who could write detailed descriptions of their crafts (i.xxxix).

20. Morris R. Brownell, *Alexander Pope and the arts of Georgian England* (Oxford 1978), p.110; 'Miller', in Huxley *et al.* (eds), *The New Royal Horticultural Society dictionary of gardening*, iii.239.

21. 'The botanical importance of Philip Miller's publications', in Le Rougetel, *The Chelsea gardener: Philip Miller 1691-1771* (Portland 1990), p.169.

Of these contributors, Pierre Daubenton (1703-1776), the elder brother of the celebrated naturalist Louis-Jean-Marie Daubenton, made the most valuable contribution to the reception of *The Gardener's dictionary* in France. Daubenton supplied an estimated forty-four articles on arboriculture to the *Encyclopédie*. It is unfortunate that these articles have 'elicited almost no comment from contemporaries or later scholars': Daubenton was an expert arboriculturalist, and from 1760 he created an international tree nursery at Montbard in Burgundy.[22] He was thus admirably qualified to assess *The Gardener's dictionary*. Daubenton could access GD39 because his close friend Buffon was a subscriber, and he regularly cites GD52 even in his earliest contributions to volume iii. At a time when Miller was continually updating his dictionary, Daubenton distinguished himself as a specialist contributor who wished to keep abreast of Miller's latest botanical and horticultural revisions, corrections, and improvements.

Daubenton consulted GD52 in order to inform himself and his readers of rare American trees which Miller described there for the first time and had attempted to cultivate. In CHATAIGNER (*Jardinage*) he introduces his readers to a rare species, now *Castanea dentata*, discovered by Charles Plumier. Daubenton remarks that 'Cet arbre n'est point encore commun en France, & il est extrèmement rare en Angleterre: on peut s'en rapporter à Miller, qui n'a parlé de cet arbre que dans la sixieme édition de son dictionnaire, qui a paru en 1752' (iii.240). He then translates Miller's description of the species in full. Daubenton could evidently depend upon Miller for early accounts of newly imported trees: when he was preparing his article, the chinquapin, now *Castanea pumila*, had been described by only Miller and the English naturalist Mark Catesby.[23] Daubenton drew from both of these sources for his description: 'le chinkapin, quoique très-commun en Amérique, est encore fort rare, même en Angleterre, où cependant on est si curieux de faire des collections d'arbres étrangers: aussi je n'en parlerai que d'après Catesby & Miller' (iii.239). Daubenton uses the same sources for his description of what Miller named the 'Virginia dogwood', now *Cornus florida*.[24] By consulting GD52, Daubenton was able to offer his readers a description of what Miller termed the 'downy Virginian mulberry', probably a variety of *Morus rubra*, which had never been seen in France. In MURIER (*Jardinage*) Daubenton remarks: 'On n'a point cet arbre encore en France; il est même extrèmement rare en Angleterre. Presque tout ce qu'on en peut savoir jusqu'à présent, se trouve dans la sixiéme édition du dictionnaire des Jardiniers de M. Miller, auteur anglois' (x.875). He also provides a synopsis from GD52 of Miller's entry on the white cedar, now *Chamaecyparis thyoides*, which Miller had enumerated in GD39 but which was still unknown in France in 1754: 'Cet arbre n'étant

---

22. Frank A. and Serena L. Kafker, *The Encyclopedists as individuals*, *SVEC* 257 (1988), p.92.
23. In Catesby, *The Natural history of Carolina, Florida, and the Bahama Islands*, 2 vols (London 1731-1743 [1748]), i.9.
24. CORNOUILLIER (*Jardinage*), iv.256.

point encore connu en France, nous avons recours pour sa description & sa culture à M. Miller.'[25] Daubenton, who was unable to observe these trees at first hand, occasionally expresses frustration at the brevity of Miller's descriptions. In ERABLE (*Jardinage*) he follows his translation of Miller's account of a variety of red maple, which had been imported by Sir Charles Wager and raised in his garden at Parson's Green, with the lament: 'C'est tout ce qu'a dit récemment M. Miller de ce bel arbre, qui auroit bien mérité quelque détail de plus' (v.898). His disappointment was all the more acute because this variety of *Acer rubrum*, which surpassed the red maple in beauty, had not yet been cultivated in France, even though it had been described by Miller in GD31 and was widespread in the tree nurseries near London.

Daubenton cites Miller not only for descriptions of imported trees but also for accounts of their progress in the northern climate of England. He remarks that Miller had seen a Portuguese cypress growing in England 'qui n'avoit qu'environ quinze piés de hauteur, & qui cependant étendoit ses branches à plus de huit piés de chaque côté du tronc'.[26] He records Miller's account of travellers bringing acorns from Asia Minor to England, 'où trois de ces especes ont réussi, & paroissent aussi robustes que nos *chênes communs*', which is noteworthy because 'ces arbres sont encore très-rares, et très-peu connus'.[27] Daubenton is particularly interested to compare the relative growth of trees which have been imported into both England and France. He illustrates his comment that the balsam poplar, now *Populus balsamifera* variety *balsamifera*, does not generally thrive in the European climate by comparing English and French specimens: 'M. Miller, auteur anglois, assure que les plus grands arbres de cet espece que l'on ait vu en Angleterre, n'avoient que quinze ou seize piés de hauteur; & on n'en a point encore vû en France qui aient atteint cet élévation.'[28] In NOYER, *nux juglans* (*Jardinage*) he notes of a variety of *Juglans nigra* that 'Je n'ai qu'un seul plan de ce *noyer* qui n'a pas encore donné de fruit, quoiqu'il soit âgé de plus de 20 ans', and records its greater progress in England: 'Selon M. Miller, cet arbre en rapporte beaucoup en Angleterre' (xi.272). Daubenton also reports Miller's observations on the progress made in England by European trees such as the Scottish maple, now *Acer pseudoplatanus*, which according to Miller 'soûtient mieux qu'aucun autre arbre les vapeurs de la mer', or the quickbeam, now *Sorbus aucuparia*, of which 'M. Miller dit en avoir vû dans quelques contrées d'Angleterre qui avoient

25. CYPRÈS (*Hist. nat. bot.*), iv.603.

26. CYPRÈS, iv.602. The species is *Cupressus lusitanica*, and is attributed to Miller.

27. CHENE, *quercus* (*Hist. nat. bot.*), iii.287. In GD39 Miller related that these seeds 'thrive, and are as hardy as the common Sort', but in GD52 he reported that since the acorns are 'subject to perish when they are kept long out of the ground, there have not been more than three of these sorts raised in England', though his own specimens 'seem to be full as hardy as our common oak'.

28. PEUPLIER, *populus* (*Jardinage*), xii.478.

près de quarante piés d'hauteur sur deux piés de diametre, mais que dans d'autres endroits cet arbre ne s'élevoit qu'à vingt piés.'[29] Daubenton occasionally cites Miller in the hope of encouraging gentlemen farmers to import foreign trees into France. In ERABLE he states that the Italian maple, now *Acer opalus*, 'est à peine connu en France; il est même très-rare en Angleterre, quoique assez robuste pour le plein air', and adds, 'Mais comme M. Miller assûre que l'on fait cas de l'opale en Italie à cause de la beauté de son feuillage, qui faisant beaucoup d'ombre engage à le planter le long des grands chemins & proche des maisons de plaisance, il faut espérer que le goût qui regne pour l'agriculture, portera les amateurs à faire venir des graines de cet arbre pour le multiplier' (v.898).

When he was unable to examine specimens himself, Daubenton clearly valued Miller as a botanist who based his descriptions upon direct observation and carried out experiments in order to identify species. Daubenton alludes to an age-old debate concerning the distinction formerly drawn between the spreading 'male' and the upright 'female' cypress, a distinction which both Theophrastus and Joseph Pitton de Tournefort had refuted on the grounds that seeds sown from one of these trees produced seedlings of both. Daubenton was unable to verify their claim because he cultivated only the more ornamental 'female' cypress, but he defers to Miller who 'l'a vérifié lui-même par plusieurs épreuves', and contrasts Miller with less reliable sources: 'Combien n'y a-t-il pas d'inconvénient en effet à s'en rapporter à des auteurs qui n'ont pas vû l'objet par eux-mêmes, & qui copient sans discernement les faits les plus absurdes?'[30]

Daubenton prized Miller's arboricultural instructions because he saw in Miller a fellow specialist who drew his recommendations from first-hand experience. In ORANGER (*Jardinage*) Daubenton describes Miller as 'très-versé dans la culture des plantes' (xi.555). Ten years before the publication of *Le Grand Dictionnaire des jardiniers*, Daubenton recognised the value of translating Miller's works into French: 'Comme ses ouvrages n'ont pas encore été traduits en notre langue, il sera avantageux de faire connoître sa méthode de cultiver les *orangers*' (xi.555). Daubenton does not merely translate Miller's advice on orange culture from GD52, however, he intimates that it may be adapted to suit the French climate: 'On pourra même s'en relâcher à quelques égards sans inconvénient, en raison de la différence

29. ERABLE, v.897; CORMIER (*Hist. nat. bot. & Jard.*), iv.243. Miller contrasts the slow growth of the quickbeam in the south with its more vigorous growth in the north and in Shropshire and Wales ('*Sorbus*', GD52).

30. CYPRÈS, iv.601. In GD52 Miller stated that 'these trees have been by all the former writers on botany put down as two distinct species; so I have also mentioned them here as such; yet, from several trials which I have lately made, I find that the seeds of one will produce plants of both kinds; therefore they should be deemed but one species'. In GD68 Miller explained that the 'male' cypress was simply a more broadly spreading variety of *Cupressus sempervirens*. It is now identified as the wild plant *Cupressus sempervirens* forma *horizontalis* which has spreading branches (David J. Mabberley, *The Plant-book*, Cambridge 1997, p.200).

du climat qui est un peu plus favorable dans ce royaume qu'en Angleterre'
(xi.555). Daubenton also enriches his translation with his own specialist
knowledge: he diverges from Miller when he recommends pinching out
the young trees to encourage the growth of laterals, though he agrees that
the trees should not be pinched out as they develop: 'mais notre auteur ne
conseille pas de pincer le sommet de toutes les branches, commes quelques-
uns le pratiquent, cela fait pousser une quantité de petits rejettons trop
foibles pour porter du fruit' (xi.556). Daubenton supplements the translation with his own remarks on pruning.

Daubenton began this process of translation with CHATAIGNER,
which is a free adaptation of '*Castanea*' from GD52.[31] Daubenton was fascinated by Miller's account of the tree's migration, which he adapts to a
French context. Miller claims that *Castanea sativa* 'was formerly in greater
plenty amongst us than at present' and cites the examples of old London
buildings made from this timber and of William Fitz-Stephen's account of
a nearby forest.[32] Daubenton omits all reference to London and to Miller:
he merely states that 'les charpentes de la plûpart des anciens bâtimens sont
faites de ce bois' and alludes to 'les forêts de plusieurs provinces, où il y a
quantité d'anciennes charpentes de *chataigner*' (iii.237). He also embellishes
Miller's account of the tree's migration with a discussion of its possible
causes, which he attributes to periods of excessive heat and drought exacer-
bated by a reduction of moisture occasioned by forest clearance. Daubenton translates Miller's advice on sowing without acknowledging him and
cites Miller directly on the method of forming chestnut groves.

In addition to translating and enriching Miller's arboricultural recommendations, Daubenton evaluates them in the light of his own observations
and experiments. He qualifies Miller's practice of rejecting chestnuts that
float as infertile with the proviso: 'quoiqu'il soit bien avéré par l'expérience
qui en a été faite, que de celles-là même il en a réussi le plus grand nombre'
(iii.238). He modifies Miller's recommendation that Italian cypress seeds
should be preserved in their cones before sowing by affirming that 'J'ai
pourtant fait l'épreuve que cette graine tirée des pommes de *cyprès*, & con-
servée dans une boîte, avoit bien levé pendant cinq annéés de suite, mais
non au-delà' (CYPRËS, iv.602). He also takes issue with Miller's claim
that swamp cypress seedlings are sturdy, and recommends that they
should be raised in boxes for the first two or three winters, 'Car quoique
M. Miller assûre que ces arbres sont extrèmement robustes, et qu'ils ne
craignent nullement le froid, je crois que cela ne peut leur être applicable
que lorsqu'ils sont parvenus à un certain âge, puisque j'ai toujours vû périr
au bout de deux ou trois ans tous ceux qu'on avoit voulu élever en plein air'
(iv.603). Daubenton realises that seedlings raised in pots have fared little

31. See also Terence M. Russell and Ann-Marie Thornton, *Gardens and landscapes in the
'Encyclopédie' of Diderot and D'Alembert* (Aldershot 1999), ii.550.
32. In *Description of the most noble city of London* (c.1173).

better because they have been unable to withstand periods of drought in spite of frequent watering, and reports that he is currently conducting an experiment in which the pots and boxes are gradually steeped in water.

Daubenton pays tribute to English agronomists' efforts to develop oak plantations, and offers a précis of Miller's recommendations (CHENE, iii.284), but only in order to highlight the difficulty of applying them. On his estate in Burgundy, Buffon 'commença à suivre exactement la direction dont on vient de voir le précis' (iii.285). Unfortunately Miller's methods were too costly: for a plantation of 100 acres, an outlay of 6000 *livres* proved insufficient to cover the costs of plantation and cultivation for the first year alone. Daubenton concludes that English authors, particularly Miller, have not devised the most cost-effective method of creating oak plantations: 'Si nous en croyons les meilleurs auteurs Anglois qui ayent traité cette matiere, Evelyn, Hougton, Laurence, Mortimer, & sur-tout M. Miller qui est entré dans un grand détail sur ce point; il faudra de grandes précautions, beaucoup de culture & bien de la dépense pour faire des plantations de *chênes*' (iii.284). Daubenton suggests that Miller's methods may be suitable for small plantations of twenty or thirty acres in the vicinity of Paris, where timber is rare and fetches a higher price. For a more extensive provincial plantation, he advocates the more effective and less expensive method of his compatriot Buffon, which he has observed at first hand: 'En essayant au contraire à faire dans un pareil terrein des plantations par une méthode toute opposée, M. de Buffon a éprouvé des succès plus satisfaisans, et peut-être vingt fois moins dispendieux, dont j'ai été témoin' (iii.285). Daubenton takes particular issue with Miller's instruction to keep oak plantations free from weeds for a period of 8-10 years: the attendant expense would make the plantation unprofitable, and frequent ploughing would render the ground more susceptible to drought and frost, especially if it were free from weeds. Miller has overlooked experiments by his countrymen Richard Bradley and William Ellis which indicate that weeds protect oak seedlings from drought and frost, though Daubenton feels that Bradley and Ellis have not gone far enough in this respect: 'Ces auteurs auroient pû dire de plus, que non-seulement on diminue la dépense par là, mais même que l'on accélere l'accroissement, surtout dans les terreins dont nous venons de parler.'[33] Daubenton explains that the shade provided by brooms, rushes, thorns, and other shrubs helps to accelerate the natural growth of the seedlings, which should be the arboriculturalist's ultimate aim.[34]

---

33. CHENE, iii.285. Bradley recommends the planting of underwood but the clearing of weeds, in *New improvements of planting and gardening*, 2 vols (London 1717), i, ch.4-5. Ellis suggests that grass and weeds will protect oak seedlings from drought and accelerate their growth, in *The Timber tree improved* (London 1738), p.20.

34. Current practice is to keep oak seedlings free from weeds until they are established (Huxley *et al.*, eds, *The New Royal Horticultural Society dictionary of gardening*, iii.777).

Pierre Daubenton's judicious use of *The Gardener's dictionary* as a privileged source for his contributions to the *Encyclopédie* makes it possible to attribute to him the unsigned article PIN (*Jardinage*). The author of this contribution consults GD52 on rare species of *Pinus*, and, like Daubenton in ERABLE, expresses disappointment at the brevity of Miller's description of what is now *Pinus echinata*: 'C'est là tout ce qu'en a dit M. Miller, et c'est le seul auteur qui soit encore entré dans quelque détail sur cet arbre' (xii.631). The author affirms that black pine seeds remain fertile for a considerable period once they have been removed from their cones, which mirrors Daubenton's comments on Italian cypress seeds. The contributor is evidently a specialist arboriculturalist, for he supports his claim by detailing one of his own experiments: each year for twenty-three years, he sowed black pine seeds which had been gathered in February 1737 and removed from their cones before being sent from Geneva. The seeds came up for the first eighteen years. This must have been a recent experiment, given that volume xii of the *Encyclopédie* was published in December 1765. It is similar to one conducted by Miller over a period of three years with Aleppo pine seeds and described in this article.

While Pierre Daubenton's articles make extensive use of *The Gardener's dictionary*, those of his younger brother Louis-Jean-Marie Daubenton make no reference to Miller, though thirteen entries serve as botanical prefaces to articles in which Miller is cited. These entries offer generic descriptions drawn exclusively from Pitton de Tournefort's three-volume *Institutiones rei herbariae*, which was published in Paris in 1700. However, in preferring Pitton de Tournefort as his taxonomic expert, Daubenton was adhering to the practice adopted by Miller for the first six editions of *The Gardener's dictionary*. Following George C. Druce and James E. Dandy, Stearn has highlighted the accidental botanical importance of the fourth abridged edition of *The Gardener's dictionary*, which appeared on 28 January 1754 and, since it post-dated Linnaeus's *Species plantarum* of 1 May 1753, 'gave valid publication to numerous Tournefortian generic names suppressed by Linnaeus', the restoration of which had previously been attributed to later post-Linnaean authors.[35] By referring, like Miller, to Pitton de Tournefort rather than to Linnaeus, Daubenton inadvertently contributed to the restoration of these genera in France. Moreover, the post-Linnaean generic descriptions which he supplied for volume iii of November 1753 predate those of Miller by two months. In CHATAIGNER (*Hist. nat.*) Daubenton offers a generic description under *Castanea*, which is now attributed to Miller. Further examination of volume iii may prompt scholars to include Daubenton among those European innovators who were Miller's contemporaries.[36]

35. Stearn, 'The botanical importance of Philip Miller's publications', p.171, 173-75; Huxley *et al.* (eds), *The New Royal Horticultural Society dictionary of gardening*, i.lvi.

36. Stearn lists these innovators as Duhamel Du Monceau (1700-1782), Abraham Gagnebin (1707-1800), Jean-Etienne Guettard (1715-1786), Giovanni Antonio Scopoli (1723-1788),

Gabriel-François Venel (1723-1775), the remaining specialist contributor who cites Miller, was born in Tourbes in Languedoc and received his doctorate from the Faculty of Medicine at Montpellier. He was one of the main contributors to articles on chemistry and medicine. Venel refers to Miller in MYRTE, *myrtus*, but not for the plant's medicinal and other properties. He chose rather to translate Miller's instructions on the cultivation of the Mediterranean myrtle, because he recognised that the English method would be more suited to the climate of northern France than that practised in the south, with which he was more familiar. Like Pierre Daubenton, Venel consulted a recent edition of *The Gardener's dictionary*, GD52, and clearly viewed Miller as an established authority, declaring: 'je ne sache pas qu'on ait donné rien de mieux à ce sujet, que ce qui a été tracé par M. Miller, dans la sixieme édition angloise de son *Dictionnaire des Jardiniers*' (x.918). Like Daubenton in ORANGER, Venel suggests that Miller's recommendations may be adapted to suit local, northern French climates: 'si on trouve les procédés trop strictes, il sera fort aisé de s'en relâcher à proportion de la température du climat où l'on se trouvera placé' (x.918). Venel also avoids relying exclusively upon Miller and cites Bradley's method of layering the myrtle.[37]

All other references to Miller are made by the chief editor Diderot and the prolific compiler Louis de Jaucourt (1704-1780) rather than by specialist contributors. Although Miller is mentioned in CAUTERE, which was composed by the influential garden theorist Antoine-Joseph Dezallier d'Argenville (1680-1765) and appended to volume xvii as an *article omis*, it is unclear whether the allusion was made by Dezallier d'Argenville or by his editor Diderot. Dezallier d'Argenville details his new method of reviving languid trees by incising the bark to the side or back of the trunk and inserting a wedge for a period of one month. Diderot then intervenes to announce Dezallier d'Argenville's forthcoming TAILLE DES ARBRES, with its exclusive précis from *abbé* Jean-Roger Schabol's book manuscript of the pruning techniques used at Montreuil.[38] It is then claimed that Dezallier d'Argenville's new method of reviving trees, particularly the peach, 'détruit entierement tout ce que nous ont enseigné la Quintinie, Liger, le frere François, la Maison-Rustique, & les livres anglois de Brandelay, de Miller, Jean Lawrence & autres' (CAUTERE, xvii.762). This reference to Miller may be read as a questionable attempt to relate Dezallier d'Argenville's new method to the contemporary debate concerning the removal of

and Jean-François Séguier (1703-1784), in 'The botanical importance of Philip Miller's publications', p.174.

37. In CARDAMINE and CERFEUIL, which refer to 'Miller *Bot. off.*' rather than to *The Gardener's dictionary*, Urbain de Vandenesse (d.1753) cites *Botanicum officinale; or a compendious herbal* (London 1722), which was composed not by Philip Miller but by the botanist Joseph Miller.

38. In the event, the précis was appended to TAILLE DES ARBRES but the article itself was composed by Pierre Daubenton. Schabol's *Dictionnaire pour la théorie et la pratique du jardinage et de l'agriculture* appeared in 1767.

gourmands, which the cited authors recommended but against which Schabol's précis remonstrates. The reference marks an attempt to evaluate past sources, challenge received authorities such as Miller, and distinguish between traditional and new arboricultural practices. However, the claim is exaggerated and overlooks the fact that Dezallier d'Argenville himself recommended the removal of gourmands in the *Encyclopédie*.[39]

Diderot refers to Miller in ANANAS, ARBRE, *le jardinier*, and CASSINE. Diderot was not a specialist in natural history, gardening or botany, and he composed these entries in his capacity as editor-compiler, but he does aspire to be a competent compiler. He cites Miller in preference to Chambers' article *Ananas* (i.84-85), which is, as Diderot complained of the *Cyclopaedia* as a whole, derived from a French author, Jean-Baptiste Du Tertre.[40] Although Diderot fails to specify any particular edition of *The Gardener's dictionary*, which does not appear in any published inventory of his books, his enumeration and description of species are drawn from GD39, while his account of the pineapple's spread to Europe and its successful cultivation by Pieter van der Voort is from GD31.[41] Diderot thus cites Miller as a botanist, natural historian, and horticulturalist. He does not simply refer his readers to Miller's article but translates it accurately, adhering closely to Miller's original text and adding phrases such as 'continue le même Botaniste' (i.406) to enable the reader to follow the progress of Miller's ideas, a practice adopted by Venel in MYRTE. Diderot also abridges aspects of Miller's descriptions that he considers to be of secondary importance. He does not list Miller's fourth species of *Ananas*, which Miller named *Ananas lucidus* in GD68 and for which he must now be cited. This may be because Miller does not describe this species. He first lists the different species of *Ananas* and then describes them, whereas Diderot blends his enumeration and description of species. Diderot also overlooks Miller's expert instructions on pineapple culture in GD31 and GD39, though he does include a few significant comments on the maturation and harvesting of the fruit. Diderot's article is not enriched with original observations; like that of Chambers it is simply compiled from a foreign source. Diderot refers to one other source, Nicolas Lémery, for the medicinal properties of the expressed and alcoholised fruit.[42]

Diderot also compiled from Miller for article CASSINE, which resembles Chambers' PARAGUAY only because Chambers and Miller drew from a common source, Amédée-François Frézier's *Relation du voyage*

---

39. GOURMAND OU †LARRON (*Jardin.*). Shoots of excess vigour are still removed completely during the training of peaches (Huxley *et al.*, eds, *The New Royal Horticultural Society dictionary of gardening*, iii.491). The symbol † here denotes a plant name that is now obsolete in a given language.

40. See *Histoire générale des isles de S. Christophe* (Paris 1654), p.191-93.

41. Pieter van der Voort instructed Miller on the successful cultivation of pineapples during Miller's visit to Meerburg in 1727 (Le Rougetel, *The Chelsea gardener*, p.50).

42. See Lémery, *Dictionnaire, ou Traité universel des drogues simples mises en ordre alphabétique*, 4th edn (Rotterdam 1727), p.27.

de la mer du Sud, which was first published in Paris in 1716. Although Diderot refers to both Frézier and Miller, his entry is translated entirely from Miller's †CASSINE, perhaps due to the relative ease of consulting a dictionary article.[43] Diderot's article is far shorter than that of Miller, which is almost three columns long. Diderot gives priority to clear definitions of local terms such as the silver-tipped calabash cup or *mate*, the silver drinking pipe called *bombilla*, and the skimmer used for removing tea leaves known as the *apartador* (ii.747). He again omits details of cultivation, in this case of what is now *Ilex paraguayensis*.

In ARBRE Diderot offers practical advice on the selection, preparation, planting, and maintenance of trees, enumerates different categories of tree, and reports and debates ten particular observations on trees made by a number of specialists. Though a non-specialist, Diderot evidently read extensively to prepare for this article: his reference to Miller is an indirect product of his admiration for Duhamel Du Monceau, who cites Miller in a manual on raising trees from cuttings and layers.[44] Diderot includes a lengthy extract from the manual at the end of his commentary on the tenth particular observation on trees concerning the relative merits of girdled and ungirdled trees. Duhamel Du Monceau notes Miller's recommendation that cuttings from evergreens should be taken in autumn and adds 'peut-être a-t-il raison' (i.588). Miller reasoned that it was preferable to obtain cuttings at the end of August rather than 'in the winter, when the sap stirs but little, or in the spring, when it begins to rise, because then it is apt to come too suddenly'.[45] Miller attributed this recommendation to John Mortimer in GFD24, where he made a virtue of scrupulously acknowledging his sources, a practice that was dropped from GD31. The extent to which Miller compiled his dictionary from other sources is therefore frequently overlooked, particularly in view of the accepted practice of considering GD31 as the first edition of the work.

Louis de Jaucourt supplied sixty-four entries that refer to Miller under each of the subject headings listed above.[46] Jaucourt was not a specialist in all of these disciplines, though he did study under Hermann Boerhaave at Leyden where he obtained a doctorate in medicine in 1730, and he composed the celebrated article MÉDECINE (*Art & Science*). He was also qualified to translate *The Gardener's dictionary*, for in 1727 he learned English in London and also studied in Cambridge. Although Jaucourt's contributions to the *Encyclopédie* are known to be 'filled with acknowledged and unacknowledged excerpts from other sources', Kafker's assessment that 'many

---

43. Diderot draws from Miller's version of a letter dated April 6 1717 from Edmund Halley to Jonah Bowyer which Frézier had included in the second edition of his *Relation*, which appeared in Amsterdam in 1717 in 2 vols in 12°.
44. This manual was later incorporated into *La Physique des arbres, où il est traité de l'anatomie des plantes et de l'économie végétale*, 2 pts in 1 vol. (Paris 1758).
45. 'Laying of trees', GD31.
46. See above, p.213.

of his articles are far from simple borrowings from others ineptly strung together' is borne out by Jaucourt's use of *The Gardener's dictionary*, which he judiciously consults as a recognised authority in preference to Chambers' *Cyclopaedia*.[47] Moreover, Jaucourt does not rely too heavily upon this source. Although Miller was recognised as an expert in melon culture, Jaucourt also praises Jean-Baptiste La Quintinie's pioneering contribution in MELON (*Agricult.*). He cites Pierre Morin's *Instruction pour la culture des fleurs* together with *The Gardener's dictionary* as authoritative texts on tulips and adds Plumier's descriptions of *Guaiacum* species to Miller's methods of raising them.[48] Jaucourt was the only contributor to highlight Miller's debt to Bradley, which Miller himself only fully acknowledged in GFD24. He cites Bradley as well as Miller in MELON, ŒILLET (*Jardin.*), and OREILLE DOURS, and recommends Bradley's *Historia plantarum succulentarum* of 1717-1734 along with *The Gardener's dictionary* for the cultivation of what is now *Mesembryanthemum*.[49]

Jaucourt evaluates his sources and usually distinguishes Miller as the most outstanding. He concludes FLEUR (*Agricult.*) with a list of references which ends with the flourish 'et sur-tout Miller, dans son *Dictionnaire du jardinage*' (vi.858). In GRENADILLE (*Bot. exot.*), he alludes to Bradley but refers the reader to Miller for the cultivation of the passion flower, since 'il a donné les meilleures & les plus exactes instructions qu'on puisse desirer' (vii.937). Unlike Diderot, Jaucourt recognised the horticultural, and also the arboricultural and agricultural, significance of *The Gardener's dictionary*, and the validity of introducing Miller's recommendations to France. In MOUSSE he provides an accurate translation of Miller's instructions for the effective treatment of moss-covered fruit trees. He particularly wished to inform French readers of Miller's success in cultivating exotics such as the calabash, which had only just been introduced into Europe. In CALEBASSIER *d'Amérique* he remarks: 'voici la méthode enseignée par Miller, & que tout le monde ne connoît pas' (ii.549). Recognising the difficulty of raising *Guaiacum* species in Europe, he details in a comprehensive translation, 'les soins & les précautions avec lesquelles Miller est parvenu à élever des arbres de gayac dans le jardin de medecine de Chelséa' (GAYAC, vi.531). He also explains Miller's original method of propagating the tropical American *Melocactus* from its offsets, since raising the plant from seed produced in 'Europe' (Miller's text reads 'England') gave only slow-growing specimens.[50] Jaucourt is solicitous to correct harmful practices in melon culture, remarking that 'Quoique la culture des *melons* soit

47. Kafker and Kafker, *The Encyclopedists as individuals*, p.176.
48. TULIPE (*Jardin des Fleuristes*) and †GAYAC (*Botan. exot.*). Morin's treatise was published in La Quintinie, *Instruction pour les jardins fruitiers et potagers, avec un traité des orangers*, 2 vols (Paris 1700). Plumier's descriptions are drawn from his *Nova plantarum americanarum genera* (Paris 1703).
49. †FICOÏDES (*Bot. exot.*).
50. MELOCACTUS (*Botan. exot.*), x.319.

très-perfectionnée, MM. Bradley & Miller y reprennent encore des pratiques, qui, pour être d'un usage presque universel, n'en sont pas moins contraires aux lois de la nature' (MELON, x.320). Following Bradley as cited by Miller in GFD24, Jaucourt objects firstly to the removal of so-called 'fausses fleurs' in order to retain the herb's vigour, since this may lead to a shortage of male flowers. Secondly, Jaucourt complains that frequent lifting of the laterals (which it was then customary to lay out) for the purpose of inspecting the young fruit may impede the flow of sap, since their conducting tissue is fragile and prone to bruising. Thirdly, Jaucourt condemns the practice of exposing young fruit to the sun prior to ripening, since this leads to dessication.

As an encyclopedist, Jaucourt was anxious to report new experiments that might prove useful to French agriculture. In GRAINE (*Agricul.*), Jaucourt introduces Miller's methods for prolonging the life of seeds as a 'secret qui intéresse les Botanistes' (vii.836). He informs the reader that seeds must be kept in their shells in a dry place, and details the manner in which Miller experimented with fresh vegetable seeds, half of which were hermetically sealed in bottles and half of which were hung up in bags so that they maintained some contact with the atmosphere. The following year, and for two years subsequently, only the latter germinated, a finding of which Jaucourt appreciated the practical significance: 'Il suit de cette expérience, que ceux qui ont à recevoir des *graines* des pays étrangers, doivent avertir leurs correspondans de se bien garder de les leur envoyer enfermées dans des pots ou des bouteilles bouchées' (vii.836). Jaucourt also recounts Miller's preferred method of preserving seeds for a period of up to twenty years by burying them to a depth of three or four feet in order to shelter them from rain and sun. Lastly, Jaucourt reports Miller's 'method for raising such seeds which have hard coats or shells surrounding them, and that have been judged very difficult, if not impossible, to be raised in England'.[51] Jaucourt carefully explains Miller's method of planting cocoa beans in a bed of tanner's bark, though he unfortunately omits to mention that the seeds must be turned sideways so that descending moisture does not rot the radicles. This was a method that Miller had perfected following two failed attempts. Jaucourt clearly admired Miller as a reliable and determined scientist who repeated his experiments in order to verify them and was not discouraged by failure.

Jaucourt at times includes a simple cross-reference to Miller's horticultural instructions, and some of his contributions thereby lose their value as a vehicle for the transmission of Miller's recommendations. In †FICOÏDES, Jaucourt relates that Miller has discovered the secret of perfecting the culture of the ice-plant, now *Mesembryanthemum crystallinum*, '& de faire venir en Angleterre la tige, les branches & les feuilles de cette espece, plus belles qu'en Afrique' (vi.679). However, for the details of this

---

51. 'Seed', GD31.

method he makes a simple *renvoi*. Jaucourt follows this practice in FENOUIL (*Jardinage*), even though he acknowledged that the French were deficient in the cultivation of Florence fennel, which was considered a delicacy. French readers may have found Miller's recommendations for raising the American persimmon useful given that what is now *Diospyros virginiana* was more common in the tree nurseries of London than of Paris, but Jaucourt refers the reader directly to the English authority (†GUJACANA). Jaucourt compiled over 17,000 articles for the *Encyclopédie* and was restricted in the amount of material he could include, as he himself lamented in GERANIUM (*Botan.*): 'Miller vous enseignera la culture de toutes les especes de *geranium* dont il fait mention. Il ne nous est pas possible d'entrer dans ce détail' (vii.641). Jaucourt's lament was justified: Miller's article listed forty species and was five columns long. Similarly, Jaucourt makes some general points concerning the culture and ornamental uses of a number of *Hibiscus* species before adding, 'mais Miller vous instruira de toutes ces particularités, que les bornes de cet ouvrage ne permettent pas même de parcourir' (†KETMIA, ix.124).

The least satisfactory aspect of Jaucourt's use of *The Gardener's dictionary* is his almost exclusive reliance upon early editions of *The Gardener's dictionary*, notably GD24 and GD31. Jaucourt must also have had access to GD39 in time for the publication of the last ten letterpress volumes, because, citing Miller, he lists two species of *Parthenium*, one species of *Randia*, five species of †*Telephioides* (now *Andrachne*), and two species of *Tabernaemontana* which Miller enumerated there for the first time. However, Jaucourt refers infrequently to GD52, causing him to repeat anecdotes that were topical when they first appeared in GD31 but no longer relevant when they resurfaced in the *Encyclopédie*. Jaucourt thus relates that in 1729, two varieties of what is now *Myrica cerifera* had flowered regularly and one had even fruited in Peter Collinson's garden, an outdated anecdote that Miller chose to omit from GD52, which appeared five years before Jaucourt's article GALE (*Botanique*). Jaucourt may have had access to GD52 by November 1757, since he appears to have consulted it for FRAISIER, *fragaria* (*Hist. nat. bot.*), in which he pays tribute to Miller's successful cultivation of a fruiting *Fragaria chiloensis* or beach strawberry: 'Cette plante a produit du fruit au jardin royal de Paris, & en porte aujourd'hui dans le jardin de Chelesca [*sic*] par les soins de Miller' (vii.276). In FRAGARIA from GD31, Miller related that his specimens had borne flowers but no fruit, whereas in GD52 he commented that they 'bear very indifferently'. Jaucourt refers directly to GD52 in JASMIN, *jasminum* with respect to a Carolina jasmine of which Miller actually makes no mention in GD52 or GD59.

Jaucourt's failure to consistently consult GD52 or the even more important GD59 which incorporated many Linnaean indices, also leads him to make outdated references to Miller's lists of species. In EUPHORBE (*Hist. nat. bot.*) Jaucourt cites Miller and Boerhaave as listing from ten to twelve species, but in GD52 which had appeared four years earlier, Miller listed no fewer than twenty-seven, and in GD59 he listed thirty-two. In GALE Jaucourt states that Miller lists three species of the shrub, but in GD52 Miller enumerated five species and referred the reader to the genus *Myrica*. In GD59 seven species of *Myrica* are listed. The point is somewhat academic given that contemporary taxonomists name approximately 2000 species of *Euphorbia* and fifty-five species of *Myrica*. However, it does shows that Jaucourt, unlike the arboriculturalist Pierre Daubenton, failed to record Miller's most recent botanical and horticultural improvements.

In spite of these deficiencies the eighty-five articles that cite Philip Miller clearly played a pioneering role in making translated extracts from *The Gardener's dictionary* available as the seventeen letterpress volumes of the *Encyclopédie* appeared, some ten or twenty years before the first separate French translation of Miller's dictionary. Pierre Daubenton ensured that translated extracts from the important sixth edition became available from as early as November 1753. The articles provided an effective means of cross-cultural exchange to the extent that they followed Diderot's recommendations on the appropriate use of source material in the construction and communication of knowledge. The contributors do not always use *The Gardener's dictionary* in the manner set forth by Diderot: their articles contain that irregular mixture of compilation and originality which Diderot found characteristic of the first four volumes of the *Encyclopédie*.[52] Simple *renvois* and unacknowledged compilations accompany extended translations and transformations, sometimes within the body of a single article, such as CHATAIGNER. Diderot himself does not escape stricture on this point, since he does not acknowledge his full debt to Miller in CASSINE. Moreover, the translations are forcibly partial, since the encyclopedists incorporated only those aspects of Miller's dictionary that pertained to their own contributions. However, *The Gardener's dictionary*, like the *Encyclopédie*, was meant to be consulted article by article rather than read as a whole, as Miller explained in the 'Preface' to GD52: 'a work of this nature is supposed rather to be referred article by article than to be read through in series'. For the most part, the articles that refer to Miller admirably demonstrate how the collaborative encyclopedic project disseminated specialist knowledge. Although English editions of *The Gardener's dictionary* were available in France, Jaucourt and Pierre Daubenton emphasised the value of translating Miller's botanical, horticultural, and agricultural recommendations into French for the benefit of their privileged readers. The encyclopedists clearly prized *The Gardener's dictionary* as an exemplary source and generally translated Miller's recommendations accurately, knowing them to be of great use to French estate owners who invested considerable sums in the cultivation of imported plants.[53] Accomplished specialists such as Pierre

52. ENCYCLOPÉDIE, v.645.
53. See Chandra Mukerji, *Territorial ambitions and the gardens of Versailles* (Cambridge 1997), p.163.

Daubenton also assessed Miller's contribution. Daubenton appreciated that GD52 contained important descriptions of newly imported American trees which were not yet known in France and tried to encourage his compatriots to cultivate trees which Miller reported to be thriving in the northern climate of England, but he also sought to dissuade his readers from adopting Miller's method of forming oak plantations. He also enriched his translations with accounts of his own experiments with different methods of sowing or preserving seeds. With Pierre Daubenton and Venel, the act of translation sometimes involved a cultural transfer in which Miller's original text was adapted to suit the French climate or include French place names. Just as successive editions of Miller's dictionary helped to popularise in England the principles of French formal garden design as expounded by Dezallier d'Argenville, so too the *Encyclopédie* made known to a generation of French readers 'the most important horticultural work of the eighteenth century',[54] though Dezallier d'Argenville contributed little, if anything, to this process.

---

54. Stearn, 'The botanical importance of Philip Miller's publications', p.169. Miller's references to Dezallier d'Argenville, *La Théorie et la pratique du jardinage* (Paris 1709) were drawn from John James's translation, *The Theory and practice of gardening* (London 1712).

JANIE VANPÉE

La Femme mode d'emploi:
how to read the article FEMME
in the Encyclopédie

In the 'Prospectus' to the *Encyclopédie* and its 'Discours préliminaire', Diderot and D'Alembert articulated the goals of the encyclopedic project and inaugurated a new epistemology by redefining the telos of knowledge. Collecting, classifying, explaining, and disseminating all extant knowledge, the *Encyclopédie* would supplant a sclerotic way of thinking based on sacred texts, revelation, superstition and prejudice with a new order founded on reason, empirical observation, and science. This intellectual project moved man from the subordinate and peripheral position he had occupied in the previous dominant hierarchical order of things to its centre, both as the object of its inquiry and as the subject directing and reading the project.

Certainly, the major task confronting the editors of the *Encyclopédie* was reorganising knowledge so as to highlight the links between its different parts. But the readers faced the equally daunting challenge of learning to read such a text. Directives or a 'mode d'emploi' was sorely needed. However, unlike the editors who from the beginning of the project used both the 'Prospectus' and the 'Discours préliminaire' as a blueprint for organising the different branches of knowledge and the articles written by the many contributors, readers would have to wait until the article ENCYCLOPÉDIE, published in the fifth volume in 1755, for Diderot to outline a 'mode d'emploi' for their use and guidance.

In contrast to the optimistic and idealistic programme set forth in both the 'Prospectus' and the 'Discours préliminaire', the metadiscursive article ENCYCLOPÉDIE discloses an obsessive awareness of the difficulties of following and reading the programme previously outlined.[1] Seven years from the project's inception, five years into its publication, and three years since the onset of problems with censorship, Diderot now had the practical experience to understand more fully the obstacles blocking not only the project's potential to reorder knowledge, but also its actual realisation. Although in the 'Discours préliminaire' D'Alembert had acknowledged

1. As the project encountered resistance, criticism and censorship, the editors used the 'Avertissement' of volumes iii and viii as well as self-referential articles such as ENCYCLOPÉDIE to defend their project and to voice an increasing anxiety about its conception.

the difficulties the editors might have in ordering such a massive amount of information and knowledge by comparing the task to losing one's way in a labyrinth, he had also immediately offered the solution of the 'arbre généalogique ou encyclopédique qui [...] rassemble [les connaissances] sous un même point de vue et qui ser[t] à marquer leur origine et les liaisons qu'elles ont entre elles' as an antidote.[2] The 'Discours préliminaire' thus repeatedly offered metaphors of spatial order – the map, the 'mappe-monde', the tree of knowledge with its roots and branches, and the plan of a rationally designed park or road system with the long perspectives of large avenues leading to distant but visible points of interest – to help the editor and, subsequently, the reader visualise the organisation of knowledge and locate an object of inquiry in relation to the total system. By the time of the publication of the fifth volume in 1755, with the editorial task of ordering and classifying the articles in the encyclopedic system functioning well, Diderot turned his attention to the reader's point of view, which differed significantly from the editors' lofty perspective.

The original metaphors of spatial order and visual clarity for representing the system of knowledge that D'Alembert and Diderot had favored in the 'Discours préliminaire' and the 'Prospectus' now give way to a practical programme of reading through *renvois* or cross-references that lead the reader to consult or 'jump' to other articles that, without the explicit direction of being read in conjunction with the original article, might not appear connected to it. The actual process of reading the *Encyclopédie* plunges the reader from the high perch that the *système figuré* provides back into a plethora of information difficult to sort or classify at first sight. Although D'Alembert had already discussed the usefulness of cross-references for the reader in the 'Discours préliminaire', he had conceived of them primarily as signposts making the links between an article and the branch of knowledge to which it belonged in the encyclopedic tree as explicit as possible. In other words, for D'Alembert the cross-references were to function like a copulative conjunction in the grammar that is the *système figuré* or classificatory structure of the encyclopedic order. Diderot's conception in ENCYCLO-PÉDIE complicates matters considerably. It suggests that the *renvois* can not only indicate evident links between an article and its science, they can also juxtapose articles with no apparent relation or with opposing ideas or arguments, and thus uncover hidden or secret links. Rather than provide shortcuts between articles, they inevitably lead the reader on detours and 'excursions' far from the original article and towards unexpected discoveries and areas of knowledge. The immediacy, clarity, and totalisation afforded by the visual metaphors and the grammatical conception of the cross-references of the 'Discours préliminaire' yield to the temporality,

2. 'Discours préliminaire', i.xiv-xv. For a recent analysis of the introductory role of the 'Discours préliminaire' to the *Encyclopédie*, see Michel Malherbe, 'Introduction', *D'Alembert: Discours préliminaire de l'Encyclopédie* (Paris 2000), p.9-77.

partiality, deferral, and ambiguity inherent in Diderot's more rhetorical conception of the *renvois*. But the new emphasis on the cross-references also inflects the original goals of the encyclopedic project. For the *renvois*, which Diderot describes as 'the most important element of the encyclopedic order', are to 'change the common way of thinking' (ENCYCLOPÉDIE, v.642b). Not only will the *Encyclopédie* represent in an ordered fashion all extant knowledge, through its system of *renvois* it will also affect and influence the reader. Indeed, following the cross-references will shape or reorder the reader's reading, and by implication, our thinking. How will this happen?

i. The rhetoric of the *renvois*

Taken together, the four types of cross-references (*les renvois de choses, de mots, de génie*, and *les renvois épigrammatiques*) that Diderot defines propose a set of explicit directives for reading that function much like a rhetorical system of literary figures that defer meaning elsewhere or in relation to two or more signifieds. Although Diderot himself does not use rhetorical terms to describe the types of *renvois*, his descriptions evoke those used by Dumarsais in his reflections on figures of thought and tropes, and later developed by Fontanier in his *Commentaire raisonné* to analyse how extended tropes and figures of thought operate to change or multiply meaning.[3] The first type of cross-reference, *les renvois de choses*, contains the basic rhetorical structures of the other types and of the overall system. For example, in Diderot's description of a first type of effect of the *renvois de choses*, the correspondences, correlations, and links made between two articles work like extended tropes – metonymy, metaphor, synecdoche – and other figures of speech – analogy and comparison: 'Les renvois de choses éclaircissent l'objet, indiquent *les liaisons prochaines* avec ceux qui le touchent immédiatement, et ses liaisons éloignées avec d'autres qu'on en croirait isolées, rappellent *les notions communes* et *les principes analogues*; fortifient les *conséquences*; entrelacent la branche au tronc, et donnent au tout cette unité si favorable à l'établissement de la vérité, et à la persuasion' (v.642b; emphasis added). Diderot continues to describe the second, and completely contrary, possible effect of this first type of *renvois*, evoking a different set of figures of speech, those that Fontanier especially elaborates upon in his *Commentaire raisonné* as 'figures d'expression par opposition', that is *la prétérition, l'épitrope*, and irony. Diderot writes (v.642a-b):

Mais, quand il le faudra, ils produiront aussi un effet tout contraire; ils opposeront les notions; ils feront contraster les principes; ils attaqueront, ébranleront, renverseront secrètement quelques opinions ridicules qu'on n'oserait insulter ouvertement. Si l'auteur est impartial, ils auront toujours la double fonction de confirmer

---

3. See Dumarsais-Fontanier, *Les Tropes* 2 vols (Geneva 1967). Volume i reprints Dumarsais's original treatise, while volume ii adds Fontanier's commentaries and elucidations.

et de réfuter, de troubler et de concilier [...]. Toutes les fois, par exemple, qu'un préjugé national mériterait du respect, il faudrait, à son article particulier, l'exposer respectueusement, et avec tout son cortège de vraisemblance et de séduction; mais renverser l'édifice de fange, dissiper un vain amas de poussière, en renvoyant aux articles où des principes solides servent de base aux vérités opposées.

The other types of *renvois* that Diderot describes next are, in fact, more precise applications of the first category. For example, the *renvois de génie* put into play figures of resemblance where no immediate correspondence comes to mind, thereby inventing strikingly new comparisons, links and analogies between fields of knowledge. Likewise, the *renvois épigrammatiques* refine the first type of *renvois* to a satiric end.

According to Diderot's description, one of the most powerful functions of the *renvois de choses*, and by extension, the *renvois épigrammatiques*, is, like irony, to signify two contrary meanings at one and the same time. Confronted with two meanings, whether they are opposite or simply different, the reader is forced to compare, question, and think. The ultimate significance of the juxtaposition of contrary meanings is neither evident, direct or transparent but must be interpreted. Such a model of reading the *Encyclopédie* subverts the project's fundamental aim to compile and disseminate knowledge as clearly and directly as possible.[4] Indeed, caught within the system of cross-references, the articles cannot stand on their own, nor even within the larger framework of the totalising images suggested in the 'Discours préliminaire'; they must be read in conjunction with, through, and against their cross-references. Far from being immediate, transparent, and literal, their meaning is always deferred until confirmed, contradicted or further cross-referenced elsewhere. As James Creech so clearly analysed, encyclopedic knowledge, contrary to the ideology its name implies, is never total, never complete, never past.[5] The reader trying to acquire some knowledge or to simply inform herself is always pointed toward another entry or article, repeatedly forced to defer any judgement or closure.

Even more problematic is what this rhetorical model implies for the reader's interpretations. The author and editor can lay out the signposts of the detours for the reader to follow through the cross-references, but they cannot control the reader's interpretation of the differences or contradictions she then encounters between articles. How the reader interprets an article that both 'confirms and refutes', 'unsettles and reconciles' explicit or implicit statements and arguments, exceeds the editor's and the author's

4. For a discussion of the subversive aims of the *renvois'* discursive strategy, see Daniel Brewer, 'Language and grammar: Diderot and the discourse of encyclopedism', in *Eighteenth-century studies* 13 (1980), p.1-19; see also Christie Vance McDonald, 'The utopia of the text: Diderot's *Encyclopédie*', *The Eighteenth century: theory and interpretation* 21, no.2 (1980), p.128-44.

5. See James Creech's fine analysis of how temporality figures in the encyclopedic discourse, 'Chasing after advances: Diderot's article "Encyclopédie"', *Yale French studies* 63 (1982), p.183-97.

command. Furthermore, the same problem applies to the author who makes cross-references to future articles not yet written. While he may intend a meaning, he too may not be able to control what finally does get written or the effect of the juxtaposition of the cross-referenced articles. Thus, this model of reading, which directs the reader to and through the contradictions and differences in the encyclopedic system, frees the reader as it loses control over him.[6]

Numerous critics have analysed the tensions and contradictions raised by the *Encyclopédie*'s programme and the impossible directives for achieving and reading it.[7] Indeed, one may well ask, is it even possible to follow Diderot's directives for reading and deciphering the cross-references? Were we to follow them literally, how would a reading of an article be achieved? How would the cross-references shape the knowledge conveyed in the various articles and the reader's understanding of this knowledge? How would the figurative readings resulting from the juxtaposition of articles according to the rhetoric of the cross-references develop, deepen or inflect the meanings of the different articles?

ii. A test case: the article FEMME

Diderot's ambition 'to change the common way of thinking' through this programme has always been a challenge to the reader. I propose to take Diderot's prescription at his word and to follow the intratextual *renvois* from article to article, charting the paths and detours from an original article to and through its subsequent cross-references. As my test case, I will focus on the article FEMME, published in the sixth volume (1756), a year after the volume in which ENCYCLOPÉDIE had appeared. Readers would thus have had the opportunity to consult Diderot's directions for reading the cross-references and could have applied them, hypothetically at least, to their own reading of FEMME.

The choice of this particular article is, of course, not arbitrary. In fact, I would argue that I am led to choose FEMME precisely because of Diderot's reading programme. In the same article, ENCYCLOPÉDIE, where he both proposes his subversive reading programme and anxiously examines the difficulties inherent in such a programme, Diderot boldly locates man to be the centre of the encyclopedic enterprise (v.641a):

6. For a longer discussion of the hidden contradiction in Diderot's reading programme, see Isabelle Regis, Maryse Guerlais, Jean-Yves Cochais and Jean Biou, 'Lire l'*Encylopédie*', *Littérature* 42 (1981), p.20-38.
7. Among the most interesting, see Wilda Anderson, *Between the Library and the laboratory* (Baltimore 1984), p.40-47; Daniel Brewer, 'Representing knowledge', in *The Discourse of Enlightenment in eighteenth-century France: Diderot and the art of philosophizing* (Cambridge 1993), p.1-55; Walter Moser, 'D'Alembert: l'ordre philosophique de ce discours', *Modern language notes* 91, no.4 (1976), p.723-33, and 'Les Discours dans le *Discours préliminaire*', *Romanic review* 67 (1976), p.102-15; as well as the pieces by Brewer and McDonald mentioned in note 4.

Pourquoi n'introduirons-nous pas l'homme dans notre ouvrage, comme il est placé dans l'univers? Pourquoi n'en ferons-nous pas un centre commun? Est-il dans l'espace infini, quelque point d'où nous puissions, avec plus d'avantage, faire partir les lignes immenses que nous nous proposons d'étendre à tous les autres points? Quelle vive et douce réaction n'en résultera-t-il pas des êtres vers l'homme, de l'homme vers les êtres? [...]. L'homme est le terme unique d'où il faut partir, et auquel il faut tout ramener.

Following Diderot's directions, and beginning with HOMME as the first and central term (or article) from which to enter the *Encyclopédie*, it is impossible not to remark that 'woman' is absent from this centre. In this very long article whose two subentries (*histoire naturelle, politique*) are penned by Diderot, man is defined anatomically, morally, politically, and biologically as the model for universal mankind. A few cross-references to genitalia barely suggest that he has a sexuality. Woman figures only as a synecdoche in the four cross-references that point to her sexual specificity – HYMEN, MAMMELLES, MENSTRUES, NYMPHES. In every other aspect, she is subsumed and her specificity subordinated under the category HOMME as mankind in general. This self-evident, unexamined subordination of woman had, indeed, been affirmed in the chronologically earlier article FEMME, where Boucher d'Argis, the lawyer responsible for the jurisprudential entry, stated unequivocally: 'Toutes les femmes et les filles sont quelquefois comprises sous le terme d'hommes.' One could argue that the article FEMME, preceding HOMME, informed and structured it proleptically. Thus, although the article HOMME does not refer the reader to FEMME, this very lacuna functions as a hidden signpost, directing the reader to FEMME. Following Diderot's directives to their logical consequences, I read the lacuna as the figure of a blatantly missing cross-reference and the actual cross-references to woman's sexed body as synecdoches alluding to FEMME.

In taking the article FEMME as a test case, my primary objective is not to assess what knowledge the encyclopedists possessed and communicated about woman. Indeed, most scholars who have studied how woman is portrayed in the *Encyclopédie* agree that, despite claims of subversive and radical new thinking, the knowledge that the encyclopedists disseminate about woman is rather tame and orthodox.[8] As Badinter argued in *L'Amour en plus*, women's status has never been absolute, but to the contrary

---

8. For a summary of the contents of the article FEMME and of woman's overall place in the *Encyclopédie*, see Sara Ellen Procious Malueg, 'Women and the *Encyclopédie*', in Samia Spencer, *French women and the age of Enlightenment* (Bloomington, Ind. 1984), p.259-71, and P. Charbonnel's excellent analysis in 'Repères pour une étude du statut de la femme dans quelques écrits théoriques des "philosophes"', *Etudes sur le 18ᵉ siècle* 3 (Université Libre de Bruxelles 1976), p.93-110. See also Lieselotte Steinbrugge *The Moral sex: woman's nature in the French Enlightenment* (New York, Oxford 1995), ch.2: 'Dividing the human race: the anthropological definition of woman in the *Encyclopédie*'. For a more impressionistic interpretation of the article, see '*Qui peut définir les femmes': L'Article FEMME de l'Encyclopédie (1756), Sur les femmes de Diderot (1772)*, ed. Catherine Cusset (Paris 1999).

always relative and dependent on current social attitudes toward men in power.[9] According to her, growing interest in children and women in the mid-eighteenth century reflected changing attitudes toward absolutism and paternal authority rather than a radical shift of interest in women themselves. The *Encyclopédie*'s presentation of woman is no anomaly. With the exception of the plates where representations of women working reflect their active participation in the contemporary economy, woman is disproportionately absent from the text, and when she is represented it is in mostly conventional ways.

Since I argue, however, that the system of cross-references potentially subverts or at the least weakens discursive authority by always deferring absolute meaning or knowledge to another article, the meaning of a particular article, in this case FEMME, exceeds its content. Although it is impossible to ignore the content of the entries and their cross-references completely, I intend to focus more on the relations between them and how these modulate their possible meaning(s). I propose to concentrate instead on how knowledge about woman is conveyed through the *renvois* and in particular, how the web and circuit of cross-references in the article situate FEMME in the encyclopedic programme.

Like most entries in the *Encyclopédie*, FEMME is a composite of contributions, in this instance, five essays by four different authors, each analysing woman from a particular epistemological perspective. A very recent graduate of the famous Faculty of Medecine at Montpellier, Barthez contributed the first entry under the rubric *anthropologie*. The chevalier de Jaucourt, also a doctor but a graduate of the medical school of Leyden, wrote the second entry, *droit naturel*, and the last, *femme en couche*. The poet and playwright Desmahis wrote the third and central essay under the rubric *morale*. Finally, Boucher d'Argis contributed his legal expertise for the fourth and longest entry on woman's legal status under the rubric *jurisprudence*.

There are a total of 53 cross-references, unevenly distributed among the five essays. The first three essays, the more philosophically speculative, contain fewer cross-references, with five in the first (*anthropologie*), two in the second (*droit naturel*), and none in the central essay (*morale*). The last two rubrics, *jurisprudence* and *femme en couche* contain the majority of the *renvois*, with thirty-five in the legal entry, and eleven in the medical entry. If, however, according to the logic of reading the cross-references, the reader should follow the cross-references of the cross-references, their number more than triples, and the reading sequences or paths from cross-reference to cross-reference stray farther from the original article into subject areas that at first glance might not appear to be related to it. While four out of five of the cross-references in the first essay (*anthropologie*) loop back to the main entry and thus do not lead beyond themselves, and the third (*morale*) with no cross-references at all is completely self-contained,

9. Elisabeth Badinter, *L'Amour en plus: histoire de l'amour maternel* (Paris 1980).

the three other essays (*droit naturel, jurisprudence,* and *femme en couche (méd.)*) direct the reader to a plethora of articles, which in turn refer the reader to yet further articles. Although today the ARTFL search engine greatly facilitates the mapping out of the cross-references, the approximately two hundred *renvois*, charted to the fifth degree, produce a massive amount of information that challenges if not defies the rhetorical system of reading that Diderot proposes for the *Encyclopédie*.[10] Multiple and diverging paths from article to article lead to multiple readings with potentially different meanings. At the very least, Diderot's 'method' actively prevents any one path or any one meaning from prevailing. With this difficulty in mind, I will chart my own navigation through the cross-references and propose one direction among many for reading this article, beginning with the two essays that have the fewest cross-references, and concluding with some observations about the circularity of the cross-references of the other three essays.

iii. Following the *renvois*, reading the rhetoric

Barthez begins the first essay (*anthropologie*) by summarily dismissing what might have been most expected from such a brilliant student versed in the latest medical knowledge and theories about human anatomy and physiology – descriptions of the skeleton and the reproductive organs founded on scientific evidence. Instead, he focuses on long-standing controversial speculations about the difference between male and female reproductive organs. Referring both to contemporary and ancient medical experts, Barthez reviews the debate whether a woman's uterus makes of her 'un homme manqué'. This debate allows him to slip easily into the second part of his essay, a compendium of ''préjugés sur le rapport d'excellence de l'homme à la femme' culled from an array of traditions and cultures. As in the first part of the essay, Barthez simply enumerates the opinions of the authorities and refers the reader to a great number of other extratextual references. It is unclear from the content of Barthez's contribution what he thinks of these stereotypical pronouncements on woman or of the references he invokes. Is he condoning or condemning these prejudices? Does he invoke traditions and the authorities in order to uphold them, or on the contrary to call them into question? Are we to infer that because Barthez offers neither opinion nor argument, his essay does not articulate a position?

If, however, we consider how Barthez (or the editor) establishes links between his essay and others, and within parts of the essay, inviting the reader to ponder what he means, a different, though not necessarily

10. While ARTFL realises perfectly Diderot's visionary programme of reading the *Encyclopédie* by facilitating immediate access to the cross-references, it also suggests additional links or circuits that the editors had not thought of originally by bringing up other rubrics where the word searched is not the head word. For a discussion on ARTFL's effect on reading the *Encyclopédie*, see Philip Stewart's article in this volume.

absolute or clearer, interpretation emerges. That is, a position emerges on some of the issues, and contradictions between implied positions become more evident.

Let me turn first to the essay's use of cross-references. Although Barthez starts off by stating that he will not broach the controversial subject of comparative anatomy, his position is far from neutral, for he refers the reader to Daubenton, the leading comparative anatomist of the time, whose findings and observations are firmly grounded on empirical evidence. In fact Barthez's essay is full of precise references to other extratextual sources. These references are not official cross-references within the *Encyclopédie*, but nothing prevents them from extending Diderot's system of cross-references outside the encyclopedic system and thus incorporating within its order these referrals to books outside the *Encyclopédie*. Indeed, Diderot's system cannot be contained or limited to the *Encyclopédie*. Thus the reference to Daubenton's findings on the skeleton certainly functions as a *renvoi de choses*, which Barthez then reinforces with an explicit cross-reference to SQUELETE. Now, volume xv in which SQUELETE appears would not be distributed until 1765, and Barthez could not really have controlled nor known what its author would argue, but that does not matter. SQUELETE is a loaded word, which at the time immediately evoked the controversy about man's origin pitting scientific arguments based on precise anatomical observation against sacred revelation.[11] A cross-reference to SQUELETE here functions as a trope summarising the debate between those believers in the Biblical account of creation who would expect all male descendants of Adam to have one less rib than Eve's descendants and those who rejected revelation in preference for the scientific and anatomical observations that male and female skeletons are highly similar.

Despite the term's implicit subversion of religious dogma, the article itself generates a new and different but equally pernicious dogma. If it contests the religious revelation of woman's origin from Adam's rib, it does so by using scientific authority to establish that the female skeleton proves that 'la destination des femmes est d'avoir des enfans & de les nourrir' (xv.483). Yet the article's author, the chevalier de Jaucourt, repeatedly confuses cause and effect, taking the physical effects of childbearing on the skeleton to be the signs of the natural suitability of the female skeleton to bear children.

The cross-reference to HERMAPHRODITE, although not as efficiently condensed as SQUELETE, also alludes to contemporary debates about sexuality, in particular to the debate on whether the male reproductive organs are a simple inversion of the female, or whether the difference

---

11. For a review of the history of the skeleton in establishing sexual difference, see Londa Schiebinger, 'More than skin deep: the scientific search for sexual difference', in *The Mind has no sex* (Cambridge, Mass. 1989), p.189-213.

between male and female reproductive organs is fundamental.[12] By referring to HERMAPHRODITE, Barthez indicates his position on the debate to be with those experts who believe in difference. Moreover, given that the article HERMAPHRODITE conveys an obsessive interest in defining difference as a deviation from nature and as monstrous, the reference to it here associates woman, albeit indirectly, with the underside of nature, and by extension with what escapes scientific understanding and containment. As in the case with the cross-reference to SQUELETE, the author had little control over the eventual meaning produced by juxtaposing his article with an as yet unwritten essay. This particular reference to HERMAPHRODITE complicated matters even more for another article on the same subject, accompanied by illustrations, would be added in the supplemental volumes of text and plates, both distributed in 1777. While the first article argues firmly from scientific evidence that two-sexed beings do not exist, the second article is more equivocal, suggesting even that masturbation might increase the size of the clitoris to such an extent that it could be taken for a penis: 'On a vu cependant des personnes dont il n'etoit pas aisé de déterminer le sexe. Un nombre assez grand de femmes naissent avec l'organe analogue du mâle, porté à une grandeur extraordinaire; il y en a d'autres où des turpitudes secretes ont augmenté le volume d'une partie qui naturellement ne se présente pas à la vue' (iii.359, H. D. G. le Baron de Haller).

The dominant figure organising Barthez's essay and its relation to the cross-references thus appears to be contradiction. As we have just seen, Barthez uses some of the *renvois* to draw attention to a contradiction or a controversial debate that he will not or dare not discuss otherwise. But the articulations between parts of his essay also proceed by contradiction, or more precisely, *prétérition*.[13] For example, he immediately refutes his opening declaration about what he will not do by discussing precisely what he has dismissed, but in an indirect way. Thus he alludes to a complex controversy in one word – *squelette*. He repeats the same rhetorical ploy when he states that he will not describe the reproductive organs and nonetheless reviews various theories, ancient and contemporary, with regard to their differences. More important, he refers to authorities in this discussion not to endorse them but rather to pit them against one another to show how they contradict each other, thereby discrediting both their authority and

---

12. For a succinct summary of the major scientific debates concerning the function of male and female sexual organs in human reproduction before the female ovum was discovered by von Baer in 1827, see Maryanne Cline Horowitz, 'The "science" of embryology before the discovery of the ovum', in *Connecting spheres: women in the western world, 1500 to the present*, ed. Marilyn J. Boxer and Jean H. Quataert (New York 1987), p.86-94. See also L. Jordanova, *Sexual visions: images of gender in science and medicine between the eighteenth and twentieth centuries* (New York 1989), and T. Laqueur, *Making sex: body and gender from the Greeks to Freud* (Cambridge, Mass. 1990).

13. 'La prétérition [...] consiste à feindre de ne pas vouloir dire ce que néanmoins on dit très clairement, et souvent même avec force' (Dumarsais-Fontanier, *Les Tropes*, ii.425).

their pronouncements. The total effect of Barthez's use of contradiction in this first part of his essay is to put into question the authorities who do not agree with the leading comparative anatomists of the time. Barthez would seem to refer the reader to a contemporary scientific description of woman. The paradox is that he himself does not do so directly.

The second part of Barthez's essay also relies on direct and indirect citations of the authorities' conflicting theories and justifications of the unjust treatment of woman in different religious and cultural traditions to put into question their foundation in absolute truth. By making an exception for the Christian religion, however, Barthez weakens his implicit critique of other religions' perspectives on and treatment of woman. Overall, then, Barthez suggests that scientific observation and evidence can contradict sacred revelation, only to revert to religious orthodoxy in the last part of his essay.

Let me now return to the other cross-references at the very beginning of the article – HOMME, FEMELLE, SEXE – and follow the various paths they suggest. All three place the article, and by implication woman, in a subordinate position either to man or to her sex. Coming immediately after the definition, 'c'est la femelle de l'homme', the first cross-reference, to HOMME, doubly defines woman in relation to man, by stressing the genitive and by subsuming woman under the central article of the encyclo-pedic system. The latter does not, as I have already remarked, make a reci-procal cross-reference back to FEMME. The brief article FEMELLE, defines her as 'le correlatif de mâle. C'est celui qui conçoit & met au monde le petit.' The article thus reiterates the female's definition in terms of the male and in the process strangely loses her grammatical gender. The article then appends the cross-reference SEXE, thereby emphasising this reference, and woman's sexuality, twice. The article does not, as we might have anticipated, refer the reader to MALE. But if, out of curiosity or desire for symmetry, we were to go to MALE anyway, we would discover first that the term is categorised under *grammaire* and not as its female correlative under *histoire naturelle*, and second that it has acquired a metaphorical meaning: 'Le *mâle* dans les especes animales ayant plus de courage & de force que la femelle, on a transporté ce terme aux choses intellectuelles, & l'on a dit, un esprit *mâle*, un style *mâle*, une pensée *mâle*.' Unlike its correla-tive term, then, MALE escapes its primary grammatical and sexual mean-ings, by metaphorically transposing physical and sexual characteristics to the intellect. This asymmetrical treatment of terms that are otherwise said to be correlatives of one another is clearly figurative of woman's subordi-nate position in the encyclopedic system.

The most obvious circuit of cross-references thus goes from FEMME to FEMELLE to SEXE, by way of SQUELETEand HERMAPHRODITE, progressively identifying woman's difference with her sexuality to the exclusion of all else. Indeed, when the article SEXE appeared in volume xv in 1765, the focus on woman's sexuality continued. This cross-reference alludes to woman as 'le sexe absolument parlant, ou plutôt le beau-sexe,

[...] l'épithete qu'on donne aux femmes, & qu'on ne peut leur ôter, puisqu'elles sont le principal ornement du monde'. With this epithet, woman does not have a sex, rather, she *is* sex. Although as the primary definition of FEMME emphasises, and as the cross-reference to FEMELLE reiterates, she is one of two sexes; the cross-reference to SEXE transforms her through synecdoche into all, or both, or only sex. Yet by figuring sex in general, woman is curiously dispossessed of sex or desexualised.

If, however, the reader were to take the shorter and more direct path to SEXE by following the cross-reference from FEMME, the figurative meaning of SEXE imparts a figurative meaning to FEMME, or at least suggests that the whole article could be read in that light. That is, indeed, the interpretation that the playwright Desmahis offers in his essay, the third and central entry under the rubric *morale*, in which he conceives the figure of a woman, Chloé, who would embody the epithet of the 'beau-sexe' described under the rubric SEXE. The superficial, amoral, and unhappy life that he imagines for her, however, contrasts completely with the happy, virtuous, and edifying role attributed to the 'beau-sexe', thereby contradicting, correcting or possibly parodying the article SEXE. Of course, the parodic overtones of Desmahis's essay would depend on the order in which the reader reads the entries and cross-references, in this instance, after attending to the earlier cross-reference to SEXE. As this last example demonstrates, the path one follows to cross-references can alter their meanings.

If the reader reads sequentially the five essays of the article FEMME without following the cross-references or leaving them for a later perusal, Desmahis's central essay will, nonetheless, appear more self-contained than the others and openly diverges from the encyclopedic project. Not only is it the only essay without any cross-references; it also reflects upon the futility of classifying or defining such a subject as woman. Unlike the authors of the other sections, who approach their topic with the impersonal, objective, and dispassionate perspective of the philosopher or scientist, Desmahis declares the philosophical contemplation of woman to be impossible. For woman, as an object of contemplation or study, transforms the scientist or philosopher who contemplates her into a sentimental dreamer or passionate lover: 'et le philosophe qui croit contempler, n'est bientôt qu'un homme qui désire, ou qu'un amant qui rêve' (vi.472a). With this assertion, Desmahis not only undermines the authority of the 'philosophe'by suggesting that the object of knowledge can affect or transform the observer and thus warp his objectivity, he also subverts his own authority as well as removes himself from the coterie of 'gens de lettres' working together on this project. This essay and one other, FAT, which could be read as a pendant to his reveries in FEMME, will be his only contributions to the *Encyclopédie*.[14]

14. As of the mid-1750s Desmahis suffered from ill health and this may have prevented him from participating more fully in the *Encyclopédie*; he died after a long illness in 1761. He

In the first part of his essay, Desmahis can do nothing better than prove his declaration to be true by insisting that he cannot define woman: 'Qui peut définir les femmes?' he asks, implying that no one can. Indeed, in the space immediately following the entry FEMME (*morale*), traditionally reserved for the definition of the term, Desmahis substitutes an observation about the name, 'ce nom seul touche l'âme', revealing his poetic sensibility. At the very least, Desmahis is conscious of the paradox in which he finds himself, as his comparison of the writer's task to the painter's impossible imperative of painting a woman's portrait both as faithfully and as flatteringly as possible demonstrates. But his declaration that woman 'ne [fait] apercevoir que pour laisser imaginer' also casts doubt on those philosophers who, before and after him, have ventured to meet the challenge. Are they but dreamers or lovers? And if they are, what should be made of their discourses on woman? Thus at the heart of the article on woman, Desmahis disputes the *Encyclopédie*'s attempt to define, describe, and locate woman in its epistemological system. The absence of any cross-references in the essay illustrates powerfully the consequences of Desmahis's contentions; unable to be represented as objective and classifiable knowledge, woman is isolated, severed from the rest of the encyclopedic system and its discourse, and abandoned to a poet's reverie.

It follows from Desmahis's assertion that if the study of woman redefines the philosopher as a dreamer or a lover, then his discourse must be a dream or a fiction. And a dream (more precisely, an erotic dream) is indeed what Desmahis's essay most resembles with its unconnected sequence of observations and comparisons leading up to the long, and slightly surreal, narrative featuring the ingenue, Chloé. It is not surprising that Desmahis should turn to a fictive portrait created from his imagination rather than from empirical observation, since for him woman is first and foremost a text, whether simply a name ('ce nom seul touche l'âme') or a whole language, whose ambiguity demands interpretation. 'Tout à la vérité parle en elles, mais un langage équivoque', declares Desmahis of woman, and his story of Chloé attempts, as a painter would do, to portray as well as interpret that 'langage équivoque'.

Desmahis recounts the story of Chloé's introduction to society after her ineffective convent education, and once married, her awakening to love, her betrayal and disillusionment, and finally her dissolution and bitterness. Although Desmahis critiques the completely conventional path of Chloé's life, it is unclear whether he knowingly or unknowingly evokes all the clichés of the genre. Since the 'philosophe' who writes about woman does so out of desire or love, he relates to his love object much as Chloé does to her lover; both Chloé and the 'philosophe' are seduced and deceived by the

was by any definition an odd choice for contributing to the encyclopedic project since his interests were primarily literary and not philosophical. He wrote a volume's worth of occasional verse and four social comedies, only one of which was ever staged (*Le Billet perdu ou l'impertinent*, 1750). See *Les Œuvres de M. Desmahis*, première édition complète (Paris 1778).

mirage that love produces. Chloé, then, and by implication woman for whom she is a figure, are mirages, dreams or fictions. Indeed, Chloé evokes not concrete scientific or legalistic facts, but the moral weaknesses of certain mythical or literary heroines. The only references pointing out from this otherwise hermetic entry are to the two most infamous Greek courtesans, Aspasia and Phryné, and to the literary heroines best known for their deceptions, mendacity, and trickery, Tasso's Armide, Molière's Célimène, and 'la femme trompeuse' in the Greek poet Archilochos's poetry.

Desmahis concludes his essay by imagining an alternative but equally fictive portrait of a happier woman, a projection of the writer's dream of the perfectly domesticated wife. Hidden from society and ignorant of its ways and pleasures, she devotes herself exclusively to home, husband, and children to the point that she has no identity, no name other than the generic ones of wife and mother: '[S]on bonheur est d'ignorer ce que le monde appelle *les plaisirs*, sa gloire est de vivre ignorée. Renfermée dans les devoirs de *femme* & de mère' (vi.475a). Domestic tranquillity and happiness do not, however, inspire the writer to 'dream' to the same extent that Chloé's dissolute mores did; one paragraph suffices to describe this more virtuous and happier woman. With this double portrait, Desmahis suggests the two alternative identities open to woman, each exclusive of the other – 'le beau sexe' or wife and mother – and each equally defined by man's desires, imagination, and possessiveness.

Desmahis's contribution is the least informative, the most personal and subjective of the essays, and the least 'encyclopedic' in its refusal to locate woman in the encyclopedic system or to define her in relation to other knowledge in the *Encyclopédie*. It is also the most openly frank and troubling in its challenge to the encyclopedic goal of defining the world in an ordered, objective way and in its admission of failure to meet this goal for woman. As such it is emblematic of the problem of representing the world of things and objects through discourse that Diderot understood so well. If empirical observation, reason, and science fail to define woman, let alone understand her, it is because language, the philosopher's tool, is not only referential and descriptive but also figurative. Both Barthez and Desmahis face this paradox of the encyclopedic project, but Desmahis the poet alone reflects upon it.

Less troubled by the limited ability of language to define and classify empirical reality and objects as knowledge, the three remaining entries immediately refer the reader to other articles that lead to yet more articles and thus firmly anchor their contribution in the encyclopedic system of knowledge. Unlike Barthez's and Desmahis's more speculative epistemological perspectives (*anthropologie* and *morale*), which underscore the non-scientific and subjective aspects of their approach to the subject, the chevalier de Jaucourt and Boucher d'Argis draw upon pre-existing legal realities and medical knowledge and terms to describe and classify woman's various legal statuses and the particular physical condition that affects her – child-birth. The epistemological perspectives of these three entries – *droit naturel*, *jurisprudence*, and *femme en couche* (*medecine*) – govern the way the subject is treated and impose upon it the specific terms of two established professions, law and medicine.

Initially Jaucourt's first essay under the rubric *droit naturel* appears to be as speculative as Barthez's and Desmahis's contributions. Jaucourt aims to debunk the sacredness of marriage and to redefine it firmly as a contract. While respecting divine and civil law, he nevertheless questions their relation to natural law, suggesting that natural law is as fundamental as divine law and certainly more so than civil law: 'On peut donc soutenir qu'il n'y a point d'autre subordination dans la société conjugale, que celle de la loi civile', he argues, 'et par conséquent rien n'empêche que des conventions particulières ne puissent changer la loi civile, dès que la loi naturelle et la religion ne déterminent rien au contraire' (vi.471a). This speculation allows him to challenge the principle of woman's subordination to man that subtends established civil law, claiming that it lacks any foundation in natural law. This in turn leads him to define marriage not as a sacrament but as a contract agreed upon by the two contracting parties. Jaucourt concludes his essay with a radical statement: 'Le mariage est de sa nature un contrat, et par conséquent dans tout ce qui n'est point défendu par la loi naturelle, les engagements contractés entre le mari et la femme en déterminent les droits réciproques' (vi.471b). Radical as it is, this statement does not lead to a liberating understanding of marriage for women, but rather prepares the way for the legalistic and reductive perspective presented by Boucher d'Argis in the fourth entry (*jurisprudence*). Still, an alternative reading is possible; if the reader comes to MARI or MARIAGE by following the cross-references from Jaucourt's entry on FEMME, her reading of the laws regulating marriage, *puissance maritale*, and woman's legal subordination to father and husband may be inflected by Jaucourt's argument against *puissance maritale* being founded in natural law.

A 'working' map of the reading directions for Jaucourt's entry (*droit naturel*) and the last two contributions reveals two main trajectories, one leading to a cluster of articles dealing with women's legal status in relation to marriage, the other leading to a series of articles concerning childbearing. Indeed, the two cross-references in Jaucourt's entry, MARI and MARIAGE, both point the reader to many of the same cross-references that Boucher d'Argis makes in his entry; and by way of 'abuses' in marriage or MANSTUPRATION further references eventually lead to several of the main cross-references in Jaucourt's medical contribution – MATRICE and ENFANTEMENT. In contrast to the cross-references in HOMME, which as I've remarked are for the most part sex and gender neutral, the numerous cross-references in these three entries once again highlight woman's gendered and sexed identity. For example the repeated references to MARI, to FEMME in relation to MARI or PUISSANCE MARITALE, and especially to MARIAGE (at least nine times) bring to the fore the second meaning of 'femme' – wife. Thus, FEMME must necessarily refer to MARI whereas HOMME does not imply husband, nor therefore marriage or wife. In Jaucourt's medical entry, the path of cross-references leads four times to MATRICE, and many of the other cross-references examine the illnesses that originate in the womb, thereby implying that woman is essentially defined by the functions and dysfunctions of one organ. As the great number of cross-references point to legal issues of marriage, to childbearing, and to inheritance problems stemming from marriage and childbearing, it becomes increasingly clear that the whole article FEMME should be understood in its second meaning, as wife, and as subordinated entirely to gender and sex. Bound by an identity of wife, her sexuality is defined and confined to the goal, act, and problems of childbirth, and her legal status determined solely by marriage.[15] This is all the more striking in view of the general absence of gendered or sexual marking of HOMME.

For the most part, then, the cross-references of these last three entries limit rather than transform radically the contemporary understandings of FEMME. The overwhelmingly legal and medical cross-references anticipate the way woman will be increasingly defined and limited by medical and legal discourse in the nineteenth century, as Michel Foucault analyses in *The History of sexuality*.[16] The knowledge that the *Encyclopédie* seeks to disseminate may indeed debunk superstitions, prejudices, religious dogma, and errors of the past concerning woman, but it also imprisons her in new, and perhaps more insidious, discourses.

While this observation is certainly not a new discovery about how woman was perceived and identified at this time in France, it reveals how the encyclopedists, despite their claims to dispel prejudices, advanced mostly reductive views on woman. This is not to say that the contributors to this article were hypocritical or cynical. On the contrary, Barthez, Boucher d'Argis, and Jaucourt especially, summarised well the most current legal and scientific knowledge on woman. The reductive or limited perspective becomes fully evident only when we heed Diderot's directives

15. For another analysis that corroborates this reductive understanding of woman's sexuality, see Christine Birnbaum, 'La vision médicale de l'amour dans l'*Encyclopédie*', in *Encyclopédie: aimer en France 1760-1860*, ed. Paul Viallaneix and Jean Ehrard, 2 vols (Clermont-Ferrand 1980), ii.307-13.
16. Foucault could be criticised for neglecting the gendered character of the disciplinary discourses and techniques he identifies and studies in his *History of sexuality*. Yet his analyses do suggest that the agencies of control and mechanisms of surveillance that, according to his argument, begin to proliferate in the eighteenth and nineteenth centuries, affected woman's sexuality in the ways already suggested by the *Encyclopédie*'s FEMME. Certainly, the article contributes to turning 'sex into discourse', Foucault's other major observation. See *The History of sexuality*, volume i, in particular Part Four, 'Deployment of sexuality' (New York 1980; original French edition 1976).

and follow the paths of the cross-references, which makes certain repetitions of circuits as well as multiple referrals to the same articles inevitably stand out. I doubt that the editors were aware of these repetitions and patterns and how they could inflect the meaning of the original article. They are, however, a perfect example of how following the cross-references can lead not only to unsettling juxtapositions and contradictions but also to unexpected meanings that, in turn, force us to think anew. Whether these effects were intended or not, whether they were programmed as part of a larger ideological project, seems irrelevant. Whether Diderot understood the full implications of his reading programme or not, the fact is that by simply following his directions, we do, indeed, come to question, if not transform 'the common way of thinking'.

ANNE C. VILA

The body in crisis:
vitalism, hydrotherapy and medical
discourse in the *Encyclopédie*

OVER the past decade, through inspirations as diverse as Foucault, feminism, psychoanalysis, and cultural studies, scholars have taken a renewed interest in the body and the meanings it held during the French Enlightenment.[1] This interest has in turn brought about a rediscovery of eighteenth-century French biomedical theory, a field that did much to shape knowledge during an era when the mind-body relation, the physical contours of the psyche, and the forms, limits, and mechanisms of knowledge were all subjects of intense scrutiny and speculation. In the empiricist, secular, monistic intellectual climate that was cultivated by the *philosophes*, medicine and physiology were influential not just in discussions of materialism, sensationalist philosophy, and scientific method, but also in the period's lively debates on human nature and diversity, on civilisation's ambiguous effects on the mind and morality, and on the widespread, multifaceted culture of sensibility. As one literary critic has aptly put it, 'like theology in the Middle Ages, medicine in the Enlightenment approached the condition of a master discourse': by virtue of its own philosophical aspirations – and its practitioners' unstinting efforts to publicise the field's recent advances – medical knowledge seemed to supply 'the cornerstone for an entire philosophy of man, in which improved public health would be indivisible from enlightened morality and from political reform'.[2]

Not surprisingly, medicine also occupied a central place in the *Encyclopédie*, the period's most ambitious attempt to present knowledge in a manner that would revolve entirely around the human being, the figure that, within the encyclopedic order as described by Denis Diderot, was to be 'le terme unique d'où il faut partir, et auquel il faut tout ramener, si l'on veut plaire, intéresser, toucher jusque dans les considérations les plus arides

1. See, for example, Barbara Stafford, *Body criticism: imaging the unseen in Enlightenment art and medicine* (Cambridge, Mass. 1991); Marie-Hélène Huet, *Monstrous imagination* (Cambridge, Mass.1993); Dorinda Outram, *The Body and the French Revolution: sex, class, and political culture* (New Haven, Conn.1989); and, looking at the body in a more metaphorical sense, Anne Deneys-Tunney, *Écritures du corps: de Descartes à Laclos* (Paris 1992).

2. David B. Morris, 'The marquis de Sade and the discourses of pain: literature and medicine at the revolution', in *The Languages of Psyche: mind and body in Enlightenment thought*, ed. G. S. Rousseau (Berkeley, Cal. 1990), p.297-98.

et les détails les plus secs'.[3] Some historians have suggested that, in its medical content, the *Encyclopédie* was primarily a work of vulgarisation, designed to translate conventional medical wisdom into terms that could be grasped by a general readership.[4] Vulgarisation is, however, too passive a term for describing the way in which contemporary medical knowledge was represented in the *Encyclopédie*, a work that served as a vehicle both for disseminating the most dynamic ideas of this field – particularly those emanating from the vitalist Montpellier medical school – and for constituting medical knowledge as a unique, authoritative way of conveying the body's true language. By exploiting the system of internal and external cross-references that Diderot had created to aid readers in negotiating their way around this enormous work, the medical encyclope-dists who championed Montpellier medicine also forged an intriguing relationship between the subject matter of their articles and the form in which that subject matter was imparted. That is, they deployed the *Encyclo-pédie*'s cross-referencing system not just to highlight vitalist principles like organic action and reaction but to demonstrate, in a formal register, the body's dynamic, resonating mode of functioning.

The campaign to use the *Encyclopédie* to promote the new 'philosophical' medicine was conducted by a mere handful of authors. The most prominent of the group was Théophile de Bordeu, a physician whose concept of vital sensibility dominated the medical thought of this period and attracted the interest of Diderot, who probably first became aware of Bordeu's work through the *Encyclopédie*.[5] Sensibility, according to Bordeu, directed the operations of the living body at both a general and a local level, such that the body could be seen as a federation of semi-independent parts, each endowed with its own distinct mode of 'feeling' or ability to respond to stimuli. Bordeu's sensibility theory, expounded in such ground-breaking works as his *Recherches anatomiques sur les glandes* (1752), led him to conceive of all body organs as 'glandular', on the model of the penis: every organ, he reasoned, acted and reacted according to a four-part mechanism of stimu-lation, arousal, an orgasmic-like crisis, and resolution in the form of a secretion or excretion; and nature used the same mechanism of crisis to

---

3. Denis Diderot, ENCYCLOPÉDIE, v.213. Daniel Brewer examines the 'powerfully cen-tralising concept of man' that the encyclopedists used to organise their text and its repres-entation of 'useful' knowledge, in *The Discourse of Enlightenment in eighteenth-century France* (Cambridge 1993), esp. p.13-25. On Diderot's innovative conception of the encyclopedic cross-referencing system, see Wilda Anderson, *Diderot's dream* (Baltimore, Md. 1990), p.91-124.

4. See William Coleman, 'Health and hygiene in the *Encyclopédie*', *Journal of the history of medicine* 29 (1974), p.399-421. Coleman focuses on the articles on hygiene written by Arnulfe d'Aumont, another graduate of the Montpellier medical faculty but one who remained theor-etically aligned with iatromechanism.

5. Jacques Roger ventures this hypothesis in his discussion of the relationship between Bordeu and Diderot, in *Les Sciences de la vie dans la pensée française au XVIIIᵉ siècle* (Paris 1963), p.630-31.

cure the body of inflammations and other diseased states.[6] Although he contributed only the article CRISE to the *Encyclopédie*, Bordeu is one of the authors most frequently cited throughout the network of Montpellier-based medical articles.

As for the other Montpellier encyclopedists, Henri Fouquet made six contributions, most notably SECRÉTION, an abstract of Bordeu's treatise on glands, and the long entry SENSIBILITÉ, SENTIMENT (*Médecine*). The physician and chemist Gabriel-François Venel, Bordeu's close friend and former classmate, wrote at least sixty-three articles (signed 'b') including EAU (*Chimie*), EAU COMMUNE (*Diète*), and EAU COMMUNE (*Mat. méd.*), all three of which concerned balneology and other forms of hydrotherapy.[7] However, the true driving force behind the effort to promote Montpellier medicine was unquestionably Jean-Jacques Ménuret de Chambaud, who wrote at least eighty-five articles for the last ten volumes of the *Encyclopédie* (volumes 8-17, letters H to Z, all published in 1765). Although he was only moderately successful as a practitioner and left little else to posterity beyond his numerous *Encyclopédie* entries, Ménuret's contributions are far more significant than has generally been acknowledged.[8] Ménuret used his individual articles to manoeuvre vitalist medicine into a position of prominence over other, more established natural sciences, and he deployed the cross-referencing system with a singular deftness.

After exploring one example of Ménuret's strategy to draw attention to the fundamental principles of Montpellier theory, I will turn my focus to a particular application of that doctrine, hydrotherapy, a therapeutic technique that enjoyed a remarkable revival in mid-to-late eighteenth-century France for reasons that were directly linked to the contemporary prestige of medical vitalism. Like Ménuret's entries on medical semiotics, physiology, and diagnostics, the hydrotherapy articles of the *Encyclopédie* and the *Supplément* created through their cross-references an intricate intertextual web that involved major medico-philosophical articles as well as the most important recent treatises on mineral waters. The discourse on hydrotherapy that took place in and beyond the *Encyclopédie* attested to the

6. Théophile de Bordeu, *Recherches anatomiques sur la position des glandes et sur leur action*, in *Œuvres complètes* (Paris 1818), i.125-26 and 194-96.
7. Maxime Laignel-Lavastine provides this count of Venel's contributions in 'Les médecins collaborateurs de l'*Encyclopédie*', *Revue d'histoire des sciences* 4 (1951), p.353.
8. Ménuret signed seventy of his articles by name or with an 'm'. The rest of the articles that can be attributed to him are either referred to as his in other articles, or extremely similar in style and theme. R. N. Schwab and W. E. Rex attribute eighty-five articles to Ménuret in *Inventory of Diderot's Encyclopédie*, *SVEC* 93 (1972), p.216-17. In her more recent, exceptionally detailed portrait of Ménuret, Roselyne Rey estimates that he wrote close to a hundred *Encyclopédie* entries; see Rey, *Naissance et développement du vitalisme en France de la deuxième moitié du 18ᵉ siècle à la fin du Premier Empire*, *SVEC* 381 (2000), p.63-89. Jacques Roger was one of the first scholars to emphasise Ménuret's role in the *Encyclopédie*; see *Les Sciences de la vie*, p.631-41. See also Pierre Astruc, 'Les sciences médicales et leurs représentants dans l'*Encyclopédie*', *Revue d'histoire des sciences* (1951), p.359-68.

emergence of a new, energetic, and vigorous model of the body – a body now deemed capable of using its inner forces to defend itself against external stimuli and pathogens, and to recover its flagging vital energies by undergoing salutary crises.[9] Although these writings present hydrotherapy as one of the most progressive, most theoretically sound curative treatments ever to be devised, they are tinged with ancient ideas about humours, sympathies, and the mysterious fluid workings of the universe. In that sense, they offer a powerful reminder of the archaic quality of Enlightenment thinking about nature, the body, and the best way to study them.

i. Promoting vitalism through the *Encyclopédie*

The Montpellier encyclopedists clearly saw the *Encyclopédie* as an excellent tool for establishing medicine as the foundation of the 'sciences de l'homme' – that is, for depicting medical knowledge as the key to understanding all aspects of the human being.[10] They designed their articles both to underscore the innovative physio-pathology to which vitalism gave rise and to sketch the elements of the newly reformed art of medical semiotics. The latter part of their campaign took place in a series of texts that include Ménuret's articles OBSERVATEUR, OBSERVATION, POULS, and PROGNOSTIC, as well as the anonymous essay SEMEIOTIQUE and Bordeu's entry on CRISE. These articles served to publicise the new semiotic system put forth in Bordeu's *Recherches sur le pouls par rapport aux crises* (1757), while also portraying the *médecin philosophe* as a heroic figure uniquely qualified to read the natural signs sent out by the body.

SEMEIOTIQUE is relatively short, but its reformist bent is immediately apparent. The author (most probably Ménuret) begins by declaring that semiotics should be recognised as a powerful instrument for penetrating into the inner recesses of the healthy or ailing body.[11] This approach to semiotics stems directly from the new Montpellier doctrine of sensibility, which invested both the patient's body and the practitioner's with a special, dynamic mode of operation. The patient's body is thus held to be driven by inner phenomena that have a 'correspondance réciproque', an 'enchaînement mutuel', and a 'gradation naturelle' (xiv.937). The signs emitted by this body are likewise naturally interrelated, such that a

9. Georges Vigarello notes that this model of the body shaped eighteenth-century inoculation theory as well as hygiene and hydrotherapy; see *Le Propre et le sale: l'hygiène du corps depuis le moyen âge* (Paris 1985), p.140-43.

10. An expanded version of this discussion can be found in chapter 2 of my book *Enlightenment and pathology: sensibility in the literature and medicine of eighteenth-century France* (Baltimore, Md. 1998), p.45-65. Elizabeth A. Williams provides a compelling historical explanation of the influence of Montpellier vitalism and other schools of 'philosophical' medicine in *The Physical and the moral: anthropology, physiology, and philosophical medicine in France, 1750-1850* (Cambridge 1994). See also her forthcoming study *A Cultural history of medical vitalism in Enlightenment Montpellier*.

11. SEMEOTIQUE, *ou* SEMEIOLOGIE (*Médecin. Semeiotiq.*), in *Encyclopédie*, xiv.937.

physician need only follow the pattern of actions and reactions formed by these signs in order to decipher what is causing the ailment with which he is confronted. Only a certain kind of physician, however, is able to detect those patterns: 'l'observateur éclairé [...] peut seul porter une vue pénétrante dans les replis les plus cachés du corps, y distinguer l'état et les dérangemens des différentes parties, connoître par des signes extérieurs les maladies qui attaquent les organes internes, et en déterminer le caractère propre et le siège particulier.' The body is a transparent machine for such an observer because he possesses a vision of its inner workings that goes beyond the usual limits of human understanding (xiv.937):

le voile mystérieux qui cache aux foibles mortels la connoissance de l'avenir se déchire devant lui; il voit d'un œil assuré les changemens divers qui doivent arriver dans la santé ou la maladie; il tient la chaîne qui lie tous les événemens, et les premiers chaînons qui sont sous sa main lui font connoître la nature de ceux qui viennent après, parce que la nature n'a que les dehors variés, et qu'elle est dans le fond toujours uniforme, toujours attachée à la même marche.

The science of medical semiotics is thus predicated on the assumption that every action, every movement, and every reaction of the body is a richly significant link in an ongoing chain of physiological or pathological events. The physician's task accordingly consists in garnering as much information as he can from the body's perceptible qualities and functions – its excretions and secretions, its colour and heat, its respiratory rhythms, and above all its pulses (the reader is referred at this point to 'POULS, RESPIRATION, SUEUR, URINE, etc.', xiv.938). These signs are to be judged not by traditional symptomalogical divisions, decried here as arbitrary and metaphysical, but rather on the basis of a painstaking observation of the same body over time – one that takes into account its temperamental type, its habits of sleep, digestion, excretion and so on, and the illnesses it may have suffered in the past. Having assembled those facts and compared them with the present signs, the observing physician should be able to determine how best to maintain that patient's health, or guide him or her through an impending pathological crisis.

Ménuret's article PROGNOSTIC offers yet another glorifying scenario of the physician at work, this time as a prognosticator who, using the 'flambeau lumineux' of his observations and experience, can see that the triumph of nature and health is often underway even through the gravest, most frightening complications.[12] As Ménuret elaborates this tableau, his physician becomes more and more heroic in character, using his unique divinatory talents to instil order into both the patient's illness and the familial entourage. The physician's exceptional physical and intellectual qualities also come to the fore – most particularly his uniquely attuned sense organs, which allow him to pick up on the signs of the various disease events occurring in the patient's body, to understand their natural

12. Jean-Jacques Ménuret de Chambaud, PROGNOSTIC, in *Encyclopédie*, xiii.429.

interrelation, and to predict the manner in which the illness will be resolved through evacuation from the body. Once he has reconstructed the script that fits the patient's specific ailment, the skilled physician acts not to interfere in the illness, but rather to guide it to its most complete denouement: 'Sans cesse occupé à suivre la nature, à éloigner tout ce qui peut retarder ses opérations et en empêcher la réussite, il proportionnera habilement ses secours et au besoin de la nature, et à la longueur de la maladie; il préparera de loin une crise complette et salutaire, une convalescence prochaine et courte, et une santé ferme et constante' (xiii.429).

Ménuret thus paints a remarkably optimistic picture of medical treatment as a mutually beneficial team effort between nature and an enlightened attending physician, who deploys his semiotic talents in order to guide the patient's impending bodily crisis to a felicitous outcome. To succeed in this endeavour, the physician must be equipped with both a reliable bank of diligently reiterated clinical observations and a sure command of the body's most important signs. Those two related medical arts – observation and semiotic skill – have, Ménuret asserts, fallen into disuse since the days of Hippocrates, largely because so many theorists have promoted frivolous, arbitrary or nonexistent signs. Fortunately, however, a handful of contemporary physicians more philosophical in temper have revived the principles of sound prognosis: 'Ce n'est que dans ces derniers tems, le prognostic a reçu un *nouveau lustre* et plus de certitude par les observations sur le pouls par rapport aux crises' (xiii.429) – an obvious allusion to Bordeu's treatise on pulses, published eight years earlier. In Ménuret's view, one can excel in the art of prognosis only by embracing the basic tenets of Montpellier vitalism: the idea that every disease state follows a specific 'critical' pattern, and the belief that, of all medical signs, pulses are the most significant.

Before ending PROGNOSTIC, Ménuret ventures the intriguing suggestion that it might be possible to use the medically-based methodology of semiotic prognosis outside the field of medicine itself, in the form of a systematic moral semiotics. This would, he argues, vastly improve the understanding of human society by revealing 'les ressorts cachés qui font mouvoir les hommes', which depend as much on the individual's physical disposition as on his or her present circumstances and dominant passions (xiii.430). Although Ménuret only toys with this possibility here, he nonetheless provides a glimpse of one of his major preoccupations as an encyclopedist: to champion medicine and its divinely gifted practitioner as shining examples for all the human sciences.

This project is most explicitly carried out in the centrepiece article OBSERVATION, an essay designed to dramatise the philosophical spirit that, in Ménuret's view, has recently reinvigorated medical thinking.[13] As he presents it, that spirit is destined to remake the medical field not just

13. OBSERVATION, in *Encyclopédie*, xi.313-23.

from within but also from without, by giving it a new place of prominence in the larger framework of human knowledge. Ménuret accordingly composes OBSERVATION to illustrate both aspects of this revolution: he continues his effort to manoeuvre semiotics into a privileged position in relation to the other branches of medicine, while redefining the general science of observation so as to depict medicine – the art of observing and coding the human body – as the alpha and omega of all natural-philosophical studies.

Although OBSERVATION is categorised as a medical article, medicine is not announced as its primary concern, at least not at the outset. Rather, Ménuret begins by denouncing experimentation, an approach to nature that he considers artificial and distorting, in marked contrast to plain and natural observation (xi.313).[14] He compares the experimenter and the observer by way of synecdoche: each is reduced to the main sensory organ he uses for his investigations. The experimenter is thus represented by his hand – an organ that manipulates and disfigures – whereas the observer is depicted as an eye, the organ that has the most distant and unobtrusive relation to its object. Experimental methods, Ménuret insists, blind their practitioner to the virtues of simple observation and denature the object observed, producing phenomena that are artificial, arbitrary, and 'pour l'ordinaire démenti[s] par l'observation' (xi.313-14). Given the multiple risks involved in experimenting, Ménuret proclaims observation to be a far surer path to knowledge. Following that principle, he presents a programme for investigating nature that resembles Diderot's *De l'interprétation de la nature* (written a decade earlier) – with the difference that Ménuret gives a distinctly organic twist to the way that the facts of natural philosophy should interact: 'plusieurs faits pris séparément paroissent secs, stériles et infructueux; dès qu'on les rapproche, ils acquierent une certaine action, prennent une vie qui par-tout résulte de l'accord mutuel, de l'appui réciproque, et d'un enchaînement qui les lie les uns aux autres' (xi.314). By the end of this article, the homology between the facts of organic matter and the organic-like interaction of facts themselves becomes something like a founding principle for medical discourse in general.

Ménuret's discussion in OBSERVATION moves steadily from fields of inorganic natural observation (astronomy, geology, physics) into the organic realm of the science of man, where the medical observer reigns supreme. 'L'Homme', Ménuret declares, 'de quelque côté qu'on l'envisage, est le moins propre à être sujet d'*expérience*; il est l'objet le plus convenable, le plus noble, et le plus intéressant de l'*observation*, et ce n'est que par elle qu'on

---

14. This part of Ménuret's discussion reflects the methodological debate then raging over the virtues of experimental investigative methods in natural philosophy. See, by contrast, D'Alembert's article EXPÉRIMENTAL, which was written to praise the king's recent establishment of a university chair in experimental physics; in *Encyclopédie*, vi.298-301. See also Haller's *Supplément* article ŒCONOMIE ANIMALE, where he defends vivisectionist experimentation in physiology; in *Supplément* to the *Encyclopédie*, iv.104-105.

peut faire quelque progrès dans les sciences qui le regardent' (xi.315). The 'noble' and 'divine' science of medicine is, he continues, the field that most excels in observing humankind, and thus warrants a particularly close examination. Ménuret then proceeds to list every type of medical observation imaginable (anatomical, physiological, hygienic, pathological, meteorological, and therapeutic) in such a way that all appear to be united under the globalising rubric of semiotics, which he presents as a system into which every observed bodily fact can be fit (xi.319). If it were properly designed, such a system of facts would not be a system at all, but rather the true language of nature (xi.320).

Sensibility, as Ménuret describes it here, provides 'un point de vue général qui sert de point de ralliement pour tous les faits que l'observation vient d'offrir' (xi.318). This vitalist theory has, he adds, been endorsed by two distinguished contemporary thinkers (xi.318):

> Un médecin célèbre (M. de Bordeu) et un illustre physicien (M. de Maupertuis) se sont accordés à comparer l'homme envisagé sous ce point de vue lumineux et philosophique à un groupe d'abeilles qui font leurs efforts pour s'attacher à une branche d'arbre; on les voit se presser, se soutenir mutuellement, et former une espèce de tout, dans lequel chaque partie vivante à sa maniere, contribue par la correspondance et la direction de ses mouvemens à entretenir cette espèce de *vie* de tout le corps, si l'on peut appeler ainsi une simple liaison d'action.

The specific works to which Ménuret is alluding here are Bordeu's *Recherches sur les glandes* and Maupertuis's *Système de la nature, ou, essai sur la formation des corps organisés* (1756), both of which use a version of the bee swarm metaphor that Diderot would later incorporate into the dialogue *Le Rêve de d'Alembert* (1769). What is most intriguing about Ménuret's use of this image in OBSERVATION is the way he applies it not just to the organic body, but also to the body of facts that physician-philosophers cull through their semiotic observations. A curious operational equivalence emerges in this article between the physical body being observed, and the textual body that is formed by a well-assembled group of medical facts: those facts, Ménuret declares, should 'communicate' via natural connections and affinities, because they refer to a living body that is likewise driven by a set pattern of sympathetic physiological resonances – all of which links its parts into an economic whole. Unlike the plain, inert theories of old-style iatromechanism – metaphorically represented as a 'troupe de grues qui volent ensemble dans un certain ordre mais sans s'entr'aider réciproquement et sans dépendre des uns des autres' (xi.318) – the ideas that arise from vitalist medicine are destined to come to life. Ultimately, therefore, the force of bodily sensibility co-ordinates not only the physio-pathological phenomena that the physician seeks to decipher, but also the way in which he obtains and disseminates his particular kind of knowledge. The bee swarm image thus figures twice in OBSERVATION: once as a model for the animal economy, and once as a model for organising medical discourse in the most simple, natural form possible.

Ménuret's lively resonating model of medical discourse is based, in part, on an intriguing application of Condillacian analysis, in which all facts are predestined to take their proper, natural place in the observer's mind – in this case, because they emanate directly from a similarly ordered animal economy. It is also a particularly dynamic realisation of what Diderot envisioned an encyclopaedia should be: a work that would literally arouse its readers and stimulate them to see all sorts of new connections among ideas and in nature. The textual network that Ménuret and his medical collaborators construct in the *Encyclopédie* literally embodies such connections, because it is composed of articles that not only describe but mimic, through their 'sympathetic' interactions, the active-reactive resonating quality of the body itself.

ii. Hydrotherapy in and beyond the *Encyclopédie*

Given their allegiance to 'expectant' medicine – that is, the doctrine that the body heals best when Nature is left to her own devices – it is not surprising that the Montpellier-based vitalists who collaborated on the *Encyclopédie* were sceptical about most contemporary therapeutic practices (harsh purgatives, blood-letting, and so on). They were nonetheless quite enthusiastic about hydrotherapy, a cluster of curative techniques that enjoyed a remarkable renaissance during the decades in which the *Encyclopédie* and its addenda were written and published. Water, in the eyes of Enlightenment physicians, was hardly a simple substance: until chemists undertook to develop standards for analysing mineral water springs late in the century, waters were, as historian Christopher Hamlin puts it, 'conceived as a complicated and changing mixture including a watery principle, various dissolved and suspended salts and earths, and a "spirit", the "life" or "soul" of the water as it was called, that transcended analysis or capture'.[15] Perhaps the most soulful and thus most mysterious of all waters was that found in the sea: sea bathing, particularly if it was involuntary, was deemed capable of curing the most intractable illnesses of both body and mind. As Hughes Maret explained in the article BAIN that he composed for the *Supplément* to the *Encyclopédie*, a sudden bath in the ocean exerted two healthful effects upon an ailing individual: first, the ocean's salty water stimulated the vessels, fortified the solids, and favoured secretion by invigorating the humoral mass; and second, the experience of being thrown into this immense and awesome substance created such an acute agitation in the soul that 'il se fait dans le corps un bouleversement général [...]. C'est par cette action que le bain de mer peut être utile dans

---

15. Christopher Hamlin, 'Chemistry, medicine, and the legitimisation of English spas, 1740-1840', in *The Medical history of waters and spas*, ed. Roy Porter (London 1990), p.71.

la rage et dans la folie.'[16] Fear and anxiety, as Alain Corbin has aptly noted, thus figured prominently in the medical 'discovery' of the sea that began in the mid-eighteenth century.[17] Yet the effort to exploit the sea's putatively unlimited healing powers was also rooted in a long-standing fascination with the therapeutic potential of all manner of vital fluids, whether frightening or familiar, external or internal. To understand the hydrotherapy movement as it evolved in Enlightenment medical thought, we should therefore view it in the context of the period's larger inquiry into the human body's organic and super-organic driving principles, an inquiry founded on the hope that nature's forces could be directly tapped to cure disease and to restore or improve the constitution of the human race.

Because they were so actively exploited for the purposes of scientific and medical popularisation, the *Encyclopédie* and its *Supplément* provide a convenient point of entry into the theories and practices that underlay hydrotherapy during the second half of the century. Although they sometimes sounded a note of caution about this movement, the medical writers who described it to the *Encyclopédie*'s readers generally believed that seabathing, mineral-water therapy and related techniques held great medical promise. They also continued the practice of abundant cross-referencing both to articles within the *Encyclopédie* – Maret's BAIN, for example, refers the reader to FIBRE, IRRITABILITÉ, NERFS, and SENSIBILITÉ – and to major treatises, typically works whose authors also belonged to the Montpellier circle. They thus give a striking demonstration of vitalist medicine at work on both a therapeutic and a discursive, intertextual level.

In BAIN, Maret characterises the benefits of balneology in these terms (ii.758):

il n'est peut-être point de remède d'une utilité plus étendue; [les bains] sont capables non seulement de guérir, mais encore de prévenir une infinité de maladies [...] un usage réfléchi et bien raisonné des différentes espèces de bains peut réformer les tempéraments et produire dans nos corps des révolutions favorables aux fonctions corporelles et mêmes aux intellectuelles.

However, in the cultural climate of eighteenth-century France, bathing was not an activity to be undertaken lightly. Given the persistent influence of the Church's doctrinal prejudice against this fleshly pursuit – and of the idea that robust people had to maintain the protective 'aura' provided by their own pungent bodily effluvia[18] – only a clearly perceived medical

---

16. Hughes Maret, BAIN (*Médecine*) in *Supplément* to the *Encyclopédie*, i.758. The mark at the beginning of this article indicates that it is an addition or correction to Vandenesse's much shorter article BAIN *de santé* ou *de propreté* (*en Médecine*), which appeared in the original *Encyclopédie*. Maret's article is based on his *Mémoire sur la manière d'agir des bains d'eau douce et d'eau de mer et sur leur usage* (Paris 1769).

17. Alain Corbin, *Le Territoire du vide: l'occident et le désir du rivage (1750-1840)* (Paris 1990), p.71-113.

18. Bordeu, for example, spoke admiringly of the 'odeur fétide qui s'exhale des mâles vigoureux', attributing it directly to the healthy man's semen, which he described as 'un

need could persuade a person to subject him- or herself to the often violent effects of baths, showers, and other forms of hydrotherapy. Taking the waters was, moreover, a distinctly elite practice, both because travelling to a mineral water spring required substantial time and financial means, and because membership in the well-to-do, leisure class was a virtual precondition for suffering the stomach ailments, melancholia, and other symptoms of excessive sensibility that brought most patients to France's spas.[19]

Although it was not a specifically French invention, the spa had already acquired a distinct national flavour in France since its revival in the sixteenth century, when mineral water springs from Bourbonne-les-Bains in Champagne to Barèges in the Pyrenees began to reclaim the popularity and renown they had held in ancient times.[20] The French spa, as historian Laurence Brockliss has described it, 'was the *physicians'* brainchild. The physicians wanted to create centres of therapy not sociability, and this they achieved [...]. There would be no eighteenth-century French Bath.'[21] That is, whereas British watering places like Bath and Brighton drew clients as much for their social whirl as for their supposed health benefits, their French counterparts were sober establishments where a patient's existence was not only highly regimented, but full of affronts to aristocratic dignity – like having to expose one's body in public, to imbibe huge quantities of bitter, briny water, and to spend long hours with one's afflicted part submerged in a vapour bath, pounded by a painfully hot shower or wrapped in cold, damp cloths. For the French elite, therefore, 'attendance at the spa was a penance – a short, sharp reminder to those who had failed to regulate their life-styles in the [medically] approved fashion'.[22] What prompted French patients to subject themselves to the harrowing methods

---

stimulus particulier de la machine [...] auquel les médecins n'ont pas regardé d'assez près'; yet he ridiculed d'Aumont's *Encyclopédie* article SEMENCE and Le Camus's *La Médecine de l'esprit* (1753/1769) for advancing the idea that semen was strictly equivalent to nervous fluid. See 'Analyse médicinale du sang', part 6 of *Recherches sur les maladies chroniques* in Bordeu, *Œuvres complètes*, ii.957-58.

19. On the social makeup of France's spa clientele during and after the Old Regime, see Douglas Peter Mackaman, *Leisure settings: bourgeois culture and the spa in modern France* (Chicago, Ill. 1998).

20. French physicians first undertook during the 1770s to legislate and manage the country's springs, which had come to be seen as an important national resource. See four pertinent essays in *Villes d'eaux: histoire du thermalisme* (Paris 1994): Catherine Goédo-Thomas, 'Le thermalisme médiéval, de Flamence à Michel de Montaigne, récits et images', p.11-26; Jacqueline Boucher, 'Voyages et cures thermales dans la haute société française à la fin du XVIe siècle et au début du XVIIe siècle', p.41-54; Jacqueline Bayon, 'Villes d'eaux et thermalisme en pays forezien sous l'Ancien Régime', p.55-66; and Françoise Bayard, 'Prendre les eaux en Forez à la fin du XVIIIe siècle', p.67-79.

21. L. W. B. Brockliss, 'The development of the spa in seventeenth-century France' in *The Medical history of waters and spas*, p.39. Using sources like baron von Pollnitz's *Les Amusements des eaux d'Aix-en-Chapelle* (1736), E. S. Turner offers a more lighthearted description of the regimens to which patients were subjected at seventeenth- and eighteenth-century French spas, in *Taking the cure* (London 1967), p.72-87.

22. Brockliss, 'The Development of the spa', p.47.

of eighteenth-century hydrotherapy was an anxiety greater than that inspired by the methods themselves: namely, the fear of remaining irremediably afflicted with one of the many chronic illnesses that seemed to be running rampant among the nation's upper crust.

Chief among the ailments that plagued eighteenth-century French culture were the vapours, an umbrella term for all of the nervous affections held to stem from a pathological over-sensitivity of the nervous system, including melancholic lethargy, excessive nervousness, nausea and indigestion, and hysteria. Most contemporary medical theorists believed that the vapours struck only wealthy, urban-dwelling women, and men who had 'degenerated' to a similarly delicate temperament; only women, however, got vapours of the hysterical variety. Pierre Pomme, for one, maintained in his *Traité des affections vaporeuses des deux sexes* (republished four times during the 1760s) that worldly women led an existence so soft, over-stimulating and denaturing that it literally dried out and stiffened their nerves, thus triggering the spasms, convulsions, obstructions in the viscera, and general irritability that he called hysteria. One of Pomme's principal cures for this condition was a cold-bath therapy dubbed the 'méthode glaciale' by his rivals: it consisted in subjecting his patients to daily baths in very cold, plain water for a duration of three to four hours during their menstrual periods, and sometimes longer when necessary, 'suivant le degré de racornissement [des nerfs] que j'attaque'.[23] 'Aux maux violents', Pomme declared, 'il faut de violents remèdes.' Pomme's glacial method for curing hysterical vapours (cited, with mild reservations, by Maret in BAIN, ii.758) thus typified the belief pervasive in Enlightenment medical philosophy that the best way to treat a chronic pain or illness was to transform it into an *acute* distress, in order to induce a crisis – a healthful process that would, in principle, rid the patient of the affliction once and for all.

The medical encyclopedists did not view hydrotherapy with unqualified enthusiasm. In BAIN *de santé* ou *de propreté*, Vandenesse underscores the many precautions the patient must take to draw some benefit from a mineral water bath:

Il faut se faire saigner et purger, le prendre le matin à jeun, ou si c'est le soir, quatre heures après le repas, afin que la digestion des alimens soit entierement finie; se reposer, ou ne faire qu'un exercice très-modéré après qu'on est sorti du bain; enfin ne se livrer à aucun excès pendant tout le temps que l'on le prendra, et dans quelque saison que ce soit, ne point se baigner lorsque l'on est fatigué par quelque exercice violent.[24]

Nor did these authors endorse all of the hydrotherapeutic theories and practices circulating at the time. In EAU COMMUNE, for example, Venel rebukes Friedrich Hoffmann for declaring water to be a universal remedy and disparages certain other ideas as quackish if not downright dangerous:

---

23. Pierre Pomme, *Traité des affections vaporeuses des deux sexes*, 3rd edn (Lyon 1768), p.58.
24. Vandenesse, BAIN *de santé* ou *de propreté*, in *Encyclopédie*, ii.21.

he dismisses as 'vaine, inefficace, et souvent meurtrière' the technique of treating acute illnesses by having patients drink copious amounts of aqueous remedies; and he warns legitimate doctors not to embrace the faddish sweat-inducing or laxative water methods invented, respectively, by an English ecclesiastic named Mr Hancock, and the Sicilian Capuchin Bernardo-Maria de Castrogianne.[25] Venel nonetheless maintains that water can be very effective in preparing the organs and humours to 'se prêter plus aisément aux mouvements de la nature, ou à l'action des remèdes curatifs'; he therefore approves of giving patients warm 'infusions théiformes' to promote gentle transpiration in the skin and lungs, of using tepid water to clean the stomach 'des restes d'une mauvaise digestion', and of prescribing one or two glasses of cold water to be taken two hours after a meal in order to prevent 'les mauvais effets des digestions fougueuses chez les personnes vaporeuses de l'un et de l'autre sexe' (v.195-96). Venel thus regards a judicious use of water as a valuable means of bringing about the salutary evacuation necessary to restore health.

Historian Roselyne Rey sums up the eighteenth-century theory of the *crise salutaire* in these terms: 'Il s'agit [...] d'exacerber la sensibilité, d'activer une énergie vitale languissante qui n'a pas d'elle-même suffisamment de force pour accomplir le travail de lutte contre la maladie.'[26] There were, Rey notes, two distinct conceptual paradigms underlying this medical theory. The first followed the logic of humoral etiology, which dictated that the physician's task was to displace a pathological humour from a vital organ to a less important organ that was more accessible to the doctor – a secretory gland, preferably. The second paradigm derived from a more recently developed nervous etiology: it entailed a strategy of stimulation designed to counterbalance one point of extreme sensitivity or irritation in the body by artificially creating another that was more intense and energetic. Mineral waters, as many eighteenth-century French physicians perceived them, were uniquely suited to accomplishing both aims: they were, depending on the virtues particular to their *source*, capable of favouring general excretion, of cleaning out the stomach and blood vessels, of invigorating selected body organs, or, in mental illness, of counteracting a deranged imagination. In all cases, the basic goal of crisis therapy was the same: to restore the vigour of a patient's organs, to eliminate any lingering vicious humours, and to bring his or her sensibility back in line with the healthful norms dictated by nature.

One finds a strikingly comprehensive fusion of crisis theory and hydrotherapy in a 1775 treatise by Bordeu entitled *Recherches sur les maladies chroniques*, revealingly subtitled 'Leurs rapports avec les maladies aiguës, leurs

25. Venel, EAU COMMUNE (*Mat. méd.*), in *Encyclopédie*, v.195. C. Hamlin argues that Friedrich Hoffmann was, in fact, quite influential in giving 'plausibility to the view that the medicinal properties of any spring were unique, irreducible, and inimitable' ('Chemistry, medicine, and the legitimisation of English spas', p.70).
26. Roselyne Rey, *Histoire de la douleur* (Paris 1993), p.153.

périodes, leur nature, et sur la manière dont on les traite aux eaux minérales de Barèges, et des autres sources de l'Aquitaine'. Diseases, Bordeu
explains, fit the same pattern as that which he had earlier discerned in
glands: 'L'on peut raisonnablement comparer une maladie à la fonction
d'une glande, et nommer son dernier temps, temps d'excrétion, puisqu'il
est certain que toute affection, soit aiguë ou chronique, qui se guérit bien,
ou selon les vœux de la nature, finit toujours par quelque excrétion.'[27] The
best means of healing a chronic illness is consequently to force it to follow
the pattern of a natural excretion, by causing a critical 'revolution' in the
body. No single class of remedy, Bordeu declares, is better suited for that
purpose than the mineral waters that abound throughout France: 'le traite-
ment des eaux minérales employées à leurs sources, est, sans contredit, de
tous les secours de la médecine, le mieux en état d'opérer, pour le physique
et le moral, toutes les révolutions nécessaires et possibles dans les maladies
chroniques' (p.806). And, he insists, no single region is richer in waters with
excellent crisis-triggering qualities than his native Béarn – where Bordeu
just happened to hold the title of 'surintendant des eaux minérales' and
where his father and brother made a living as local spa overseers.[28]

Bordeu's underlying purpose in writing the *Recherches sur les maladies chroniques* is thus twofold: he seeks both to synthesise his physiological doctrine
of sensibility with his theory of chronic and acute disease, and to promote
the supposedly unique healing powers of the springs in the region of the
Pyrenees and Aquitaine, where he (like many medical authors who wrote
about particular waters) had a vested professional interest. Bordeu
acknowledges that one of the main benefits of mineral water therapy is the
act of travelling it involves, thanks to which rich city dwellers can escape,
for a time, from their bad living habits, excessive passions, and 'détraque-
ments habituels de la partie sensible [qui] énervent les fonctions [et] aggra-
vent les maladies longues et lentes' (p.806).[29] At the same time, he clearly
believes that the best chance for the chronically ill to restore their health is

27. Bordeu, *Recherches sur les maladies chroniques*, in *Œuvres complètes*, ii.845. A similar argument underlies Bordeu's article CRISE, where he initially takes a sceptical position on the
ancient doctrine of crises but ultimately endorses it; in *Encyclopédie*, iv.471-89. Bordeu also
wrote a *Dissertation sur l'usage des eaux de Barèges et du mercure* (Paris 1757) which focused on the
use of hydrotherapy to treat scrofula; this treatise is cited by Leroy (another Montpellier
physician) in MINÉRALES, EAUX, in *Encyclopédie*, x.540.

28. According to Anthelme-Balthasar Richerand's 'Notice sur la vie et les ouvrages de
Bordeu', Bordeu went to Paris shortly after getting his medical degree in Montpellier in
1744, and obtained the title of 'surintendant des eaux minérales de l'Aquitaine'. After returning to the Béarn he zealously undertook to attract more clients to the mineral waters of the
Pyrenees and Aquitaine. Richerand comments: 'C'est dans ce projet louable et patriotique, et
pour remplir les devoirs qui lui imposoit le titre pompeux dont il était revêtu, qu'il composa
cette foule d'ouvrages dont ses *Recherches sur les maladies chroniques* présentent le résumé et
l'analyse'; in Bordeu, *Œuvres complètes*, i.v.

29. 'Le voyage, l'espoir de réussir, la diversité des nourritures, l'air surtout qu'on respire et
qui baigne et pénètre les corps, l'étonnement où l'on se trouve sur les lieux, le changement des
sensations habituelles, les connaissances nouvelles qu'on fait, les petites passions qui naissent
dans ces occasions, l'honnête liberté dont on jouit, tout cela change, bouleverse, détruit les

by taking the waters of the Eaux Bonnes, the Eaux Chaudes, Cauteret, Bagnères, Luz, or his apparent favourite, Barèges, each of which is specifically suited to a particular temperament and ailment. In short, although they have yet to be scientifically analysed, 'les eaux des Pyrénées sont d'un grand secours dans les maladies lentes et longues [...] elles opèrent quelquefois des guérisons inattendues, et qui étonnent les connoisseurs' (p.929).

Bordeu is well informed about the latest developments in the field of hydrotherapy: he proudly announces the 'masterly' comprehensive analysis of France's mineral waters that is forthcoming from the chemists Venel and Baïen; and he appeals to the physicians who have recently been appointed to Louis XV's hydrotherapy commission to step up their efforts to develop a complete system for managing *sources* throughout the French kingdom (p.825-27).[30] 'Jamais', Bordeu declares, 'il ne fut autant question d'eaux minérales que dans ce siècle', and never has any century been better poised for tapping the full curative potential of mineral waters – both because chronic disease has never been more widespread, and because medicine has never been so philosophical in its understanding of the vital workings of the human body and mind.

Eighteenth-century French hydrotherapy was a complex conceptual movement that was promoted through a rich array of rhetorical techniques, including scare tactics, the blatant advertising of certain waters, exhaustive classifications of the country's springs, and above all appeals to the 'enlightened', vitalist conception of the body and its energies. The writings on this subject that one finds in and beyond the *Encyclopédie* illuminate several key currents in this period's medical thought as well as in the culture that surrounded it. First, they portray the Enlightenment physician as a distinctive figure who seemed to master nature with his penetrating mind and senses, and who sought to have a comprehensive influence over his patients' physical and moral hygiene and an authoritative voice on issues of public health.[31] Hence, perhaps, the keen rivalries that often developed over particular spas or water treatments: Jean-Baptiste Chevalier, for example, devoted his *Mémoires et observations sur les effets des eaux de Bourbonne-les-Bains* to denouncing Pomme's 'méthode glaciale' and its underlying *racornissement* theory, the better to promote his own method for using the waters of

habitudes d'incommodités et de maladies auxquelles sont surtout sujets les habitants des villes' (*Recherches sur les maladies chroniques*, p.806).

30. This royal commission, appointed by Louis XV in 1772, was led by Joseph Raulin, who was previously known primarily as a specialist in female maladies and author of works like the *Traité des affections vaporeuses du sexe* (1758). After becoming commission president, Raulin wrote four treatises promoting French mineral waters, published from 1772 to 1778; see Bayard, 'Prendre les eaux en Forez', p.68-71.

31. Maret, for example, ends his *Supplément* article BAIN by urging the government to favour the establishment of public baths, although he notes that precautions will have to be taken to avoid compromising the public's morality, especially in cities, 'où la dépravation des mœurs rend plus nécessaires les moyens de s'opposer à la dégénération de l'espèce humaine, et à la dépopulation, qui en est une suite inévitable' (*Supp.*, i.758).

Bourbonne, which Pomme had rudely dismissed a year earlier.[32] The hydrotherapy movement also illustrates medicine's gradual evolution away from purely speculative (and sometimes fraudulent) theories and toward more scientific approaches: Venel's work, in particular, reflects the growing effort to use chemistry as a means of establishing neutral, common standards by which to evaluate famous springs, and of inventing ways to imitate or improve their waters.[33]

At the same time, this movement highlights the powerful fluidist mindset that continued to imbue the healing arts of eighteenth-century France – a rubric that included both mainstream medicine and therapeutic fads like animal magnetism, which Franz-Anton Mesmer and his disciples introduced with great success and scandal in fashionable Paris during the 1780s. As Jean Starobinski has underscored, Mesmer devised his doctrine simply by replacing the period's reigning imaginary fluid – nervous fluid – with another, which he called 'universal'.[34] Mesmer then reconfigured the existing vitalist notion of crisis to create a curative scenario in which the patient's true ailment, a blockage in his or her universal fluid that interrupted communication with the fluids of the cosmos, was supposedly corrected through the artificial 'tide' that the magnetiser produced in the patient's body.[35] In many ways, the mysterious, seductive power that animal magnetisers held over their eager subjects echoed the extraordinary control that contemporary spa doctors and *intendants* strove to exert over their patients: both movements can be seen as preludes to the very hierarchical brand of physician-patient relationship that has come to dominate modern medicine and psychotherapy.

32. Jean-Baptiste Chevalier, *Mémoires et observations sur les effets des eaux de Bourbonne-les-Bains, en Champagne, dans les maladies hystériques et chroniques* (Paris 1772). The dispute also involved the distinguished Swiss physician Samuel-Auguste Tissot: in his widely read *Essai sur les maladies des gens du monde* (Lausanne 1770) Tissot praised 'mon ami M. Pomme' for successfully treating hysterical illnesses through the use of 'des bains tiedes ou froids, longs et multipliés, et des quantités presque effrayantes de boissons purement acqueuses'; in *Œuvres de M. Tissot* (1788), 135. However, Tissot also cautioned that the glacial cure was not universally applicable and, in a passage cited by Chevalier (p.xxi), warned physicians not to be slavishly devoted to a single therapeutic method.

33. The reservations Venel expressed about Hoffmann in EAU COMMUNE reflect the more neutral, objective view of mineral waters that emerged in the latter half of the century through the development of pneumatic chemistry by Lavoisier and others chemists; see Hamlin, 'Chemistry, medicine, and the legitimisation of English spas', p.72. Venel is praised by Leroy in MINÉRALES, EAUX for devising an 'invention très-ingénieuse' that created effervescence in flat water, thus allowing chemists and physicians to imitate the healthful salty, bubbly waters of Spa, Pyrmont or Camares; in *Encyclopédie*, x.535.

34. Jean Starobinski, 'Note sur l'histoire des fluides imaginaires (des esprits animaux à la libido)', *Gesnerus* 23 (1966), p.180.

35. See, for example, Mesmer's remarks in 'Mémoire sur la découverte du magnétisme animal' on the phenomena of flux and reflux he perceived in the human body; Mesmer, *Le Magnétisme animal*, ed. Robert Amadou (Paris 1971), p.61. See also François Azouvi's incisive study, 'Magnétisme animal: la sensation infinie', *Dix-huitième siècle* 23 (1991), p.107-18.

Finally, the eighteenth-century hydrotherapy movement reflects the anxieties and ambivalence that were then associated with the French social elite and with its preferred habitat, the city, a place that was generally deemed unwholesome by Enlightenment physicians. In that sense, this movement represents a curious expression of this period's larger effort to ameliorate humanity and correct the perceived ills or excesses of civilisation. Hydrotherapy was not, of course, strictly equivalent to Diderot's project of improving minds by changing 'la façon commune de penser' (ENCYCLOPÉDIE, v.222); yet it was rooted in the optimistic belief that good hygiene and the strategic use of nature's often dramatic curative capacities would eventually allow all individuals to find a new, healthier equilibrium between themselves and society – that is, between their physical existence as sentient beings, and their moral-intellectual activities as social beings.[36] Examining hydrotherapy on its own, peculiar terms thus helps us to uncover the intriguing concepts of the body, the patient, and the 'civilised' versus 'natural' self on which medical knowledge was constructed in eighteenth-century France – a period when medicine was intimately connected to all aspects of culture, from moral theory to literary criticism;[37] when penetrating into the secrets of the human being seemed as simple as deciphering a pulse or a secretion; when medical knowledge was accessible to the educated public in a way that it had never been before, and probably has not been since; and when physicians offered patients of a certain social stratum the promise that they could master all aspects of their well-being, simply by following nature.

36. Roselyne Rey emphasises this aspect of mid-to-late eighteenth-century hygienist discourse in her suggestive essay, 'Hygiène et souci de soi', *Communications* 56 (1993), p.25-39.

37. Many eighteenth-century physicians engaged in literary criticism among their various 'philosophical' pursuits. For one example, see my essay 'The *médecin philosophe* as drama critic: Pierre Fabre's natural history of French theatre', *SVEC* 314 (1993), p.231-48.

STEPHEN WERNER

The *Encyclopédie* 'index'

In 1780 a Protestant pastor named Pierre Mouchon published a *Table analytique et raisonnée du dictionnaire des sciences, des arts et des métiers*. Two thick folio volumes in size, the work was designed as an index to an edition of Diderot's *Encyclopédie* brought out by the well-known firm of Panckoucke. In addition to providing a list of the articles of Diderot's great 'war-machine' against ignorance and intolerance, Mouton's text also contained a catalogue of famous names mentioned in their pages as well as several new entries formed by combining information contained in previous articles.

The importance of Mouchon's *Table analytique* to the history of the *Encyclopédie* cannot be underestimated. The *Journal des savants*, in a contemporary review, termed it 'un vrai dictionnaire [...] utile à ceux qui n'auraient pas *L'Encyclopédie*, mais [...] indispensablement nécessaire pour ceux qui ont ce grand ouvrage et qui veulent le consulter'.[1] No bibliography of the different editions of Diderot's text, from those of Lucca to later digests such as *L'Esprit de l'Encyclopédie*, would be complete without reference to it. Yet the relationship of Mouchon's index to Diderot's conception of *encyclopédisme* cannot but be thought of as anecdotal (a condition in no way limited to Mouchon's dubious practice of having completed his work without Diderot's permission or his use of a different publisher than the ones who had produced the seventeen volumes of text and the eleven volumes of plates that made up the first edition of the *Encyclopédie*).

Introduced as a 'true' volume of the *Encyclopédie*, Mouchon's index robs Diderot's work of its authenticity and purpose. For the *Encyclopédie* was specifically conceived as a book of knowledge without an index. An alphabetical listing of contents looked back to an older and outmoded way of representing knowledge. It was first introduced in 1614 by Antonio Zara's *Anatomia ingeniorum et scientiarum*, followed up not long afterwards by Johann Jacob Hoffman's *Lexicon universale* (1677)[2] and kept alive in the early eighteenth century by Chambers, whose *Cyclopaedia*, the source or founding influence of the *Encyclopédie*, contained long double columns of text meant

---

1. George B. Watts, 'The Supplément and the table analytique et raisonnée of the *Encyclopédie*', *French review* 28 (1954-1955), p.4-19. See, too, Jean Ehrard, 'De Diderot à Panckoucke: deux pratiques de l'alphabet', in *L'Encyclopédisme*, ed. A. Becq (Paris 1991), p.243-52, and F. A. Kafker, 'The role of the *Encyclopédie* in the making of a modern encyclopedia', in *The 'Encyclopédie' and the age of revolution*, ed. C. Donato and R. M. Maniquis (Boston 1992), p.21.

2. *Encyclopedia Britannica*, 15th edn, vol.18.

to furnish readers with detailed summaries of the articles contained within.[3]

As Diderot was to deepen the point of many dictionary techniques bequeathed to him by his encyclopedic forebears (a vastly expanded coverage of matters relating to the manual arts, more extensive reliance on illustrations, rejection of a single editor in favour of a 'society of men of letters'), so too was he, in his task as editor-in-chief, to redesign this key principle of ordering knowledge. Gone now in the fresh or modern version of an encyclopedia was the idea of a closed-off or final text for which an index stood as the exemplary symbol. What was now to be validated was a more open or fluid style of encyclopedia writing, one committed to the ironies always to direct the Diderot *œuvre*. Reliance on *renvois*, or articles cross-referenced to one another, was at the heart of this approach.

Diderot did not of course invent cross-references. The mode was introduced to English lexicography by Harris's *Lexicon technicum* (another key influence on the *Encyclopédie*) and, not surprisingly, Chambers. The latter viewed cross-references as central to his compendium. They gave his work, he said, a sense of unity and comprehensiveness, a condition referred to in the text as a way of treating articles as:

so many Wholes, and as so many Parts of some greater Whole; their Connexion with which is pointed out by a Reference. So that by a Course of References, from Generals to Particulars; from Premises to Conclusions; from Cause to Effect; and vice versa, i.e. in one word, from more to less complex, and from less to more, a Communication is opened between the several Parts of the Work; and the several Articles are in some measure replaced in their natural Order of Science, out of which the Technical or Alphabetical one had remov'd them.[4]

Yet here too Diderot brought to the technique distinct powers of critical invention. *Renvois* now fit into two formal categories rather than the older single pattern. The first, *renvois de mots*, served to clarify meanings and avoid repetitions. A second category was called *renvois de choses*. Its function was to establish connections between related ideas or concepts. The more important change, though, concerned the function of the *renvois*. They were not to be thought of as a mere convenience to readers. Cross-references were now to be understood as 'the secret utility and inner force of the entire work'.[5]

Definitions were no longer fixed in a single dictionary entry but spread out over many volumes. The full meaning of any one subject thus partook of a kind of dialogue between separate though related entries. What was

3. The index, twenty pages long, comes in the second of Chambers' two folio volumes. It provides an overview of the numerous entries on science, philosophy and technology contained in this work first brought out in London in 1727. A good introduction to the world of Chambers is the article by Lael Ely Bradshaw, 'Ephraim Chambers' *Cyclopaedia*', in *Notable encyclopedias of the seventeenth and eighteenth centuries: nine predecessors of the Encyclopédie* (hereafter *NE*), ed. F. Kafker, *SVEC* 194 (1981), p.123-40.

4. Ephraim Chambers, *Cyclopaedia*, 2 vols, vol.ii (London 1728).

5. Diderot's article ENCYCLOPÉDIE provides the classic justification of the new role assigned to the *renvois*.

established was a kind of counterpoint between readers and text. Those who purchased the *Encyclopédie* gave up their position as passive consumers of an 'absolute book' of knowledge. Their status was now that of active participants in the construction of such a work. Readers were to coordinate related entries and put together their hidden, or at least underground, shape. The *renvoi* in CORDELIERS, for example, a seemingly innocuous piece on the history of the Franciscan order, sent readers to CAPUCHON, a satirical account of a battle that raged among the Franciscans as to whether cowls ought to have been broad or narrow (a dispute 'barely settled', the author says, by papal bulls issued by Nicholas IV, Clement V, John XXII, and Benedict XII). AGNUS SCYTHICUS, a brief commentary about an imaginary plant said to possess mythical properties, and accepted as such by gullible scholars, offers a justification of Bacon's experimental method and is to be completed by a second thrust at scientific error entitled CERTITUDE. PRÊTRE, an unsigned article generally attributed to Diderot but doubtless written by d'Holbach, expounds anti-clerical themes later to be fleshed out by readings in ORACLES and SUPERSTITIONS. A mild-mannered entry on BELBUCH ET ZEOMBUCH (Vandal divinities) suggests cross-references to IMMORTALITÉ and ÂME and through them, the controversial theme of Manicheism.

What is significant to note is that the dispersive qualities brought into play by the *renvois* were by no means linked to philosophical articles like CAPUCHON or AGNUS SCYTHICUS. Entries on steel furnaces, stocking frames, shipbuilding, and hundreds of other technical subjects given prominence in the full title of Diderot's text – *Encyclopédie, ou dictionnaire raisonné des sciences, des arts et des métiers* – also had a vital role in the condition. These articles did of course deepen the theoretical underpinnings of Diderot's text through insights – drawn from Bacon – about the complexity of technical operations, the knowledge of workmen and, as stated in the 'Prospectus', the value of technology as a central branch of knowledge:

On a trop écrit sur les sciences: on n'a pas assez bien écrit sur la plupart des arts libéraux: on n'a presque rien écrit sur les arts mécaniques; car Qu'est-ce que le peu qu'on en rencontre dans les auteurs, en comparaison de l'étendue & de la fécondité du sujet? Entre ceux qui en ont traité, l'un n'était pas assez instruit de ce qu'il avait à dire, & a moins rempli son objet que montré la nécessité d'un meilleur ouvrage: un autre n'a qu'effleuré la matière, en la traitant plutôt en grammairien & en homme de lettres, qu'en artiste; un troisième est à la vérité plus riche & plus ouvrier; mais il est en même temps si court, que les opérations des artistes & la description de leurs machines, cette manière capable de fournir seule des ouvrages considérables, n'occupe que la très petite partie du sien. Chambers n'a presque rien ajouté à ce qu'il a traduit de nos auteurs. Tout nous déterminait donc à recourir aux ouvriers.[6]

They also influenced issues bearing on the representation of the newly acclaimed virtues of technical knowledge. Central to an understanding of

6. Diderot, v.99.

this point is the curiously dual status of the technical *renvois*. Cross-references on these subjects not only sent readers to related written articles for information on any one industrial process or machine. More often than not, when amplification on a subject was called for it was also necessary to refer to illustrated plates or, as they were called, *planches*: some, single drawings, others, sets containing upwards of fifty or more engravings, the entire complex of drawings providing the first edition of the *Encyclopédie* with no fewer than half of its folio tomes.

Many of the technical plates, CHARPENTE for example or POTIER DE TERRE, are one-dimensional affairs. They endorse a style of detailed line-drawing influenced by Renaissance technical dictionaries like Ramelli's *Le Diverse et artificiose machine*, Leupold's *Theatrum machinarum* or Jacques Besson's *Théâtre des instruments mathématiques et mécaniques* (all crucial sources for Diderot's work), and clearly subordinate art, or any aesthetic instinct, to the requirements of the written texts they back up and support.

The same cannot be said for the more imaginatively probing plates of the *Encyclopédie* such as FORGES, SOIERIE or BAS. These illustrations possess the Socratic qualities Diderot was always to validate and to which he was to call attention in a key passage in the *Encyclopédie* under the heading OBSTETRIX ANIMORUM. The phrase refers to dialectical agents able to bring into being or 'birth' a spirit of modernity: 'Il nous a fallu exercer avec eux la fonction dont se glorifiait Socrate, la fonction pénible et délicate de faire accoucher les esprits, *obstetrix animorum*.'[7]

Plates endowed with this quality use the pictorial as an independent mode of expression. They grant drawings qualities of animation and colour, indeed endow them with an instinct for expression in some way beyond the sway of the merely illustrative or 'written'. The engravings for FORGES and GAZIER, for example, expand the boundaries of the articles they refer to with interests in cross-cuts, overhead views, sectionals and other techniques of perspective. Sequences like SOIERIE stress the value of industrial operations that evolve over many stages and thus bring into play a temporal complexity unknown to the more closed-in drawings (an 'action-oriented' approach Diderot was specifically to stress when, in speaking of the plates, he said: 'il n'y a rien ici de superflu, ni de suranné, ni d'idéal; tout y est en action et vivant'). One of the thirty-five plates of SOIE offers a juxtaposition of a frontal view of the machine called a 'métier pour fabriquer les étoffes brochées' with a sequence of squares that show the range of colours raw silk takes on when manufactured. They thus bring movement and a dynamic sense to dictionary making (qualities also demonstrated in the numerous variations in page and format size found in plates like TOURNEUR and MONNAYAGE[8]).

7. Diderot, v.100.
8. For an analysis of these and other *planches*, see Stephen Werner, *Blueprint: a study of Diderot and the Encyclopédie plates* (Birmingham 1993), p.63-69.

The entry on BAS or the stocking machine revealed the most striking example of the new importance of *le pictural* as a mode of representation. The text, an effort at providing an inventory of the hundreds of parts of the stocking machine from 'la traverse d'en bas où se tiennent les marches' to 'les écrous à l'oreille', and offering illustrations of all of their many *assemblages*,[9] is the longest of Diderot's many technical articles and is justly celebrated for its novelty. Diderot had never seen the machine in operation or visited a factory where it was used. The book of plates on which he based his account lacked a vital first page illustration of a 'tricot à la main: deux aiguilles sur lesquelles se montent succesivement la première, la deuxième, la troisième, la quatrième mailles'.

But it was the conclusion reached in what Jacques Proust has called this 'représentation du philosophe devant la machine et sur la machine'[10] that is surely most stunning. Diderot's exhaustive reporting on the stocking machine, his complex summaries of its parts and systems, all backed up by huge line-drawings (some three folio sheets in size), could not supply an authoritative account of the device for manufacturing stockings. This banal industrial object had properties that lay outside the framework of an inventory, however encyclopedic or complete. Here was a device that transcended the encyclopedic goal of full and accurate representation:

On conçoit, après ce que je viens de dire de la liaison & de la forme des parties du métier à *bas*, qu'on se promettrait en vain quelque connaissance de la machine entière, sans entrer dans le détail & la description de ces parties: mais elles sont en si grand nombre, qu'il semble que cet ouvrage doive excéder les bornes que nous nous sommes prescrites, & dans l'étendue du discours, & dans la quantité des planches. D'ailleurs, par où entamer ce discours? comment faire exécuter ces planches? La liaison des parties demanderait qu'on dît & qu'on montrât tout à la fois; ce qui n'est possible, ni dans le discours, où les choses se suivent nécessairement, ni dans les planches, où les parties se couvrent les unes les autres.[11]

A conception of an encyclopedia as an exercise in irony between a first philosophical entry and its later supplemental texts (both written and pictorial) is clearly being worked out in the volumes of the *Encyclopédie*, a tactic the more striking because of the contrast it offered with the alphabetical order in which the volumes were issued, their imposing scientific tables and the majestic frontispiece, baroque in style, didactic in conception yet ultimately to be understood less as a design that sealed off the text in a timeless classical order than as an ironic flourish that opened it up to 'l'activité toute moderne de l'appropriation discontinue, oublieuse des anciennes exigences d'unité organique'.[12]

9. Diderot, vi.76.
10. Jacques Proust, 'L'article "Bas" de Diderot', in *Langue et langages de Leibnitz à l'Encyclopédie*, ed. Michèle Duchet et Michèle Jalley (Paris 1977), p.271.
11. Diderot, vi.76-77.
12. Jean Starobinski, 'Remarques sur l'*Encyclopédie*', *Revue de métaphysique et de morale* 75 (1970), p.288.

The arrangement draws attention to the dramatic style always to animate the Diderot *œuvre* from *Le Neveu de Rameau* to *Jacques le fataliste*, indeed to the existence of the *livre-théâtre* so well defined by Jean Starobinski in his reading of a passage (already striking in its sense of theatre) from the article ENCYCLOPÉDIE:

Il faut considérer un dictionnaire universel des sciences et des arts, comme une campagne immense couverte de montagnes, de plaines, de rochers, d'eau, de forêts, d'animaux, et de tous les objets qui font la variété d'un grand paysage. La lumière du ciel les éclaire tous; mais ils en sont tous frappés diversement. Les uns s'avancent par leur nature et leur exposition, jusque sur le devant de la scène; d'autres sont distribués sur une infinité de plans intermédiaires; il y en a qui se perdent dans le lointain; tous se font valoir réciproquement.[13]

The connection of Diderot's text with the history of encyclopedias is no less telling. Here is a work that not only provides a variation on the theme of absolute knowledge at the heart of so much Enlightenment theorising, but stands as its exemplary form of expression. In these volumes a view of a 'circle of knowledge' as open and complete gives way to a conception of *encyclopédisme* as discontinuous and hidden. Here readers surrender their position as 'passive spectators of representation before whom the total meaning of all signs is played out' to become 'an integral part in the machine's production of narratives of knowledge'.[14] In these pages, above all, styles of representing and ordering of knowledge congenial to Chambers or Bayle's *Dictionnaire historique et critique* merge, owing to the plates, with pictorial or 'romantic' interests soon to surface in Rees's *New Cyclopaedia or a universal dictionary of the arts* and Coleridge's *Encyclopaedia metropolitana*.[15] Diderot is thus the creator of an encyclopedia often to be copied and translated in turn, but never, as Jean Thomas has stated, fully imitated.[16] The missing or absent index supplies a vital clue to this justly celebrated (and already 'modern') Enlightenment text.

13. Diderot, vii.254.

14. Daniel Brewer, *The Discourse of Enlightenment in eighteenth-century France* (Cambridge 1993), p.54.

15. For study of the pictorial or 'romantic' encyclopedia, see Stephen Werner, 'Abraham Rees's eighteenth-century *Cyclopaedia*', in *NE*, p.183-97.

16. Jean Thomas, 'Un moment du développement culturel de l'humanité: l'*Encyclopédie*', *Cahiers d'histoire mondiale* 9, no.3 (1966), p.695.

List of works cited

Adorno, Theodor W., *Aesthetic theory*, ed. G. Adorno and R. Tiedemann, ed. and translated by R. Hullot-Kentor (Minneapolis, Minn. 1997).

Agamben, Giorgio, *The Man without content*, translated by G. Albert (Stanford, Calif. 1999).

Alembert, Jean Le Rond D', 'Essai sur la société des gens de lettres et des grands' in *Œuvres complètes* (Paris 1822).

— 'Observations préliminaires sur l'art de traduire en général', in *Mélanges de littérature, d'histoire et de philosophie*, 3 vols (Amsterdam 1763).

— *Essai sur les éléments de philosophie*, in *Œuvres complètes* (Paris 1821).

Althusser, Louis, *For Marx*, translated by Ben Brewster (London 1969).

Anderson, Wilda, *Between the library and the laboratory* (Baltimore, Md. 1984).

— *Diderot's dream* (Baltimore, Md, 1990).

Appiah, K. Anthony, 'Battle of the bien-pensant', *The New York review of books* 47:7 (27 April 2000).

Argenville, Dezallier d', *La Théorie et la pratique du jardinage* (Paris 1709).

Arnold, Duane W. H., and Pamela Bright (eds), *De doctrina christiana: a classic of western culture* (Notre Dame, Ind. 1995).

Astruc, Pierre, 'Les sciences médicales et leurs représentants dans l'Encyclopédie', *Revue d'histoire des sciences* (1951), p.359-68.

Augustine, Saint, *On Christian teaching*, translated by R. P. H. Green (Oxford 1997).

Auroux, Sylvain, *La Sémiotique des ency-clopédistes* (Paris 1979).

Azouvi, François, 'Magnétisme animal: la sensation infinie', *Dix-huitième siècle* 23 (1991), p.107-18.

Badinter, Elisabeth, *L'Amour en plus: histoire de l'amour maternel* (Paris 1980).

Baker, Keith, 'Enlightenment and the institution of society: notes for a conceptual history', in *Main trends in cultural history: ten essays*, ed. Willem Melching and Wyger Velema (Amsterdam 1994), p.95-120.

— *Inventing the French revolution: essays on French political culture in the eighteenth century* (Cambridge 1990).

Barbey d'Aurevilly, Jules, *Contre Diderot* (Paris 1986).

Baridon, Michel, 'L'imaginaire scienti-fique et la voix humaine dans *Le Rêve de d'Alembert*', in *L'Encyclopédie, Diderot, l'esthétique*, ed. Sylvain Auroux, Dominique Bourel, and Charles Porset (Paris 1991).

Barret-Kriegel, Blandine, *La République incertaine* (Paris 1988).

Barthes, Roland, 'Image, raison, dérai-son', in *L'Univers de l'"Encyclopédie"* (Paris 1964).

— 'Le Dernier des écrivains heureux', in *Essais critiques* (Paris 1964).

Batteux, Charles, *Cours de belles-lettres, ou principes de la littérature*, 4 vols (Paris 1763).

— *Les Beaux arts réduits à un même principe* (1773; Geneva 1969).

Baudrillard, Jean, *Simulacra and simula-tion*, translated by Sheila Faria Glaser (Ann Arbor, Mich. 1994).

Bell, David, *The Cult of the nation in France: inventing nationalism, 1680-1800* (Cambridge, Mass. 2001)

Benedict, Barbara M., *Framing feeling: sentiment and style in English prose fiction, 1745-1800* (New York 1994).

Bénichou, Paul, *Le Sacre de l'écrivain: 1750-1830* (Paris 1985).

Benjamin, Walter, 'On language as such and the language of man', translated

by Edmund Jephcott, in *Reflections*, ed. Peter Demetz (New York 1978).
– 'The task of the translator', translated by Harry Zohn, in *Illuminations*, ed. Hannah Arendt (New York 1968).
Benrekassa, Georges, 'La pratique philosophique de Diderot dans l'article "Encyclopédie" de l'*Encyclopédie*', *Stanford French review* 8:2-3 (1984), p.189-212.
– *La Politique et sa mémoire: le politique et l'historique dans la pensée des Lumières* (Paris 1983).
– *Le Langage des Lumières* (Paris 1995).
Berman, Antoine, *L'Epreuve de l'étranger* (Paris 1984).
– *La Traduction à la lettre ou l'auberge du lointain* (Paris 1999).
Bernstein, J. M., *The Fate of art: aesthetic alienation from Kant to Derrida and Adorno* (University Park, Pa. 1992).
Birnbaum, Christine, 'La vision médicale de l'amour dans l'*Encyclopédie*', in *Encyclopédie: aimer en France 1760-1860*, ed. Paul Viallaneix and Jean Ehrard, 2 vols (Clermont-Ferrand 1980), ii.307-13.
Blackmore, Richard, *The Lay-monastery* (London 1714).
Bonnet, Jean-Claude, *Naissance du Panthéon, essai sur le culte des grands hommes* (Paris 1998).
Bono, James J., *The Word of God and the languages of man: interpreting nature in early modern science and medicine* (Madison, Wis. 1995).
Bordeu, Théophile de, 'Analyse médicinale du sang', *Recherches sur les maladies chroniques* in *Œuvres complètes*, 2 vols (Paris 1818).
– *Dissertation sur l'usage des eaux de Barèges et du mercure* (Paris 1757).
– *Recherches anatomiques sur la position des glandes et sur leur action* in *Œuvres complètes*, 2 vols (Paris 1818).
Borges, Jorge Luis, 'Of exactitude in science', in *A universal history of infamy*, translated by Norman Thomas di Giovanni (New York 1972).
– 'The analytical language of John Wilkins', in *Other inquisitions, 1937-*

1952, translated by Ruth L. C. Simms (Austin, Tex. 1964).
Bourdieu, Pierre, *Distinction: a social critique of the judgement of taste*, translated by Richard Nice (Cambridge, Mass. 1984).
Bradley, Richard, *New improvements of planting and gardening*, 2 vols (London 1717).
Bradshaw, Lael Ely, 'Ephraim Chambers' *Cyclopaedia*', in *Notable encyclopedias of the seventeenth and eighteenth centuries*, ed. Frank A. Kafker, *SVEC* 194 (1981), p.123-40.
Brewer, Daniel, '1751: ordering knowledge', in *A new history of French literature*, ed. Denis Hollier (Cambridge, Mass. 1989), p.447-55.
– 'Language and grammar: Diderot and the discourse of encyclopedism', *Eighteenth-century studies* 13 (1979), p.1-19.
– 'The French intellectual, history, and the reproduction of culture', *L'Esprit créateur* 37:2 (1997), p.16-33.
– *The Discourse of Enlightenment in eighteenth-century France* (Cambridge 1993).
Brockliss, L. W. B., 'The development of the spa in seventeenth-century France', in *The Medical history of waters and spas*, ed. Roy Porter (London 1990).
Brown, Gregory, 'Reconsidering the censorship of writers in eighteenth-century France' (unpublished paper).
Brownell, Morris R., *Alexander Pope and the arts of Georgian England* (Oxford 1978).
Bruckner, Pascal, and Alain Finkielkraut, *Au coin de la rue l'aventure* (Paris 1979).
Buffon, Georges Louis Leclerc, comte de, *De l'homme*, ed. Michèle Duchet (Paris 1971).
Buisseret, David (ed.), *Monarchs, ministers, and maps: the emergence of cartography as a tool of government in early modern Europe* (Chicago, Ill. 1992).
Burnett, James, *Of the origin and progress of language* (1773; Menston 1967).

Butler, Judith, *Bodies that matter* (New York, N.Y. 1993).

Callinicos, Alex, *Against postmodernism* (Cambridge 1989).

Casey, Edward S., 'Smooth spaces and rough-edged places: the hidden history of place', *Review of metaphysics* 51:2 (1997), p.267-97.

Cassirer, Ernst, *The Philosophy of the Enlightenment*, translated by Fritz C. A. Koelln and James P. Pettegrove (Princeton, N.J. 1951).

Catesby, Mark, *The Natural history of Carolina, Florida, and the Bahama Islands*, 2 vols (London 1731-1743 [1748]).

Cavaillès, Henri, *La Route française: son histoire, sa fonction* (Paris 1946).

Chambers, Ephraim, *Cyclopaedia*, 2 vols (London 1728).

Charbonnel, P., 'Repères pour une étude du statut de la femme dans quelques écrits théoriques des "philosophes"', *Etudes sur le 18ᵉ siècle* 3 (Université Libre de Bruxelles 1976), p.93-110.

Charle, Christophe, *Naissance des 'intellectuels' 1880-1900* (Paris 1990).

Charpentier, Louis, *Causes de la decadence du goût sur le théâtre* (Paris 1768).

Chartier, Roger, 'Distinction et divulgation: la civilité et ses livres', *Lectures et lecteurs dans la France d'Ancien Régime* (Paris 1987).

– 'The man of letters', in *Enlightenment portraits*, ed. Michel Vovelle, translated by Lydia Cochrane (Chicago, Ill. 1997), p.142-89.

– *Culture écrite et société* (Paris 1996).

– *Lectures et lecteurs dans la France d'Ancien Régime* (Paris 1987).

– *The Cultural origins of the French revolution*, translated by Lydia G. Cochrane (Durham, N.C. 1991).

Chevalier, Jean-Baptiste, *Mémoires et observations sur les effets des eaux de Bourbonne-les-Bains, en Champagne, dans les maladies hystériques et chroniques* (1772).

Chisick, Harvey, *The Limits of reform in the Enlightenment: attitudes toward the education of the lower classes in eighteenth-century France* (Princeton, N.J. 1981).

Christensen, Thomas, *Rameau and musical thought in the Enlightenment* (Cambridge 1993).

Coleman, Patrick, 'The idea of character in the *Encyclopédie*', *Eighteenth-century studies* 13 (1979), p.21-47.

Coleman, William, 'Health and hygiene in the *Encyclopédie*', *Journal of the history of medicine* 29 (1974), p.399-421.

Condillac, Etienne Bonnot de, *Essai sur l'origine des connaissances humaines* (Paris 1998).

Conner, Rebecca E., ' "Can you apply arithmetick to everything?" *Moll Flanders*, William Petty, and social accounting,' *Studies in eighteenth-century culture* 27 (1998), p.169-94.

Contamine, Philippe, 'Mourir pour la patrie, Xᵉ-XXᵉ siècle', in *Les Lieux de mémoire* II, *La Nation*, iii, ed. Pierre Nora (Paris 1986), p.11-23.

Cooper, Anthony Ashley, Earl of Shaftesbury, *Characteristics of men, manners, opinions, times*, ed. P. Eyres (Oxford 1999).

Corbin, Alain, *Le Territoire du vide: L'Occident et le désir du rivage (1750-1840)* (Paris 1990).

Coyer, Gabriel François, abbé, *Dissertations pour être lues: la première, sur le vieux mot de 'patrie'; la seconde, sur la nature du 'peuple'* (The Hague 1755).

Creech, James, 'Chasing after advances: Diderot's article "Encyclopédie" ', *Yale French studies* 63 (1982), p.183-97.

– *Diderot: thresholds of representation* (Columbus 1986).

Cusset, Catherine, ed., '*Qui peut définir les femmes': l'article FEMME de l'Encyclopédie (1756), Sur les femmes de Diderot (1772)* (Paris 1999).

Dapper, Olfert, *Kaffraria or land of the kafirs, also named hottentots* (1668), in *The Early Cape hottentots*, ed. I. Schapera (Cape Town 1933).

Darnton, Robert, 'Philosophers trim the tree of knowledge: the epistemological strategy of the Encyclopédie',

in *The Great cat massacre and other episodes in French cultural history* (New York 1984).
- *The Business of Enlightenment: a publishing history of the 'Encyclopédie', 1775-1800* (Cambridge, Mass. 1979).
- *The Literary underground of the old regime* (Cambridge, Mass. 1982).
Debray, Régis, *Teachers, writers, celebrities: the intellectuals of modern France* (London 1981).
DeJean, Joan, *Tender geographies: women and the origins of the novel in France* (New York 1991).
Deleuze, Gilles, *Pourparlers* (Paris 1990).
- and Félix Guattari, *Capitalisme et schizophrénie* (Paris 1972-1980).
- *Mille plateaux* (Paris 1980)
Deneys-Tunney, Anne, *Ecritures du corps: de Descartes à Laclos* (Paris 1992).
De Rozoi, Barnabé Farmian, *Les Sens, poème en six chants* (London 1766).
Description of the most noble city of London (1772).
Desmahis, Joseph François Edouard, *Les Œuvres de M. Desmahis* (Paris 1778).
Diderot encyclopedia: the complete illustrations, 1762-1777, 5 vols (New York 1978).
Diderot, Denis, 'Plan d'une université pour le gouvernement de Russie', in *Œuvres complètes de Diderot*, 20 vols, ed. J. Assézat (Paris 1875-1877), iii.429-535.
- *Le Neveu de Rameau*, DPV, xii.169-96.
- *Mémoires sur différents sujets de mathématiques*, DPV, ii.231-338.
- *Pensées sur l'interprétation de la nature*, DPV, ix.26-111.
Dieckman, Herbert, *Le Philosophe: texts and interpretation* (Saint Louis, Mo. 1948).
Dizionario universale delle arti e delle scienze, 9 vols in 4° (Venice 1748-1749).
Droixhe, Daniel, *La Linguistique et l'appel de l'histoire (1600-1800)* (Geneva 1978).
Du Bos, Jean-Baptiste, *Réflexions critiques sur la poésie et sur la peinture*, pref. by Etienne Wolff (Paris 1993).

Duetti, Clinio L., 'Work noble and ignoble: an introduction to the history of the modern idea of work' (doctoral dissertation, University of Wisconsin, 1954).
Duhamel Du Monceau, Henri Louis, *Eléments d'agriculture* (Paris 1762.)
- *La Physique des arbres, où il est traité de l'anatomie des plantes et de l'économie végétale* (Paris 1758).
Dumarsais, César Chesneau, *Exposition de la doctrine de l'église gallicane par rapport aux prétentions de la cour de Rome*, 3 vols (Geneva 1757).
- *Les Tropes*, with commentary by Pierre Fontanier, 2 vols (Geneva 1967).
Du Ryer, Pierre, preface to Claude Favre de Vaugelas, trans, *Quinte-Curce, De la vie et des actions d'Alexandre le Grand*, 2 vols (Paris 1653).
Du Tertre, Jean Baptiste, *Histoire générale des isles de S. Christophe* (Paris 1654).
Edney, Matthew H., 'Cartography without "progress": reinterpreting the nature and historical development of mapmaking', *Cartographica* 30:2-3 (1993), p.54-68.
- *Mapping an empire: the geographical construction of British India, 1765-1843* (Chicago, Ill. 1997).
Ehrard, Jean, 'De Diderot à Panckoucke: deux pratiques de l'alphabet', in *L'Encyclopédisme*, ed. Annie Becq (Paris 1991), p.243-52.
- 'L'arbre et le labyrinthe', in *L'Encyclopédie, Diderot, l'esthétique*, ed. Sylvain Auroux, Dominique Bourel, and Charles Porset (Paris 1991).
Eisenstein, Elizabeth L., *Print culture and Enlightenment thought* (Chapel Hill, N.C. 1986).
- *Grub street abroad: aspects of the French cosmopolitan press from the age of Louis XIV to the French revolution* (New York 1992).
Elias, Norbert, *La Civilisation des mœurs*, translated by Pierre Kamnitzer (Paris 1973).
- *Norbert Elias par lui-même* (Paris 1991).

– *The Court society*, translated by Edmund Jephcott (New York, N.Y. 1983).

Ellis, Harold, *Boulainvilliers and the French monarchy: aristocratic politics in early eighteenth-century France* (Ithaca, N.Y. 1988).

Ellis, William, *The Timber tree improved* (London 1738).

The Encyclopedia: selections, ed. and translated by Stephen Gendzier (New York 1967).

Escolar, Marcelo, 'Exploration, cartography, and the modernization of state power', *International social science journal* 49 (1997), p.55-75.

Febvre, Lucien, and H.-J. Martin, *The Coming of the book: the impact of printing, 1450-1800*, ed. G. Nowell-Smith and D. Wooton, translated by D. Gerard (London 1984).

Fellows, Otis E., and Norman L. Torrey, ed., *The Age of Enlightenment* (New York 1942).

Ferry, Luc, *Homo aestheticus: l'invention du goût à l'âge démocratique* (Paris 1990).

Finkielkraut, Alain, *La Défaite de la pensée* (Paris 1987).

Fischer, Jean-Louis, 'L'*Encyclopédie* présente-t-elle une pré-science des monstres?' *Recherches sur Diderot et sur l'Encyclopédie* 16 (1994), p.133-52.

La Folie des dictionnaires, *Critique* 608-9 (1998).

Force, Pierre, 'Self-love, identification, and the origin of political economy', *Yale French studies* 92 (1997), p.46-64.

Forrest, Alan, 'Respect et reconnaissance dans la France révolutionnaire' in *La Considération*, ed. C. Haroche and J.-C. Vatin (Paris 1998).

Foucault, Michel, *Les Mots et les choses* (Paris 1966).

– *La Pensée du dehors* (Paris 1986).

– *L'Usage des plaisirs* (Paris 1984).

Frei, Hans W., *The Eclipse of biblical narrative: a study in eighteenth- and nineteenth-century hermeneutics* (New Haven, Conn. 1974).

Frézier, Amédée François, *Relation du voyage de la mer du sud*, 2 vols (Paris 1717).

Gauchet, Marcel, *Le Désenchantement du monde* (Paris 1985).

Gay, Peter, *The Enlightenment: an interpretation*, 2 vols (New York 1966-1969).

Genette, Gérard, 'Bonnet blanc *versus* blanc bonnet', in *Mimologiques: voyages en Cratylie* (Paris 1976).

– *L'Œuvre de l'art: la relation esthétique* (Paris 1997).

Gilman, Sander, 'Black bodies, white bodies: toward an iconography of female sexuality in late nineteenth-century art, medicine, and literature', in *'Race', writing, and difference*, ed. Henry Louis Gates, Jr. (Chicago, Ill. 1985), p.223-61.

Goodman, Dena, *The Republic of letters: a cultural history of the French Enlightenment* (Ithaca, N.Y. 1994).

Gordon, Daniel, *Citizens without sovereignty: equality and sociability in French thought, 1670-1789* (Princeton, N.J. 1994).

Gossman, Lionel, *Medievalism and the ideologies of the Enlightenment: the world and work of La Curne de Sainte-Palaye* (Baltimore, Md. 1968).

Goulemot, Jean Marie, 'Histoire littéraire et histoire des idées du XVIIIe siècle à l'épreuve de la Révolution', *Modern language notes* 114 (1999), p.629-46.

– and Daniel Oster, *Gens de lettres, écrivains et bohèmes: l'imaginaire littéraire, 1630-1900* (Paris 1992).

Grandière, Marcel, *L'Idéal pédagogique en France au dix-huitième siècle*, *SVEC* 361 (1998).

Gregory, Derek, *Geographical imaginations* (Cambridge 1994).

Grevenbroek, J. G., *An Elegant and accurate account of the African race living round the Cape of Good Hope*, translated by B. Farrington (n.p. 1695).

Grimm, Friedrich Melchior, Freiherr von, *Lettre sur Omphale* (n.p. 1752), in *La Querelle des bouffons*, ed. D. Launay, 3 vols (Geneva 1973), i.1-54.

Groot en algemeen kruidkundig, hoveniers, en bloemisten woorden boek, 2 vols (Leiden 1745).

Guenée, Bernard, 'Etat et nation en France au moyen âge', in *Politique et histoire au moyen âge: recueil d'articles sur l'histoire politique et l'historiographie médiévale (1956-1981)* (Paris 1981), p.151-64.

Habermas, Jürgen, *The Structural transformation of the public sphere*, translated by T. Burger (Cambridge, Mass. 1989).

Hacking, Ian, 'How, why, when, and where did language go public', *Common knowledge* 1 (1992), p.74-91.

Hamlin, Christopher, 'Chemistry, medicine, and the legitimization of English spas, 1740-1840', in *The Medical history of waters and spas*, ed. Roy Porter (London 1990).

Hampson, Norman, *A cultural history of the Enlightenment* (New York 1968).

Haraway, Donna J., *Modest-witness@ second-millennium.femaleman-meets-oncomouse: feminism and technoscience* (New York, N.Y. 1997).

Hardesty, Kathleen, *The Supplément to the Encyclopédie* (The Hague 1977).

Harley, J. B., 'Deconstructing the map', *Cartographica* 26:2 (1982), p.1-20.

Haroche, Claudine, 'Egards, respect, considération: les formes du souci de l'autre', *Magazine littéraire* 345 (1996).

Harvey, David, *The Condition of postmodernity: an enquiry into the origins of cultural change* (Oxford 1989).

Hayes, Julie Candler, *Reading the French Enlightenment: system and subversion* (Cambridge 1999).

Healy, F. G., 'The Enlightenment view of *homo faber*', *SVEC* 25 (1963), p.837-59.

Henrey, Blanche, *British botanical and horticultural literature before 1800*, 2nd edn (Oxford 1999).

Hillman, David, and Carla Mazzio (eds), *The Body in parts* (New York, N.Y. 1997).

Hobson, Marian, 'La *Lettre sur les sourds et les muets* de Diderot: labyrinthe et langage', *Semiotica* 16:4 (1976), p.291-327.

Holly, Grant, 'The allegory in realism', in *Enlightening allegory: theory, practice, and contexts of allegory in the late seventeenth and eighteenth centuries*, ed. Kevin L. Cope (New York, N.Y. 1992).

Horguelin, Paul A. (ed.), *Anthologie de la manière de traduire: domaine français* (Montreal 1981).

Horkheimer, Max, and Theodor W. Adorno, *Dialectic of Enlightenment*, translated by J. Cumming (1972; New York, N.Y. 1991).

Horowitz, Maryanne Cline, 'The "science" of embryology before the discovery of the ovum', in *Connecting spheres: women in the western world, 1500 to the present*, ed. Marilyn J. Boxer and Jean H. Quataert (New York, N.Y. 1987), p.86-94.

Huet, Marie-Hélène, *Monstrous imagination* (Cambridge, Mass.1993).

Hume, David. *Of the standard of taste and other essays*, ed. J. W. Lenz (Indianapolis, Ind. 1965).

Huxley, Anthony, Mark Griffiths, and Margot Levy, ed., *The New Royal Horticultural Society dictionary of gardening*, 4 vols (London 1992).

Iverson, John, *Voltaire's heroes: violence and politics in the age of Enlightenment* (Ph.D. thesis, University of Chicago, 1998).

Jameson, Fredric, *Postmodernism, or the cultural logic of late capitalism* (Durham, N. C. 1991).

Jameson, Fredric, *The Political unconscious* (Ithaca, N.Y. 1981).

Jellicoe, Geoffrey, and Susan Jellicoe *et al.*, ed., *The Oxford companion to gardens* (Oxford 1991).

Jordanova, Ludmilla, *Sexual visions: images of gender in science and medicine between the eighteenth and twentieth centuries* (New York 1989).

Kafker, Frank A., *The Encyclopedists as individuals: a biographical dictionary of the authors of the 'Encyclopédie'*, *SVEC* 257 (1988).

– *The Encyclopedists as a group: a collective biography of the authors of the 'Encyclopédie'*, SVEC 345 (1996).

– 'The role of the *Encyclopédie* in the making of a modern encyclopedia', in *The 'Encyclopédie' and the Age of Revolution*, ed. C. Donato and R. M. Maniquis (Boston 1992).

– and Serena Kafker, *The Encyclopedists as individuals*, SVEC 257 (1988).

Kant, Immanuel, *Critique of judgment*, translated by W. S. Pluhar (Indianapolis, Ind. 1987).

– *Critique of pure reason*, translated by Norman Kemp Smith (New York 1965).

Kaplan, Steven L., *La Fin des corporations* (Paris 2001).

– *Provisioning Paris: merchants and millers in the grain and flour trade during the eighteenth century* (Ithaca 1984).

Kavanagh, Thomas, *Esthetics of the moment: literature and art in the French Enlightenment* (Philadelphia, Penn. 1996).

Keates, J. S., *Understanding maps* (New York, N.Y. 1982).

Kelly, L. G., *The True interpreter: a history of translation in the West* (Oxford 1979).

King, Geoff, *Mapping reality: an exploration of cultural cartographies* (New York 1996).

Kircher, Athanasius, *De mystico-allegorico-tropologica arcae expositione, or Arca Noë, in tres libros digesta* (1675).

Klossowski, Pierre, translator's preface to *L'Enéide* (Paris 1989).

Koepp, Cynthia, 'Anticipating the *Encyclopédie*: artisans and the mechanical arts in Pluche's *Le Spectacle de la nature*' (forthcoming).

– 'Before liberty: the ideology of work, taste, and the social order', in *Naissances des libertés économiques: liberté du travail et liberté d'entreprendre: le décret d'Allard et le loi Le Chapelier*, ed. Alain Plessis (Paris 1993).

Kolb, Peter, *The Present state of the Cape of Good Hope* (London 1731).

Konvitz, Josef, *Cartography in France, 1660-1848: science, engineering and statecraft* (Chicago, Ill. 1987).

Kors, Alan C., *Atheism in France 1650-1729*, vol 1 (Princeton, N.J. 1990).

Korzybski, Alfred, *Science and sanity: an introduction to non-aristotelian systems and general semantics*, 2nd edn (Lancaster, Penn. 1941).

Kundera, Milan, *Jacques et son maître, hommage à Denis Diderot en trois actes* (Paris 1981).

La Quintinie, Jean de, *Instruction pour les jardins fruitiers et potagers, avec un traité des orangers*, 2 vols (Amsterdam 1700).

Laignel-Lavastine, Maxime, 'Les médecins collaborateurs de l'*Encyclopédie*', *Revue d'histoire des sciences* 4 (1951).

Lambert, José, 'Le discours implicite sur la traduction dans l'*Encyclopédie*', in *La Traduction en France à l'âge classique*, ed. Michel Ballard and Lieven D'Hulst (Villeneuve d'Ascq 1996), p.101-19.

Laqueur, Thomas, *Making sex: body and gender from the Greeks to Freud* (Cambridge, Mass. 1990).

Larrère, Catherine, *L'Invention de l'économie au XVIIIᵉ: du droit naturel à la physiocratie* (Paris 1992).

Le Goff, Jacques, 'Memory' in *History and memory*, translated by Steven Rendall and Elizabeth Claman (New York 1992).

Le Guern, Michel, 'Le mot *nation* dans les six premières éditions du *Dictionnaire de l'Académie*', in Sylvianne Rémi-Giraud and Pierre Rétat, *Les Mots de la nation* (Lyon 1998), p.161-67.

Le Rougetel, Hazel, *The Chelsea gardener: Philip Miller, 1691-1771* (London 1990).

Le Ru, Véronique, *Jean Le Rond d'Alembert philosophe* (Paris 1994).

Leca-Tsiomis, Marie, *Ecrire l'Encyclopédie: Diderot: de l'usage des dictionnaires à la grammaire philosophique* (Oxford 1999).

Leclerc, André, 'Le problème de la traduction au siècle des Lumières:

obstacles pratiques et limites théoriques', *TTR* 1 (1988), p.41-62.

Lémery, Nicolas, *Dictionnaire, ou traité universel des drogues simples mises en ordre alphabétique*, 4th edn (Rotterdam 1727).

Lougee, Carolyn, *Le Paradis des femmes: women, salons, and social stratification in seventeenth-century France* (Princeton, N.J. 1976).

Lough, John, *Essays in the 'Encyclopédie' of Diderot and d'Alembert* (London 1968).

Lovejoy, Arthur O., *The Great chain of being* (Cambridge, Mass. 1936).

Loyseau, Charles, *Traité des ordres simples dignitez* (Chasteaudun 1610).

Lyotard, Jean-François, 'Discussions, ou: phraser "après Auschwitz"', in *Les Fins de l'homme* (Paris 1981).

– *Le Différend* (Paris 1983).

– *The Postmodern condition*, translated by Geoff Bennington and Brian Massumi (Minneapolis. Minn. 1984).

– *Tombeau de l'intellectuel* (Paris 1984).

Mabberley, D. J., *The Plant-book* (Cambridge 1987).

McDonald, Christie Vance, 'The utopia of the text: Diderot's *Encyclopédie*', *The Eighteenth century: theory and interpretation* 21:2 (1980), p.128-44.

MacEachren, Alan, *How maps work: representation, visualization, and design* (New York 1995).

MacIntyre, Alasdair, *Three rival versions of moral enquiry: encyclopedia, genealogy, and tradition* (Notre Dame, Ind. 1990).

Mackaman, Douglas Peter, *Leisure settings: bourgeois culture and the spa in modern France* (Chicago 1998).

Maire, Catherine, *De la cause de Dieu à la cause de la nation: le jansénisme au XVIIIe siècle* (Paris 1998).

Malherbe, Michel, 'Introduction', in D'Alembert, *Discours préliminaire de l'Encyclopédie* (Paris 2000), p.9-77.

Malueg, Sara Ellen Procious, 'Women and the *Encyclopédie*', in Samia Spencer, *French women and the age of Enlightenment* (Bloomington, Ind. 1984), p.259-71.

Maret, Hughes, *Mémoire sur la manière d'agir des bains d'eau douce et d'eau de mer et sur leur usage* (Paris 1769).

Mason, H. T. (ed.), *The Darnton debate: books and revolution in the eighteenth century* (Oxford 1999).

Masseau, Didier, *L'Invention de l'intellectuel dans l'Europe du XVIIIe siècle* (Paris 1994).

Mercier, Daniel, 'La problématique de l'équivalence des langues au XVIIe et XVIIIe siècles', in *La Traduction en France à l'âge classique*, ed. Michel Ballard and Lieven D'Hulst (Villeneuve d'Ascq 1996), p.63-81.

Mesmer, Franz Aton, *Le Magnétisme animal*, ed. Robert Amadou (Paris 1971).

Miller, Philip, *The Gardener's and florist's dictionary* (London 1724).

Monmonier, Mark, *How to lie with maps*, 2nd edn (Chicago, Ill. 1996).

Montesquieu, Charles de Secondat, baron de, *Essai sur le goût*, ed. C.-J. Beyer (Geneva 1967).

– *Œuvres complètes*, ed. Roger. Caillois, 2 vols (Paris 1949-1951).

Moriarty, Michael, *Taste and ideology in seventeenth-century France* (Cambridge 1988).

Mornet, Daniel, *Les Origines intellectuelles de la révolution française* (Paris 1954).

Morris, David B., 'The marquis de Sade and the discourses of pain: literature and medicine at the Revolution', in *The Languages of Psyche: mind and body in Enlightenment thought*, ed. G. S. Rousseau (Berkeley, Calif. 1990).

Morrissey, Robert, John Iverson, and Mark Olsen, 'L'Encyclopédie de Diderot sur Internet', *RDE* 25 (1998), p.163-68.

Moser, Walter, 'D'Alembert: l'ordre philosophique de ce discours', *Modern language notes* 91:4 (1976), p.723-33.

– 'Les discours dans le Discours préliminaire', *Romanic review* 67 (1976), p.102-15.

Mouchon, Pierre, *Table analytique et raisonnée du dictionnaire des sciences, des arts et des métiers* (Paris 1780).

Muehrcke, Phillip C., and Juliana O. Muehrcke, *Map use: reading, analysis, and interpretation*, 4th edn (Madison, Wis. 1998).

Mukerji, Candra, *Territorial ambitions and the gardens of Versailles* (Cambridge 1997).

Nora, Pierre, 'Entre mémoire et histoire: la problématique des lieux', in *Les Lieux de mémoire* (Paris 1984-1992), i.xvii-xlii.

Norris, Christopher, *Paul de Man* (New York 1988).

– *What's wrong with postmodernism* (New York 1990).

O'Dea, Michael, *Jean-Jacques Rousseau: music, illusion and desire* (New York 1995).

Outram, Dorinda, *The Body and the French revolution: sex, class, and political culture* (New Haven, Conn. 1989).

Payne, Harry C., *The Philosophes and the people* (Princeton, N.J. 1976).

Pellegrin, Simon Joseph, *Dissertation sur la musique françoise et italienne* (Amsterdam 1754), in *La Querelle des bouffons*, ed. D. Launay, 3 vols (Geneva 1973), iii.1669-1729.

Petty, Sir William, *The Petty papers* (New York 1927).

Placher, William, *The Domestication of transcendence: how modern thinking about God went wrong* (Louisville, Ky. 1996).

Plumier, Charles, *Nova plantarum americanarum genera* (Paris 1703).

Pomme, Pierre, *Traité des affections vaporeuses des deux sexes*, 3rd edn (1768).

Poovey, Mary, *A History of the modern fact: problems in the sciences of wealth and society* (Chicago 1998).

Proust, Jacques, 'L'article *Bas de Diderot', in *Langue et langages de Leibniz à l'Encyclopédie*, ed. Michèle Duchet and Michèle Jalley (Paris 1977), p.245-71.

– *Diderot et l'Encyclopédie* (Paris 1962).

– *Marges d'une utopie: pour une lecture critique des planches de l'Encyclopédie* (Cognac 1985).

Quintili, Paolo, 'Machines et "métamachines": le rêve de l'industrie

mécanisée dans *l'Encyclopédie*', in *La Matière de l'homme dans l'Encyclopédie*, ed. Sylviane Coppola and Anne-Marie Chouillet (Paris 1998), p.247-74.

Raulin, Joseph, *Traité des affections vaporeuses du sexe* (1758).

Regis, Isabelle, *et al.*, 'Lire l'*Encylopédie*', *Littérature* 42 (1981), p.20-38.

Rey, Roselyne, *Histoire de la douleur* (Paris 1993).

– 'Hygiène et souci de soi', *Communications* 56 (1993), p.25-39.

– *Naissance et développement du vitalisme en France de la deuxième moitié du 18ᵉ siècle à la fin du Premier Empire*, SVEC 381 (2000), p.63-89.

Richerand, Anthelme-Balthasar, 'Notice sur la vie et les ouvrages de Bordeu', in Théophile de Bordeu, *Œuvres complètes*, 2 vols (Paris 1818).

Ricken, Ulrich, *Grammaire et philosophie au siècle des Lumières* (Villeneuve d'Ascq 1978).

– *Linguistics, anthropology and philosophy in the French Enlightenment: language theory and ideology*, translated by Robert E. Norton (London 1994).

Robinson, Douglas, *Translation and taboo* (DeKalb, Ill. 1996).

Roche, Daniel, *France in the Enlightenment*, translated by Arthur Goldhammer (Cambridge, Mass. 1998).

Roger, Jacques, *Les Sciences de la vie dans la pensée française au XVIIIᵉ siècle* (Paris 1963).

Rosenband, Leonard N., *Papermaking in eighteenth-century France: management, labor, and revolution at the Montgolfier mill, 1761-1805* (Baltimore 2000).

Rosenberg, Daniel, 'An eighteenth-century time machine: the *Encyclopédie* of Denis Diderot', *Historical reflections / réflexions historiques* 25:2 (1999), p.227-50.

Rotman, Brian, *Ad infinitum – the ghost in Turing's machine: taking God out of mathematics and putting the body back in: an essay in corporeal semiotics* (Stanford, Calif. 1993).

Rousseau, Jean-Jacques, *Œuvres complètes*, ed. B. Gagnebin and M. Raymond, 5 vols (Paris 1959-1995).

Russell, D. A., *Ancient literary criticism: the principal texts in new translations* (Oxford 1972).

Russell, Terence M., and Ann-Marie Thornton, *Gardens and landscapes in the 'Encyclopédie' of Diderot and d'Alembert* (Aldershot 1999).

Russo, Elena, 'The self, real and imaginary: social sentiment in Marivaux and Hume', *Yale French studies* 92 (1997), p.126-48.

Said, Edward, *Representations of the intellectual* (New York 1994).

Saint-Amand, Pierre, *Diderot, le labyrinthe de la relation* (Paris 1984).

– *Les Lois de l'hostilité* (Paris 1992).

Saisselin, Rémy, *The Literary enterprise in eighteenth-century France* (Detroit, Mich. 1979).

Sartre, Jean-Paul, *Qu'est-ce que la littérature?* (Paris 1945).

Scarry, Elaine, *On beauty and being just* (Princeton, N.J. 1999).

Schabol, Jean Roger, *Dictionnaire pour la théorie et la pratique du jardinage et de l'agriculture* (Paris 1767).

Schiebinger, Londa, 'More than skin deep: the scientific search for sexual difference', in *The Mind has no sex* (Cambridge, Mass. 1989), p.189-213.

– *Nature's body* (Boston, Mass. 1993).

Schleiermacher, Friedrich, 'On the different methods of translating' (excerpts), in *Translation / history / culture: a sourcebook*, ed. André Lefevere (London 1992).

Schwab, Richard N., Walter E. Rex, and John Lough, *Inventory of Diderot's Encyclopédie*, SVEC 80, 83, 85, 91, 92, 93 (1971-1972); 223 (1984).

Sewell, William H., jr, *Work and revolution in France: the language of labor from the Old Regime to 1848* (Cambridge 1980).

Shackleton, Robert, 'The Enlightenment and the artisan', *SVEC* 190 (1980), p.53-62.

Smith, Samuel Stanhope, *Essay on the causes of the variety of complexion and figure in the human species* (Cambridge, Mass. 1965).

Sonenscher, Michael, *The Hatters of eighteenth-century France* (Berkeley 1987).

Soper, Kate, *Humanism and anti-humanism* (London 1986).

Speir, Hans, 'Magic geography', *Social research* 8 (1941), p.310-30.

Spink, J. S., 'Philosophical speculation and literary technique: the systematic context of Dumarsais's *Des tropes*', *Voltaire and his world: studies presented to W. H. Barber*, ed. R. J. Howells *et al.* (Oxford 1985), p.241-60.

Stafford, Barbara Marie, *Body criticism: imaging the unseen in Enlightenment art and medicine* (Cambridge, Mass. 1991).

Stafleu, Frans A., and Richard S. Cowan, *Taxonomic literature: a selective guide to botanical publications and collections*, 2nd edn, 7 vols (Utrecht 1981).

Starobinski, Jean, 'Note sur l'histoire des fluides imaginaires (des esprits animaux à la libido)', *Gesnerus* 23 (1966).

– 'Remarques sur l'*Encyclopédie*', *Revue de métaphysique et de morale* 75 (1970), p.284-91.

Stearn, William T., 'The botanical importance of Philip Miller's publications', in Hazel Le Rougetel, *The Chelsea gardener: Philip Miller 1691-1771* (London 1990).

Steinbrugge, Lieselotte. *The Moral sex: woman's nature in the French Enlightenment* (New York and Oxford 1995).

Steiner, George, *After Babel: aspects of language and translation*, 2nd edn (Oxford 1992).

Sulzer, Johann Georg, *Allgemeine Theorie der schönen Künste*, in *Aesthetics and the art of musical composition in the German Enlightenment*, ed. N. K. Baker and T. Christensen (Cambridge 1995).

Taylor, Charles, 'The need for recognition', in *The Ethics of authenticity* (Cambridge, Mass. 1991).

Ten Rhyne, William, *A Short account of the Cape of Good Hope and of the hottentots who inhabit that region* (1686), in *The*

Early Cape hottentots, ed. I. Schapera, translated by I. Schapera and B. Farrington (Cape Town 1993).

Thomas, Jean, 'Un moment du développement culturel de l'humanité: l'*Encyclopédie*', *Cahiers d'histoire mondiale* 9 no.3 (1966).

Tissot, Samuel-Auguste, *Essai sur les maladies des gens du monde* (1770).

Treue, Wilhelm, 'D'Alemberts Einleitungen zur Enzyclopädie – heute gelesen', *Blätter für Techniksgeschichte*, 51-52 (1989-90), p.173-86.

Trinkle, Dennis, 'Noël-Antoine Pluche's *Le Spectacle de la nature*: an encyclopaedic best seller', *SVEC* 358 (1997), p.93-134.

Truant, Cynthia M., *The Rites of labor: brotherhoods of compagnonnage in old and new regime France* (Ithaca 1994).

Turner, E. S., *Taking the cure* (London 1967).

Turnovsky, Geoffrey, 'Reconsidering the literary underground in France, 1750-1789' (unpublished paper).

Undank, Jack, and Herbert Josephs (eds), *Diderot, digression and dispersion: a bicentenial tribute* (Lexington, Ky. 1984).

L'Univers de l'Encyclopédie, ed. Roland Barthes, Robert Mauzi et Jean-Pierre Seguin (Paris 1964).

Van Kley, Dale, *The Religious origins of the French Revolution: from Calvin to the civil constitution 1560-1791* (New Haven, Conn. 1996).

Venuti, Lawrence, *The Translator's invisibility* (London 1995).

Versini, Laurent, introduction to the *Encyclopédie*, in Diderot, *Œuvres*, 5 vols (Paris 1994-1997), i.199-210.

Viala, Alain, *La Naissance de l'écrivain: sociologie de la littérature à l'âge classique* (Paris 1985).

Vigarello, Georges, *Le Propre et le sale: l'hygiène du corps depuis le moyen âge* (Paris 1985).

Vila, Anne, *Enlightenment and pathology: sensibility in the literature and medicine of eighteenth-century France* (Baltimore, Md. 1998).

– 'The *médecin philosophe* as drama critic: Pierre Fabre's natural history of French theatre', *SVEC* 314 (1993), p.231-48.

Villes d'eaux: histoire du thermalisme (Paris 1994).

Voltaire, *Candide* in *Contes en vers et en prose*, ed. S. Menant (Paris 1992).

– *Défense du Mondain* (1737).

– *Discours en vers sur l'homme* (1738).

Voss, Jürgen, *Das Mittelalter im historischen Denken Frankreichs: Untersuchungen zur Geschichte des Mittelalterbewertung von der zweiten Hälfte des 16. bis zur Mitte des 19. Jahrhunderts* (Munich 1972).

Wade, Ira O., *The Clandestine organization and diffusion of philosophic ideas in France from 1700 to 1750* (Princeton, N.J. 1938).

Walter, Eric, 'Les auteurs et le champ littéraire', in *Histoire de l'édition française*, ed. Henri-Jean Martin, vol. ii, *Le Livre triomphant (1660-1830)* (Paris 1984), p.383-409.

Watts, George B., 'The Supplément and the table analytique et raisonnée of the *Encyclopédie*', *French review* 28 (1954-55), p.4-19.

Werner, Stephen, 'Abraham Rees' eighteenth-century *Cyclopaedia*', in *Notable encyclopedias of the seventeenth and eighteenth centuries*, ed Frank A. Kafker, *SVEC* 194 (1981), p.183-97.

– *Blueprint: a study of Diderot and the 'Encyclopédie' plates* (Birmingham, Ala. 1993).

Williams, Elizabeth, *The Physical and the moral: anthropology, physiology, and philosophical medicine in France, 1750-1850* (Cambridge 1994).

Wilson, Arthur M., *Diderot* (Oxford 1972).

Woodward, David, 'Medieval mappaemundi', in *The History of cartography*, vol. i, ed. David Woodward and J. B. Harley (Chicago, Ill., 1987).

Zuber, Roger, *Les 'Belles infidèles' et la formation du goût classique*, 2nd edn (Paris 1995).